# Food Security in India

## Myth and Reality

# Food Security in India
## Myth and Reality

Vikas Bajpai
Anoop Saraya

AAKAR

Food Security in India: Myth and Reality
*Vikas Bajpai and Anoop Saraya*



First Published 2018

ISBN 978-93-5002-513-0



Published by
**AAKAR BOOKS**
28 E Pocket IV, Mayur Vihar Phase I
Delhi 110 091
aakarbooks@gmail.com
www.aakarbooks.com

Designed by
Limited Colors, Delhi 110 092

Printed at
Sapra Brothers, Delhi 110 092

# Contents

# Contents

# Foreword

Books and reports of various descriptions are available on global food security, and in poor countries especially in India. This is only natural because India is not only the second most populous country in the world. It is also as the country where most of the desperately poor live. With the present trends continuing, India is not an emergent global power but a global cripple with the majority of its children mal nourished, stunted and many crippled while persistent hunger and morbidity caused by inadequate food is the normal state of existence for the majority of adult men and women in the country. And yet, it is a democracy which in theory is supposed to respond to the most basic need of its people—Food. This state of affairs have continued for seven decades, and the thing that is most visible is sadly not any dramatic change in the ground reality, but the growth of a huge industry, official and non-official centred around counting the number of 'poor'.

The body counting of poor people from various angles got its biggest impetus from the World Bank when McNamara, one of the main architects of the Vietnam War came from the US State Department to the World Bank as its President. He brought with him the habit of getting counted the daily body-bags of US dead soldiers that arrived from Vietnam. As the main architect of the failed US war policy in Vietnam, blood had still not dried on his hand; yet habits die hard and, he now brought his old habit and mode of thinking to counting the number of poor in the world. In this he was supported enthusiastically by several young eager beaver colleagues who were desperate to rise in their career in the World Bank by being in the good book of its president (Dr. Montek Singh Aluwaliah the former deputy chairman of the Indian Planning Commission was one among them). World over in governments, in academia, and in non-government organizations the tendency grew, no doubt supported greatly by fat consultancy fees on how to define and count the number of poor. And this continues to date.

The academic discussion on these matters reached great subtleties no doubt. And yet, it was almost uncanny in at least ways. It tried as far as possible to define the 'poor' without mentioning the 'why' of hunger and poverty, for example what keeps so many people persistently poor and hungry in Indian democracy decade after decade? This book is refreshingly different on this count because it tries to identify clearly without unnecessary obfuscation the basic 'structural causes' of hunger and poverty. Second, because of the structural perspective it adopts the arguments in this volume also help us to recognize why government policies which try to alleviate poverty and malnutrition, e.g. through recent measures like food security bill, national rural employment guarantee etc miss the wood for the trees. They are usually not only dishonest in intent and corrupt in practice, their main purpose is to gather temporary electoral support without even touching the structural causes that generate such enormous poverty and mal nutrition. Not to question the power structure that results in persistent poverty but to benefit by preserving it seems to be the essence of these government policies. Indeed corruption and governance failure are its inevitable consequence not the cause. The book is welcome because it is bold enough to raise this question candidly, and call a spade a spade without mincing words whenever necessary. It is refreshingly honest and yet thorough in its analysis based on carefully documented evidence from a variety of sources it helps the reader to have an informed opinion about that overwhelming question that India continues to face. That question is not high or low rate of economic growth, fiscal or current account deficit as is made out by the media, but what needs to be done to not just pretend to alleviate poverty and hunger as an election gimmick but to demolish that evil structure that nurtures it in the name of democracy. Identifying clearly that structure is the first step of a longer journey that has to start here. Anyone interested in living in a healthy Indian democracy must read it.

**Amit Bhaduri**
Professor Emeritus
Jawaharlal Nehru University
New Delhi

# Acknowledgement

The authors feel that for long there has been a need for the narrative on India's food security presented in this book to be brought in public realm to expose the chicanery of the ruling classes who seem content and happy at having normalized huge problems of hunger and chronic under-nutrition prevalent in our society. We do not believe that efforts such as ours shall bring about any change of heart on part of the political and policy elite of the country. However, it may help those fighting on the side of the people to give the right direction to the fight against massive problem of chronic hunger, apart from impressing upon them the need for a revolutionary change of Indian society. The importance of this struggle cannot possibly be overemphasized. The fate of impoverished Indian masses rests on it. Indeed, they are the motive force behind it and the most crucial force whose endeavor shall make this struggle successful. It is only natural that we express our gratitude to the laboring masses of India whose trials and travails motivated us to write this book. This is a debt that can never be acknowledged enough, let alone be repaid.

Acknowledgement is also due to other friends and colleagues who helped us in this endeavor. Among them we would like to acknowledge Prof. Amit Bhaduri, who has written the foreword and whose numerous suggestions helped us to further refine the content. Very special thanks for Prof. K.B. Saxena who readily acceded to our request to write an essay on the food policy of the country by way of an introduction to the book. We express our gratitude to Shri M.V. Kannan for having very diligently edited the proof of the book, besides his insightful observations regarding the work. We also express our gratitude to Shri Shyam Bihari Rai of Granth Shilpi Prakashan who not only nudged us constantly to write this book but also volunteered to publish its Hindi translation soon after the English publication.

Last but not the least we would like to acknowledge friends and colleagues at the Centre for Social Medicine and Community Health, Jawaharlal Nehru University and our comrades who have contributed immensely towards the development of our intellectual capabilities in order to undertake a work of such complexity.

Vikas Bajpai

Anoop Saraya

# Authors' Note

After nearly twenty-five years of implementation of the neoliberal economic and development policy paradigm, the situation across the world is poised for a change once again. Capitalism has lost much of its sheen as an engine of economic growth with the economies of the world's leading capitalist countries being deeper in crisis than earlier.

The worldwide economic crisis that exploded in 2008 has refused to ebb and the subsequent developments in Europe and other leading economies show that the economic crisis is only deepening further, threatening in its wake the economic and social security of not only the working masses but also of even a section of the middle classes across the world.

Food security is an issue that has closely dovetailed these developments. The year 2008 was also witness to a major worldwide food crisis with food riots being reported from several countries.

Food security is one issue that cuts through the very core of the lives of the poor and given the fact that it is home to the largest number of hungry and malnourished people in the world, food security issues in India have acquired prominence in public and policy debate resulting in promulgation of schemes like the National Rural Health Mission, the Mahatma Gandhi National Rural Employment Guarantee Act and the National Food Security Bill.

While the Government itself portrays these initiatives as part of its commitment to usher in inclusive growth, there is no dearth of people who tagged the label of 'the new hope' to these policy initiatives. Among these are the radical sounding civil society activists and the Parliamentary Left.

Initiation of these measures by the ruling dispensation itself and projection of high hopes from them almost completely absolve the present social, economic and political system of its role in leading to the precarious situation of the people. So tightly is the debate on poverty and hunger sequestered within the safe margins of the present system that there appears little scope for an alternative opinion to be interjected in the given scheme of things.

Contrary to this, the revolutionary Left, which admittedly constitutes a minority opinion, holds the present social, economic and political system responsible for the state of poverty and hunger in the country and considers a radical restructuring of the society to be the solution to the present crisis. This book *Food Security in India: Myth and Reality* is an effort to articulate this alternative for which there is little scope in the mainstream debate.

This book is essentially a political treatise on food security and an argument for the implementation of radical land reforms as the basis of India's transformation. Since the papers included in the book were written over a fairly long period of time, newer data on some aspects has appeared which could not be updated in various chapters, the reason being that subsequent developments in no way dent the validity of the arguments presented in this study. By and large the later developments do not represent a qualitative break from the past albeit there being some instances wherein an improvement in the picture may be claimed by some. For example, the Government recently released the results of a rapid survey of children, conducted by the Ministry of Women and Child Welfare with the help of UNICEF in 2013-14, which show notable improvement in the parameters of child malnutrition in the country compared to those registered in National Family Health Survey 3 in 2004-05.

It would be imprudent to comment loosely about these results; however, it is agreed by other commentators as well that these results do not represent a qualitative change in the situation. In fact, based on much evidence that is available from the latest round of agricultural census and the socio-economic caste census, the performance of the economy and the high food inflation call for caution in interpretation of the latest malnutrition figures. After all, it was only in 2011 that the 'Hungama' report on child malnutrition had shown worsening of child malnutrition since NFHS 3, obliging the then Prime Minister to call the high prevalence of child malnutrition in India a national shame.

The present study has also not dealt with the actions taken by the present Modi government at the Centre that came to power in May 2014. However, rather than representing a break from the past, backed by its brutal majority in the Parliament, Modi Government seems intent on giving the go by to whatever may have been the perceived gains of the social sector initiatives taken by the erstwhile UPA Government. The recommendations of the Shanta Kumar Committee on restructuring of Food Corporation of India and further dilution of the Public Distribution System are cases in point.

The argument of the book is mainly political and the technical nitty-gritty of existing policies or legal provisions has been kept to the necessary minimum, the reason being that the impediments to ensuring food security are mainly political and not technical. Hence in trying to solve the problem of food insecurity we have to keep politics in command. Once the politics that leverages the interests of the masses is grasped, there is enough talent available in the country to tailor technically sound policies.

We may however caution the readers that our argument is 'polemical', 'tendentious' and 'value laden'. At least regarding issues that hinge on the power relations in the society, we strongly believe that there can be no a-polemical and value-neutral position. Our credentials lie in the fact that we forthrightly claim this to be our departure point in the great divide on the issues of poverty and hunger.

With these opening remarks we present this work for your scrutiny.

Vikas Bajpai
Anoop Saraya

# Introduction
## Chronic Hunger is Structural Violence—Inadequate State Response to Eliminate it

### Changing Concept of Food Security

Food Security is the most essential requirement of life. Ensuring food security for its members is the most compelling engagement of the head of a household. It is also a vital public policy issue for a developing country. What constitutes food security for a nation has undergone conceptual change over a period of time from just availability of sufficient food for its people to provision of access to and basic services for absorption of food and includes nutritional and health security. The internationally accepted definition of food security as articulated by World Food Summit, 1996 convened by FAO is "Physical and economic access at all times, to sufficient, safe and nutritious food to meet dietary needs and food preferences for an active and healthy life." (Singh, 2005) This has been further improved upon by the National Commission for Farmers in its report of 2006 which defines it as a situation where every individual has the physical, economic, social and environmental access to a balanced diet that includes macro and micro nutrients, safe drinking water, sanitation, environmental hygiene, primary hygiene, health care and education so as to lead a healthy and productive life. A situation where these or some of these conditions do not exist would be regarded as Food Insecurity. The situation of Food Insecurity manifests itself in various layers. The most elementary one is inability to command food when one is hungry. This is usually termed as explicit food insecurity which is not serious if it is a momentary and temporary phenomenon and gets neutralized soon. But its extreme form is when this insecurity becomes long lasting, chronic or endemic hunger and may lead to starvation. It is the latter part which is an issue of serious concern and has engaged attention of thinkers, policy makers and socially conscious citizens at national and International levels. This heightened concern to address endemic hunger caused by natural calamities, or public policies or struggles for survival is a post-world war II phenomenon. However, situations where large sections of populations are exposed to hunger as well as under nourishment has been a recurrent phenomenon in the world which resulted in low life expectancy of people, with neither adequate response from the rulers nor their capacity in terms of availability of food and ability to reach to the affected population to prevent mortality. No such excuse exists for the present day governments. Also the level of consciousness, national and international, would not permit them to take the matter lightly. (Drézé and Sen, 1993)

It is in this context that a very large and, in some states, alarming, incidence of hunger in India is shocking and has been a major political issue for a long time. IFPRI (International Food Policy Research Institute) which has been mapping the Global Hunger Index as a multi-dimensional statistical tool, composed of percentage of undernourished population, underweight children under the age of five and mortality rate of children under the age of 5, to describe the state of countries' hunger situation has placed India on the top of the World Hunger List with 194 million hungry people in 2016. It ranks India 97 of 118 countries in GHI with 28.5% of people labeled as 'serious'. India's rank has risen from level of 23 in 2008 (IFPRI, 2016). It is higher than even Sri Lanka,

Bangladesh and Nepal in South Asia. Two other studies, though of 2005, estimated a much higher number of hungry at 320 and 327 million. (Cheriyan, 2006). This 'hunger' status covers both types: (1) a condition of the body where desire to consume food is not fulfilled as well as (2) inadequate intake of food over time which results in lack of demand for more food leading to physical and mental under-development. The latter condition is considered as malnutrition which is manifested in low BMI, stunted growth and early mortality. Global Hunger Index is calculated using indicators of calorie consumption, underweight and mortality of children. That such a situation exists (and continues) despite national level food sufficiency, high economic growth and policy interventions over a long period of time calls for a serious scrutiny of policy and governance as well as strong political commitment to eliminate endemic hunger. This is all the more necessary in the context of Goal two of SDGs which commits the country to eliminate hunger and ensure access to safe, nutritious and sufficient food all year around by 2030. It may be recalled that India was not able to meet the MDGS on this score.

## Dimensions of Food Insecurity

Food security has three inter-dependent dimensions (a) at the macro-level (country) (b) household level (c) individual level. The macro-level food security is determined by sufficiency of local availability of food through domestic production and or procurement and ability to reach it to the population. The household level food security is determined by physical and economic access to food. Besides physical availability and economic access, individual level food security within the household is influenced by social factors such as gender discrimination in intra-family distribution of food. An environmental dimension has also been added to food security in recent years which links it to method of food production i.e., food production and distribution should have been the outcome of technology and processes that are instrumental in sustaining its natural resource base (Singh, 2006). Since Food Security is essential for a healthy and productive life, the wider conceptual dimension of food and nutritional security now also includes conditions for absorption of food i.e., access to safe drinking water and sanitation and health care. Food security at the individual and household level is measured by per-capita availability and consumption of food, level of calorie intake, anthropometric indicators (BMI, stunting, underweight, and anemia) and the extent of variety in food to take care of the nutritional requirements and access to safe drinking water and sanitation and health care.

In terms of the above indicators, India's score at macro-level food security is currently satisfied since India produces sufficient food to feed its population and also makes it available to its people through an elaborate system of storage and distributional network. Some deficiencies in particular crop varieties are met with imports. This creates broad ability to prevent mass hunger or starvation. This achievement by itself is an improvement over the past as India had inherited a highly deficient level of macro food security at the time of independence. This achievement, however, gets diminished , as it emerged later, because the increase in food production was at the cost of the use of technologies and processes (Green Revolution) which have been highly degrading to the natural resource base and which are detrimental to the further growth of food output and may even threaten macro-level food security later. The economic growth paradigm which is fast degrading the production resource base—land, forest, inland water, sea and rapid warming of the globe further compound this threat in the absence of comparable seriousness to address this challenge. This puts question mark on the environmental dimension of food security. But the macro-level food sufficiency has not eliminated or even significantly reduced chronic food insecurity and nutritional deficiency at the household and individual levels. This is evident from the negative score in terms of all indicators. The per capita availability as well as consumption of food grains has declined. There is a high level of inequity in cereal intake between the bottom two deciles and top two deciles and ability to access higher quality of food such as fruits, vegetables milk and meat. The calorie consumption of lower half of population has been declining consistently during the last three decades. The anthropometric indicators show no sign of getting significantly improved outcomes as evidenced by the last three NFHS data. However, the conditions for absorption of food are characterized by skewness as the social groups at the lower end of the social hierarchy continue to operate with social barriers in access to drinking water, sanitation and health care Therefore, the magnitude of chronic food insecurity or endemic hunger that pervades in India has to be located in the ability of the households and individuals to access sufficient and nutritious food and basic services to absorb food. This lack of access therefore is not physical as it is available in the PDS or the market but economic—in the lack of purchasing power. This lack of purchasing power is the outcome of poverty, lack of employment and low wages. Poverty itself is caused by, among other factors, lack of employment or inadequate employment and low level of wages. Notwithstanding the sizable reduction of poverty as officially claimed in the period of high growth during the first decade of the century, the jobless nature of the current growth, insecure nature of available employment, low level of wages on the one hand and the low rate of agricultural growth where 2/3 of the population tries to earn a living cause lack of purchasing power to access food. This lack of economic access also includes those who are forcibly deprived of their livelihood by acquisition of their productive assets, degradation and diversion of their resources base, and impoverishment of farmers and small producers on account of unviability of their vocation due to high cost of inputs and volatility of output market, dumping of cheap imports and withdrawal of state support, etc. Besides there is a section of people who are unable to work and, therefore, lack purchasing power to access food. This includes elderly people, people with disability, widows, children without a guardian or family support, persons afflicted with serious illness, destitutes, people displaced by natural calamities, war and internal strife, etc. These constitute a large section of people which explains the magnitude of endemic hunger. It is not that state intervention has not been made to address this lack of purchasing power by way of providing wage employment on public works, credit and input support to self-employed and social security; but these intervention are both inadequate considering the level of need or fail to reach the deserving due to targeting and identification problem, procedural bottlenecks and corruption which indicates governance failure. The ideological opposition to such interventions in the current market centric paradigm of economy is shrinking rather than enlarging the ambit of these interventions.

This explains why IFPRI's Global Hunger Index (2016) termed it 'serious' even though it had declined from 36% in 2008 to 28.5% in 2016 and was worse than many sub-saharen countries with smaller size and lower GDP and even Sri Lanka, Bangladesh and Nepal. IFPRI also estimated hunger index for 17 major states in India covering more than 95% of the population to map out the low, moderate, and alarming categories with a view to locating the distress areas. Other studies including national level statistical surveys have thrown up additional information which helps in not only identification of areas with chronic food insecurity but also particular social groups which are affected by chronic hunger. These studies show no sign of improvement. This body of information brings out various dimensions of food insecure people and areas. This information is valuable in targeting interventions and public action to eliminate it. The first dimension emerging from this information is territorial i.e., the area of chronic food insecurity and the gradation of level of chronic food insecurity across states. The IFPRI Index places all seventeen states well above 'low' and 'moderate' hunger categories implying that the affliction is widespread in India and no state is free from it, and also that the incidence is not influenced by state's level of economic growth as high level of hunger prevails in high economic growth states also. The second dimension is the economic status of food insecure people. The GHI scores broadly concide with poverty levels of the 17 states of which 12 are labeled as 'alarming'. The five states outside this ambit are Punjab, Kerala, AP, Assam and Haryana in that order whose poverty levels are below 20% Chhatisgarh (with 26.65%) Bihar (with 27.80%), Jharkhand (with 28.67%) and MP (with 30%, people affected by chronic hunger are among the worst whose GHI scores are above 25 with MP being termed as 'extremely alarming'. But, as per this index, in case of Odisha the correlation between percentage of people below poverty line and Hunger Index score did not converge as it was not in the 'alarming' category even though its percentage of people below poverty line was the highest (46.37) and Hunger Index ranking was 12 (with 23.79% of population) (Saxena, 2009). Notwithstanding the decline in the levels of poverty both in rural areas and urban areas, rural areas consistently have higher incidence of poverty and its decline is also slower in rural households. 69% of the population lives in rural areas and they depend upon agriculture for income generation. Due to lower agricultural growth rates there is substantial difference in rural-urban productively and wage levels which determine income. With insufficient opportunities for wage employment outside agriculture in rural areas, they suffer from the persistence of poverty and higher level of its incidence.

The third dimension of chronic hunger is age and gender. Older people and children suffer more from food insecurity as they are unable to engage in work and earn income with which to purchase their food requirements. They are dependent upon the bread earner of the family. When the head of the family migrates for work, he usually leaves behind his wife, children and other relations. The situation is worse when the husband and wife with children migrate for work, but leave behind older relations who have to depend upon the kindness of people in the village to occasionally provide them some food. The gender dimension of food security lies in intra-family distribution of food which persists even when the woman is working. Women get least food as they are the last to eat in the family whatever is left over when others in the family have eaten. This is reflected in the anthropometric indicators of nutritional status of women and children in India. India has 46-47% underweight children in the age group of 0.3 years (NFHS III) and 35.7% (38.3% in rural areas) of the children are under-weight in the age group of 0-5 years. 38.4% (41.2% in rural areas) of all children are stunted in the country (NFHS IV). More than half of India's women 53% in the age-group of 15-49 years and 58.4%of children under 6 years are anemic and children aged 5 years or less account for 56% deaths in rural areas. The percentage of women in rural areas with BMI below 18.5 in 2015-16 was 26.7% (MOHFW, 2016).

Food Insecurity also has an identity dimension. As a social group, Tribals are the most food insecure community. The next are the Dalits. This converges with the figures of persons below poverty line in the official documents and lately with the caste and economic census. SCs and STs have the largest number of below poverty line households and have the highest percentage of food insecure people with STs scoring worse than SCs. The convergence also extends to BMI< 18.5, with STs being 60.9%in this category and SCs 53.2% as against 46.8% in other social groups. Women in these communities share a double disadvantage and therefore are more vulnerable to hunger. 21.2% of ST women have Chronic Energy deficiency

(CED) and 68.5% of them are anemic while 18.5% of SC women have CED and 58.3% are anemic. This is in contrast to 29.4% of women in other social groups having CED and 51.1% in these groups being anemic MOHFW (NFHS-III 2006). STs are at the bottom of all indicators in the Human Development Index too. SCs and STs share in the incidence of poverty is the largest and therefore they are most vulnerable to food insecurity shocks. They are also disadvantaged by poor health, discrimination and exclusion, political powerlessness, physical insecurity and disarticulation. Poverty alleviation programme have made no significant impact on this situation. They are also not well integrated with food security programmes at the delivery level. The efforts for combating exclusion and discrimination continue to be weak and lacking in political thrust and social mobilization. This accounts for both poverty and food insecurity persistently co-existing at high levels in these two communities.

There is a seasonal dimension of hunger too. It pertains to rural areas in respect of persons dependent upon agriculture and includes small and marginal farmers and agricultural labourers who face starvation during months between harvesting of major Rabi and Kharif crops and during lean agricultural seasons. This is the period when they need wage employment the most as there is no farm work available and they do not have food stocks to survive. This is the period when they migrate for work under the most exploitative conditions just to stave off hunger Seasonal hunger has a regional sub-text. This hunger, overall and particularly in ST and SC households, is higher in rural than in the urban areas (Sagar, 2015). But for STs, chronic hunger in urban areas is higher than in rural areas. This is explained by their access to forest resources (roots and tubers) in rural areas (Sagar, 2005). The regional dimension of hunger is conveyed by greater vulnerability of rural people compared to those in the urban areas as the former have lesser income earning opportunities to be able to purchase food.

There are occupational aspects of hunger as well. The incidence of hunger is higher in rural labour households particularly landless agricultural labourers, artisans and other non-labour categories (Sagar, 2005). Self-employed in agriculture and non-agricultural vocations, agricultural labour and other labour in rural areas are the most vulnerable compared to urban areas because the latter have greater possibility to find casual work. But in urban areas casual labour faces the greatest threat of hunger both seasonal and chronic, even though the incidence of both type of hunger has declined. Overall, the incidence of hunger is concentrated in eastern states and it is the highest in agricultural labour and other labour households in rural areas and casual labour households in urban areas (Sagar, 2005). The income dimension of poverty is relatable to the poverty levels. The socio-economic groups which share higher level of poverty are food insecure. SCs and STs are, therefore, the most food insecure and the incidence of endemic hunger is also the highest among them. Judging by the norm of calorie intake, more than 60% of rural population is food insecure despite reduction in poverty levels. Judging by the norm of food absorption as reflected in anthropometric indicators, there is convergence between caloric in take, access to basic services and incidence of child malnutrition (Sagar, 2005).

The discourse on hunger usually leaves out the vulnerability dimension in terms of capacity to access food. The extreme extent of chronic food insecurity and starvation deaths are concentrated in groups who are most vulnerable because they are unable to purchase food. There are homeless persons, beggars, persons with disability (with no family support/weak family support), persons suffering from chronic illness, widows, battered and abandoned women, sex workers, street children. Some of these people are forced to sell their children or push them to labour market. In rural areas, they are forced survive on edible grasses, roots and rat meat. In urban areas they engage in begging, low and underpaid work, scrounge for leftover food from dust bins, feed opium to their children to stop them for crying and abandon them on the streets and at times take their lives in desperation. We shall now scrutinize how the state has responded to address their food security, whether the measures taken have been adequate and what has been their impact?

## Political Economy of Hunger

The inability of people to access food and other essential necessities in any country can be directly related to the nature of economy and society. The paradox of food availability at the macro-level and high incidence of chronic hunger in India can only be explained by a large number of causes which have contributed to lack of access to food. These causes have arisen from and have been sustained by State policies which have undermined the power of particular sections of the population to command food. Foremost among these policies is the forcible acquisition of land of peasants in the name of development leading not only to the loss of the individual household's ability to produce food for its consumption but also loss of livelihood since land was the only means for such households to produce food and have some income. With state neither providing alternative livelihood to persons losing their land or access to forest resources nor providing sufficient financial compensation and rehabilitation these households were exposed to lack of power to purchase food from the PDS or open market. The rapidly growing cash economy replacing the pre-wage economy has also deprived several small groups of the income which they earned from many traditional vocations especially as these groups were not provided any alternate source of livelihood. This segment has been the most vulnerable to chronic hunger. The changes in the labour market conditions leading to decline in wages compared to food prices or increase in the unemployment have the most negative impact on the food security of the wage labour solely dependent on selling its labour power to purchase food. This vulnerability increases enormously with market economy. In India, this is particularly so because there is no institutionalized social security arrangement such as unemployment insurance or food vouchers which are helpful in absorbing this shock especially as the traditional mechanisms of social security in pre-wage economies have broken down. The advances in technology contributing not only to increase in food production and enhancing food security but also other improvements in life, while raising standard of living have caused enormous environmental degradation of productive resources such as degradation of soil, pollution of water sources, deforestation and desertification and lately, the climate change which have negatively impacted on the food security and livelihood of the people in the rural areas. The increasing integration of country's economy with global market has exposed farmers to increase in input cost of cultivation and volatility of output prices, liberalized imports and competition with producers across the world. This has rendered farming unviable and farmers impoverished with sharp fall in income and increasing debt leading to not only food insecurity of the farming households but also to farmers' suicides. A large number of them leave farming to seek livelihood as wage labour and therefore become victims of chronic food insecurity. The sharply increasing inequalities produced by the economy have resulted in some sections enjoying access to choicest food of quality, while others are lacking even the means to purchase food such as situation results not from natural calamities but from man made decisions which render some sections enormously rich while many others losing their access to food suddenly and rapidly. Much of this is the outcome of ideological shifts in policy and governance. The lack of sensitivity and concern to address these debilitating inequalities, but as also other reasons for widespread hunger, in particular the absence of a comprehensive social security to ensure that no household is permitted to fall into the category of endemic hunger emanates from the skewed power relations in society in which those who are negatively impacted by economy and political decision making are powerless to counteract the mortifying phenomenon of chronic hunger on such a large scale. State is therefore complicit in creating this situation as its policies are responsible for increasing food insecurity on such as widespread scale. A scrutiny of state action since independence would show how the state has betrayed its responsibility comprehensively and to a devastating effect.

## State Polices to Address Endemic Hunger

While the modern day consciousness about food and nutritional insecurity of people did not exist in ancient times, large scale deprivation of food entitlements leading to starvation deaths or deaths due to disease to which lack of food contributed in the form of famines did attract attention of the rulers. There is some evidence, though scanty, of how pre-colonial rulers responded to such catastrophic episodes. These responses included employment creation in large size public works like temples/mosques, forts or irrigation works to recreate purchasing power, distribution of raw grains to those who could not work, opening of free kitchens and public food grain stores and payment of advances and remission of taxes. But their scale, reach and effectiveness was limited due to lack of a large number of factors which included lack of accurate information, inadequate resources and governance capacity, lack of connectivity, etc. Besides, these measures were adhoc and confined to certain locations which did not show any systemic response. Such a systemic response though considerably late and after initial periods of inaction was introduced during the colonial period which witnessed recurrent famines starting from 1770 large scale Bengal Famine to the most acute Bengal Famine of 1943 leading to lakhs of deaths. These famines as many earlier famines resulted largely from crop failure due to drought leading to reduced food availability in the region and lack of employment for agricultural labourers as farm activity was disrupted. This was compounded by rise in food prices. This happened most unfortunately despite the fact that there was no shortage of food in the country as a whole. The intervention to address such situations emerged as the colonial government was under pressure to prevent political instability, revenue loss as also to assuage public opinion in England besides some humanitarian concerns. This action emanated from the recommendations of the Famine Commission Reports in the form of 'selective intervention' focused primarily on providing contingency employment on public works for income generation. The policy instrument designed for such action was introduction of Famine Codes which were quite comprehensive. The strategy of famine relief contained in it basically focused on the organization of public works directed to creation of public assets on a large scale, to provide employment at subsistence wages and 'Gratuitous relief' for those unable to work in the form of doles or kitchen (Drézé, 1995) Doles in cash and grain were preferred over cooked meals. The twin action also fulfilled the objective of financial economy as only the very needy and willing would come forward to claim them. But the utility of these provisions was limited in preventing starvation deaths as these provisions were not enforced speedily and effectively due to reluctance and sluggishness and at times deliberate delay in declaring a 'famine' despite clear guidelines laying down conditions requiring such a declaration. Other factors which limited the utility of famine provisions were very low level of wages paid on public works, failure to regulate trade in food grains to ensure their availability, checking rise in food grain prices in the affected area and lack of action, beyond restoration of food entitlements, to check vulnerability to epidemics due to emasciated condition of people living in the area resulting from deprivation of food. But above all the famine code provisions were niggardly and did not show the requisite understanding of the value attached to human life. (Drézé, 1995)

India inherited this legacy of tackling hunger and starvation in a situation of a precariously low level of food production which was aggravated by partition as the production rich part of Punjab went over to Pakistan. This situation continued until at a macro-level, production started increasing moderately after the Green Revolution. Yet Independent India was able to prevent famine which the colonial government could not. This could be attributed to improved availability of food at a macro-level through imports and later through accumulation of large stocks through procurement. But improvement in availability of food through increased production as a result of Green Revolution was regionally uneven as it did not cover non-irrigated areas—roughly two third of the country, which neither experienced rise in rural employment nor wages besides facing ecological degradation—deforestation, soil erosions, falling water tables along with periodic crop failures in one part or the other. These gains in production could not have prevented chronic food insecurity or famine like conditions which are caused by factors relating to access food. The success in preventing famine could only be attributed to the timely and effective state intervention. This intervention was effected on the lines of famine code of the colonial government. But this intervention depended on an early declaration that such a condition had occurred and to putting into effect the famine code provisions focused on generating the purchasing power of the people in affected areas through employment in public works, physical supply of food facilitated by private trade and gratuitous relief for the those who could not work. State action was deficient on both these counts. The consideration of financial economy usually weighed in resulting in delay in introducing these measures as well as the scale of operations. As a result, starvation in vulnerable households may not have been prevented entirely though governments never admit it (Drézé, 1995). But post-Independence India moved beyond the legacy of colonial mode of famine prevention by regulating private trade in food grains and maintaining price stability, Public distribution system, and, later, by other measures to protect the vulnerable sections (Children and those who could not work) and more broad based employment generation programmes. Additionally, political and civil society pressure, within a limited democracy also played a role in increasing state intervention to not only prevent starvation and famine but also to address chronic food and nutritional insecurity among vulnerable victims due to persistence of mass poverty. However, the continuing phenomenon of India having the largest number of hungry people and nutritionally deficient children and adults has to be situated in the entitlements that the state has created, their scale, eligibility of access and effectiveness of their implementation.

## Issues of Food Security Availability

Food security at the national level needs to address four issues. These are availability of food grains, environmentally sustainable method of food production, access of hungry population to food and absorption of food consumed. As regards availability, the total food grains production in the country during the year 2014-15 was 252.02 million tones with a storage capacity of 823.17 lakh tonnes. There was a short fall in production from the level reached in 2013-14 which was 265.04 million tonnes and of 259.28 million tones in 2011-12. Per capita net availability of food grains per annum in 2013 was 146.5 kg which was a decline from 165.6 kg in 2011 and per captia net availability of food grains per day was 401.4 gms in 2013, a decline from 453.6 gms in 2011 and 510.1 gm in 1991 (MoA, 2015) per day. While the population growth rate has declined from 2.24% in 1961-71 to 1.03% in 2001-2011, the overall rate of growth of food grains has also declined. Even so, it is projected that the total food grains demand will increase to about 291 million tonnes by 2025 and per capita per month from 16.7 kg to 19.9 kg (Khatkar et al., 2016). Food Grain production has almost stagnated and production gaps exist despite decline in the population growth. The country would require to increase food grain production by 5 million tonnes per year so as to satisfy the demand for food grains per capita and overall as projected. Between 1950-51 and 2006-07, production of food grains increased at an average annual rate of 2.5% compared to the growth of population averaging 2.1% during the year. This provided a reasonable degree of self-sufficiency. However, between 1990-2007 rate of growth of food grains production decelerated to 1.2% while the annual rate of population growth was higher at 1.9%. Food grain 'availability' therefore declined by 4.5% and per capita availability declined by 13% from 468 gms per capita per day in 1992 to 422 gms per capita per day in 2005 and to 401 gms in 2013 (MOA, 2015, Swaminathan and Bhavani 2013). The availability decline during this period could also be on account of exports besides deficient production. The deficiency had to be bridged by a ban on exports and by resorting to imports. The stagnation in food grain production represents the state of agriculture which is in crisis. Improvement in yields holds the key for India to remain self-sufficient in food grain. (MoF 2012-13) Various measures such as National Food Security Mission, Rashtriya Krishi Vikas Yojana, Rainfed Area Development Programme etc were taken to increase food grain production to address this crisis. Some more programmes have been added by the NDA government.

Yet another dimension of food grains availability lies in the unevenness of food grain production across different parts. Green Revolution, the prime contributor to food grain production in the country through significant increases in yields and total output was confined to irrigated regions while the unirrigated (Dry land) areas which constitute two thirds of the total cropped area have experienced virtual stagnation in production with little evidence of increasing rural incomes and employment. These regions also suffered ecological degradation (deforestation, soil erosion and falling water table) and periodic episodes of droughts and crop failures causing huge problems of access to food (Drézé, 1995). While Green Revolution strategy to cover these regions was introduced in the recent years, regional food grains deficits were met by procurement, building buffer stocks and sale through public distribution system.

Thus production along with public stock building determine food availability. For this purpose government has issued guidelines on the norms for buffer stocking of wheat and rice as on the first day of January, April, July, October. The optimum level of stocking as per this norm since January 2015 has been 41.12 million tonnes which includes the strategic reserves (MOA, 2015). Usually, government procures far more food grains than this level and therefore the buffer stock with the FCI at any given time is much higher than this limit. The buffer stock primarily consists of wheat and rice but, from the view point of nutrition, coarse grains are important for which there is negligible procurement and buffer stocking.

## Sustainability of Food Production

The achievement in food production which underlies macro-level availability of food has a huge environmental cost which threatens its sustainability. The drivers of unsustainability are declining availability of cultivable land, degradation of productive resources—land, water forest and marine resources and injudicious use of inputs. Between 1970-71 and 2009-2012, diversion of agricultural land for non-agricultural purposes has increased from 16 million hectares to 26 mha (IDFC, 2013). This has led to significant intensification of land use to increase yield through increased use of irrigation and use of other inputs. While the net sown area continues to remain at 46% of total geographical area since 1970-71, higher cropping intensity has led to significant increase in gross cropped area. The productive potential of land has reduced due to degradation which affects 57% of the total area of which 25% is subject to desertification. The leading cause of land degradation is soil erosion by water which affects 70% of such degradation. The other cause is inappropriate use of inputs with disproportionate use of chemical fertilizers, particularly nitrogen which has reduced soil fertility. Increasing pressure for fodder and fuel wood has also degraded arid and semi-arid regions. Mining has also degraded land by dumping of overburden soil and water logging. The area under Common Property Resources (CPRs) has declined by 31-55% (IDFC, 2013). Surface and sub-surface water used in agriculture has been degraded by discharge of industrial effluents.

Inefficient use of water has led to water logging (2.46 mha), surface water stagnation (3.4 mha) and accumulation of soft and alkalinity in soil (Reddy, 2011). Rapid increase in tube wells has led to lowering of ground water table and irrigation with saline water. There was a loss of forest cover of around, 1, 40, 000 ha per year between 1951-1980 and around 53, 000 ha between 1999-2007 (Srivastava and Kothari, 2012). Marine resources have also degraded due to excessive extraction of catch, overfishing in territorial waters and illegal fishing by trawler owners leading to upsetting of salinity balance in coastral area, which has damaged farm lands, lowered rice production besides causing loss of livelihood (Srivastava & Kothari, 2012).

## Access

But food security at the level of individuals and households is not ensured by mere physical availability of food grains in the market or the local PDS shop. Where the households are able to produce food for all its members, availability of and access to food grains are ensured. Where this is not the case, the access to food depends upon income to purchase food. This purchasing power determines access to food and its quality and quantity which are reflected in level of consumption of food. The real per capita food consumption has registered a decline during the last two decades in respect of cereals, pulses and edible oils with no signs of adequate intake of other foods meat, milk, eggs, fruits and vegetables (Singh, 2006, NSSO, 2007). This is particularly so in respect of lower 10% of the population compared to the top decile. This can be attributed to lack of income to purchase food. The incidence and magnitude of hunger in India is directly related to this lack of purchasing power despite the physical availability of food. This lack of purchasing power is on account of low income of farming households as reflected in NSSO estimates and lack of sufficient employment opportunities as well as low level of wages of those employed. This explains why despite the growth in food grain production falling behind rate of population growth, there is rising levels of procurement by the government leading to higher than prescribed norm of buffer stocks, and even exports and inadequate lifting of food grains by the PDS shops. In 2012-13, 52.8 million tonnes of food grains were procured to build buffer stock but the off take level reached only 47.16 million tonnes (MoF, 2013). This reflects effective contraction of demand which is indicative of the level of poverty caused by unemployment and income decline (Saxena, 2009). Based on the planning commission estimates in 2007, nearly 260.27 million people in both rural and urban areas can be assumed to be unable to buy sufficient food to ensure their food and nutritional security (Singh, 2005). While lack of purchasing power constrains ability to purchase food, lack of effective access may also be caused by inefficiency of public distribution system particularly in the hilly, tribal and remote areas.

## Absorption

Another facet of Food Insecurity is nutritional insecurity which is caused by inability of the body to absorb the nutrients from food consumed. This insecurity depends upon non-food factors such as access to drinking water, sanitation, health services, basic education. The wider conceptualization of food insecurity includes this dimension as well. The lack of absorption of food even when adequate food is taken on account of lack of access to these amenities produce malnutrition, cause ill health, lower productivity and generate an overall absence of well-being. The high incidence of nutritional deficiency in the population is manifested in below normal BMI, under nourished children (suffering from underweight and stunting), and chronic energy deficiency among women leading to anemia, and malnutrition among children leading to child mortality. Therefore, the absence of hunger is to be measured not merely by adequate calorie intake but by absorption of food in the body which is enabled by easy access to safe drinking water, sanitation facilities and health care.

## Government Responsibility

Colonial government was not very responsive to addressing chronic food insecurity of people which was manifested in large number of famines'. Being a subject, Indian people had no mechanism to convey their suffering to the government and demand its alleviation. This was particularly so during the company rule which saw a larger number of famines as there was no accountability of its action. Post 1858, with direct assumption of rule by the crown, notionally at least, there was accountability of the Indian government to British Parliament and therefore to the people there. The famines during this period therefore attracted some attention, though belatedly, which eventually led to the setting up of Famine Commissions and introduction of Famine codes on the basis their recommendations (Drézé, 1994). During this period, national movement towards the latter half of British rule in $20^{th}$ century had also gathered momentum and could put some pressure through public action on the government for its intervention. Though inadequate these measures were able to limit the severity of the impact of famines in later years. Even so, it was a fire fighting operation to preempt public criticism in England and not to address the chronic food Insecurity of the people which was caused not merely by adverse weather conditions but also by government's agrarian, industrial and trade policies.

After Independence, India embraced a democratic polity governed by the Constitution. Its policies were influenced both by the provisions of the Constitution as well as public action manifested in pressure exerted by representative institutions and other entities representing public interest. The rulers were also more responsive to suffering of the people. Ensuring food availability therefore received their priority attention. The country was also conscious of its international obligation under the Covenant on Economic Social, Culture Rights to protect and fulfill the right to food for every citizen of India. However, government's intervention to tackle food security of people faced serious shortages of food grains availability which had to be met by imports. But the government also focused on increasing production and introduction of Green Revolution was the main policy intervention to achieve it. Later, it put in place a Public Distribution System to ensure availability of food grains to the people at controlled prices throughout the country. Over a period of time, a number of schemes were introduced to address problems of access to food, its absorption and under nutrition. The aggressive campaigns by social activists and public interest litigation in the Supreme court resulted in the apex court monitoring the measures to ensure food security to the people and issuing several directions to expand the food and nutritional entitlements of the people. But there was still no guaranteed right to food embedded in law which could be enforced in case of denial. The public campaign had pitched for a such a law.

## Right to Food

The Indian Constitution does not incorporate Right to Food as one of the Fundamental Rights though Art 47 in the Directive Principles of State Policy does consider it as 'the duty of the State to raise the level of nutrition and standard of living and to improve public health'. But the Supreme Court has interpreted the Fundamental Right to life in Art 21 to imply life with dignity which includes access to adequate food. Besides, since 2001, in response to a PIL filed by PUCL (Peoples Union for Civil Liberties) on inadequate food relief in drought affected six States, Supreme Court expanded its ambit to eliminate hunger and under nutrition in the whole country through interim orders (over 40 so far) directing central and state governments to effectively implement existing food and nutrition related schemes. Yet, the State till recently did not recognize an enforceable right to food for its people.

### Intervention to provide Food Security

Government Interventions over a period of time to provide food security to the people have been varied and wide ranging covering virtually from pre-birth stage to old age through its development planning. They have also covered three dimensions of food and nutritional security—production, access and absorption. The Intervention at the level of production came first in the form of Green Revolution. This was a technological intervention to increase production through input of high yielding hybrid seeds in selected areas where irrigation water was available. Prior to that government had launched a Grow More Food campaign through its community development programme. Separately, irrigation development was also undertaken covering all three type of projects-large irrigation through construction of dams and network of canals, medium irrigation projects through smaller size water storage and distribution projects, and minor irrigation projects covering check dams, ponds, tanks, lift irrigation, dykes, etc. The third intervention for enhancing agricultural production was supply of subsidized inputs like seeds, fertilizers and extension of technology and information. Agricultural universities were established to undertake research for development of high yielding and pest resistant seeds, etc. Seeds Development Corporations were set up to produce seeds based on the technology developed by the universities for distribution to farmers. Subsidized fertilizers was also distributed to the farmers for which fertilizer factories were established Production and land development credit was arranged through a network of cooperative and commercial banks. Trained extension workers were posted at the village level to carry the fruits of research to the farmers and gather farmer's feedback to the policy makers and universities, Agricultural development officials constituted integral part of Block, Subdivision and District level administration. To provide incentives to the farmers and assure them of remunerative price for their produce and to insulate them from the vagaries of the market, Minimum Support Price was declared for major cereal crops to influence market prices and procurement was undertaken to prevent distress sale of produce. Food availability at micro-level was arranged through four major interventions (1) procurement of food grains from the farmers and mandating rice and sugar mills to deliver prescribed quantum of production so as to build a buffer stock for distribution along with storage structures at national and regional levels. (2) setting up a country wide network of fair price shops for supply of food grains at prescribed prices. (3) fixing prices of commodities to be supplied to households. (4) Setting up of state agencies to draw the required quantity of food grains from national depots and their transportation to the PDS.

Lately, sustainability of food production has also been attended to for ensuring stability in food production. This has been attempted through efforts to reverse land degradation and construction of soil and water conservation structure. These include watershed development programme particularly in rainfed and resource poor areas to improve water retention in soil, soil fertility and crop productivity and reduce soil erosion in cropped areas, changes in the subsidy pattern of fertilizer use to check imbalance in fertiliser use from a regime of subsidy per fertiliser product to a regime of nutrient based subsidy, promotion of organic farming, financial assistance for creation of compost units and bio-fertiliser and bio-pesticide production units and compensating farmers for a part of cultivation costs under its agricultural development schemes, converting waste lands into cropped lands and promoting cultivation of non-food crops such as Jatropha and Pongamia. Forest degradation was checked through compensatory afforestation programmes and other initiative for afforestation and forest protection. Water crisis is being tackled through regulation of ground water, river conservation and lake conservation plans to check pollution. Marine resources degradation is being addressed through various regulatory measures. The effect of Climate change is also sought to be counteracted by a comprehensive National Action Plan to mitigate hardships caused to farmers (IDFC, 2012-13).

The interventions for access to food have centered around creating purchasing power to buy food grains from PDS or the market. The main approach of this intervention was targeting. Each of the instruments introduced for access was designed to be selective and confined to a specific target group. Poverty alleviation programmes for income generation through self and wage employment (IRDP & Food & Wage for Work Programmes now rechristened as NRLM and MNREGS respectively) were made eligible only to those below a certain threshold of income considered bare minimum for procuring requisite items of food basket for subsistence. A BPL list was prepared for this purpose. The households included in the list were entitled to avail of the programs. The children's food and nutritional security was ensured through supply of food in the age group of 0-5 years under ICDS and for school group children under Mid-Day Meals. For older persons not capable of doing physical labour, National Social Assistance Programme provided a small amount as monthly pension. Pregnant women's additional food and nutritional needs were catered to under the Maternity Benefit scheme Adolescent girls nutritional requirements were addressed through SABLA scheme those households who lost their bread winner were provided one time financial assistance under National Family Benefit Scheme. The indigent and most vulnerable persons' food needs were met through Annapurna and Antyodya Schemes.

Absorption of food consumed to get the requisite nutrients was facilitated through provision of safe drinking water to each village and urban residential colonies and sanitation facilities under its National Drinking Water Mission and Total Sanitation Programmes. Access to health care was provided through a five tier infrastructure with Sub centre at the bottom level, primary health centre, community health centre, District Hospital in the middle level and the Medical College and hospital at the apex level which catered to preventive and promotive and curative dimensions of health. Access to education has been arranged through network of schools at primary and secondary levels.

## Existing Food Security Schemes

Prior to the enactment of National Food Security Act (NFSA), a total of nine schemes were in operation which included Targeted Public Distribution System, Antodyaya Anna Yojana (AAY), Annapoorna Yojana, Integrated Child Development Services (ICDS), Mid-Day Meal Scheme (MDM), National Maternity Benefit Scheme, SABLA, National Family Benefit

Scheme (NFBS), and National old age Pension Scheme. Targeted Public Distribution System (TPDS) supplied essential commodities—rice, wheat, sugar, edible oil, kerosene to consumers through fair price shops at fixed prices so as to insulate the consumers from price inflation. Annapoorna Yojana provided 10 kg of food grains free of charge per month to indigent citizens living alone. Antyodya Yojana provided to the poorest of the poor households 35 kg of food grains per month at very low prices of ₹ 2 per kg rice and ₹ 3 per kg for wheat. Integrated Child Development Services programme provided children in the age group of 0-3 free food along with health services. Mid-Day Meal Scheme is applicable to all government and government assisted schools where free hot cooked meal is made available to children for at least 200 days per year. National Family Benefit Scheme provided one time assistance to families who have lost a bread earner, while National Maternity Benefit Scheme (NMBS) extended cash assistance to pregnant women for improving their nutrition. SABLA provide package of services including health and nutrition to adolescent girls in the age group of 11-14 years for out of school girls and 15-18 years for all girls. National Old Age Scheme provided monthly pension to elderly above 60 years who have no family support, widows and disabled persons as an economic support. The latter three being cash assistance schemes addressed the food security indirectly by making purchasing power available to them to address their vulnerable conditions. Since access to food is contingent upon availability of Income to purchase it, a wage employment programme with a guaranteed 100 days of work for unskilled labourers in rural areas has been provided as a legal entitlement under MNREGS. National Rural Livelihood Mission extended assistance for improving skills and bank credit to the self-employed persons for enhancing their income. Both schemes addressed lack of adequate purchasing power of the needy households.

## Status of Implementation of These Schemes

The above eleven schemes have not been able to ensure food and nutritional security to all the needy people because of conceptual limitations, operational problems, and deficient coverage and inadequate resource allocation which have left large gaps between those who need these services and those who are able to get their benefit. Among the conceptual issues, the eligibility test tops the list. Its chief instrument, the BPL list, has been the most controversial due to inclusion and exclusion errors. The other issues which have constrained access are low coverage on account of inadequate resource allocation such as with NSAP (National Social Assistance Programme), ICDS, MDM, design factor such as only one time benefit as in the case of NFBS (National Family Benefit Scheme) and conditionalities imposed for accessing benefits as in the case of NMBS (National Maternity Benefit Scheme), Antyodya and Annapurna Yojana and very small area coverage as in the case of SABLA (Rajiv Gandhi Scheme for empowerment of adolescent girls—sabla), IGMSY (Indira Gandhi Matritva Sahyog Yojana) which are only pilot projects. The operational bottlenecks include procedural requirements for access and difficulties faced by the poor in complying with them, unresponsiveness of the lower level bureaucracy and omissions result in inadequate attention being paid to address food security of the vulnerable categories of the poor. These categories include destitute urban poor, migrants, street children, slum residents, unorganized workers due to difficulties associated with identification in the absence of any permanent address. This is in addition to those who are excluded on account of the flawed process of identification in the BPL list. Besides, the Supreme Court orders to cover certain categories of vulnerable persons such as the aged, infirm, disabled, pregnant and lactating women, destitute women, widows and other single women with no regular support, older persons above 60 years with no assured means of subsistence, households with a disabled adult but no regular support or assured means of subsistence, households where, due to a variety of reasons, no adult member is available for gainful employment, pre-agricultural tribes etc are also not covered or are inadequately covered by the existing social security schemes.

Besides, these limitations, implementation of individual schemes bring out other negative features which limit their effectiveness in addressing food security of the people. The Targeted Public Distribution System (TPDS) supplied food grains at subsidized prices only to poor persons included in the Below Poverty Line list. Persons above this line were supplied food grains at a higher price. This poverty line was prepared on the basis of income poverty i.e. the level of Income required to access specified calories from food basket. The official poverty line suffered from a large degree of exclusion of the genuinely poor and inclusion of the underserving. The nutritional studies showed that a far larger number of people suffered from food insecurity than the number included in the list. The functioning of Fair Price Shops, was extremely dismal. Some of the problems noted were shops remaining closed, bogus ration cards, poor quality of food grains supplies from F.P. shops, short weighting of food grains, Price charged in the TPDS being higher than the notified price were some of the problems which afflicted TPDS. Besides, the existing level of entitlement provided inadequate quantity of food grains. It was 35 kg per household for BPL households and certain groups above poverty line. (APL) while the ICMR has laid down a norm of 55 kg for a family of five as the need. Several states refused to issue ration cards to urban destitute and homeless persons and migrant labour due to identity related problems such as lack a shelter and verifiable antecedents. There was also a differential pricing system for grains supplied to different categories of beneficiaries. It was lower for BPL families but higher for APL households. A third price was introduced for Antodya Anna Yojana, which is lower than those for BPL families. The differential pricing facilitated leakage and malpractices, caused confusion among consumers, created social discontent due to perceived unfairness by different households, besides complexity of administering the scheme. The TPDS also suffered from inefficiency, pilferage and corruption and diversion of food grains from TPDS network, depriving the eligible beneficiaries of their entitlement (Cheriyan, 2006). A number of state governments were not lifting their entitled share of food grains due to lack of working capital with the nodal agency and adequate storage, handling and transportation facilities. FP shops were also not provided storage, handling and transportation charges. FP shops were also not supplied with food grains on time. FP shopkeepers complained of economic unviability of this business due to a very low level of commission admissible to them. Low purchasing capacity of consumers forced them not to claim their entitled quota of food grains and other commodities. The most damaging aspect of current management of PDS is the increase in the quantity of food grains rotting in the godowns of FCI while millions of people go hungry (UN, 2012).

Mid-Day Meals Programme suffered from non-implementation in many states citing reasons of lack of cash resources to run it and disruption of school activities, etc. despite the Supreme Court orders. Where it was implemented, coverage was not universal. Other features which affected the reach of this benefit to school going children included disruption due to delay in supply of food grains and release of funds by the state governments to implementing agencies, poor quality of food and frequent complaints of children falling ill, number of children taking food coming down, absence of infrastructure for cooking, drinking water and sanitation facilities, demotivated cooks and helpers due to low remuneration and its late payment and being burdened with tasks of procuring food grains, cooking, serving and cleaning, disinterested school staff who considered this responsibility a waste of time, multiple and disconnected channels of monitoring, absence of clearly established system of accountability and lack of facilitating mechanism for community participation. Corruption also plagued the implementation.

ICDS Programme encountered more or less the same set of problems i.e insufficient resource allocation to comply with Supreme Court order of universal coverage, poor quality and palatability of food, insanitary conditions of cooking, irregular supply of food material, absence of proper infrastructure—building, weighing machine, educational and recreational material, drinking water and sanitation facilities, overburdened Anganwadi Workers and low honorarium and that too not paid timely beside corruption. In addition, the Programme implementation also brought out that take home ration in place of cooked food was also of poor quality, long delay in serving food, health and education part of the programme badly neglected, supplementary nutrition not provided, growth monitoring not carried out, lack of coordination between ANM, AWW and ASHA.

Maternity Benefit Scheme was only implemented as a pilot project in select 52 districts and not universalized. Even in these districts restrictions in claiming entitlement were impacted by conditions of eligibility—(1) minimum age of entitlement being fixed at 19 years 2) not being adminissible for more than one child birth and (3) for child birth having taken place through institutional delivery with required vaccination. Besides, the amount provided was inadequate to provide care and nutrition. Further the procedural hassals encountered in procuring prescribed certificates for registration of claims and verification for eligibility acted as a further barrier in seeking it. There was no crèche facility which prevented breast feeding by unorganized women workers who are forced to work shortly after delivery. Similarly SABLA scheme suffered from inadequate coverage, low reach, low financial allocation, deficient implementation of package, etc.

Antyodya Anna Yojana failed to provide food security to many of the poorest of the poor due to a ceiling fixed on its coverage as only 5% of the population could avail of it. This implied selective coverage of the eligible resulting in selection being influenced by local power structure. Annapoorna Yojana though not beset with restricted coverage is eligible only for individuals without an assured pension or a regular source of income or those with a family that earns less than a specified annual income. States found selection on the basis of these conditions among a large number of claimants extremely difficult and wanted to cover all destitute individuals above 65 years of age. But central government did not expand the ambit of coverage. The Scheme therefore failed to provide food security to such indigent groups and the scheme was therefore virtually unimplemented.

The National Social Assistance Programme which targets persons of old age, widows and those with disability faces a huge unmet demand due to restricted coverage caused by (current coverage only 33%) inadequate resource allocation, deficient targeting process leading to exclusion of many deserving persons and inclusion of some underserving ones, very low amount of assistance provided which has not been increased since the inception of the scheme, inter-state disparity in the amount of assistance paid to the pensioners as some states provided a higher amount by supplementing their own resources, unwillingness to relate the amount with inflation leading to diminishing purchasing power from the amount, disrupted payment and non-payment in some states due to budget constraints.

MNREGS, the only programme which provides wage employment to enable access to food security has not succeeded in providing even 100 days of assured employment, the average number of days per year has been around 40-

45. The Programme implementation is also constrained by failure to provide employment when the poor need it the most to stave off starvation, huge unmet demand, virtual non-implementation during the agricultural season, skewed coverage across panchayats, blocks and districts, delayed payment, inadequate staff support, and indifference of implementing agencies in many areas besides corruption, actual wage payment based on output being less than the mandated wage, payment of wages solely on the basis of number of days prescribed in the SoR (Schedule of Rates) irrespective of number of days for which the worker has worked.

National Rural Livelihood Mission has been ineffective in providing credit and technology and escorting support for self-employment due to absence of inadequate training, lack of cooperation from banks, lack of dedicated field staff to implement, SHGs not transiting from micro-finance meeting contingencies to livelihood creation/support. Even the few well-functioning SHGs which make financial support available for small needs/contingencies are unable to assist the beneficiaries for higher level of livelihood activities. The programme lacked capability to provide this kind of support. The SHGs are even unable to get the prescribed 2-5 lakhs as community investment fund and end up getting a much lower amount. The programme has no potential to create assured purchasing power for access to food.

National Family Benefit Scheme has a very low reach with benefits extended to 1-2 lakhs beneficiaries in a year which indicates low level of awareness, lack of social support to claim entitlement, procedural requirement including those of verification leading to intermediation by touts and cheating. The low amount of entitlement in any case is onetime payment and does into ensure assured purchasing power on a continuing basis.

## Limitations of Policy Interventions

The measures for enhancement of agricultural production have failed to boost up growth of production so as to keep pace with the rate of growth of population due to stagnation in yields in the absence of any further technology break-through, serious gaps in productivity potential and improvement of dry land agriculture, lack of appropriate technology for adaptability to climate change, severe degradation of land, water, forest and marine resources, unviability of agriculture due to high cost of production and low returns, high indebtedness of farmers and frequent failure of crops, declining State support in terms of subsidized inputs, poor delivery of services such as credit and inputs to small and marginal farmers, skewed distribution of land and fragmentation of holdings, adverse trade policies, etc.

Measures for promoting sustainable agricultural production have failed to make an impact. Watershed development projects focused on engineering and constructional activities without community participation. Maintenance in post implementation phase was poor. Nutrient based subsidy regime for fertilizers did not include urea and therefore farmers replaced decontrolled fertilisers with it. Organic farming accounts for less than 1% of total cultivated area. Conversion of waste land into cropped land ignored equity. It denied villagers access to grazing land and other resources for livelihood. Efforts to check degradation of forests ignored livelihood needs of communities which led to their marginalization and therefore opposition. Measures to check pollution of water resources and depletion of ground water and degradation of marine resources have produced no visible positive change. (IDFC, 2013).

The interventions made for creating purchasing power to access food through provision of wage employment and Self-employment have been inadequate and have failed to achieve their objectives as indicated above. The economy failing to provide adequate employment due to jobless nature of growth, very low growth rates in agriculture compared to the growth rates of the overall economy further diminish the prospects of increase in employment and improvement in wages. Therefore, access to food emerges as the most formidable cause of all three types of food insecurity viz endemic hunger (Poverty induced), hidden hunger (caused by nutritional deficiency), and transient hunger (due to seasonal disruption in access). This dismal picture in respect of lack of purchasing power is all the more acute in respect vulnerable sections including the elderly persons who cannot work. This issue therefore calls for foremost massive intervention to prevent starvation deaths.

The interventions for absorption of food have been constrained by social barriers in access to basic services experienced by marginalized groups such as SCs, STs, migrants and destitutes and the physical barriers due to non-availability of a facility such as sanitation in the vicinity (distance factor), non-functionality of services (health education, drinking water) and poor quality of services (health and education) due to inadequate resource allocation for improvement in infrastructure, discriminatory behavior of the service providers, increasing privatization of service provisioning and shrinking state commitment to enhance access through pubic provisioning.

## New Legislation

Due to a massive Right to food campaign launched by the civil society activists, the National Advisory Council, a Think Tank of UPA which had as its members some of the social activists involved in this campaign took up the matter and recommended a comprehensive proposal to the Central government for a right based legislation guaranting food security to all citizens without discrimination. A new law, National Food Security Act which is a diluted version of the NAC proposal was enacted in 2013. Its major features include enhanced coverage of population with 75% of population in rural areas and 50% in urban areas, thus extending the coverage of TPDS to 67% of the population. The old categorization of population into BPL and APL has been done away with. The excluded group would consist of 25% of rural and 50% of urban population. The targeted groups (leaving aside the excluded category) have been divided into two categories: Antyodya Group and Priority Group.

Antyodya Group would be restricted to 10% of all households. The norms of food grain supply to this group would be 35 kg of food grains per family per month at subsidized rates of rice at ₹ 3 kg for rice, at ₹ 2 kg for wheat and at Re. 1 kg for Jowar. The priority group would receive 5 kg of food grains per person per month at subsidised rates. Separate entitlements for women and children have been provided. The maternal entitlements will be universal. Pregnant and lactating women will be entitled to free meals during pregnancy and upto six months after child birth. They will also receive maternity benefit of at least ₹ 6,000. The eldest woman of the household would be considered head of the household for issuing ration cards. Children aged 6 months to 6 years will get Take Home Ration or hot cooked meal. Children in the age group 6-14 years shall get one midday meal free of charge every day except holidays upto class VIII in all government managed and government aided schools. In urban areas, facilities for centralized kitchens may be used. The nutritional norms of take home ration/cooked meal/morning snack have also been specified. The new law provided clear division of responsibility between Central government, state governments and Local authorities. Centre government will procure food grains and allocate them to state governments based on the number of persons to be covered in each state. However, if the existing quantity of food grains which a state has been lifting from stocks for the last three years is more than the quantity allocated by the central government as per the Food Security Act, then the State's existing entitlement shall be protected. The Central government will also be responsible for transporting food grains to the central depots in each state. It shall create and maintain required modern scientific storage facilities. The state government would be responsible for the last mile delivery—from these depots to ration shops. The law has also introduced compensatory arrangement for non-supply of food grains. In the case of non-supply of food grains, the Central government will provide cash to the states which will be passed on to the beneficiaries. The Central government shall also provide assistance to state governments for meeting their expenditure on intra-state movement, handling of food grains, and margins paid to fair price shop dealers. The responsibility of state governments was to decide on the eligibility criteria for the households to get the required quantity of food grains based on a socio-economic and caste census within the state to cover the population decided by the Central government. The State shall take delivery of supply of food grains from the Central government, organize intra-state allocation and ensure delivery to the entitled persons. In the case of non-supply of entitled quantities of food grains/meals, they shall pay food security allowances to the beneficiaries. They are also required to create scientific storage capacity at state, district and block levels and establish institutionalized licensing arrangements and suitably strengthen capacities of their Food and Civil supplies corporations to handle storage and transportation of food grains. They shall establish institutionalized licensing arrangement for FP shops. Local authorities shall be responsible for implementation of the Act in their respective areas.

The law also lays down requirements of transparency and mechanism of accountability. As regards transparency, all PDS related records are required to be placed in public domain for inspection. There is also a provision of social audit to be conducted by the local authority as well as a provision for setting up a State Food Commission for monitoring of the

Act. The mechanism for accountability is provided by putting in place Grievance Redressal System at the District and State levels, setting up of call centres, helplines and nodal officers at State level and constituting vigilance committees at state, district, block and F.P. shop levels.

Four Schedules are also attached to the law. Schedule I specifies the subsidized price at which food grains would be supplied. Schedule II lays down nutritional standards for Take Home Ration, Hot Cooked Meal and Morning Snack. Schedule III makes provisions for measures required for revitalization of agriculture, procurement, storage and movement of food grains, reforms in PDS, access to drinking water, sanitation, nutritional supplements, health care and educational services and pension for senior citizens. Every Anganwadi centre and school shall have facilities for cooking, drinking water and sanitation. Schedule IV indicates state wise allocation of food grains.

While the law is an improvement over the existing food security schemes in terms of larger coverage and incorporation of entitlements of women and children, there are serious gaps in the legislation. The Act disregarded the demand for universal coverage excluding the privileged classes. It does not specify criteria for the identification of households eligible for food entitlements. As per the law, the central government will determine state wise coverage of population only and allocation of food grains on that basis. Prior fixation of state wise coverage of population and allocation of food grains without taking into account number of eligible persons that would emerge from the caste and economic census would leave scope for exclusion of the deserving. The Act provides food grain security but not nutritional security as there is no provision for supply of pulses and edible oil in the entitlement package. There is no protection against increase in prices of food grains. The objective of the law is also threatened by pressure to introduce cash transfers as a substitute for distribution of food grains (UN, 2012). Access to entitlement only with Aadhar linkage strikes at the root of the right based law and would bring in exclusion through the backdoor. Retention of GM foods creates apprehension about possible adverse impact on health. An escape route for withdrawal of the right to food in the case of natural calamities and war has been incorporated which creates apprehension about scrapping or dilution of the entitlement if the government so decides. No entitlement for destitute, homeless persons and those suffering from disabling diseases etc has been provided. Besides the above, the Act entitles a family only 25 kg of food grains at cheap rates per month and thus reduces the existing entitlement under Supreme Court orders of 35 kg per family per month. For children's Right to Food, provision of cooked hot meal in ICDS centres and supply of other nutrients has not been explicitly made. The expression used in the Act is 'appropriate meal.' As the commercial interests in Food sector have been provided an opening in the Act, this may be used to substitute hot cooked meal by readymade packaged commercial product. There is no provision for free meals to starving persons and no protocol has been laid down to investigate starvation deaths. No measures for protection of farmers access to productive resources and against dumping of subsidized imports, diversion of natural resources from food production, prevention of introduction of GM seeds, speculation and futures trading in food items have been included to ensure that food production in sustained.

## Current State of Implementation of NFSA

The NFSA was enacted on September 10, 2013. It was to have been operationalized within 365 days from its commencement on 15 July 2013 during which states were required to complete identification of eligible households for Priority Category and Antyodya Anna Yojana Category on the basis of socio-economic and caste census. As per the latest information on the website of the nodel Ministry, 33 States and UTs are implementing provisions of NFSA out of which two—Chandigarh and Puduchery are implementing in it DBT mode i.e., by providing direct cash transfer of food subsidy in place of food grains to the beneficiaries (DoFPD, 2017; Hindu, 2017). But not all implementation in other states (UTs) is as per the provisions of the Act, since many States have not yet identified AAY and Priority Household beneficiaries but continue to use old data base of beneficiaries. Similarly, new ration cards with eldest women of the family as head of the households have not yet been issued to all the beneficiaries. Maternity benefit has not yet been implemented. Government proposes to partially implement it by introducing the conditionality of being admissibile only for the birth of the first child disregarding the provisions of the Act. Only 54.5% children and 70.3% pregnant mothers are being provided free meals at Aanganwadi centres 25% of eligible school going children are not receiving entitled mid-day meals. Infrastructure in schools and Aanganwadi centes interms of buildings, cooking facilities, drinking water and sanitation continues to be poor. There is acute shortage of front level implementation staff in most states (RFC, 2017) Central budgetary allocation for ICDS and Mid-Day Meals has been reduced which threatens even the existing level of implementation let alone its universalization as per the law. Commercial interests are intruding into the programme with Political backing. As per CAG Audit Report 2015, storage capacity of food grains was not adequate for even holding three months food grains requirement (CAG, 2016). Door step delivery was also not being implemented in some states. Computerization of PDS operation was not completed in some states. The Grievances Redressal Mechanism has not been put in place in many states and where established it is not functional. Vigilance committees were not in existence in most states. Monitoring of Implementation is yet to start either at Central or state level. The push for mandatory Aadhar based identification for accessing food grains and other benefits has resulted in sizable number of beneficiaries having been declared fake which is exclusion by other name. In Kerala, which was implementing PDS on a near universal basis, many of the existing beneficiaries who are in excess of the targeted coverage are left out due to cut back in food grain allocation. This allocation is based on the targeted percentage beneficiaries for the State. In states where existing coverage of beneficiaries is larger than the targeted percentage determined by the Central government the concerned State governments would have to purchase required food grains from the market if they wish to protect the entitlements of such persons (Suresh, 2017). Most significant development is the declining commitment of the governments, central and state, to implement NFSA in its entirety for which even the supreme court has recently reprimanded them (Rajagopal, 2017). With regard to a number of measures suggested in the Schedules of the Act for enhancing production, reforms in PDS promoting access and protecting resource base, there has been no action at the central or state levels.

## Would NFSA Ensure Food Security to all Citizens

Quite apart from the partial implementation of the NFSA manifested in non-compliance of a number of its provisions, the problem of endemic hunger would not cease though its incidence may lessen in magnitude even if the right based entitlements in NFSA are implemented in their entirety. This is because the coverage is not universal (excluding the privileged classes). A ceiling has been fixed on the coverage of population for each state and food grains are allocated to the state governments from the Central government on that basis within which the eligible beneficiaries are required to be identified. It has been left to the state governments to cover additional beneficiaries if they wish from their own resources. States governments with a poor resource base would find it difficult to do so. The identification of beneficiaries is to be done on the basis of socio-economic and caste census. This would inevitably leave scope for exclusion of the deserving. Mandatory requirement of Aadhar linkage has added to this threat. Besides no such census has been carried out for the urban areas where the identification process is going to be more problematic and therefore prone to exclusion of the deserving. With Central government slashing its share in respect of ICDS, MDM schemes, even the existing level of coverage of these programmes is threatened. Besides, there are problems of portability of entitlements in respect of migrant labour with no clear guidelines issued by the Centre government. Vulnerable category of Persons such as homeless and destitutes would continue to be exposed to chronic food insecurity due to absence of entitlement emerging from lack of a permanent address and verifiable identity. But a determined push towards cash transfer in place of food as a part of neo-liberal reforms agenda aimed at eliminating welfare subsidies threatens to dismantle the entire PDS which is the back bone of the current food security arrangement. It would knock off the utility of the right based legislation for provision of food security itself.

The long term food security is also threatened by the ongoing crisis In agriculture. There is no light at the end of the tunnel. This crisis would not only threaten macro-level food availability for the growing population and therefore overall food security of the country but also food security of many marginal and small farmers who abandon agriculture due to its unviability or became agricultural labourers due to displacement from their land and or deprivation of access to forest resources. The Act does not address the issue of access at all. Its focus is on entitlement, availability and reach of food. The access is provided by income to purchase food whether from PDS or the market. The income can be earned only from assured employment and decent wages. In an economy of jobless growth, this poses aformidable constraint. The access of elderly, widows, disabled persons and those households losing the bread winner is even more seriously constrained due to inadequacy of assistance in the case of the former and one time nature of assistance in the case of the latter in the existing schemes of social security. These constraints remain unaddressed. The Antyodya category would still continue to be exposed to food insecurity due to inadequate coverage resulting from a cap imposed on the optimum number of persons who would be entitled to it. Nutritional security continues to remain neglected due to inadequate resources with many states to universalize coverage of existing schemes and enhance food supplements and declining central commitment to meet this resource gap. The only effective access enabling programme for the working age population prepared to do manual labour though limited to only 100 days of entitled employment is MNREGS. This assurance itself is inadequate in creating requisite purchasing power. Besides, MNREGS does not address lack of purchasing power of those who cannot do manual labour. But even with MNREGS the latest reports suggest that this access is shrinking due to illegal deletion of a large number of ration cards due to non-linkage with Aadhar identification system, delays in payment of wages and denial of entitled payment by payment of less than the locally declared minimum wage, wage suppression, underfunding and non-payment of compensation for delay in providing employment. (Dey and Roy, 2017) With low rate of agricultural growth and an overall growth which fails to create required number of jobs, the access problem is going to mount.

The absorption dimension of the food security may deteriorate with drinking water problem becoming more acute due to drying up of sources, falling underground water levels, diversion of water for industrial purposes and quality related problem of water in many places due to pollution and where arsenic and fluoride content in water is very high. The current level of coverage may therefore go down sharply if new water sources are not found and quality problems are not addressed.

The access to sanitation, though considerably enhanced with increased resource allocation by the present government, is directly linked to regular availability of water even if toilets are constructed. The access to health care is unlikely to improve due to push towards privatization, underfunding of public sector, failure to reform medical education to make doctors available for rural areas and a large out of pocket expenditure. Insurance cannot address these issues and promote access due to the limited coverage and ambit of care it caters to and its high cost, etc.

Thus, the overall prospects of ensuring food security to the people and eliminate chronic hunger do not appear to be bright notwithstanding some gains having been achieved in right based and legally enforceable food entitlements in NFSA over the earlier arrangement. This pessimism emerges from the ground reality that is unfolding.

## Endemic Hunger is Structural Violence

Millions of People continuing to suffer endemic hunger due to their poverty, destitution and despite the centrality to democratic politics, State's legitimacy is grounded in its responsibility to ensure the welfare of the people. Violation of this legitimacy constitutes structural violence because this suffering is 'not only tolerated but also taken as normal'. Not only the State actors but the elites and middle classes supporting this and allowing this situation to continue, not getting outraged to see it changed are complicit in this violence (Gupta, 2016). They are fully aware that the interventions made by the state are inadequate and are unlikely to eliminate hunger as required under SDG2. Yet the ideological underpinnings of economic governance blinds them to the reality that inadequate resource provisioning, limiting coverage of beneficiaries, aggressive pursuit of Aadhar linkage, cash transfer, reduction in subsidy and withdrawl of State from welfare provisioning would strike at the very root of a systematically evolved Public

Distribution System and would expose the affected groups to the market forces and resultant worsening of their food insecurity. In the absence of a comprehensive and adequate social security and provisioning of guaranteed employment with decent wages, there would be severe constraints to access food. The continuing crisis of agriculture puts in jeopardy the sufficiency of production of food itself which is not being squarely faced. The right based food security programme (NFSA) is therefore unlikely to eliminate structural violence unless all dimensions of food insecurity of affected population are addressed seriously and in an integrated manner and effectively enforced, monitored and evaluated with informed participation of beneficiaries and their interlocutors. There is little indication that this is on the political horizon.

## References

Cheriyan, George (2006), Enforcing Right to Food in India: Bottlenecks in Delivering the Expected Outcome, UN University, UNU—WIDER Research Paper No. 2006/132, November 2006.

Comptroller and Auditor General of India (2016), 'CAG Compliance Audit Report on Preparedness for Implementation of National Food Security Act presented', Press Release, April 29, 2016

Department of Food and Public Distribution, Ministry of Consumer Affairs, Food and Public Distribution, Government of India (2017): *National Food Security Act, 2013* retrieved from http://dfpdnic.in/nfsa-act-htm and accessed on April 19, 2017.

Dey Nikhil and Roy, Aruna (2017), 'Excluded by Aadhar', *Indian Express*, June 5, 2017

Dey, Nikhil (2017), 'Government trying to finish off rural employment scheme', News item in *The Hindu*, dated April 20, 2017 p. 7.

Dréze, Jean (1995), 'Famine Prevention in India, in Dréze, Jean and Amartya Sen (1993): *Hunger and Public Action*, Oxford University Press, Delhi.

Dréze, Jean, Amartya Sen and Athar Hussain (eds), (1995), *The Political Economy of Hunger: Selected Essays*. Oxford, Clarandon Press (1995).

Gupta, Akhil (2016), 'Structural Violence', in Kannabiran, Kalpna (ed), *Violence Studies*, Oxford, New Delhi, 2016.

IDFC (Infrastructure Development Finance Company) Rural Development Network (2013), *India Rural Development Report*

*2012-13,* IDFC Rural Development Network, Orient BlackSwan, Delhi, 2013.

International Food Policy Research Institute (2016), *Global Hunger Index,* retrieved from http\\ghi.ifpri.org/countries/IND/ and accessed on March 28, 2007.

Khatkar, B.S., Chaudhury, N. and Dangi, P. (2016), Production and Consumption of Grains: India, *Encyclopedia of Food Grains,* Vol. 1, pp. 367-373

Ministry of Agriculture, Directorate of Economics and Statistics, Government of India (2015): *Agricultural Statistics at a Glance 2015.*

Ministry of Finance (2013), *Economic Survey 2012-13.*

Ministry of Health and Family Welfare, Government of India, *National Family Health Survey* IV and III (2015-16), (2005-06) International Institute for Population Services, Mumbai.

Ministry of Law and Justice (2013), *The National Food Security Act, 2013,* No. 20 of 2013, 10th September, 2013.

Rajagopal, Krishnadas (2017) : 'Food Security: SC Raps Centre, States', *The Hindu,* August 07.

Reddy, V. Ratna (2011), 'Land Degradation in India: Extent Cost and Determinants' *Economic and Political Weekly,* Nov. 1, 2003.

Right to Food Campaign (2017), Situation of Hunger and Malnutrition in India, April, 2016.

Sagar, Vidya, (2005), 'Food Security in India' in Vyas, Vijay (ed), *Food Security in Asian Countries in the Context of Millennium Goals,* Academic Foundation, New Delhi.

Saxena, N.C. (2009), Hunger, Under-Nutrition and Food Security in India, CPRC—IIPA Working Paper 44, IIPA, Delhi.

Singh, R.B. (2005), Towards a Food Secure India and South Asia: Making Hunger History, retrieved from http://India environment portal.org.in/files/towards—a food secure—India-making—hunger—history and accessed on 28th March, 2017.

Srivastava, Aseem and Kothari, Ashish (2012), *Churning the Earth: Making of Global India,* Penguin, New Delhi.

Suresh, Neenu (2017), 'How a Flawed National Food Security Act is undermining Kerala's PDS' Life Line, *The Wire,* Feb. 18, 2017.

Swaminathan, M.S. and Bhavani, R.V. (2013), Food Production and Availability—Essential prerequisite for sustainable food security, *Indian Journal of Medical Research,* 138 (3), September.

*The Hindu* (2013), 'Food Act to be implemented in all States by next month'. Paswan, PTA, Ajmer, October, 2016 *The Hindu* April 19, 2017.

United Nations (2012), *Human Rights in India: Status Report,* 2012.

# 1

# Food the Elixir of Health
## Understanding the Crucial Bondage*

## Introduction

Highlighting the importance of food, Joan Gussow famously remarked, 'if there is not enough food, it doesn't matter if there is enough of everything else—including oil and money' (Gussow, 1981). Indeed, so much taken for granted is the availability of food in the lives of the 'haves' that they seem to have made peace with the fact that nearly 1.2 billion people i.e. nearly a fifth of humanity suffered from abject poverty at the dawn of the 21st century and around 800 million of these in the developing world suffered from chronic hunger (FAO, 2002). Around 842 million people i.e. one in eight of the humankind do not get enough food to remain healthy and lead an active life (WFP, 2014). Even in the richest country on the globe, the United States, according to the government statistics, one in seven households i.e. 17.5 million households were food insecure in 2012 (Coleman-Jensen et al., 2013). This gives enough of a reason to refresh and re-emphasise the central importance of food in human well-being. 'Human

---

*Another version of this paper had earlier been published in *Global Journal of Medicine and Public Health* (GJMEDPH) IN 2015. The full reference of that paper is as under: Vikas Bajpai, Anoop Saraya, Re-emphasizing food as the basic medicine of public health to reclaim hunger in health discourse. GJMEDPH, 2015, Vol. 4(2): 20 pages.

health' is perhaps the best marker of human well-being. To come to a reasoned understanding of the centrality of food to human well-being, we shall explore the relationship between 'human health' and the factors impacting on it.

Talking of the factors impacting on human health, indeed so spectacular have been some of the achievements of the modern medical science that in popular imagination availability and access to modern healthcare and health technologies has come to be considered as a precondition for ensuring the health of the society. It is not our intention here to contest the immense contribution of modern medical technologies in preventing and curing many a disease and thereby reducing human suffering and improving the quality of human life. However, to the extent this popular perception regarding 'modern medicine' tends to distort our understanding of human health and well-being, it mandates a closer scrutiny of things as they are.

In the long history of human health, the advent of modern medicine comes at a much later stage, say with the mid to late 18th century. The more spectacular period of western medicine can be loosely categorised to have started even later, say with the rise of the germ theory of disease in 1870. An understanding of the factors contributing to human health and the relative role of modern medicine in the same requires an examination of the entire history of human health. This mandates the question: what is the running thread through the history of human health that facilitates study of human health in different phases of human civilisation notwithstanding the immense changes through these phases?

It would be prudent to begin with the way WHO (World Health Organisation) defines health. WHO states, 'Health is a state of complete physical, mental and social well-being and not merely the absence of disease or infirmity' (WHO, 1946). This definition makes it eminently clear that health is a multidimensional and a far more complex phenomenon. Health services, inclusive of the medical technologies, are only a part of the overall conditions that determine human health. The one outcome variable that encapsulates the extent of completeness of physical, mental and social well-being of people i.e. their health is the longevity of their lives, which in public health terminology is known as 'life expectancy.'

Sheila Zubrigg, a health historian, has used this understanding of health in 'the most elemental sense of physical survival' (Sheila Zubrigg, 1998) as a tool to study the history of health. Taken as such, the history of human health can then be taken as the study of secular trends in human life expectancy (Sheila Zubrigg, 1998).

It is equally true that through much of human history, the infectious diseases have posed a major deterrent to health and longevity of human life. History of human health thus becomes coterminus with the dynamics of what is called in epidemiology of disease as the 'epidemic equation', which has on one side the human exposure to infectious disease, and on the other side the ability of the human body to resist infectious disease agents (Sheila Zubrigg, 1998).

The question then is what the other factors are that have helped tilt the epidemiological equation in favour of the human race, thereby enhancing its life expectancy and what is the relative contribution of modern medicine to this?

Thankfully, the existence of a rich body of literature on this issue makes answering these questions much easier.

## Factors Influencing Human Life Expectancy: Food versus the Rest

Figure 1.1 below shows the growth of human population through history.

More than three-fourth of the rise in human population has occurred in less than last two hundred years i.e. after

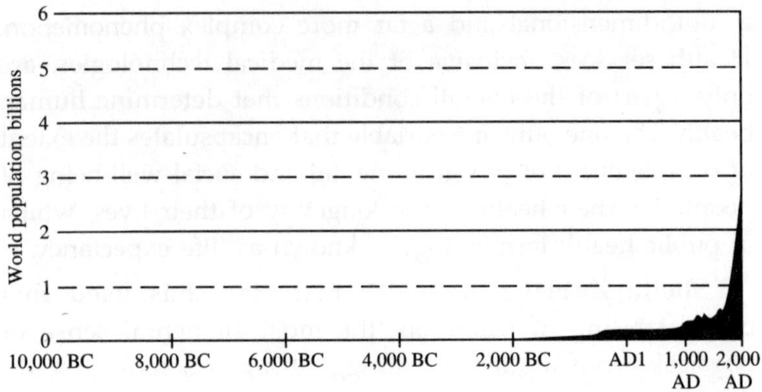


Figure 1.1

*Source:* Wikipedia, the free encyclopedia, quoted in Bajpai and Saraya (2012).

AD 1800, a period we may refer to as the period of modern rise of human population. This means that for much of the human history the means of subsistence seem to have been grossly inadequate to support a larger human population. Through much of the history of human civilisation, total human population hovered around not more than a few tens of millions, crossing the 100 million mark somewhere around 1000 BC. In fact, through much of human civilisation the average life expectancy varied between a mere 20 to 25 years (Sheila Zurbrigg, 1994). So the question is what spurred the modern rise of human population, or shall we say the rise in human life expectancy, and thereby human well-being?

Thomas McKeown, a British professor of social medicine and a medical historian studied the modern rise of population in England and Wales and some other European countries. It can be seen from Figure 1.2 that the life expectancy in England and Wales rose sharply since the latter half of 19th century. McKeown argued that the greatly accelerated rise in the population of these countries observed since the latter half of the 19th century, was the result of a huge decline in mortality due to improved human resistance to infectious diseases consequent to improvements in socio-economic conditions, availability of food in the main, rather than due to interventions of modern medicine (Thomas McKeown, 1976). McKeown's formulation later came to be known as the 'McKeown Thesis.'

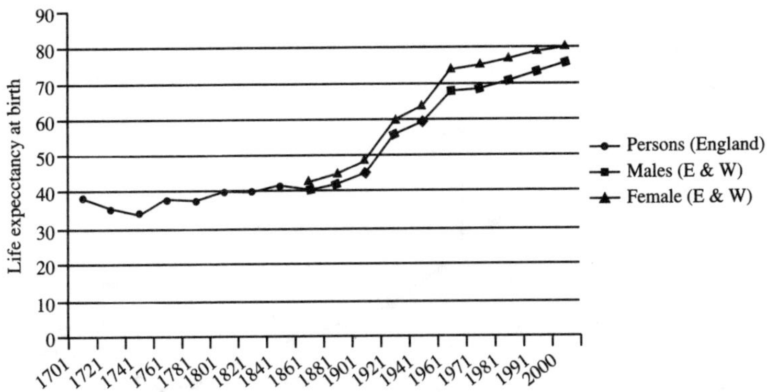


Figure 1.2: Life expectancy at birth in England/England and Wales, 1701-2000.

*Source:* Emily Grundy, 2005. 'Commentary: The McKeown debate: time for burial,' *International Journal of Epidemiology*, Vol. 34: 529-533.

Mckeown's methodology was simple—he plotted the decline in mortality due to specific infectious diseases that were the major killers at that time, and on the graph of declining mortality, he marked the year when the technological interventions of modern medicine against the particular disease became available for the first time. Figures 1.3, 1.4 and 1.5 show the declining mortality due to respiratory tuberculosis, whooping cough and measles in England and Wales and the specific time when modern medical interventions against these diseases became available. It was observed that the secular trend in the decline of mortality due to the major diseases of the time (tuberculosis, measles, whooping cough, bronchitis and others) occurred much before any of the medical interventions—antibiotics, immunisation, vitamin supplements, intravenous rehydration, etc., came into existence.

Having demonstrated this, McKeown excluded other possible causes of decline in death rates e.g. decline in virulence of pathogenic microorganisms, or increase in specific immunity against these diseases in the population. In the light of improving socio-economic conditions of the

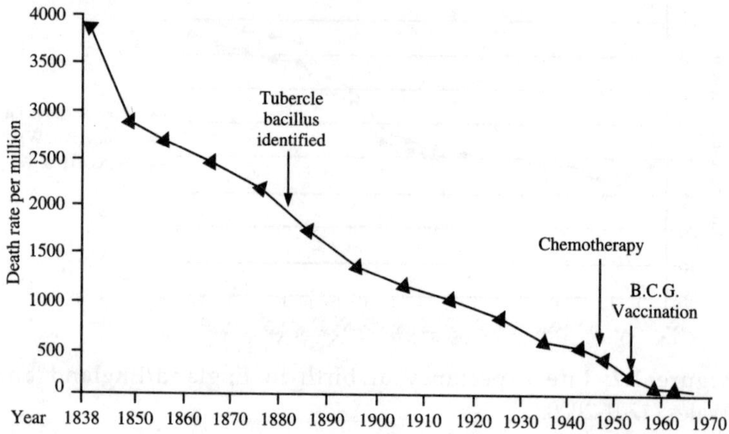


Figure 1.3: Secular decline in death rates due to respiratory tuberculosis in England and Wales.

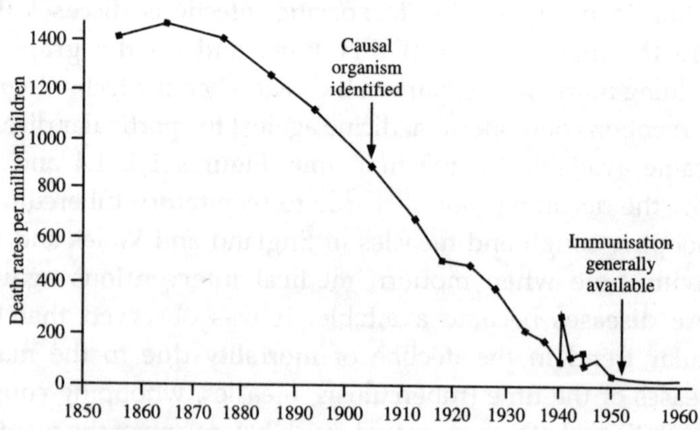


Figure 1.4: Secular decline in death rates due to whooping cough in England and Wales.

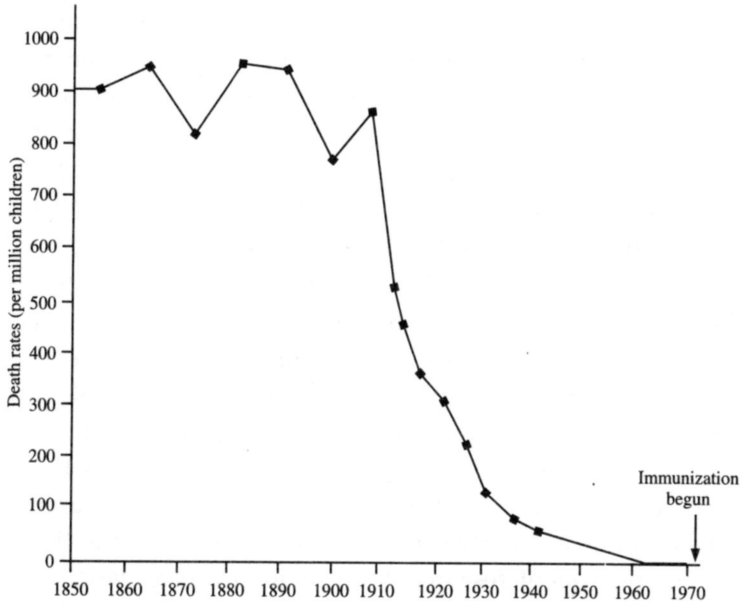


Figure 1.5: Secular decline in death rates due to measles in England and Wales.

time, advancements in agricultural production and thereby availability of food under the impact of the enclosure movement and associated technological innovations in agriculture, McKeown concluded that improvements in human resistance to these diseases due to improved nutrition was the major reason for the steady decline in deaths due to these diseases (Thomas McKeown, 1976).[1]

The many public health measures, such as availability of safe drinking water that had been undertaken in Great Britain since the beginning of Chadwickian sanitary reforms in 1848, also contributed to the mortality decline due to infectious diseases, however, these measures could account for at best one-third to one-fourth of the decline in deaths (Thomas McKeown, 1976).[2]

Further credence to McKeown's thesis is lent by evidence that points to better availability of food being a predominant factor in the decline of mortality in other countries of the world that underwent a similar development trajectory as that of England and Wales. Vallin showed that similar patterns of mortality decline were also observed in virtually all the European countries (Vallin J., 1991).

Likewise, in case of US, referring to the period between 1900 and 1970, McKinley and McKinley showed that much of the decline in mortality due to infectious diseases had occurred much in advance of the introduction of specific technological interventions of modern medicine. They estimated that no more than 3 percent of the mortality decline in the US in 20th century could be attributed to preventive or curative interventions of modern medicine (McKinley and McKinley, 1977). Subsequent research has provided direct evidence of the overriding importance of food as the most important influence in increasing life expectancy.

In the United States, after an increase in the life expectancy up to 50 to 55 years in the second half of the eighteenth century, it declined to about 45 yrs during 1830 to 1860. This has been attributed primarily to increased urbanisation, immigration and most importantly to considerable rise in income inequality (Fogel R., 1986, Steckel, 1983). However, the period beginning from 1870 marks a period of sustained rise in life expectancy in the US along with rising wages and establishment of wider public health measures in urban areas. An important distinction to this view was made by Higgs who noted that there was a decline in mortality rates even in the rural areas despite the fact that 'the 1890-1920 public health movement. . . almost completely bypassed the countryside' (Higgs R., 1973, 1979). Additionally, there was a poor correlation between the timing of establishment of public health services and the decline in mortality observed in the late nineteenth century in the major

US cities (Higgs R., 1973, 1979).

Studies in the field of historical anthropometry have provided more direct evidence of the impact of changes in access to food on mortality. Stature, and conversely nutritional stunting, provide a direct measure of access to food, especially chronic undernourishment. Studies in historical anthropometry have provided secular trends of stature in European and American populations, which have proved important for assessing the role of increased access to food in the decline of mortality. Data shows a secular trend of increasing stature in different countries of Europe (Floud 1983) and the United States (Floud 1986) respectively. Statistical analysis has shown that overall, secular rise in statures explains nearly two-thirds of the decline in mortality in Western Europe since late eighteenth century (Fogel R., 1992).

These findings are further confirmed by the fact that increase in stature and the declining trend in mortality across the nineteenth century Europe occurred in conditions when in all likelihood people were exposed to much higher levels of infections due to rapid and unplanned development of cities with huge slums with unhygienic conditions and high levels of population mobility during the early years of industrialisation (Burnett J, 1991, Fredrick Engels, 1845). The observed increase in statures and declining mortality are indeed remarkable as they occurred in conditions in which we would have expected mortality to soar.

Pointing to a much more deep-rooted relationship between food and health outcomes, studies have now established anthropometric indicators (height at given ages, weight at given ages, and weight-for-height) as predictors of morbidity and mortality among children below the age of 5 years (Sommer and Lowenstein 1975, Chen, Chowdhury, and Huffman 1980, Billewicz and MacGregor 1982, Kielmann et al., 1983, Martorell 1985). Other studies showed that height at maturity was a predictor of mortality risk or the risk of developing chronic disease in middle or older age (Marmot, Shipley, and Rose 1984, Waaler 1984, John 1988, Costa 1993), and even BMI has been shown to have well-defined predictive properties (Heywood 1983, Waaler 1984, Martorell 1985, Payne 1992, Osmani 1992, Srinivasan 1992).

## Evidence From India

There is evidence from pre-independence India to show the huge impact that state policies affecting food intake can make on the well-being of the people.

Work done by Sheila Zurbrigg on epidemic malaria mortality in Punjab between 1868 and 1940 helps strengthen the McKewonite understanding of the relationship between food intake and health in India's context (Sheila Zurbrigg, 1992). During the span between 1868 and 1940, it was observed that the most dramatic decline in epidemic malaria mortality began around 1908. This was statistically shown to have been on account of the decline in intensity of famine and epidemic hunger that accompanied drought and/or floods due to changes in famine relief policy, all other factors related to malaria mortality (epidemiological, entomological, preventive and curative) remaining the same.

Concern for people's health was in the least the motivation of the British colonisers in introducing these reforms, since they did little to initiate any measures directed at improving the overall preventive or curative facilities, indeed the incidence and prevalence of diseases in general saw little change. Moreover, the per capita food availability in India undoubtedly declined in the colonial era. Irrespective of the compulsions of the British colonial government, these reforms did help in tilting the balance in favour of the people by preventing excess mortality due to starvation in an otherwise distressing situation.

More importantly, this highlights the crucial role of State intervention in the well-being of the people. It is most regrettable that the health policy paradigm pursued in the country since independence has feigned ignorance of this crucial relationship between food and disease. None of the disease control programmes in the country leverages the role of adequate food intake in control of diseases. Falling back on technological interventions has been the easier way out for the health administrators and the results continue to be less than satisfactory with an exception or two.

By way of an example, while there remains much consternation among health administrators in India to improve coverage of measles vaccination (among other vaccine preventable diseases), there is much wisdom in pondering over the threat that measles is to a well-fed child! Even though measles mortality in India has declined, our country still accounts for 47 percent of measles deaths in the world (Sinha, 2012).

## Hunger and its Socio-economic Roots

Ensuring adequate supply of food is supposedly one of the most important reasons why human society came into being in the first place (Gussow, 1981, Behar, 1976). In fact, the society grew more complex and the need for an effective social order was that much more as the food systems became more and more complex. It is indeed tragic that at a time when the human race is equipped as never before to best feed all its members, we seem to be becoming oblivious to this most fundamental role of human society.

Rene Laennec has said, 'Do not fear to repeat what has already been said. Men need (the truth) dinned into their ears many times and from all sides' (quoted in Douglas et al., 1987). Hence, even if only to reiterate the obvious, there is great merit in demonstrating the socio-economic roots of the problem of hunger. Figure 1.6 clearly shows that hunger is largely concentrated in the global South i.e. primarily in the developing countries of Asia and Africa, and to a lesser extent in Latin America. That hunger is largely concentrated in the developing countries, while the developed countries have largely[3] overcome this, is not merely an empirical fact; this fact has a history as also a present. The colonial domination of global South by the global North in the past and the continuing neo-colonial dispensation of global governance wherein the developed countries dominate over the developing countries of Asia, Africa and Latin America politically and economically in order to maintain their stranglehold over the resources of these countries is responsible for the picture as seen in Figure 1.6. It need also to be highlighted that the ruling classes of many Third World countries have been willing partners in this state of affairs as can be illustrated from the example of India itself.

Even though the British, who ruled over India for nearly 200 years, claimed that they rescued India from timeless hunger, their claims rang hollow in face of the results of an 1878 study that was published in the Journal of the Statistical Society. The study documented that till that time while there had been as many as 31 famines during the 120 years of colonial rule of the British in India, there were only 17 recorded famines in the previous two millennia of Indian history (Walford, 1878). Geographer Michael Watts has observed, 'Famines are social crises that represent the failures of particular economic and political systems' (Watts, 1983).

The sweeping downhill change that India underwent under colonialism can be gauged by the fact that while in 1750 India produced nearly 25 percent of world's industrial output, by the year 1900 this was reduced to barely 2 percent (Clingingsmith and Williamson, 2005). What this meant in terms of the well-being of the people is demonstrated to an

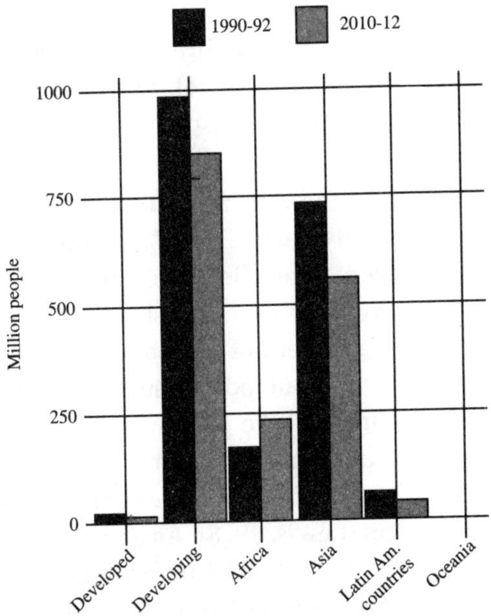


Figure 1.6: Number of people Undernourished 1990-92 and 2010-12.

*Source:* FAO, 2013. Part 2, 'Hunger Dimensions' in *FAO Statistical Yearbook* 2013, Rome 2013, p. 70.)

extent by Parthasarthi in his work (Parthasarthi, 1998). As against the popular imagination of an Indian labourer being a semi-starved, loincloth clad wretch, Parthasarthi notes, 'Indeed, there is compelling evidence that South Indian labourers had higher earnings than their British counterparts in the 18th century and lived lives of greater financial security' (Parthasarthi, 1998). Parthasarthi gives further evidence to suggest that due to better productivity of land in South India the diets consumed by weavers and other artisans were better than those of average Europeans. On account of enjoying superior rights of contract and greater economic power, the rates of unemployment among the weavers and artisans were lower as compared to those in Europe. Vis-à-vis English farm labourers, even the outcaste farm labourers in Madras had higher real earnings. By 1900 however, the picture was totally reversed, income of the average British household was about 21 times higher (Parthasarthi, 1998). Such changes could not have been without adverse consequences to the food security of the people.

The Indian smallholder agricultural and industrial producer was forcefully sucked in to commodity production and markets that were controlled from overseas to serve the interests of the colonial powers. Cash crops were enforced on farmers, besides a system of high and fixed rent collected through landlords who doubled as usurers in conditions that led to high indebtedness of the peasantry, and of course there was increasing alienation of the peasantry from land (Medick, 1981). The terms of global trade were totally loaded against the Indian producers (Lewis, 1978). As a matter of fact, India's Viceroy during 1898-1905, Lord Curzon himself complained in the House of Lords, 'Tariffs 'were decided in London, not in India, in England's interests, not in India's' (Dewey, 1978).

What is dismaying however are the policies pursued by the Indian ruling classes since 1947, which undermined the food security of India's working masses, especially since the beginning of the accelerated phase of the neoliberal economic reforms in 1990. The dichotomy between the 'Shining India' and the 'Struggling India' is well known, even then, since the beginning of the economic reforms, the gap between the 'Shining' and the 'Struggling' India has widened ever more.

Among the multifarious impacts of this widening gap between the rich and the poor, the most dramatic has been the deepening agrarian crisis in the country which has undermined the food security of Indians as nothing else has. In what has been described as a 'A Policy-induced Disaster of Epic Proportions' (The Sanhati Collective, 2012) more than a quarter million of farmers committed suicide in the country between 1995 and 2011 alone and the numbers continue to increase by the year (*The Indian Express*, 2012). The de-facto unanimity of all ruling class parties regarding these economic policies has ensured that despite its magnitude, farmers' suicides have never become an electoral issue in the country. The agrarian crisis is deeply rooted in the socio-economic policies pursued by India's ruling elite (Dhas, 2009, Bhalla amd Singh, 2009, Patnaik, 2003, Perspectives, 2009).

It needs little imagination to configure its implications for food security and hunger in a country where nearly 70 percent of people live in villages and more than 50 percent of the workforce directly depends on agriculture for sustenance. The peasantry, especially the small, marginal and the landless peasants in India are not just the producers of food, but also the largest social and economic group in the population that is the first to go hungry.

However, there are instances to show how the subservience of Indian rulers to the international neoliberal economic order lorded over by the developed countries has compromised food security of India's poor. Though ridden with corruption, the Public Distribution System (PDS) in India has been the cornerstone of food security of the poor in the country. Since the beginning of the neoliberal economic reforms, there have been persistent efforts by successive governments to weaken and dismantle PDS under pressure from the World Bank in order to open food grain sector to the market forces (Jafri, 2008). There was a shortage of wheat in India in 2005-07 because the Government systematically reduced the food grain buffer stocks by reducing the procurement of food grains from farmers to much below the targeted off-take. The Government was under pressure from the US to import wheat and as a prelude to the same Government slowed down the procurement of wheat in 2005-07 by deliberately keeping its minimum support price for the farmers low in order to facilitate the entry of the multinational corporations in food trade (Debate on price rise in the Rajya Sabha, the Parliament of India, 16 April 2008, quoted in Jafri, 2008.). It is noteworthy that in 2006, Cargill India, the Australian Wheat Board, ITC and Adani Export, the latter two being Indian companies with considerable foreign equity, together procured 30 lakh tones of wheat in India. This stands in sharp contrast to persistently declining Government procurement which was 16.8 million tons in 2003-04, 14.8 million tons in 2004-05, 11.1 million tons in 2005-06 and a mere 9.2 million tons in 2006-07 (Debate on price rise in the Rajya Sabha, the Parliament of India, 16 April 2008, quoted in Jafri, 2008.). Thus the Government deliberately created a situation of food insecurity in the country only to facilitate the entry of agribusiness corporations in food grain trade in the country.

Such macro and microeconomic policies further reinforce inequities and inequalities already prevalent in the society, much to the detriment of the marginalised sections. Table 1.1 clearly shows the gradients in health outcomes, which can be taken as measures of prevalence of hunger in the society, along caste and economic statuses, with the most deprived castes and economic categories being the worst off. In view of these facts, it need be emphasised that the fight against hunger is not as much a technical question of production, processing,

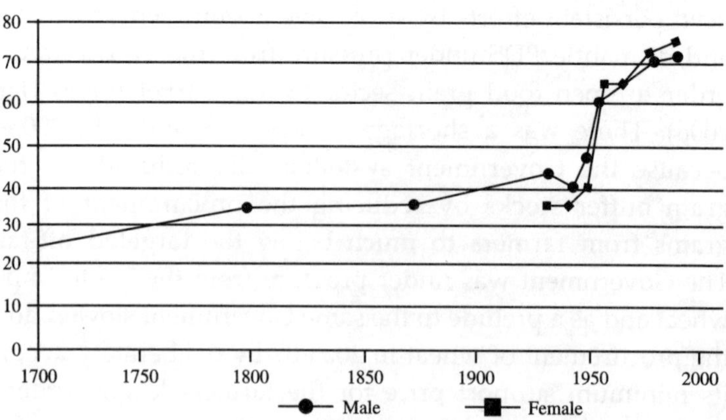


Figure 1.7: Life expectancy in China from 1700 to 1990.

Table 1.1: Gradation of Health Outcomes Reflecting Hunger/Nutritional Status by Caste and Wealth Index in India

| *Category* | *IMR (per 1,000 live births* | *Under 5 yrs mortality (per 1,000 live births)* | *Chronic malnutrition (low height for age) in children below 5 yrs (% children below 2 SD)* | *Anemia in children 6 to 59 months of age (%)* | *Anemia in 15 to 49 yrs old* | | *BMI less than 18.5 in 15 to 45 yrs old* | |
|---|---|---|---|---|---|---|---|---|
| | | | | | *Men (%)* | *Women (%)* | *Men (%)* | *Women (%)* |
| Caste/Tribals[4] | | | | | | | | |
| SC | 66.4 | 88.1 | 53.9 | 72.2 | 58.3 | 26.6 | 41.1 | 39.1 |
| ST | 62.1 | 95.7 | 53.9 | 76.8 | 68.5 | 39.6 | 46.6 | 41.3 |
| OBC | 56.6 | 72.8 | 48.8 | 70.3 | 54.4 | 22.3 | 35.7 | 34.6 |
| Others | 48.9 | 59.2 | 40.7 | 63.8 | 51.3 | 20.9 | 29.4 | 28.9 |
| Wealth index | | | | | | | | |
| Lowest | 70.4 | 100.5 | 59.9 | 76.4 | 64.3 | 37.9 | 51.5 | 48.3 |
| Second | 68.5 | 89.6 | 54.3 | 73.6 | 60.3 | 30.2 | 46.3 | 42.4 |
| Middle | 58.3 | 71.9 | 48.9 | 69.3 | 56.0 | 24.8 | 38.3 | 37.4 |
| Fourth | 44.0 | 51.2 | 40.8 | 64.8 | 52.2 | 18.8 | 28.9 | 29.6 |
| Highest | 29.2 | 33.8 | 25.3 | 56.2 | 46.1 | 14.2 | 18.2 | 19.1 |

*Source:* International Institute for Population Sciences (IIPS) and Macro International (2005-06): '*National Family Health Survey (NFHS–3), India', Vol. I. Mumbai.* Compiled from tables: 7.2 (p. 182), 8.12 (p. 208), 10.1 (p. 270), 10.12 (p. 289), 10.22.1 (p. 304), 10.22.2 (p. 306), 10.24.1 (p. 311), 10.24.2 (p. 312).

*Note:* IMR = Infant Mortality Rate, SD = Standard Deviation, BMI = Body Mass Index, SC = Scheduled Castes, ST = Scheduled Tribes, OBC = Other Backward Castes.

preservation, transportation and distribution of food, even as these are important aspects, it is a social, structural and a political question in the main. Just how dramatic can be the impact of changed socio-economic conditions on hunger is clearly evident from Figure 1.7 which shows a huge decline in the chronic and endemic acute hunger in China as reflected in a sharp rise in life expectancy in the country, especially in the immediate aftermath of the Revolution in 1949. The redistribution of the productive resources, most importantly, equitable distribution of land among the peasantry and freedom from feudal oppression of the landlords, was the factor that played a major role in ameliorating hunger in China.

## From Hunger to Nutrition, Unravelling the Transition

Moises Behar said:

> If it is accepted that the fundamental role of any society is to ensure the well-being of all its members, including their adequate nutrition, then the presence of malnutrition to any significant extent must be interpreted as a failure of that society. This is really the problem we are facing today: that it is the structure of society itself that limits the capabilities of many of its members to obtain their basic needs, including enough and adequate food, because power and the utilisation of resources is concentrated in the hands of a minority (Behar, 1976).

These words of Behar hit the ruling classes, around the world, where it hurts them the most. Admission of one's failure is difficult in general, but doubly so for the ruling elite who are always anxious to project the success of the systems they lord over, despite its obvious failures. However, when wishing away is not the available option, the way out sought by the establishment (scientists, teaching establishment and other professionals included) is to twist the discourse around these obvious failures and to regulate it in a manner that helps in soft-pedalling the failures. Making issues highly technical, replacing the commonly understood vocabulary and idioms in which common people can express their suffering and experiences, with esoteric terms and jargon is a time-tested method of regulating a potentially threatening discourse into safe channels. This cliché, albeit is practised and perfected in an 'academic', 'logical' and 'scientific' rubric which confounds the subtlety of this change. The discourse on hunger is but another example of this phenomenon.

To understand the transition in question, it would be good to begin by looking at some definitions:

- **Hunger** (Hunger Task Force, 2003): 'A condition, in which people lack the basic food intake to provide them with the energy and nutrients for fully productive lives.'
- **Hunger** (WFP, 2014): 'Hunger is the body's way of signaling that it is running short of food and needs to eat something.' Hunger can lead to malnutrition.
- **Nutrition/Nutritional Status:** 'Nutrients provided by food combine with other factors, including the health state of the person consuming the food, to produce 'nutritional status.'' Nutritional status can be assessed by measurement of body size or composition, or physiological dysfunction of the body on account of deficiency of one or many nutrients (Behrman, et al., 2004).
- **Malnutrition:** It is defined as a 'state in which the physical function of an individual is impaired to the point where he or she can no longer maintain natural bodily capacities such as growth, pregnancy, lactation, learning abilities, physical work and resisting and recovering from disease' (WFP, 2014).

Without going into the complexity of issues related to these definitions, our purpose here is to emphasise that those going without food know what is happening to their bodies and can articulate their plight better in terms of their bodily feeling. The term 'Hunger', by definition, lends itself better to such an expression. 'Hunger' is well understood by the laity and is easily communicable.

Nutrition/malnutrition on other hand are a clinical condition that is a consequence of how well the people are able to eat. It lends itself to clinical assessment and measurement, but the terminology nutritionists deploy is something that the hungry do not have the chance to be familiar with. In as much as the larger policy discourse on 'Hunger' and its impact on people is dominated by the 'Nutrition' terminology, it alienates the sufferers of 'Hunger' from this discourse.

Talking of this change Sheila Zurbrrig writes:

> With this shift in scientific focus, so also in language itself, hunger, an eminently concrete condition, both acute and chronic, became sidelined by 'nutrition', term which in its general and often poorly defined usage has tended to obscure the two central human predicaments of little or nothing to eat. Without a conceptual vocabulary, hunger became in effect very difficult to talk about, and in the process even more problematic to measure . . . The reluctance to address hunger conceptually and analytically stems perhaps from a sense that the term is unscientific, imprecise, worse, emotional. 'Nutrition', or 'malnutrition' has the cachet of 'scientific respectability', Diana Wylie has recently remarked, while 'hunger does not' (Sheila Zurbrigg, 1994).

Human race has come to inhabit the remotest and even the most uninhabitable corners of the earth like the Arctic region, remote mountains with little arable land and the scorching deserts. Yet there is no literature to show that all those who inhabited these regions were nutritionally crippled. These people have physiologically adapted their bodies to successfully bear the harsh ecological conditions over generations. All said and done, appreciable sections of these populations at any point in time are free of nutritional disorders so long as they have enough to eat of the food available in their respective environments (Mann et al., 1962, Sauberlich et al., 1972, Guo et al., 2014). And if it is true of human populations living in remote regions, it ought to be even truer of the densely populated and more productive regions. It is the widespread disruption of the ecological context of these populations, more specifically that associated with the exploitative relations of production (these decide who eats enough and who does not), which is at the root of all nutritional disorders (Banerji, 1988). Further, the 'Social and economic forces which create such conditions also ensured that such issues are kept out of the body of knowledge of nutrition sciences.' The situation was further manipulated by the 'market forces', which were responsible for disruption of ecology of human nutrition in first place, to develop the epistemology of nutrition in a manner that was conducive to increasing the sales of food and drugs industry (Banerji, 1988).

This new epistemology uprooted the problems of nutrition from their ecological moorings (poverty, discrimination, exploitation) and parcelled them into atomised entities along with the new age curative agents offered by the industry. This process was furthered by the marriage of science of 'nutrition' with sciences like chemistry, biochemistry, physiology and other medical sciences (as Banerji puts it, 'apparently to gain respectability as a science'). This resulted in a long list of scientific breakthroughs: various nutritional elements, balanced diets, processes and pathways of digestion and metabolism of nutritional elements and ever new nutritional disorders identified on the basis of the breakdown of these complex pathways due to malfunctioning of molecular components at any of the several steps constituting individual pathways. While one cannot help but marvel at these amazing achievements of science, the direction of progress was clear: from the macro to micro, from the society to atomised entities, from the felt experiences of the hungry masses to sanitised environs of the scientist's laboratory.

It need be pondered at this stage as to what proportion of malnutrition is due to 'inadequacy of food consumption' and what is the extent of malnutrition attributable to 'molecular' factors, yet the weight of knowledge of human nutrition has moved away from societal factors to the atomised nutritional components. Rather than study human nutrition, or the lack of it at the level of the society, the, 'Biochemical laboratories and animal houses became the major places for study of human nutrition,' including some spillover to hospital wards (Banerji, 1988). This phenomenon has been referred to as the 'scientification of food.' Is it surprising then that the 'hungry' have simply slipped away from the memory of nutrition scientists and the larger discourse on hunger?

The context of hunger and malnutrition in the West and in the developing world is entirely different. Yet as in various fields of science, and in nutrition science as well, the flow of knowledge has been from the developed to the developing world. This is because the development of indigenous science in these countries stagnated during colonialism and the colonial period led to a world system wherein the countries of the Third World became subservient to and dependent on the developed countries. So while in the developed countries, attention shifted to nutritional disorders due to deficiency of individual nutrients or molecular deficiencies at the cellular level, consequent to overcoming of energy deficiency in people's diets, this paradigm came to be adopted as such in the Third World countries where the principal nutritional problem continues to be insufficient dietary energy intake due to shortfall in the overall food intake on account of people's poverty—put simply, the problem of hunger.

It has taken a long time to unequivocally establish the dietary energy deficiency as the principal nutritional problem in the Third World, and this could be done only by the Third World scientists (Gopalan et al., 1971, Sukahtme 1978, and Narasingarao et al., 1989), once they broke from the dominant western paradigm of conceptualising nutritional problems. Even till date, attempts are being made to confound poverty induced inadequate dietary energy intake as a voluntary 'diversification of diets' in favour of high value foods by Indian consumers, unmindful of compromise in the dietary energy (GOI, 2001-02, Suryanarayana, 1995).

These trends are not inadvertent acts of omission or commission; they have an underlying base of politics and a design that we need to elucidate here. If a person has sufficient food to meet his/her dietary calorie requirement, it would be impossible for him/her not to consume the required amounts of proteins, vitamins and minerals for normal bodily functions (Banerji, 1988). Banerji writes:

> It can thus be concluded that if people get opportunities to get enough food to satisfy their hunger and meet their calorie needs, the need for intervention from nutritionists will be limited only to a few special conditions. For dealing with the rest of the problems they will have to get involved in social, economic and political issues that come in the way of satiation of hunger and meeting the calorie needs (Banerji, 1988).

However, the problems have not always been viewed with deference to privileging common sense and rationality in finding solutions that are required and are workable. For example, it is widely recognised that micronutrient deficiency is invariably associated with poverty, food insecurity and undernutrition that is so very characteristic of the people who invariably do not have sufficient food to eat (Aphane et al., 2011, FAO, 2000, West, 2006) It is equally true that seldom does a single nutrient deficiency express itself in isolation from deficiency of other nutrients (Aphane et al., 2011). The logical approach should then be to try and increase the overall food intake of those suffering from inadequate food intake in order to tackle their multiple nutritional deficiencies (micronutrient, protein and energy deficiencies) all at the same time. This however, would entail engaging with larger societal questions of poverty reduction, unequal and inequitable distribution of resources and mitigating social exclusion based on caste, class and gender. Such solutions do not suit the interests of the ruling elite and the dominant sections of the society who maintain their domination precisely because of the present arrangement of things. The food and drug industry will be forced to subvert them.

In fact, without leaving things to chance, the subversion begins much earlier. Rather than let the desirable solutions even be considered as an option, the food and drug industry has spawned an entire range of nutritional supplements—essential amino acids, essential fatty acids, vitamins, minerals, a broad spectrum of tonics and baby foods, as the 'new age' solution to the humongous problem of hunger and malnutrition. The dismay at the state of affairs was expressed by three leading scientists in the journal Lancet in the following words:

> . . . it is clear that we have, all too often, neglected the overriding issue of inadequate calorie intake and its determinants which continue to take such an enormous toll on vulnerable populations.
>
> We know more today about how to address PEM through food security, nutritional care of women and children, and public-health interventions than we did 20 years ago. But the attention of the nutrition community and the resources of donors are more attracted by the glamour of micronutrients,

> a largely technical and often top-down solution (as close to a quick fix magic bullet as we are likely to get in this field), than by the politically sensitive business of poverty alleviation, people's empowerment, and equity, necessary to ensure that mothers and children have access to health and educational services and adequate food to eat (Schuftan et al., 1998).

Saying this is not to condemn the superb technological achievements of nutritional science. As is acknowledged, these have helped in some dramatic improvements with regard to some of the nutritional problems, however, there remains a strong need to place things in perspective. Micronutrient supplements and the technologies to administer them may help in overcoming the symptoms of the specific nutritional disorders caused by the deficiency of these micronutrients, but they still do not address the primary cause of it in the first place i.e. the deficiency of diets. Neither is it that the deficiency of diets is something natural and unavoidable, for we know that those who suffer from this have specific socio-economic characteristics. We would like to end this section with the following words of Joan Gussow (Gussow, 1981), which make an impassioned plea for looking at food through a macroscope, in the hope that they leave some impression on the readers.

> we have attended to the ever smaller and smaller, breaking down food, food handling, food processing, food functions, into manageable, microscopic pieces, and looking at the isolated effects of the isolated behaviors on isolated food substances in isolated biological systems. I believe it is time now for some of us in the field of food and nutrition to take up our macroscopes rather than our microscopes, to begin the task of looking at connections not merely between nutrients and cells, or between food handling, food textures and food toxins, looking at the connections between farmers and producers, between food policies

> and environmental policies, between toxic wastes and the opportunity to produce safe, affordable food, between tax policies, development policies, and land use policies and our ability to retain farm land, and between that cost of energy and the cost of food.

It is only the macroscope that can bring the hungry and their narratives back in the picture.

## Conclusions

We began our argument by stating the obvious, but somewhat obscured the importance of food for human sustenance. In the figurative sense, opposite of 'food' is 'hunger.' Leveraging the politics of nutrition, we have tried to tease out the reasons and the manner in which the central importance of the question of hunger is sought to be obscured. The continued presence of hunger and undernutrition to a significant extent in our society is a testament to our failure as a society. This failure is sought to be covered up, to an extent, by deploying the sanitised vocabulary of 'nutrition.'

Never has the capacity of human kind to produce food to feed all people on the globe been more than today, yet more than a billion people on earth are compelled to go hungry. India has the largest number of hungry and malnourished people on the globe, the country also has mountains of food grains stored in its warehouses and go-downs, yet this food cannot be distributed to the hungry for one reason or the other, all of which appear to be an attempt at deception in the face of the frequent stories of food grain rotting in godowns or of its export at prices even lower than those meant for the below poverty line people, probably to feed cattle and pigs in the first world. To say the least, this shows utter lack of seriousness on the part of the rulers to address the problem of hunger.

It is the poor and the disempowered who suffer most from hunger and malnutrition. It is also well recognised that malnutrition casts its effect over generations through what is known as intergenerational cycle of malnutrition (FAO, 2012, Blossner, 2005, Delisle, 2008). Propagation of malnutrition through generations in the absence of effective remedial measures sets the stage for further propagation of social, economic and political inequities prevalent in the society. As Behar puts it:

> Seen in this light-malnutrition is not only a consequence of gross inequalities in society, but also a mechanism for maintaining them . . . The 'ruling classes' have an interest, consciously or unconsciously, in maintaining a system that works so well in their favor, while ignoring the interests and desires of society as a whole (Behar, 1976).

It is only this kind of mindset which explains the absolute nihilism with which the ruling classes have treated the raging agrarian crisis in the country and the tsunami of peasant suicides. For all those seriously working for the mitigation of the problem of hunger in the country, the message is clear, 'the fight against hunger has to be taken as a part of the overall struggle for democratisation and radical transformation of the society.

## Endnotes

1. McKewon however pointed out two notable exceptions to this general conclusion i.e., smallpox and scarlet fever. In case of smallpox, inoculation and later immunisation against the disease from the beginning of the 19th century seems to have played an important role, while with respect to scarlet fever decline in the virulence of the bacterium seems to have had a major role in the decline of lethality of the disease. However, even for these two diseases, improved human resistance due to better nutrition remained an important reason.
2. There have however been several contestations over McKewon's thesis. One of the prominent arguments against McKewon's thesis

is that he provided no direct evidence of 'improved nutrition' being the cause of rise in life expectancy at birth and thereby of the population, while there is clear evidence of improvements in public health, sanitation and improved housing that positively impacted on population health (Szreter, 1988 and Easterlin, 1999). Even more challenging was the monumental publication, 'The Population History of England, 1541-1871' brought out in 1981 by Wrigley and Schofield, wherein they claimed 'an absence of any pattern linking economic conditions and mortality in England' (Wrigley E A and Schofield R S, 1981) based on a weak statistical relationship between mortality and real wage trends. This conclusion threatened to severely undermine McKewon's hypothesis.

3. We say 'largely' overcome, rather than fully overcome, because in spite of the fact that most of the developed countries have either attained self-sufficiency in food or have enough of resources to comfortably provide for the dietary needs of their people, there still remains a sizeable section of people in these countries who are food insecure. For example according to the US Department of Agriculture in 2012 about 14.5 percent of the households in the US were food insecure, of which 5.7 percent were households with very low food security (USDA, 2014). By race or ethnicity the maximum food insecure households were Black non-Hispanics, Hispanics, White non-Hispanics and others, in that order (USDA, 2014). This is despite the fact that the United States is among the foremost nations to export enough agricultural produce to exert 'Food Power' over many vulnerable nations of the world (Wallensteen, 1976). These facts go to further reinforce the socio-economic roots of hunger.
4. Caste is an omnipotent and omnipresent social reality in India which is discriminatory in practice due to hierarchical arrangement of castes. Even though caste is characteristic of the Hindu religion, none of the other major religions in the country—Islam, Christianity and Sikhism—which are otherwise ideologically opposed to caste system have escaped the invasion of caste and have been equally prone to the vagaries of the institution of caste. The castes lowermost in social hierarchy and thereby socio-economic development have been classified as 'Scheduled Castes' while the intermediate caste categories are known as 'Other Backward Castes.' The category of 'others' includes upper caste groups which are socio-economically much better off and the uppermost section among these has a pervasive control over the state structure. The indigenous people in India (the Scheduled Tribes), though not part of the formal caste

structure, are perhaps the most marginalised of the social groups in the country.

Though caste enjoys religious sanction, the material phenomena of economic exploitation are at the root of this institution and the religious sanction only seeks to provide sanctity to the underlying economic exploitation. Even though there are numerous constitutional provisions meant for the social and economic uplift of oppressed castes and tribes, the stranglehold of the upper castes on the state, economic and social apparatus has undermined such provisions and has often led to reactionary movements to demand dissolution of such provisions.

## References

Aphane J.M., N. Pilime and N.J. Saronga (2011): 'Food-based Low cost strategies to combat micronutrient deficiencies: Evidence based Interventions in Lesotho and Malawi. In '*Combating Micronutrient Deficiencies: Food-based Approaches*', Brian Thompson and Leslie Amoroso (eds.), CAB International and FAO (pub.), Rome, Italy, p. 278.

Bajpai V. and Saraya A. (2012): 'Of the Relationship Between Population and Development: Need to Stop Vilifying the People', *Journal of Health Management*, 2012, 14(3): pp. 329-340.

Banerji D. (1988): 'The Knowledge of Human Nutrition and the Peoples of the World.' *World Rev Nutr Diet*. 57:1-23.

Barrett R. and Armelagos G. (2013): '*An Unnatural History of Emerging Infections*,' Oxford University Press.

Behar M. (1976): Nutrition: A Social Problem, Micronesian Reporter: *The Journal of Micronesia*, Vol. 24 (2).

Behrman J.R., Harold Alderman and John Hoddinott (2004): 'Hunger and Malnutrition', *Copenhagen Consensus—Challenges and Opportunities. Copenhagen Consensus Challenge Paper*, February.

Bhalla G.S. and Singh G. (2009): 'Economic Liberalisation and Indian Agriculture: A Statewise Analysis,' *Economic and Political Weekly*, Vol. 44 (52): pp. 34-44.

Billewicz, W.Z. and I.A. MacGregor. (1982): A birth to maturity longitudinal study of heights and weights in two West African (Gambian) villages, 1951-1975. *Annals of Human Biology* 9: 309-20.

Blössner M. and Mercedes de Onis (2005): 'Malnutrition: Quantifying the Health Impact at National and Local Levels', Environmental Burden of Disease Series, No. 12, World Health Organisation, Geneva.

Burnett J. (1991): 'Housing and Decline of Mortality', in R. Schofield (1991): '*Decline of Mortality*', pp. 158-76.

Chen, L., A.K.M. Chowdhury, and S.L. Huffman (1980): Anthropometric Assessment of Energy-Protein Malnutrition and Subsequent Risk of Mortality Among Preschool-aged Children, *American Journal of Clinical Nutrition,* 33: 1836-45.

Claudio Schuftan, V. Ramalingaswami, F. James Levinson (1998): 'Micronutrient deficiencies and protein-energy malnutrition', *The Lancet,* Vol. 251: 1812.

Clingingsmith, D. and Williamson, J.G. (2005). *India's Deindustrialisation in the 18th and 19th Centuries.* Cambridge: Harvard University.

Coleman-Jensen, Alisha, Mark Nord, and Anita Singh (2013): 'Household Food Security in the United States in 2012.' ERR–155. US Department of Agriculture, Economic Research Service, September.

Costa, D.L. (1993): 'Health, income, and retirement: Evidence from nineteenth century America'. Ph.D. diss., University of Chicago.

Delisle H.F. (2008): 'Poverty: The Double Burden of Malnutrition in Mothers and the Intergenerational Impact,' *Annals of the New York Academy of Sciences,* Vol. 1136: 172-84. doi: 10.1196/annals.1425.026.

Dewey, C. (1978): 'The End of the Imperialism of Free Trade', in Dewey, C. and Hopkins, A., (eds.) *The Imperial Impact: Studies in the Economic History of Africa and India,* London, 1978, p. 35.

Dhas A.C. (2009): 'Agricultural Crisis in India: The Root Cause and Consequences,' MPRA Paper No. 18930, posted 30. November. Available from http://mpra.ub.uni-muenchen.de/18930/.

Douglas M.C. Wilson, Joel Singer and J. Allan Best J. (1987): Supportive Follow-up for Cigarette Smokers in a Family Practice: Issues of Method Analysis and State of the Art. *Canadian Medical Association Journal,* Vol. 137 (1): 609-612.

Easterlin R.A. (1999): 'How beneficent is the market? A look at the modern history of mortality.' *European Journal of Economic History,* Vol. 3: 257-94.

FAO (2002): 'Reducing Poverty and Hunger: The Critical Role of Financing for Food, Agriculture and Rural Development', Paper Prepared for the International Conference on Financing for Development, Monterrey, Mexico, 18-22 March 2002, Rome, February.

FAO (2012): 'Gender and Nutrition', Draft paper, October. Available from www.fao.org/fileadmin/.../Gender-Nutrition_FAO_IssuePaper_Draft.pdf on 17 August 2014.

FAO (2013): 'Part 2, 'Hunger Dimentions' in *FAO Statistical Yearbook 2013,* Rome 2013, p. 70.

Floud R. (1983): 'The heights of Europeans since 1750: A new source for European economic history'. Mimeograph: Birkbeck College.

Fogel R. (1986): 'Nutrition and the Decline in Mortality since 1700', in S. Engerman, R. Gallman eds., *Long term factors in American Economic Growth,* University of Chicago Press, 439-555.

Fogel R. (1992): Second thoughts on the European escape from hunger: Famines, chronic malnutrition, and mortality rates. *In Nutrition and Poverty*, ed. S.R. Osmani, Oxford: Clarendon Press, 243-286.

Fogel R.W. (1993): 'Economic Growth, Population Theory, and Physiology: The Bearing of Long-Term Processes on the Making of Economic Policy,' Nobel Lecture, December 9, 1993.

Fogel, R.W., D.L. Costa, and J.M. Kim (1993): 'Secular trends in the distribution of chronic conditions and disabilities at young adult and late ages, 1860-1988: Some preliminary findings'. Paper presented at the NBER Summer Institute, Economics of Aging Program (July 26-28). Typescript, University of Chicago.

Food and Agricultural Organisation (FAO) (2000): *State of Food Insecurity in the World*, Rome, p. 9.

Fredrick Engels (1845): *The Conditions of the Working Class in England*, Published in Leipzig.

Gopalan C., Rama Sastri B.V. and Balasubramanian S.C. (1971): *Nutritive Value of Indian Foods*, National Institute of Nutrition, Hyderabad.

Government of India (GOI) (2001-02): *The Economic Survey, 2001-02*, Ministry of Finance, New Delhi.

Guo X1, Long R., Kreuzer M. et.al. (2014): 'Importance of functional ingredients in yak milk-derived food on health of Tibetan nomads living under high-altitude stress: a review.' *Crit Rev Food Sci Nutr*. Vol. 54(3):292-302. doi: 10.1080/10408398.2011.584134.

Gussow J. (1981): 'An SOS for Home Production', *Alumni News*, The University of North Carolina, November.

Heywood, P.F. (1983): 'Growth and nutrition in Papua New Guinea'. *Journal of Human Evolution* 12: 131-43.

Higgs R. (1973): Mortality in Rural America, 1870-1921, *Explorations in Economic History*, Vol. 10: 177-95.

Higgs R. (1979): 'Cycles and Trends of Mortality in 18 Large American Cities, 1871-1900,' *Explorations in Economic History*, Vol. 16: 381-408.

Hunger Task Force (2003): 'Halving Hunger by 2015: A Framework for Action, Interim Report,' Millennium Project, UNDP, New York, p. 33.

International Institute for Population Sciences (IIPS) and Macro International (2005-06): 'National Family Health Survey (NFHS–3), India', Vol. I. Mumbai. Compiled from tables: 7.2 (p. 182), 8.12 (p. 208), 10.1 (p. 270), 10.12 (p. 289), 10.22.1 (p. 304), 10.22.2 (p. 306), 10.24.1 (p. 311), 10.24.2 (p. 312).

Jafri A. (2008): 'Food Crisis Exposes Failings of India's Agricultural Reforms,' *Mainstream Weekly*, Vol. 46 (33).

John, A.M. (1988): *The plantation slaves of Trinidad, 1783-1816: A mathematical and demographic inquiry*. Cambridge: Cambridge University Press.

Kielmann, A.A., DeSweemer C., Uberoi I.S. et al. (1983). *Child and maternal health services in rural India: The Narangwal experiment. Vol. 1: Integrated nutrition and health*. Baltimore: Johns Hopkins University Press for The World Bank.

Lewis, W.A. (1978): *Growth and Fluctuations, 1870-1913*. London, Routledge Revivals, p. 189.

Mann G.V., Edward M. Scott, Lawrence M. Hursh et.al. (1958): 'The Health and Nutritional Status of Alaskan Eskimos', A Survey of the Interdepartmental Committee on Nutrition for National Defense 1958, *American Journal of Clinical Nutrition*, Vol. 11: 31-76.

Marmot, M.G., M.J. Shipley, and G. Rose. (1984): Inequalities in death-specific explanations of a general pattern? *Lancet* 8384 (May 5): 1003-6.

Martorell, R. (1985): Child growth retardation: A discussion of its causes and its relationship to health. In *Nutritional Adaptation in Man*, edited by K. Blaxter, and J.C. Waterlow. London and Paris: John Libby, 13-29.

McKinley J.B. and McKinley S.M. (1977): 'The Questionable Contribution of Medical Measures to Mortality Decline in the US in the 20th Century', *Milibank Memorial Fund Quarterly*, Summer 1977.

Medick, H. (1981): 'The Proto-Industrial Family Economy and the Structures and Functions of Population Development under the Proto-Industrial System', in Kriedte, P., et al., (eds.) *Industrialisation Before Industrialisation*, Cambridge.

Moradi A. (2006): 'On inequality in net nutritional status' Center for Study of African Economies, Department of Economics, University of Oxford, 16 March. Available from http://www.csae.ox.ac.uk/conferences/2006-EOI–RPI/papers/gprg/Moradi.pdf on 27 July, 2014.

Narasinga Rao B.S., Deosthale Y.G. and Pant K.C. (1989): 'Nutritive value of Indian foods' (Revised and updated). Eds. Gopalan, C., B.V. Rama Sastri and S.C. Balasubramanian, National Institute of Nutrition, Hyderabad. 1989.

Osmani, S.R. (1992): On some controversies in the measurement of undernutrition. In *Nutrition and Poverty*, edited by S.R. Osmani. Oxford: Clarendon Press, 121-64.

Parthasarathi P. (1998): 'Rethinking Wages and Competitiveness in the Eighteenth Century: Britain and South India,' *Past & Present*, No. 158, February, pp. 79-109.

Patnaik U. (2003): 'Food Stocks and Hunger: The Causes of Agrarian Distress', *Social Scientist*, Vol. 31 (7/8): 15-41.

Patnaik U. (2004): 'The Republic of Hunger', Public Lecture on the occasion of the 50th Birthday of Safdar Hashmi, organised by SAHMAT (Safdar Hashmi Memorial Trust) on 10 April, New Delhi.

Payne, P. (1992): 'Undernutrition: Measurement and implications'. In *Nutrition and Poverty*, edited by S.R. Osmani, Oxford: Clarendon Press.

Perspectives (2009): 'Harvesting Despair: Agrarian Crisis in India,' January.

Sauberlich H.E., W. Goad, Y.F. Herman et al. (1972): 'Biochemical Assessment of the Nutritional Status of the Eskimos of Wainwright, Alaska', *The American Journal of Clinical Nutrition*, Vol. 25: 437-445.

Shatrugna V., Balakrishna N., Krishnaswamy K. (2006): *Effect of micronutrient supplement on health and nutrition.*

Sheila Zubrigg (1998): 'Re-thinking Public Health, Food, Hunger and Mortality Decline in Indian History', *Medico Friend Circle Bulletin*, No. 258-259, Sept–Oct.

Sheila Zurbrigg (1992): 'Hunger and Epidemic Mortality in Punjab, 1869-1940,' *Economic and Political Weekly*, Vol. 32 (4): 2-26.

Sheila Zurbrigg (1994): 'The Hungry Rarely Write History, and Historians are Rarely Hungry: Reclaiming Hunger in the History of Health', Unpublished paper, Department of History, Dalhousie University, Canada, September.

Sinha K. (2012): '47% of global measles deaths in India', *The Times of India*, 24 April. Available from: timesofindia.indiatimes.com/home/science/47-of-global-measles-deaths-in-India/articleshow/12843053.cms on 3 August, 2014.

Sommer, A., and M.S. Lowenstein (1975): 'Nutritional status and mortality: A prospective validation of the QUAC stick'. *American Journal of Clinical Nutrition* 28: 287-92.

Srinivasan, T.N. (1992): Undernutrition: Concepts, measurement, and policy implications. In *Nutrition and Poverty*, edited by S. R. Osmani. Oxford: Clarendon Press, 97-120.

Steckel R.H. (1983): 'Height and per capita income', *Historical Methods*, 16: 1-70.

Sukhatme, P.V. (1978): 'Assessment of Adequacy of Diets at Different Income Levels,' *Economic and Political Weekly*, Vol. 13 (31/33): pp. 1373-1384.

Suryanarayana, M.H. (1995): 'Growth, Poverty and Levels of Living: Hypotheses, Methods and Policies', *Journal of Indian School of Political Economy*, Vol. (7) 2: 203-255.

Szreter S. (1988): 'The importance of social intervention in Britain's mortality decline c. 1850-1914: a reinterpretation of the role of public health.' *Soc Hist Med*, Vol.1:1-37.

*The Economic Times* (2013): 'Parliamentary panel pulls up government for 'outdated' malnutrition data', September 8.

*The Indian Express* (2012): '2.90 lakh farmers committed suicide during 1995-2011: Govt', 31 August. Available from http://archive.indianexpress.com/news/2.90-lakh-farmers-committed-suicide-during-19952011-govt/995981/ on 10 August, 2014.

The Sanhati Collective (2012): 'Farmer Suicides in India: A Policy-induced Disaster of Epic Proportions', *Sanhati*, January 15. Available from http://sanhati.com/excerpted/4504/ on 10 August, 2014.

Thomas McKeown (1976): 'The Modern Rise of Population', Published by E. Arnold, London.

USDA (United States Department of Agriculture) (2014): 'Food Security Status of US Households in 2012' and 'Food Insecurity by Household Characteristics,' April. Available from www.ers.usda.gov/topics/food-nutrition-assistance/food-security-in-the-us/key-statistics-graphics.aspx on 10 August, 2014.

Vallin J. (1991): 'Mortality in Europe from 1720 to 1914', in R. Schofield, D. Reher and A. Bideau (1991): *The Decline of Mortality in Europe*, Oxford, p. 38-67.

Waaler, H.T. (1984): Height, weight and mortality: The Norwegian experience. *Actu Medica Scandinavica* suppl. 679: 1-51.

Walford, C. (1878): 'The Famines of the World: Past and Present', *Journal of the Statistical Society* 41:13, pp. 434-42.

Wallensteen P. (1976): 'Scarce Goods as Political Weapons: The Case of Food', *Journal of Peace Research*, 1976, Vol. 13 p. 281.

Watts, M. (1983): *Silent Violence: Food, Famine and Peasantry in Northern Nigeria, Berkeley*, pp. 462-3. This 'negotiation' is two-sided and must include climate shock as an independent variable.

West K.P. (2006): 'Protein-Energy Malnutrition (PEM) and Under-nutrition Causes, Consequences, Interactions and Global Trends, John Hopkins Bloomberg School of Public Health, Available from ocw.jhsph.edu/courses/International Nutrition/PDFs/Lecture2.pdf on 16 Aug 2014.

WFP (World Food Program) (2014): 'Hunger Glossary.' Available from https://www.wfp.org/hunger/glossary on 14 August, 2014.

WFP (World Food Program) (2014): 'World Hunger.' Available from http://www.wfp.org/hunger on 3rd of August, 2014.

WHO (1946): Preamble to the Constitution of the World Health Organisation as adopted by the International Health Conference, New York, 19-22 June, 1946, signed on 22 July 1946 by the representatives of 61 States (Official Records of the World Health Organisation, No. 2, p. 100) and entered into force on 7 April 1948.

Wrigley, E.A. and Schofield, R.S. (1981): *The Population History of England, 1541-1871*. Cambridge University Press, p. 452.

# 2

# The Myth and the Reality of Food Security in India

Commissioners of the Supreme Court on the Right to Food have described hunger situation in India as, 'India: Paradox of Hunger Amidst Plenty' (Commissioners of the Supreme Court of India, 2001). The phrase of 'hunger amidst plenty' is a myth popular not only in the official narrations regarding India's food security but has been assiduously cultivated in popular public perception and academic discourse (Chandra, 2010, Patnaik, 2006, Drèze, 2003). There is something queer about this phrase, it carries a self-congratulatory undertone suggestive of country's leadership having succeeded in creating a situation of plenty, as to the prevalent hunger, it is just a question of fair distribution that can be taken care of any day, even as India adds on hungry millions by the day as per the *United Nations Millennium Development Goals Report, 2010* (Dhawan, 2010).

This myth engenders complacency in tackling the question of hunger in India. In order to break this complacency there is a need to unravel the myth of 'hunger amidst plenty' which is what we attempt here. The methodology adopted is simple, first average per capita food grain requirement in the country is calculated assuming all its citizens are fortunate to consume the recommended dietary calories and then, food grain requirements for consumption of poverty-line level calories are calculated. These computed values for average per capita food grain requirement are compared with the data on food grain availability in India since 1947 to draw relevant conclusions.

Subsequent to this, an attempt is made to have a closer look at another myth, it is the myth of people 'diversifying their dietary intake' even as the total calories per diem have been consistently falling in the period of neoliberalisation. Changes in food and non-food expenditure patterns have been looked at to examine their consistency with well- established laws of food consumption and draw conclusions as to the veracity of 'diversification of diet' thesis.

## Some Baseline Data

The following data is important for aforementioned calculations:

- Recommended calorie norms for different age groups in India
- Proportion of direct calories derived from cereals in the rural and urban areas and among the different classes
- The energy value of different food grains in India
- Estimates of poverty levels in India.

### Recommended Calorie Norms for Different Age Groups

Table 2.1 below gives the calorie norms for different age groups in India as recommended by ICMR (Indian Council of Medical Research) (ICMR, 1990). As per the National Institute of Nutrition guidelines, these recommendations remained unchanged even till 2004 (Gopalan, 2004). However, the latest guidelines issued in 2011 have reduced the daily calorie requirements for different groups (NIN, 2011). The following calculations are based on the earlier guidelines. While we reserve our comments on the new guidelines for later in the article (in the section on changing dietary patterns), suffice here to say that the following calculations regarding per capita food grain requirement and the inferences drawn therefrom remain valid for the period since 1947, and even for the near future.

Table 2.1: Recommended Daily Intake of Energy of Indians.

| *Group* | | *Body weight (kg)* | *Energy allowance per day (kcal)* |
|---|---|---|---|
| Infancy | | | |
| 0-6 months | | – | 118 kcal/kg/day |
| 7-12 months | | – | 108 kcal/kg/day |
| Children | | | |
| 1-3 years | | 12.03 | 1,240 |
| 4-6 years | | 18.87 | 1,690 |
| 7-9 years | | 26.37 | 1,950 |
| Adolescents | | | |
| 10-12 years | (males) | 35.4 | 2,190 |
| | (females) | 31.5 | 1,970 |
| 13-15 years | (males) | 47.8 | 2,450 |
| | (females) | 46.7 | 2,060 |
| 16-18 years | (males) | 57.1 | 2,640 |
| | (females) | 49.9 | 2,060 |
| Ref Males | (light work) | 60 | 2,425 |
| | (moderate work) | | 2,875 |
| | (heavy work) | | 3,800 |
| Ref Females | (light work) | 50 | 1,875 |
| | (moderate work) | | 2,225 |
| | (Heavy work) | | 2,925 |
| Pregnant women | | – | + 300 |
| Lactating women | (first 6 months) | – | + 550 |
| | (6-12 months) | | + 400 |
| | | | or an avg. of 475/day |

*Source:* Recommended dietary intakes for Indians. Indian Council for Medical Research, New Delhi, 1990.

The energy requirements for age groups above 40 years have been subsequently calculated in accordance with the

WHO recommendations which state that 'after the age of 40 years, requirements should be reduced by 5% per decade until the age of 60, and by 10% for each decade thereafter' (Park, 2007: 502).

Definitions pertinent to these recommendations:

*Indian Reference Man:* An Indian reference man is defined as being 'between 20 and 39 years of age and weighs 60 kg. He is free from disease and physically fit for active work. On each working day he is employed for 8 hours in occupation that usually involves moderate activity. While not at work he spends 8 hours in bed, 4 to 6 hours sitting and moving around and 2 hours in walking and in active recreation or household duties' (ICMR, 1990).

*Indian Reference Woman:* She is 'between 20 and 39 years of age, healthy and weighs 50 kg. She may be engaged for 8 hrs in general household work, in light industry or in other moderately active work. Apart from 8 hrs in bed, she spends 4 to 6 hours sitting or moving around only through light activity, and 2 hours in walking or in active recreation or in household duties (ICMR, 1990).

## Direct Calories Derived From Cereals in Indian Diets

There are variations in patterns of direct and indirect cereal consumption as a society moves up the development ladder. With rising affluence, indirect consumption of cereals in the form of animal products forms a sizable part of the diets (Patnaik, 2009). Accordingly there is lesser variation in the diets of those lower down the social ladder and the poor often derive a large part of their calories through direct food grain consumption, unable to afford the costlier animal products, vegetables and fruits. Tables 2.2 and 2.3 below give the proportion of overall calories derived from cereals in India (Deaton and Drèze, 2009).

Table 2.2: Total and Cereal Calorie Consumption by Decile and Quartile of Per Capita Expenditure, Rural India, 1983 to 2004-05 Across Different National Sample Survey rounds.

| *Year* | *Bottom decile* | *Bottom quartile* | *Second quartile* | *Third quartile* | *Top quartile* |
|---|---|---|---|---|---|
| | | | *Total calories* | | |
| 1983 | 1,359 | 1,580 | 2,007 | 2,328 | 3,044 |
| 1987-88 | 1,488 | 1,683 | 2,056 | 2,334 | 2,863 |
| 1993-94 | 1,490 | 1,659 | 2,000 | 2,251 | 2,702 |
| 1999-2000 | 1,496 | 1,658 | 1,978 | 2,250 | 2,707 |
| 2004-05 | 1,485 | 1,624 | 1,900 | 2,143 | 2,521 |
| | | | *Cereal calories* | | |
| 1983 | 1,150 | 1,309 | 1,589 | 1,738 | 1,974 |
| 1987-88 | 1,221 | 1,359 | 1,598 | 1,715 | 1,894 |
| 1993-94 | 1,203 | 1,316 | 1,504 | 1,591 | 1,690 |
| 1999-2000 | 1,197 | 1,289 | 1,591 | 1,509 | 1,566 |
| 2004-05 | 1,189 | 1,259 | 1,690 | 1,430 | 1,471 |

*Source:* Angus Deaton and Jean Drèze. *Economic and Political Weekly,* February 14, 2009, Vol XLIV (7).

Table 2.3: All India Averages for Total Calories and Calories Derived from Cereals.

| *Year* | *NSSO round* | *Total Calories* | | *Total Calories (All India)* | *Cereal Calories* | | *Cereal Calories (All India)* |
|---|---|---|---|---|---|---|---|
| | | *Rural* | *Urban* | | *Rural* | *Urban* | |
| 2004-05 | 61st | 2,047 | 2,021 | 2,040 | 1,386 | 1,147 | 1,326 |

*Source:* Compiled from Tables 2.1 and 2.3, Angus Deaton and Jean Drèze. *Economic & Political Weekly,* February 14, 2009, Vol XLIV (7).

We can see from Table 2.2 that the total calorie consumption of the bottom three quartiles in rural India is below the 2,400 calories per day which is the cut-off for determining rural poverty, while that of the top quartile is above 2,400 calories. Thus the mean calorie consumption of the bottom three quartiles can be taken as calorie consumption of the below poverty line (BPL) while that of the top quartile as that of above poverty line (APL) for rural areas. The BPL and the APL categories in rural areas thus derive 77% and 58% of their dietary calories respectively from cereals.

Disaggregated quartilewise data for total and cereal calories for urban areas was not available. However, from Table 2.3 we can see that overall calories derived from cereals constitute about 57% of the total calories in urban areas, while for the rural areas the same figure is 68%.

**The energy value of different food grains in India.**

Table 2.4 gives the calories derived from different food grains grown in India (Gopalan, 1989).

Table 2.4: Energy Value of Different Food grains Grown in India.

| *Category* | *Cereals* | | | *Pulses* | | | |
|---|---|---|---|---|---|---|---|
| *Food grain* | *Raw rice Milled* | *Wheat Whole* | *Maize dry* | *Bengal Gram* | *Black Gram* | *Red Gram* | *Soya Bean* |
| Weight | 100 | 100 | 100 | 100 | 100 | 100 | 100 |
| Energy k cal | 345 | 346 | 342 | 360 | 347 | 335 | 432 |

*Source:* Gopalan et. al (1989): Nutritional value of Indian foods, NIN, Hyderabad.

From Table 2.4 the average energy value of food grains is derived to be 3.6 kcal per gm of food grains.

## Estimates of Poverty Levels in India

The Tendulkar Committee Report of 2009 prepared by the Planning Commission has effectively reduced the poverty line level calorie norms to 1,800 calories per person per day for both the urban and the rural areas in the name of moving away from the calorie norms for determining the poverty line. Even though we shall discuss in a later chapter as to how and why the Tendulkar Committee has pulled the measures of poverty down to such abominably low levels, it should suffice here to say that per capita calorie consumption of 2,400 calories for rural areas and 2,100 calories for the urban areas (as fixed originally in 1973-74) has been taken as the minimum irreducible cut off for estimating nutritional poverty levels in India. According to Utsa Patnaik the population in rural areas consuming less than 2,400 calories is 87%, while for the urban areas the proportion of population consuming less than 2,100 calories is about 35.5% (Patnaik, 2007, 2010). These estimates are very close to other estimates of poverty in India based on same calorie norms (Deaton and Drèze, 2009; MRD, 2009). Based on consumption patterns, the Arjun Sengupta Committee came out with the finding that approximately 77% of the population in the country subsists on less than ₹ 20 a day (NCEUS, 2007).

## Estimation of Average Per Capita Calorie and Food Grain Requirement

In this section, we calculate the average per capita daily calorie and food grain requirement based on the recommendations of ICMR given in Table 2.1 and the baseline data given above. To arrive at these estimates we have to take into account the male and female composition of population in different age groups as calorie requirements vary by sex and the proportions of APL and BPL population in each age group as the nature of work and hence the calorie requirement would vary by socio-economic category. Since such data is not readily available, we have to make some reasonable assumptions. The assumptions we have made for the purpose of these calculations are as follows:

- Since age-groupwise sex ratios were not available separately for rural and urban areas, these have been assumed to be the same as the age-groupwise sex ratio of the overall population. Accordingly, the per capita daily calories for each age group has been calculated by taking the weighted average of per capita calorie requirement for males and females in each age group for both rural and urban areas.

- The BPL to APL ratio of male and female population in each age group for rural and urban areas is presumed to be the same as the overall BPL to APL ratio for rural and urban population respectively.
- Poor people invariably have to do hard manual labour for a living. Hence, the daily calorie requirement for the BPL population is accordingly taken to be 3,800 and 2,925 calories respectively for males and females (Table 2.1). Given the hardships of the rural life even the APL population in rural areas has to do moderately heavy work, while those in urban areas may get by doing light work. Accordingly, the daily calorie requirement is 2,875 and 2,225 calories for APL males and females respectively in the rural areas, while that in the urban areas is 2,425 and 1,875 calories for males and females respectively (Table 2.1).
- While calorie requirements for adults may vary by the level of activity, for children and adolescents, requirements have been taken as those necessary to meet their physiological needs for maintaining bodily functions and to meet their growth needs. Since the physiological needs should ideally be the same for all children, no difference has been made between the children from rural or urban or the BPL and APL categories.

These generalisations are not watertight and leave room for exceptions. For example, there is chronic unemployment and underemployment on a large scale, especially among the poor, for which reason it may be said that the assumption of daily calorie requirement commensurate with heavy work for BPL adults may overestimate the average per capita calorie and food grain requirement. But this is not necessarily true because let alone the energy required for income earning work, the hardships entailed even for such routine activities of daily life like arranging for water, fuel, food and other daily necessities can make them quite energy intensive for the poor.

Given these assumptions, the per capita average calorie requirement for the rural and the urban areas is arrived at by calculating series of weighted averages as shown in Table 2.5 (see Appendix 1). Average per capita daily calorie requirement thus calculated is 2,554 and 2,487 calories for the rural and the urban areas respectively.

As per the projections the proportion of rural and the urban population in India was 70.2% and 29.8% respectively as on 1st March 2010 (indiastat.com—projected total population by sex and projected urban population by sex). The average per capita daily calorie requirement for the country would be the weighted average of the average per capita daily requirement for the rural and the urban areas i.e. [2,554 × 70.2 + 2,487 × 29.8]/100 = 2,534 calories per day.

## Food Grain Requirement

Based on the calculations in Table 2.5 we can compute average per capita cereal calories as shown in Tables 2.6a and 2.6b (Appendix 2). In Table 2.6a we have calculated the cereal calories for males and females belonging to BPL and APL categories separately. In Table 2.6b, first the weighted average of cereal calories for males of BPL and APL categories and the weighted average of cereal calories for females of BPL and APL categories are calculated using the BPL/APL ratio and then the weighted average of cereal calories for males and females in each age group is calculated using the age group specific sex ratio. In the same table the weighted averages of cereal calories for different age groups have been computed using their respective proportions of rural and urban populations to arrive at average daily cereal calories consumed in rural and urban areas.

The weighted average of the direct calories of rural and urban areas would be = 1,732 kcal. Therefore the required average per capita food grain requirement = 1,732/3.6 (calories derived from 1 gm of food grains) = 481 gm per day or 176 kg per annum.

## Discussion on the Validity of the Above Results

One possible objection to our estimate of average calorie requirement of 2,554 calories for the rural areas and 2,487 in the urban areas can be that it is an overestimate because there has been a declining trend in calorie consumption over the years as revealed by different NSSO rounds (Table 2.2). So, the theory of 'voluntary choice' put forth by the government to explain the observed decline in calorie consumption over the years. *The Economic Survey 2001-02* reports that the excess of food stocks that existed then represented a 'problem of plenty' (Patnaik, 2003). It said, 'The growth rates of superior cereals have been higher than population growth owing to allegedly too high administered prices of rice and wheat, and stocks have built up because all consumers voluntarily wish to reduce their intake of cereals and rather consume fruits, vegetables and animal products (milk, eggs, chicken, etc.) as their income rises' (ibid). The suggestions are that 'The poor seem to have opted for some diversification in consumption providing a more nutritious diet though not necessarily adequate energy (Suryanarayana, 1995).'

The proposition of 'voluntary choice' is a poor attempt at weaving the myth of 'hunger amidst plenty.' There is hardly a country around the world where social and economic progress has meant a decline in calorie consumption. Even WHO projections (Table 2.7) show that dietary calories across different regions of the world, including South Asia, are increasing (WHO, 2010).

Table 2.7: Global and Regional Per Capita Food Consumption (kcal Per Capita Per Day)

| *Region* | *1964-66* | *1974-76* | *1984-86* | *1997-99* | *2015* | *2030* |
|---|---|---|---|---|---|---|
| World | 2,358 | 2,435 | 2,655 | 2,803 | 2,940 | 3,050 |
| Developing countries | 2,054 | 2,152 | 2,450 | 2,681 | 2,850 | 2,980 |
| Near East and North Africa | 2,290 | 2,591 | 2,953 | 3,006 | 3,090 | 3,170 |
| Sub-Saharan Africa | 2,058 | 2,079 | 2,057 | 2,195 | 2,360 | 2,540 |
| Latin America and Caribbean | 2,393 | 2,546 | 2,689 | 2,824 | 2,980 | 3,140 |
| East Asia | 1,957 | 2,105 | 2,559 | 2,921 | 3,060 | 3,190 |
| South Asia | 2,017 | 1,986 | 2,205 | 2,403 | 2,700 | 2,900 |
| Industrialised countries | 2,947 | 3,065 | 3,206 | 3,380 | 3,440 | 3,500 |
| Transition countries | 3,222 | 3,385 | 3,379 | 2906 | 3060 | 3180 |

*Source:* WHO (2010).

Apart from 'voluntary choice' the other reasons for decrease in calorie consumption that have been forwarded are improvements in general comforts of life even in the rural areas like better transport, better roads even to remote areas, easier availability of cooking fuel, increasing mechanisation of agriculture, decrease in fertility rates and hence lesser number of children to feed and lesser need for increased dietary allowances for pregnant and lactating women, availability of piped water and improvement in sanitary conditions that have reduced morbidity and thereby reduced the need to consume more calories (Deaton and Drèze, 2009). There is no denying the fact that all these factors impact on dietary energy needs, but their presence alone means little unless placed in perspective.

Mechanisation of agriculture with increasing concentration of land in a few hands in the absence of any land reforms worth their name could very well mean that vast numbers of rural poor who depend on agriculture for a living are thrown out of work and pushed down the poverty line, are thus unable to afford any food. Given their numbers in India, this section of landless agricultural workers and marginal peasants alone could pull the average calorie consumption down.

In their paper 'Food and Nutrition in India: Facts and Interpretations' Angus Deaton and Jean Drèze write 'Undernutrition levels in India remain higher than for most countries of sub-Saharan Africa, even though those countries are currently much poorer than India, have grown much more slowly, and have much higher levels of infant and child mortality' (Deaton and Drèze, 2009). It is queer that people should 'voluntarily' fritter away their prosperity by opting for so-called 'diversification' even at the cost of being undernourished and thereby endangering the very prosperity which is supposed to have afforded them 'voluntary choice' and 'diversification' in the first place. Clearly, there is a need to have a closer look at the changing dietary patterns, their impact on the nutritional status and the real reasons behind falling dietary intake, rather than portray fraudulently happy scenarios where they don't exist at all. Utsa Patnaik has convincingly established that the proportions of poverty, as measured by the initial calorie norms, have consistently increased since the launch of the Neoliberal Economic Reforms both in the rural and the urban India (Patnaik, 2007, 2010). With little purchasing power and given levels of food inflation, how are people expected to consume enough food let alone exercise 'voluntary choice'? The cause for falling calorie consumption over the years has been put by Patnaik as, 'a very large increase in the inequality of income distribution during the nineties owing to income deflationary policies impacting the poor, and also in the poor being institutionally denied access to grain since 1997-98 owing to the misconceived targeting system under which large numbers of the actually poor are not being identified as such and are not being issued ration cards for accessing cheap food' (Patnaik, 2003). As to the upper income groups, the same author says, 'The absorption of food grains can be safely assumed to be rising, for let us remember, this refers not only to directly absorbed grains but also to indirectly absorbed grains via conversion to animal products' (Ibid).

It needs to be mentioned here that our estimate of required daily calorie intake is barely 6% more than the prescribed minimum norm of 2,400 calories for the rural areas and about 18% more for the prescribed calorie norm for urban areas. Moreover we have not included here the increased dietary allowance in states like pregnancy, lactation and during illness, which are genuine concerns when making provision for people's nutritional needs.

It would not be out of place to expect that post-colonial India would gratify her children more than what the colonial masters did. Based on our calculation of average per capita, per day calorie requirement, 176 kg of food grains is required per capita annually to provide for per capita cereal calories, given the present consumption pattern. It is instructive to note here that this amount of per capita annual food grain requirement is much below the minimum that was considered necessary, in the report of the British appointed 'Famine Commission' of 1880, to avoid starvation deaths (Bajaj and Srinivas, 2002).

When the minimum calorie norms were first defined in 1973-74, Government of India defined the 'minimum income' as that which could be, 'considered adequate to ensure minimum energy requirements for an active and healthy life and also minimum clothing and shelter. It did not include expenditures on health and education, which are to be provided by the State as per the Indian Constitution.' It further stated that, 'The minimum itself should be revised upwards with economic progress' (Suryanarayana, 2009). It follows then that the minimum calorie norms for poverty that were set in 1973-74 should have been revised upwards by now. But the efforts have been very much in the reverse direction. It is revealing to have a look at the actual per capita daily calorie consumption of some of the developing and least developed countries in Table 2.8 (FAO, 2008). India's per capita dietary energy consumption is still a far cry from that of countries like Syria (3,000 kcal), Egypt (3,320 kcal), Cuba (3,280 kcal) and China (2,990 kcal) (Ibid). In spite of facts being what they are, the policy establishment has chosen to live in a state of denial.

Table 2.8: Per Capita Daily Calorie Consumption in Some Countries, 2003-05

| *Country* | *Per capita calories per day* | *Country* | *Per capita calories per day* |
|---|---|---|---|
| Burkina Faso | 2,620 | Mali | 2,570 |
| Gabon | 2,760 | Maldives | 2,630 |
| Ghana | 2,690 | Nepal | 2,430 |
| Guinea | 2,540 | Jamaica | 2,810 |
| Nigeria | 2,600 | Honduras | 2,590 |
| Mauritania | 2,790 | South Africa | 2,900 |
| Viet Nam | 2,650 | Samoa | 2,820 |

*Source:* FAO.

## Food Grain Requirement at Poverty Line Level Calorie Consumption

For a calorie consumption of 2,400 kcal per person per day the BPL persons in rural areas will consume 1,848 direct calories from cereals @ 77% of total calories and the APL persons will consume 1,392 direct calories from cereals @ of 58% of total calories. The average direct calories derived from cereals per person per day for rural areas would be the weighted average of the BPL and APL direct calories:

[87 × 1,848 + 13 × 1,392]/100 = 1,788.72 kcal

Likewise for urban areas the average per capita direct calories derived from cereals would be = 1,197 @ of 57% of total calories. Given the ratio rural to urban population ratio of 70.2/29.8, the average direct calories derived from food grains at poverty line level calorie consumption would be:

[70.2 × 1,788.72 + 29.8 × 1,197]/100 = 1,612.4 kcal

Therefore average per capita per day food grain requirement at poverty line cut off level = 1,612.4/3.6 = 448 gm or 163.5 kg per annum.

## The Truth of India's Self-Sufficiency in Food Production

Table 2.9 shows per capita net availability of food grains since 1951 (Indiastat.com: Per Capita Net Availability of Food grains).

The net food grain availability here includes food grains required for both direct and indirect consumption.

We have calculated above that at given rates of cereal calories, average food grain requirement is 176 Kg per person per annum if people were to consume recommended energy allowances for different age groups and 163.5 Kg per person per annum if everyone were to consume at the poverty line cut off levels for rural and urban areas. It need to be emphasised here that this is only direct food grain requirement and does not include the food grains consumed indirectly in form of animal products. It is well known that per calorie consumed in the form of animal products like meat, many more calories are consumed in the form of food grains diverted as animal feed (Patnaik, 2009). This eventually means that the actual food grain requirement is still higher than the levels calculated above.

It is seen from Table 2.9 that in first 63 years of independence, it is only in five years i.e. 1989, 1991, 1995, 1997 and 2002, that India managed to reach per capita food

Table 2.9: Per Capita net Availability of Food Grains (Per Annum) in India (1951 to 2007)

| *Year* | *Net Food grains availability Kg per year* | *Year* | *Net Food grains availability Kg per year* | *Year* | *Net Food grains availability Kg per year* | *Year* | *Net Food grains availability Kg per year* | *Year* | *Net Food grains availability Kg per year* |
|---|---|---|---|---|---|---|---|---|---|
| 1951 | 144.1 | 1963 | 162.0 | 1975 | 148.0 | 1987 | 172.0 | 1999 | 170.0 |
| 1952 | 140.7 | 1964 | 165.4 | 1976 | 155.3 | 1988 | 163.4 | 2000 | 165.9 |
| 1953 | 150.6 | 1965 | 175.3 | 1977 | 156.8 | 1989 | 180.1 | 2001 | 151.9 |
| 1954 | 167.1 | 1966 | 149.0 | 1978 | 170.8 | 1990 | 172.5 | 2002 | 180.4 |
| 1955 | 162.0 | 1967 | 146.5 | 1979 | 173.9 | 1991 | 186.2 | 2003 | 159.7 |
| 1956 | 157.6 | 1968 | 168.4 | 1980 | 150.2 | 1992 | 171.1 | 2004 | 168.9 |
| 1957 | 163.2 | 1969 | 162.5 | 1981 | 166.0 | 1993 | 169.4 | 2005 | 154.2 |
| 1958 | 149.2 | 1970 | 166.1 | 1982 | 166.1 | 1994 | 172.0 | 2006 | 162.5 |
| 1959 | 170.9 | 1971 | 171.1 | 1983 | 159.5 | 1995 | 180.8 | 2007* | 160.4 |
| 1960 | 164.6 | 1972 | 170.6 | 1984 | 175.0 | 1996 | 173.5 | | |
| 1961 | 171.1 | 1973 | 153.9 | 1985 | 165.5 | 1997 | 183.6 | | |
| 1962 | 168.2 | 1974 | 164.7 | 1986 | 174.3 | 1998 | 163.2 | | |

*Source:* indiastat.com. *Figure for 2007 is provisional.

grain availability (for both direct and indirect consumption) more than 176 kg (optimal food grain required for direct consumption only). The increase registered in 2002 seems to have been only on paper, because we can see that the figures for 2001 and 2003 are abysmally low to make the figure for 2002 tenable. For much of the first decade of 21st century the food grain availability in India has been even lower than that required to meet food grain demand for direct consumption at poverty line level of calories. In fact it is only in 23 years out of 63 that food grain availability has been more than this level and if we add to this the food grain required for indirect consumption, the total availability in all years is bound to be way below the requirement, claims of food self-sufficiency as a result of Green Revolution notwithstanding.

We have talked only of average consumption till now, but it can safely be presumed that a very high proportion of the population consumed way below these averages while a minority consumed much higher amounts.

## Analysing Poverty and the Changing Dietary Patterns

A very important issue still remains unresolved here: that is, that if the levels of poverty in the country are indeed as high as have been assumed in our calculations i.e. 87% and 35.5% in the rural and the urban areas respectively, then how do we account for the seeming affluence that is clearly visible by way of unprecedented levels of consumerism, in the face of increasing levels of poverty? Alternatively, if indeed affluence of the people has increased, then how come their calorie consumption levels are falling and there is demonstrated stagnation in nutritional outcomes in the country?

First of all, we feel that we can draw a distinction between nutritional poverty and income poverty. This is necessitated on account of an opinion that expenditure on food may not command preference beyond the basic level due to either the pressure of consumerist culture which may entice people to divert a real increase in income towards non-food consumer items or even for other necessary expenditures like education or increasing healthcare costs.

Such a demarcation acknowledges that poor nutrition could be due to factors other than income poverty and that there is a need to study the factors that influence people's spending preferences vis-a vis food or other factors impacting dietary energy intake. This perspective is lost in a rather simple conceptualisation that food is the most basic human need, that people would channelise their resources first towards the satisfaction of this basic need along with the need for housing and clothing and then divert resources towards other spending preferences.

The latter conceptualisation largely explains the scenario in case of absolute poverty where the resources hardly suffice even to provide for the most basic needs and the income elasticity for food is significant, however, it may not explain the full picture in case of sections that are slightly better off, and upon satisfaction of their basic hunger, tend to diversify their consumption pattern due to various reasons. It is pertinent to point here that due to increasing withdrawal of the State from providing for necessities like education, health and other social sector spending, people have to divert substantial portions of their incomes for such expenditure of necessity. They may yet like to have more wholesome food, much beyond the poverty line cut-offs of 2,400 and 2,100 calories for the rural and urban areas, provided there is sufficiency of resources.

The question then is, is this premise borne out by empirical data? Besides, we also need to empirically test the veracity of 'diversification of diets theory' which holds that, 'Consumers voluntarily wish to reduce their intake of cereals and rather consume fruits, vegetables and animal products' due to rising incomes during the years of neoliberal economic reforms. In this enquiry we can be guided by some well-established laws of food consumption.

## Laws of Change in Food Consumption

The two most important laws used to study changes in food consumption patterns are the Engel's Law and the Bennet's Law.

### Engel's Law

The Engel's Law holds that in a society, the proportion of expenditure on food is higher for the poor than that for the rich, while at aggregate level, poorer countries spend a larger proportion of their GDP on food than the wealthier ones, for example in the United States this proportion is around 10%, while it can be as high as 50% for very poor countries (FAO, 1999).

To put it in the words of the man himself, Engels said:

> This natural law can be stated as follows:
>
> The poorer the individual, a family, or a people, the greater must be the percentage of the income necessary for the maintenance of physical sustenance, and again of this a greater portion must be allowed for food (Zimmerman, 1932).

Secondly, although there is a decrease in the proportion of expenditure on food, the per capita expenditure on food rises with increasing per capita incomes as people tend to consume higher value foods (FAO, 1999).

What is important to note here is that consumption of higher value foods is accompanied by higher per capita expenditure on food and there is nothing to suggest that this is accompanied by a cut back on the total number of calories consumed. Moreover, we have already mentioned above WHO data to show that there has been an increase in per capita dietary calories with economic growth.

## Bennett's Law

Bennett's Law states that as there is economic growth, the proportion of calories in the diet derived from cheaper foods e.g. cereals, roots and tubers declines, while the share of calories from costlier foods like vegetables, fruits, milk and meat increases. Bennett argued that, 'General economic development and change in the composition of regional diets . . . in the direction of wider variety and greater expense, go hand in hand and are not separable one from the other' (Bennett, 1954).

Poleman proposed an extension to Bennett's Law to account for the dietary changes in a developing country situation. He suggested that a change from cheaper cereals to more costly cereals is likely to occur first before there is a changeover to non-cereal foods (Poleman, 1981). In the Indian context, this would mean a shift from the coarse cereals to the superior cereals namely wheat or rice or both.

It is said that evidence of such substitutions could be interpreted as indicative of 'perceived nutritional adequacy' (Meenakshi, 2000).

## Pattern of Dietary Changes during the Period of Economic Reforms

In this section, we present disaggregated data on changes in per capita per diem calorie consumption and monthly per capita expenditure on food and non-food items through the period of economic reforms. All the data presented here is obtained from different rounds (50th round in 1993-94 through 66th round in 2009-10) of NSSO (National Sample Survey Organisation) on household expenditure.

Notes for the figures in this section:

- We have analysed here the consumption expenditure data only for rural India. Even though there is considerable poverty, malnutrition and hunger in the urban India, but rural India is the one that forms the forte of these problems, hence the consumption data from rural areas was deemed best for illustrating the argument of this paper.

Even otherwise, the trends in consumption of and expenditure on food in urban areas are very similar to those in rural areas (Deaton and Drèze, 2009), meaning thereby that the analysis of NSSO MPCE on food for urban areas will only be a minor variant of similar analysis for rural areas. The only exception here is the conspicuous consumerism and ostensible affluence of the urban areas which does not seem to be reflected adequately in the NSSO data.

- The consumer expenditure data for the different NSSO rounds has been obtained from the respective NSSO reports (NSSO 50th Round, 1996, NSSO 53rd Round, 1998, NSSO 56th Round, 2002, NSSO 59th Round, 2005, NSSO 61st Round, 2006, NSSO 62nd Round, 2008, NSSO 64th Round, 2010, NSSO 66th Round, 2011).
- Till the 62nd Round the available NSSO data is disaggregated into 12 MPCE classes, which has been reconstituted into three groups (lower, intermediate and upper) of 4 MPCE classes each by taking weighted average of the separate expenditure classes. From the 64th Round the data is disaggregated into 10 fractile classes, which have again been reconstituted into 3 groups—lower (the lower 4 fractiles), intermediate (middle 3 fractiles) and the upper (top 3 fractiles) by taking average of the fractiles.
- Beginning from the 50th Round (1993-94 consumer data), subsequent rounds were chosen with a gap of two rounds, thus the last round with 12 MPCE classes was 62nd Round (2005-06 data). Round 64 was chosen

because it is the first NSSO round that gives consumer data by MPCE fractiles. Round 66 being the latest at the time of writing, was chosen to provide updated data, unfortunately though it does not give disaggregated consumer data by fractiles/classes.

- The expenditure on food is classified into three categories:
  1. Food grains: includes cereals, grams, pulses and their products.
  2. High value foods: includes milk and milk products, egg, fish and meat, vegetables, fresh and dry fruits.
  3. Beverages and processed food.

  Food items like cereal substitutes, edible oil, sugar, salt and spices have been left out as the concentration was largely on food grains and higher value foods. Any deviation from this has been specified at the appropriate place.
- The non-food expenditure is categorised into following heads:
  1. Pan, tobacco and intoxicants
  2. Fuel and light
  3. Clothing and footwear
  4. Miscellaneous goods and services: these include expenditure on education, medical expenditure (institutional and non-institutional), conveyance, other services, toilet articles and sundry articles
  5. Durable goods.

## Changes in Per Capita Per Day Calories

Table 2.2 shows that there has been a consistent decline in the daily calories across the expenditure quartiles since 1987-88. The fact that this data is disaggregated by quartiles, and that there is a decline even in the top quartile is of particular significance. A decline in average calorie consumption of all expenditure classes can be deceptive as this can easily mask a handsome increase in the top classes while there is a steep decline in the lower classes; but a decline even in the top quartile compels us to look carefully for the reasons of the same.

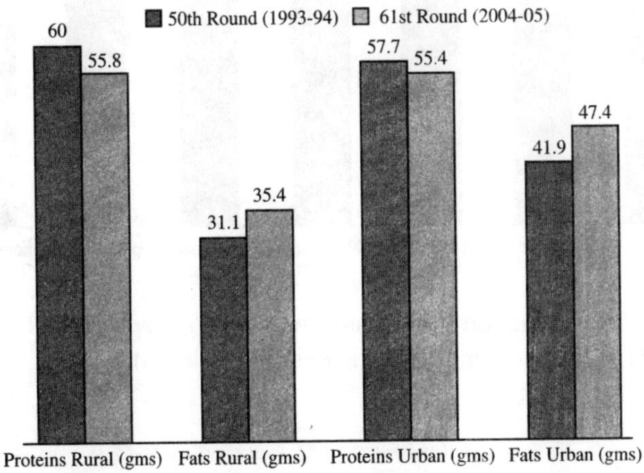


Figure 2.1: Average change in consumption of proteins and fats per capita, per day (All India).

Associated with the decline in total calories, Figure 2.1 shows that there has, on an average been a decline in consumption of dietary proteins across MPCE classes through the period of economic reforms. Even though we do not have quartile-wise decrease in consumption of dietary proteins, it is improbable that in the top expenditure quartile the consumption of dietary proteins (from animal products like milk and meat and eggs) would have increased in the presence of a decline in dietary calories. This fact puts a question mark over the 'diversification of diet' and 'voluntary reduction in cereal calories' thesis.

## Variation in Food and Non-food Expenditure

Figures 2.2a, 2.2b and 2.2c show the variation in food and non-food expenditure across different MPCE (monthly per capita

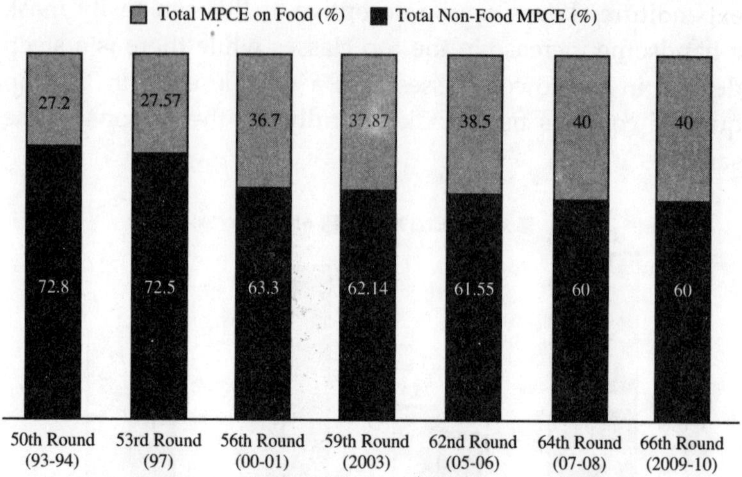


Figure 2.2a: Variation in food and non-food expenditure (% of total MPCE) among lower MPCE classes (Rural India).

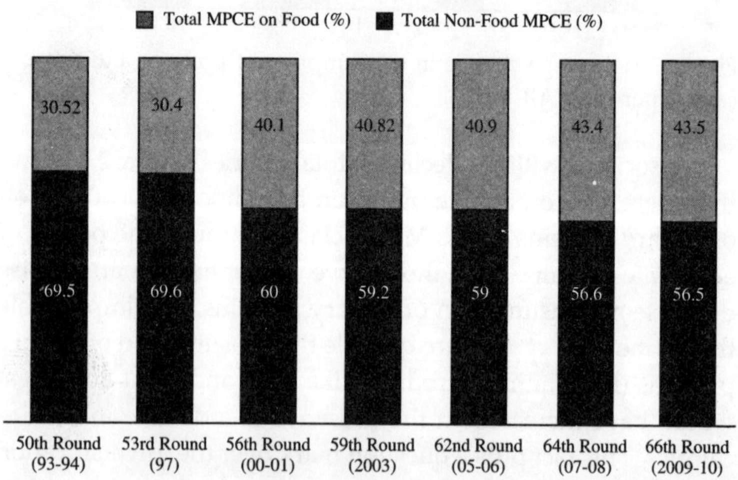


Figure 2.2b: Variation of food and non-food expenditure (% of total MPCE) in intermediate MPCE classes (Rural India).

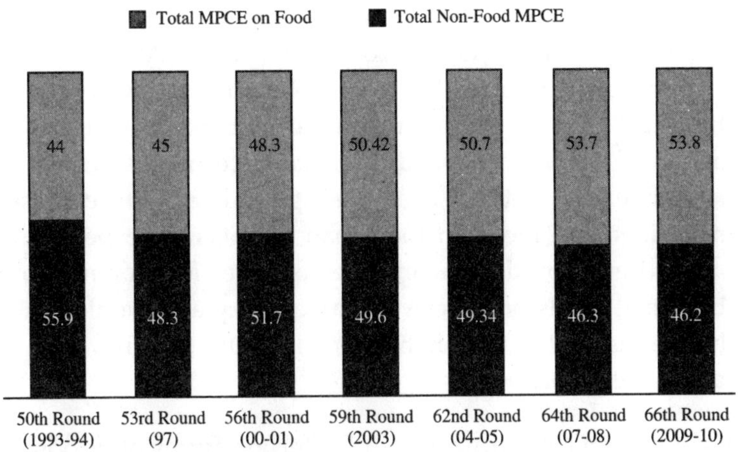


Figure 2.2c: Variation of food and non-food expenditure (% of total MPCE) in upper MPCE classes (Rural India).

expenditure) classes. It can be seen from the figures that since the 56th round in 2000-01 there has been at best a marginal change in the proportions of food and non-food expenditures for the lower and the intermediate MPCE classes, while the change is only slightly more in the upper MPCE classes for the same period. What is more worrisome is that while the low income countries (<15% of per capita US income) spent on an average 47% of the budget on food (Regmi, 2001), the corresponding figure for even the higher expenditure classes in India was 48.3% in 1997 (worrisome because even the top MPCE classes in India spend a higher proportion on food than the low income countries), while the expenditure on food for the intermediate and the lower expenditure classes amounted to as high as 69.6% and 72.5% respectively in 1997.

For the year 2005, the proportion spent on food by the low income countries was 48.5% (USDA, 2011), while that for the upper, intermediate and lower expenditure classes in India in 2005 it was 49.34%, 59% and 61.5% respectively. During the period from 1995 to 2005, the expenditures on food seem to have increased across the world, this increase being from

13% to 20% for the high income countries and from 29% to 31% for the middle income countries (USDA, 2011).

From the findings above, it is obvious that even though the Engel's Law is borne out insofar as the net change is in favour of non-food expenditure, the pace of this change is negligible. The fact that even the highest expenditure classes in India spend more on food than the average expenditure on food even by the low income countries is a comment on the actual levels of poverty in the country and would make the claims of the 'diversification of diets' theorists appear rather premature.

## Variation in Consumption of Different Types of Foods

The categorisation of foods used here, and their components have already been mentioned above. Figures 2.3a, 2.3b, 2.3c and 2.3d show the variation in the consumption of different food items during the reform years in India from 50th NSS round in 1993-94 to 66th round in 2009-10.

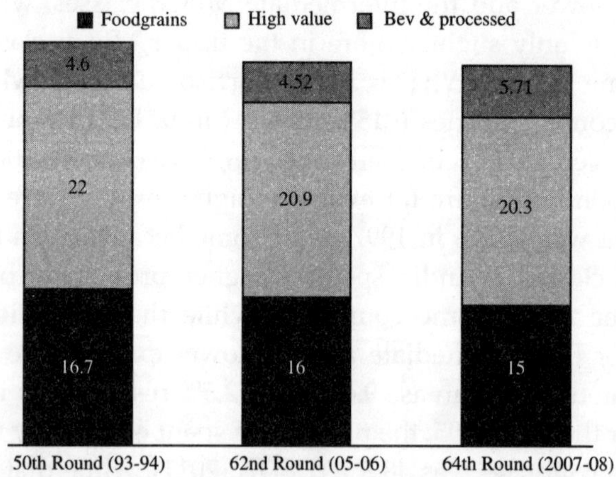


Figure 2.3a: Variation in expenditure on different types of food (% of total MPCE) across upper MPCE classes (Rural India).

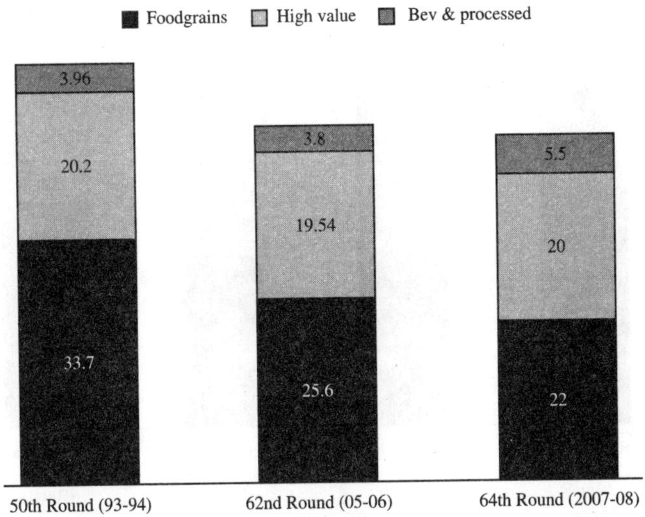


Figure 2.3b: Variation in expenditure on different types of food (% of table MPCE) across intermediate MPCE classes (Rural India).

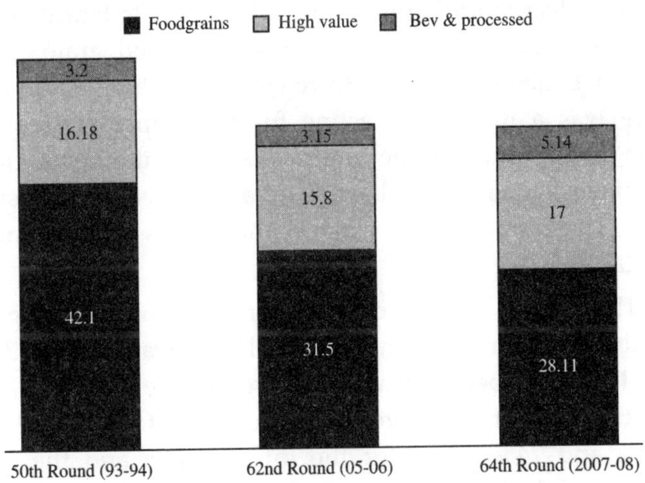


Figure 2.3c: Variation in expenditure on different types of food (% of total MPCE) across lower MPCE classes (Rural India).

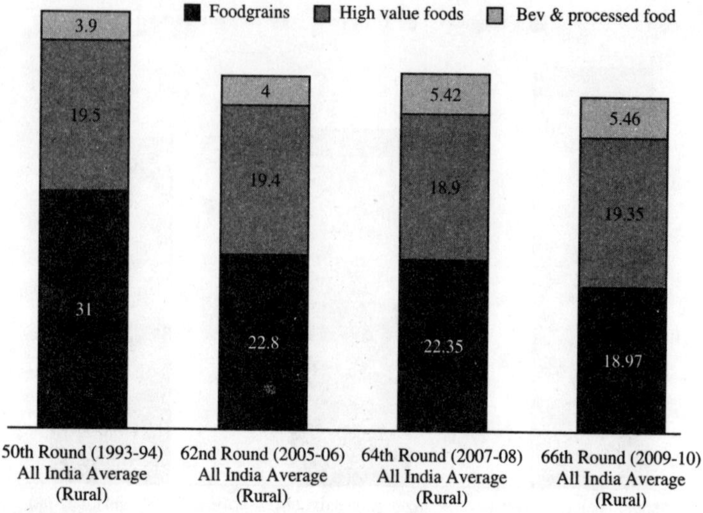


Figure 2.3d: Variation in pattern of expenditure on food items (all India average, Rural).

It is clear from Figures 2.3a, 2.3b and 2.3c that there has definitely been a fall in consumption of food grains across all MPCE classes, while with regard to the high value foods there was a marginal decline for the upper classes, and their consumption in the intermediate and the lower classes remained stagnant. Simultaneously, an increase was registered in the consumption of beverages and processed foods across all classes.

The decline registered in the consumption of food grains for the lower, middle and upper classes was 33.25%, 34.7% and 10.18% respectively while the respective increases in the consumption of beverages and processed foods were 60%, 38.9% and 24%. Thus for the intermediate and the lower classes, while food grains remained the principal source of dietary calories, their contribution to the total dietary calories declined dramatically without any compensatory increase in higher value calories. Simultaneously, the substantial increase in the consumption of beverages and processed foods is unlikely to have been nutritionally rewarding.

The pattern of changes in the average expenditure of all classes (Figure 2.3d) on different food items through different rounds is closer to that observed for the intermediate and lower MPCE classes.

This scenario can hardly be explained through the colourful imagination of 'voluntary reduction in food grain consumption' even as there is no meaningful diversification of diets. What is tenable though is that not only was the purchasing power of the majority of people compromised to afford them an increased supplement of costlier calories, but they were hard-pressed to even maintain their quota of the cheaper calories from the staple food grains as an increasing portion of incomes got diverted towards the consumption of beverages and processed foods.

This diversion of incomes towards increased consumption of beverages and processed foods seems to have had other harmful impacts as well. We can see from Figure 2.1 that consumption of fat has increased both in the rural and the urban areas between the 50th and the 61st NSSO Rounds. However, in proportionate terms the share of expenditure on edible oils has decreased over the years as can be seen from Table 2.10. As the consumption of food grains and high value foods has been declining (both in proportionate and absolute terms), the increase in consumption of fats could have only come from processed junk food and beverages, expenditure on which has increased across all expenditure classes. Since the consumption of fats remains above the recommended daily allowances, this has been adding incrementally to the public health problem of obesity, at least among the more affluent sections.

Table 2.10: Variation in Expenditure on Edible Oils through Different Rounds

| *NSSO Round* | *Expenditure on edible oil (% of MPCE)* | |
|---|---|---|
| | *All India (Rural)* | *All India (Urban)* |
| 50th Round (1993-94) | 4.4 | 4.4 |
| 61st Round (2004-05) | 4.6 | 3.5 |
| 66th Round (2009-10) | 3.6 | 2.5 |

Any argument here that people ought to be more prudent in their choice of food vis-à-vis a higher consumption of processed foods is only as worthwhile as blaming them for alcoholism after the Government has issued licenses for more liquor shops because it fetches more revenue. Consumerism, especially the kind that has been promoted during the liberalisation era can be imposing in a manner that is difficult to resist for a variety of reasons.

Bennetts Law is thus not borne out in case of India for the period of economic reforms, the only possible implication of this is that the proclaimed prosperity under the reforms has glided past a large section of India's human mass, including sections of the so-called middle classes. This is further borne out in the following exposition of consumer expenditure in India.

### *How Does India Compare with the Rest?*

Table 2.11 gives a comparison of consumer expenditure on different types of food in India and different groups of countries by income for the year 2005.

It has already been noted while discussing the Engel's Law that poorer the country, the higher is the expenditure on cheaper calories and as per the Bennett's Law higher expenditure on higher value foods comes with increasing affluence. In case of developed countries where incomes and consumption of high value foods are already high, further

Table 2.11: Comparison of Consumer Expenditure between India and Countries by Income Groups.

| *Country group* | *Cereals* | *Meat, fish, egg, dairy products, vegetables and fruits* | *Beverages, tobacco, processed and other food* | *Oils and fat* |
|---|---|---|---|---|
| Low income (< 15% of US) | 23.3 | 45.6 | 26.2 | 4.9 |
| Middle income (15%–50% of US) | 12.4 | 45.1 | 39.5 | 3 |
| High income (> 50% of US) | 8.6 | 32.3 | 57.7 | 1.4 |
| India | 31.4 | 35.9 | 25.5 | 7.5 |

*Source:* For data on different country groups: United States Department of Agriculture, 2011. For data on India: NSSO 62nd Round, 2008: Household Consumer Expenditure in India, 2005-06, Report No. 523, Ministry of Statistics and Programme Implementation, Government of India.

increase in income may lead to consumption of high value processed foods or imported food varieties of perceived/real higher value (Regmi, 2001).

Even if only to state the obvious, it can still be emphasised that the group of low income countries includes some of the poorest countries, with abysmal levels of human consumption. However, the period of reforms seems to have placed India in an unenviable position where its share of expenditure on cereals is 34.8%, more than the average for low income countries, that on high value foods is a good 21.3% less, while the expenditure on beverages, processed and other foods is also about 3% less. This would indicate that economically an average Indian was worse off compared to an average citizen of a low income country. It is anybody's guess if such a condition would afford millions of impoverished Indians any scope of 'voluntarily reducing food grain consumption', let alone afford the luxury of choosing from more expensive foods.

*Change in Consumption within Cereals*

We have quoted above Poleman's theorisation that in case of developing countries, change in consumption from cereals to more expensive calories would be preceded by change from coarse cereals to more refined cereals like rice and wheat. It would be worth examining whether this has happened in case of India.

It is important to pointout here that much of the substitution of coarse cereals with more refined cereals like rice and wheat, took place as a result of the Green Revolution. It was not necessarily as a changeover in the wake of increased prosperity, but because substitution of the cultivation of coarse cereals with cultivation of high yielding varieties of rice and wheat was proactively encouraged by the Government even in the rainfed areas. This led to changes in dietary patterns and this strategy that was adopted earlier is now being questioned increasingly as the Green Revolution is running out of steam rapidly and efforts are afoot to revive the coarse cereals in the traditional areas of its cultivation.

Having said this we turn our attention to the findings of Table 2.12. It can be computed from the table that the share of coarse cereals in the total cereal consumption in the lower, middle and upper tertiles of MPCE consumption classes dropped from 19.7%, 14.1% and 12.8% respectively in 50th Round to 10%, 10.5% and 8.8% in the 64th Round. The ratio of rice plus wheat to coarse cereals increased from 4.1:1, 6.1:1 and 6.8:1 in the lower, middle and upper tertiles respectively to 9:1, 8.6:1 and 10.2:1 respectively.

On the face of it then, Poleman's hypothesis seems to be borne out in the case of India and one might be led into believing that lack of gains in consumption of high value calories across different expenditure classes may not be such a worrisome thing after all. This would be true except that the apparent shift in favour of superior cereals is accompanied

Table 2.12: Consumption of Different Cereals (in kg Per Capita, Per Month) Over Different NSSO Rounds.

| Round/ Year | *Lower tertile* | | | | *Middle tertile* | | | | *Upper tertile* | | | |
|---|---|---|---|---|---|---|---|---|---|---|---|---|
| | *Rice* | *Wheat* | *Others* | *Total* | *Rice* | *Wheat* | *Others* | *Total* | *Rice* | *Wheat* | *Others* | *Total* |
| 50th Round (1993-94) | 6 | 3.4 | 2.3 | 11.7 | 7.5 | 4.1 | 1.9 | 13.5 | 7.3 | 5.7 | 1.9 | 14.9 |
| 62nd Round (2005-06) | 6.3 | 3.3 | 1.03 | 10.6 | 6.5 | 4.2 | 1.1 | 11.8 | 6.6 | 5 | 1 | 12.7 |
| 64th Round (2007-08) | 6.4 | 3.7 | 1.12 | 11.2 | 6.4 | 4.3 | 1.25 | 11.9 | 6.3 | 4.7 | 1.07 | 12.1 |

*Source:* Compiled from the NSSO reports for respective rounds. Note: The category 'Others' includes jowar, bajra, maize, barley, small millets, ragi, other cereals and gram.

by a net decline in their consumption. Poleman's hypothesis implies that an increase in income should enable increased consumption of superior cereals supplemented by the willingness of the people to divert their money from consuming lower cereals to consuming superior ones. To the contrary, here we notice that there has been a decline of 7.8% and 15.4% in the consumption of rice and wheat in the intermediate and upper expenditure classes respectively. It is only in the lower classes that there has been an increase in the consumption of rice and wheat by 7.5%; this too is in the face of an overall decline in consumption of cereals. The decline in consumption of rice and wheat along with a steep decline in consumption of coarse cereals only means that the nutritional security of the people was compromised even further.

## Downward Revision of Recommended Calorie Norms

The latest recommended dietary guidelines issued by NIN in 2011 have brought about moderate reductions in the recommended calorie norms for males and females in different age groups (NIN, 2011). It would only have been in the fitness of things that the scientific rationale for this revision was adequately dealt with in the guidelines, however, there is not even one sentence as to that in the whole document, while the revised norms themselves are presented in Annexure 1. Though the document itself does not draw any link between the two the mention of increasing trends in obesity due to increased consumption of processed food and sedentary lifestyles could be a possible reason for this reduction in calorie norms. Read with the evidence of increased consumption of dietary fats over and above recommended allowances, some might argue for tempering consumption patterns in the wake of newfound affluence.

The question is whose affluence, and whose consumption? Are the trends in obesity such a compelling reason for reducing the daily calories for the entire population? The evidence regarding this is unambiguous, all of which need not be gone into here. We summarise the same with the following quote:

The distribution of underweight and overweight in India remains socially segregated. Despite rapid economic growth, India has yet to experience a situation in which underweight and overweight coexist in the low-SES groups (Subramanian, 2009).

Figure 2.4 gives a clear visual impression of the social segregation of the problem of obesity (Subramanyam, 2011).

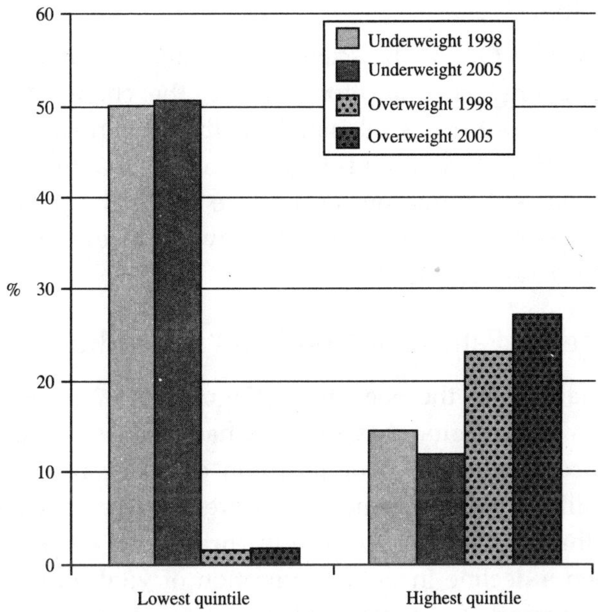


Figure 2.4: Social segregation of obesity and underweight in India.

Notes: BMI < 18.5 kg/m$^2$ is underweight and BMI ≥ 25 kg/m$^2$ is overweight. The data is taken from the 1998-1999 and 2005-2006 NFHS surveys for women in the lowest and highest household wealth quintile. Source: Subramanian, 2009.

Moreover, describing the 'Current Diet and Nutrition Scenario', authors of the latest NIN guidelines state, 'The proportion of households with energy inadequacy was about 70%, while that with protein inadequacy was about 27%. Thus, in the cereal/millet based Indian dietaries, the primary bottleneck is energy inadequacy and not protein, as was earlier believed' (NIN, 2011: 6).

It is further stated that, 'The most rational, sustainable and long term solution to the problem of malnutrition is ensuring availability, access and consumption of adequate amounts of foods' (Ibid: 7).

So where then is the scientific rationale for reducing the dietary energy consumption? Hence, the change is made quietly, without any explanation in the Appendix. It might only be a conjecture, yet it is highly probable that this revision of guidelines is borne out of an urge to toe the policy shift on calorie norms for determining poverty as exemplified in the Tendulkar Committee Report.

## Changes in Pattern of Non-Food Expenditure

While talking of the need to distinguish between nutrition poverty and income poverty, we had stressed that other than income poverty, poor nutrition could be the result of factors like non-food spending preferences. We have already noted that in food expenditure in rural India, even as there has been a decline in the consumption of vital nutrients, an increased trend of spending on beverages and processed foods was noticed. In this section, we shall discuss the changes in spending on non-food components and their implication for spending on food.

Figures 2.5a, 2.5b, 2.5c and 2.5d show the changes in non-food expenditure among the upper, intermediate, lower and average across all MPCE classes. In these figures:

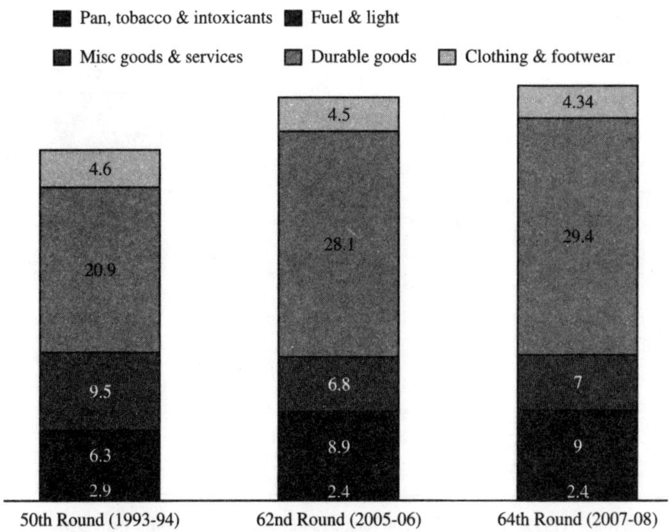


Figure 2.5a: Variation in pattern of non-food expenditure (% of total MPCE across upper MPCE classes (Rural).

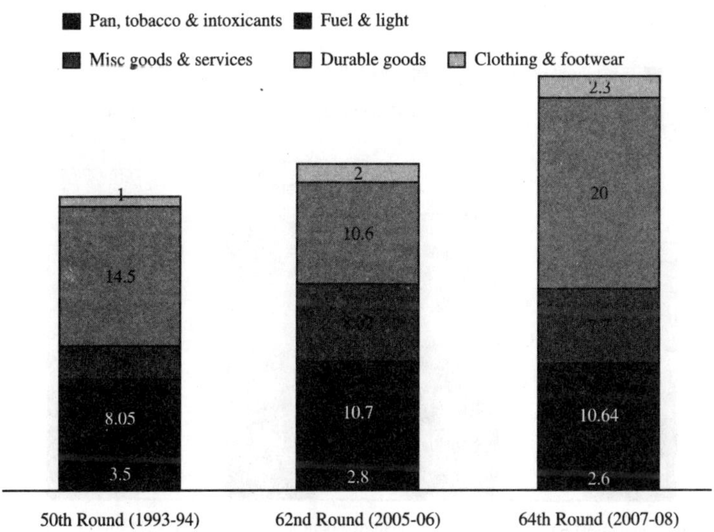


Figure 2.5b: Variation in expenditure on different non-food items (% of total MPCE) across intermediate MPCE classes (Rural India).

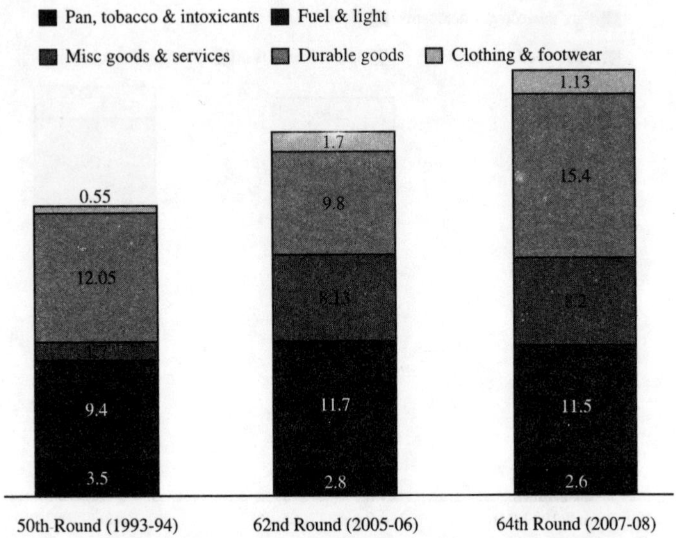


Figure 2.5c: Variation in pattern of non-food expenditure (% of total MPCE) across lower MPCE classes (Rural India).

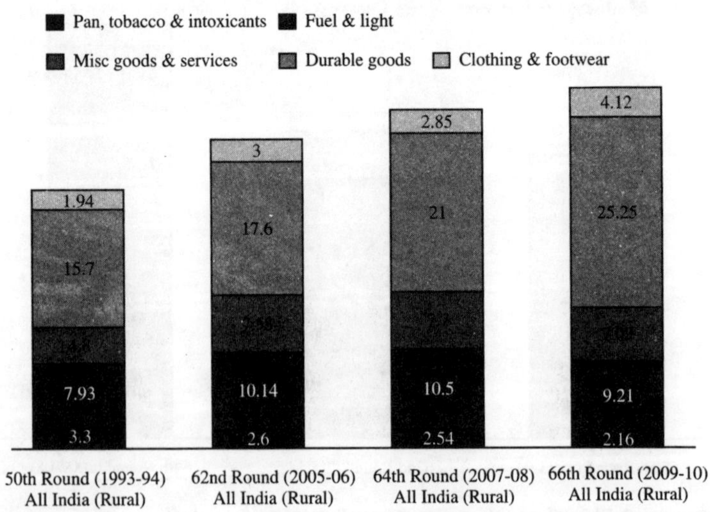


Figure 2.5d: Variation in pattern of non-food expenditure (% of total MPCE)—All India Average Rural.

Miscellaneous goods and services include the following items:

Education, medical expenses (institutional and non-institutional), entertainment, miscellaneous consumer goods (goods for personal care, toilet articles and sundry articles), consumer services (excluding conveyance), conveyance, rent, taxes and cesses.

## The Upper MPCE Classes

For the top MPCE classes, the bulk of non-food expenditure is on miscellaneous goods and services, which underwent an increase of 40.7% during the reform years, while the expenditure on fuel and light increased by 43% in the same period. The expenditure on clothing and footwear actually underwent a contraction. Table 2.12 gives a break-up of the expenditure on miscellaneous goods and services for 64th NSSO Round.

From the break-up given in Table 2.13, the expenditure on education, medical expenditure, conveyance and consumer services excluding convcyance need to be considered essential and reducible only at the cost of compromising the quality of life. 22.84% out of the total 29.4% expenditure on miscellaneous goods and services was incurred on these heads by the top expenditure fractiles. This expenditure would hardly qualify as any kind of luxury, in fact the reduction in expenditure on clothes and footwear (26%) and a marginal decline in the expenditure on durable goods (5.7%) indicates cutting of corners by the highest expenditure classes to meet the essential expenditure on education, medical expenses and other consumer services required for day-to-day life.

It is quite possible that the cut back in consumption of nutrients that we noted earlier for this section, is directly feeding into maintaining these essential services as a valiant attempt by these sections to retain their middle or lower middle class status. The decline in expenditure on durable goods and a pitiable expenditure on entertainment hardly betray a consumerist orientation of these classes, or shall we say, an inability of even the highest expenditure classes in the NSSO data to partake in the new found affluence through the economic reforms.

Table 2.13: Break-up of Expenditure on Miscellaneous Goods and Services (Round 64, 2007-08).

| *Item* | *Percentage share in total consumption expenditure* | | |
|---|---|---|---|
| | *Lower 4 fractiles* | *Middle 3 fractiles* | *Top 3 fractiles* |
| Education | 1.8 | 2.6 | 4.6 |
| Medical expenses (Inst. and non-inst.) | 3.3 | 4.7 | 7.84 |
| Entertainment | 0.32 | 0.54 | 0.9 |
| Goods for personal care | .2 | 0.23 | 0.25 |
| Toilet articles | 2.7 | 2.7 | 2.5 |
| Sundry articles | 2.2 | 2.3 | 2.14 |
| Consumer services excluding conveyance | 3 | 3.9 | 5.4 |
| Conveyance | 1.7 | 2.7 | 5 |
| Rent | 0.08 | 0.16 | 0.56 |
| Taxes and cesses | 0.12 | 0.2 | 0.3 |

## The Intermediate and the Lower MPCE Classes

Between the 50th (1993-94) and the 64th (2007-08) NSSO Rounds, for the intermediate and the lower MPCE classes, the maximum increase has been in expenditures on durable goods and clothes and footwear, followed by an increase in expenditure on miscellaneous goods and services and then fuel and light. The respective increases for expenditure under these heads is 130%, 113%, 38% and 32.2% for the intermediate classes and 287%, 382%, 27.8% and 22.34% for the lower MPCE classes. However, it is important to note that between the 62nd and the 64th Round, the bulk of the increase in non-food expenditure has been under the head of miscellaneous services and goods, as in case of the upper classes.

The steep rise in expenditure on durable goods and clothes and footwear does not seem to be fuelled as much by consumerist aspirations, as much by the fact that the initial expenditure under these heads was a pittance: 1% and .55% on durable goods and 3.6% and 1.7% on clothes and footwear for the intermediate and the lower classes respectively. There was thus much scope for an increase under these heads.

For all the expenditure classes, increasing expenditure to improve quality of nutrition does not seem to have been much of a priority beyond satisfying the minimal requirements. After fulfilling minimal nutritional requirements, the priority shifted to fulfil the minimal need for durable goods and clothing and then to spend on other essential services like education, health and conveyance etc.

Trends from all India average non-food expenditure also mimic the trends observed in non-food expenditure by the intermediate and the lower classes. Given the size of MPCE for different classes in rupee terms, the absolute expenditure on various non-food consumer items and services would remain modest. The handsome rise in proportionate expenditure on durable goods, clothing and footwear among the intermediate and the lower classes may be cited by some as evidence of rising consumerism. Given the size of the population of the country, this increase may add up to constitute a huge market for many of the lower cost consumer products. It remains a matter of further study as to how much this has helped to improve the overall quality of life of these sections. As regards food and nutrition security, the increasing diversion of resources towards beverages and processed food does not augur well for the poor.

## Who then is Firing India's Consumerist Boom?

We covered earlier the anachronism between increasing nutritional poverty accompanied by income poverty and rising consumerism in the country. Apart from the exercise undertaken to prove the insufficiency of food grain production in the country, the data presented thus far and the accompanying discussion have helped us establish a few things:

- That nutritional poverty in the country has indeed been rising with large sections of the population living with chronic dietary energy and protein deficiency.
- Even as consumption of high value calories remains static or has decreased, there is a worrisome decline in the consumption of even the staple cereals. The myth of 'diversification of diets in favour of high value calories' at the cost of reduction in staple calories fails to stand the test of hard evidence.
- Even as food has been difficult to come by, there is evidence of diversification of precious resources towards consumption of nutritionally poor processed foods and beverages.
- It can be argued, though not very strongly, that there is some evidence of incipient consumerism among the different MPCE classes vis-à-vis non-food consumer items.

This however still does not explain the conspicuous consumerism that is as real a product of the economic reforms as are the rest of the findings. At least the bigger cities and towns are booming with expenditure on automobiles, a host of electronic consumer items and gadgetry, new shopping malls opening everywhere, the multistorey residential complexes and even consumer services going by the number of costly public schools, the nature of costly and privatised professional education and the number of corporate tertiary care hospitals. There seems to be no dearth of people wanting to have their share of all this. This is the class which has an imposing presence in the society because they are the ones who get talked of in the media: television serials and even the news plays, replays and overplays the vacuous trials and travails of this class. They dominate the politics, business, educational and other public institutions and are the reigning moguls in the world of art, literature and sports. Yet, this class may constitute 4% to 5% of the country's population. The population that the NSSO data represents does not belong to this category. Given the size of the MPCE in rupees for different expenditure classes, there is little possibility of them having a share in this high-end consumerism, except for the theoretical possibility in case of the topmost expenditure class, for which we have no evidence from the present NSSO data.

This is better illustrated in the Table 2.14. In 2004-05 a middle class person with daily per capita expenditure of more than ₹ 37 or a high income person with daily per capita expenditure of ₹ 100, could not have afforded the kind of lifestyles that are typical of the middle classes and the rich in the country as we know them. For example, they could not go shopping in malls or go to cineplexes or afford to own a four wheeler or go out eating to McDonald's, Pizza Hut and other such eateries or send their children to public schools. They most certainly could not have afforded the costly coaching for medical and engineering entrance or entrance to Indian Institutes of Management for their children.

Even though the NSSO household consumption data potentially covers all the consumer classes in the country, in reality it fails to reflect the consumerism of the 'other India', those who are the 'progeny of the neoliberal reforms' and the 'motive force' powering the consumerist boom. The reason why this is so can be best answered by NSSO itself, but the

Table 2.14: Monthly and Daily Per Capita Expenditure by Poverty Status

| *Serial No.* | *Poverty status* | *Criteria* | *MPCE (₹)* | *DPCE (₹)* |
|---|---|---|---|---|
| 1 | Extremely poor | If MPCE <= 0.75 (PL) | 269 (268) | 9 (9) |
| 2 | Poor | If 0.75 PL < MPCE <= 1PL | 348 (358) | 12 (12) |
| 3 | Marginal | If 1 PL < MPCE <= 1.25 PL | 438 (449) | 15 (15) |
| 4 | Vulnerable | If 1.25 < MPCE <= 2.0 PL | 609 (631) | 20 (21) |
| 5 | Middle income | If 2.0 PL < MPCE < 4.0 PL | 1,098 (1137) | 37 (38) |
| 6 | High income | If MPCE > 4 PL | 2,776 (2879) | 93 (96) |
| 7 | Extremely poor and poor (1 + 2) | – | 325 (331) | 11 (11) |
| 8 | Marginal and Vulnerable (3 + 4) | – | 550 (570) | 18 (19) |
| 9 | Poor and Vulnerable (7 + 8) | – | 486 (500) | 16 (17) |
| 10 | Middle and High income (5 + 6) | – | 1,387 (1448) | 46 (48) |
| 11 | All | – | 696 (734) | 23 (25) |

*Source:* Sengupta A et al., 2008, computed from NSS 61st round survey on employment-unemployment, 2004-05.

PL = Poverty Line. The poverty line here means as defined by the Planning Commission, which has gained notoriety as destitution line. MPCE = Monthly per capita expenditure, DPCE = Daily per capita expenditure. Figures in brackets are based on detailed consumer expenditure.

reading of the data presented above tends to support our viewpoint.

## Examining Other Factors Impacting Calorie Intake

The important factors impacting dietary energy intake could be changes in the environmental conditions over a period of time.

### Improvements in the Epidemiological Conditions

Deaton and Drèze have emphasised the changes in the epidemiological environment impacting the morbidity and mortality due to infectious diseases and thereby a decline in calorie needs. The more important changes that have been cited in this regard are the much increased access to piped drinking water, an increase in vaccination rates of children and improvement in child health due to better education of women. Tables 2.8, 2.9 and 2.10 trace the morbidity and mortality due to infectious diseases over the period since 1993, while Table 2.11 gives the performance of the expanded programme for immunisation from 1991-92 till 2004-05. Table 2.12 shows the ordering of states by female literacy, infant mortality and mortality among children below 5 years of age.

An improvement in the epidemiological environment would be expected to bring down the share of infectious diseases in the total number of deaths and an increase in the share of non-infectious or life style diseases. It is evident from Table 2.14, between 1993 and 1998 the proportion of deaths due to diseases of respiratory system, which are mostly of the infectious nature, actually increased by 19.5%, while the deaths due to infectious and other parasitic diseases remained stagnant. Deaths due to viral infections also showed a marginal increase, as did deaths due to genito-urinary system while proportion of deaths due to conditions of pregnancy, childbirths and puerperium remained unchanged over the six

Table 2.8: Total Number of Deaths by Major Cause Group in India (Rural)—1993-98.

| *Major cause group* | *Proportion of total deaths* | | | | | |
|---|---|---|---|---|---|---|
| | *1993* | *1994* | *1995* | *1996* | *1997* | *1998* |
| Diseases of respiratory system | 14.4 | 15.1 | 16.60 | 17.8 | 16.0 | 17.2 |
| Infectious and parasitic diseases | 12.5 | 12.0 | 11.90 | 10.9 | 10.0 | 12. |
| Viral infection | 4.20 | 4.40 | 4.70 | 3.90 | 3.10 | 4.30 |
| Diseases of digestive system | 1.40 | 1.60 | 1.60 | 2.00 | 2.10 | 2.10 |
| Pregnancy, childbirth and puerperium | 1.10 | 0.90 | 0.80 | 1.00 | 0.70 | 1.10 |
| Diseases of genito-urinary system | 0.50 | 0.60 | 0.70 | 0.80 | 1.00 | 0.70 |

*Source:* Causes of death statistics, In Health Information of India, 2000-2001, Central Bureau of Health Intelligence, Director General Health Services, Ministry of Health and Family Welfare.

year period. The rise in proportion of deaths due to diseases of digestive system was alarming at 50%.

A perusal of data from the same source shows stagnation or only a slight increase in deaths due to non-infectious causes of death.

Likewise, a perusal of Table 2.9 shows that incidence of acute respiratory infections per 100,000 population increased by 20.1% between 2001 and 2009 while incidence of acute diarrheal disease (wider access to piped water would be expected to bring about a decrease in their incidence and prevalence) increased by 12.7% in the same period. The increase in incidence of pulmonary TB which is a chronic infectious condition placing a much higher demand for dietary energy consumption as compared to acute infections, was

117.4%. The increase recorded in the incidence of enteric fever, pneumonia and gonococcus infections per 100,000 populations was 93.8%, 28.3% and 8.4% respectively.

Table 2.10 shows that between 2001 and 2009 there was a decline of 23%, 43.2%, 37% and 32.25% in the mortality due to acute respiratory infection, acute diarrheal disease, enteric fever and pneumonia respectively. However, given the small proportion of mortality of less than 1 per 100,000 for all these diseases, this decline was more than undone by a massive increase of 175.16% in mortality due to pulmonary tuberculosis. Apart from these there were marginal declines in mortality due to viral hepatitis and malaria, while mortality due to Japanese encephalitis registered an increase.

A reading of figures from Table 2.11 does not reveal any spectacular increase in either the overall targets for immunisation or the proportionate achievement of these targets over the years between 1991-92 and 2004-05 that could have meaningfully contributed to the observed decline in per capita calorie consumption observed during the same period. Anyway, the vaccine preventable diseases constitute at the most about 15% of infant and under five mortality even as the bulk of mortality is due to neonatal causes, diarrheal diseases and pneumonia (Morris, 2003).

We can thus see that the hypothesis of improvements in the epidemiological environment resulting in a decline in calorie requirements and thus a decline in dietary energy consumption over the years is clearly not borne out by the epidemiological data.

## Improvement in Female Literacy

Table 2.12 gives the ranking of 10 Indian states by female literacy rates, IMR (infant mortality rates) and the under-five mortality rates, the latter being indicators of improvements in the environmental conditions. Except for three states of

Table 2.9: Incidence of Infectious Diseases—Cases Per 100,000 Population.

| *Disease* | *2001* | *2002* | *2003* | *2004* | *2005* | *2006* | *2007* | *2008* | *2009* |
|---|---|---|---|---|---|---|---|---|---|
| Acute respiratory infection | 1998 | 2118 | 2283 | 2547 | 2349 | 2351 | 2319 | 2398 | 2400 |
| Acute diarrheal disease | 903 | 903 | 989 | 972 | 1002 | 918 | 974 | 995 | 1018 |
| Pulmonary TB | 46 | 60 | 85 | 110 | 118 | 126 | 131 | 133 | 100 |
| Enteric fever | 48 | 47 | 56 | 64 | 63 | 71 | 73 | 82 | 93 |
| Pneumonia | 53 | 55 | 62 | 65 | 71 | 61 | 66 | 64 | 68 |
| Gonococcal | 12 | 12 | 14 | 15 | 13 | 12 | 14 | 12 | 13 |
| All viral hepatitis | 15 | 13 | 14 | 22 | 17 | 14 | 10 | 8 | 11 |
| Malaria | 200 | 176 | 176 | 177 | 166 | 161 | 134 | 133 | 133 |

*Source:* National Health Profile of India, 2010, Central Bureau of Health Intelligence, Director General Health Services, Ministry of Health and Family Welfare.

Table 2.10 Mortality Due to Major Diseases, Deaths Per 100,000 Population.

| *Disease* | *2001* | *2002* | *2003* | *2004* | *2005* | *2006* | *2007* | *2008* | *2009* |
|---|---|---|---|---|---|---|---|---|---|
| Acute respiratory infection | .336 | .395 | .403 | .498 | .375 | .336 | .616 | .465 | .259 |
| Acute diarrheal disease | .271 | .332 | .323 | .272 | .196 | .286 | .319 | .250 | .154 |
| Pulmonary TB | 2.049 | 2.603 | 2.961 | 3.488 | .154 | 5.803 | 5.744 | 5.783 | 5.638 |
| Enteric fever | .059 | .052 | .079 | .075 | .038 | .059 | .04 | .032 | .037 |
| Pneumonia | .372 | .389 | .392 | .334 | .321 | .3 | .306 | .338 | .252 |
| All viral hepatitis | .112 | .087 | .095 | .110 | .066 | .062 | .048 | .047 | .051 |
| Malaria | .099 | .093 | .095 | .088 | .088 | .153 | .116 | .092 | .097 |
| Japanese encephalitis | .047 | .045 | .067 | .034 | .154 | .060 | .088 | .06 | .066 |

*Source:* National Health Profile of India, 2010, Central Bureau of Health Intelligence, Director General Health Services, Ministry of Health and Family Welfare.

Table 2.11: Year-wise Targets and Achievements of Maternity Child Health Activities—all India during 1991-92 to 2004-05

(Figures in million numbers)

| *Year* | *TT pregnant women* | | *DPT* | | *Polio* | | *Measles* | |
|---|---|---|---|---|---|---|---|---|
| | *Target* | *% achieved* | *Target* | *% achieved* | *Target* | *% achieved* | *Target* | *% achieved* |
| 1991-92 | 26.13 | 77.6 | 23.33 | 90.9 | 15.97 | 91.3 | 23.33 | 85.0 |
| 1992-93 | 27.01 | 79.4 | 24.29 | 90.6 | 16.31 | 91.0 | 24.29 | 85.9 |
| 1993-94 | 27.56 | 82.6 | 24.79 | 93.2 | 16.65 | 93.6 | 24.79 | 88.5 |
| 1994-95 | 27.53 | 83.8 | 24.77 | 94.5 | 20.31 | 95.2 | 24.77 | 87.2 |
| 1995-96 | 27.53 | 80.4 | 24.86 | 90.7 | 20.72 | 91.6 | 24.86 | 82.6 |
| 1996-97 | 28.11 | 81.8 | 25.4 | 91.5 | 21.08 | 92.7 | 25.40 | 83.2 |
| 1997-98 | 28.29 | 82.6 | 25.55 | 92.9 | 21.44 | 93.9 | 25.55 | 85.8 |
| 1998-99 | 27.75 | 83.9 | 25.12 | 93.7 | 23.82 | 95.3 | 25.12 | 88.1 |
| 1999-00 | 29.24 | 81.3 | 24.72 | 95.3 | 24.23 | 95.9 | 24.72 | 89.8 |
| 2000-01 | 28.81 | 85.8 | 24.35 | 100.9* | 24.62 | 102.1* | — | — |
| 2001-02 | 28.85 | 86.9 | 24.43 | 101.5* | 25.03 | 101.3* | — | — |
| 2002-03 | 29.76 | 81.4 | 25.2 | 97.4 | 20.96 | 97.5 | — | — |
| 2003-04 | 30.29 | 78.1 | 25.69 | 91.5 | 25.84 | 93.3 | — | — |
| 2004-05 | 30.25 | 78.6 | 25.69 | 93.7 | 17.33 | 94.2 | — | — |

*Source:* Figures for TT pregnant women, DPT and Polio are from Table No. 12.02, E.P.I. Performance, Health Information of India, 2005, Central Bureau of Health Intelligence, Director General Health Services, Ministry of Health and Family Welfare and for Measles the figures are from Table 12.02, E.P.I. Performance, Health Information of India, 2000-01.

* These figures though improbable, but have been reproduced as given in original

Table 2.12: Ordering of Some States by Female Literacy, IMR and Under Five Mortality.

| *Serial No.* | *Female literacy (%)* | *IMR* | *Under five mortality* |
|---|---|---|---|
| 1. | Kerala (87.8) | Kerala (16.3) | Kerala (18.8) |
| 2. | Mizoram (86.13) | Himachal Pradesh (34.4) | Himachal Pradesh (42.4) |
| 3. | Goa (75.51) | Goa (36.7) | Goa (46.8) |
| 4. | Delhi (75) | Mizoram (37) | Mizoram (54.7) |
| 5. | Himachal Pradesh (68.08) | Nagaland (42.1) | Delhi (55.4) |
| 6. | Maharashtra (67.5) | Maharashtra (43.7) | Maharashtra (58.1) |
| 7. | Tamil Nadu (64.5) | Sikkim (43.9) | Tamil Nadu (63.3) |
| 8. | Punjab (63.5) | Delhi (46.8) | Nagaland (63.8) |
| 9. | Nagaland (61.9) | Tamil Nadu (48.2) | Sikkim (71) |
| 10. | Sikkim (61.4) | Punjab (57.1) | Punjab (72.1) |

*Source:* Female literacy figures are based on the 2001 census figures, while the infant and under five mortality figures are for the years 1998-99 obtained from NFHS–2. The figures for infant and under five mortality are per thousand live births and per thousand children of less than five years age respectively.

Kerala, Goa and Maharashtra for whom the ranks in these three parameters coincide, for the rest of the states there is no tight relation of IMR and under-five mortality with female literacy. Even though female literacy has an important bearing on the health and nutrition of children and an intergenerational impact on nutrition, there is no reason to believe that it has had an overarching impact in effecting the observed decline in daily per capita calorie consumption in India.

An important question here is that improvements in female literacy and epidemiological environment also occurred in the period earlier to the last twenty years that is under consideration here, yet why was no decline in dietary energy consumption observed for that period?

## Decrease in Physically Demanding Activities

The conclusions reached above leave only one more hypothesis for us to consider i.e. reduction in physically strenuous routine of daily lives due to expansion of road network, motorised transport, expansion of mechanised agriculture as also piped drinking water that has obviated the need to fetch water over long distances and other such developments. Intuitively speaking, this argument appears appealing, however, Deaton and Drèze have themselves admitted that there is little empirical data to corroborate this and have suggested the need for conducting detailed time use studies in this respect. This deficit could have been overcome to an extent by reflecting on the experience of other countries in this respect.

We have already noted in Table 2.2 above that the per capita, per day calorie consumption has been rising in all the regions of the world. It needs reminding that as compared to India the levels of mechanisation of either agriculture or gadgets of daily use in life that are imputed to have led to decreased need for dietary energy consumption have by far been much higher in countries like China, Taiwan, South Korea and Brazil if we were to discuss here the case of only the developing countries, yet the average dietary energy consumption in these countries has only risen and currently stands much higher as compared to that in India.

Deaton and Drèze cite the example of Britain, where in the period from 1775 to 1850, 'in spite of rising real wages, there was no apparent increase in the real consumption of food' and that of China for which it is claimed that despite improvements in nutrition indicators, calorie consumption is said to have declined in the 1980s and 1990s (Deaton and Drèze, 2009).

The point is that can these two instances outweigh the weight of evidence from the rest of the world. Secondly, there is no elaboration of important details like whether the increase in real wages in Britain was across all socio-economic strata or merely an aggregate increase due to far greater increase in the profits of the incipient capitalist class and the feudal gentry in the wake of the enclosure movement that led to development of commercial agricultural production. One cannot help but recall the description given by Friedrich Engels of widespread squalor afflicting working masses of industrial cities of Britain in his famous work on 'Conditions of Working Class in England, 1844' (Engels, 1845).

Deaton and Drèze themselves admit in their paper 'Food and Nutrition in India: Fact and Interpretations' (Deaton and Drèze, 2009) the possibility that improvements in nutritional outcomes of the present generation could be a result of improvements in diets and other factors that happened years earlier for example the nutritional well-being of today's children could be the result of good nutrition of their mothers when they were children and adolescents. Likewise before the stated improvements in nutritional outcomes had started showing in China in the 1980s and the 1990s, there had been a long period of socialist construction that vastly improved the availability of food and healthcare for the people. As a matter of fact there is enough literature to show that as a result of pro-market reforms initiated from late 1970s onwards many of the earlier benefits guaranteed to the people were gradually withdrawn. It is possible that the breaking up of the communes resulted in stagnation of dietary energy consumption for some Chinese. However, the claim that the dietary energy consumption in China declined in the 80s

Table 2.13: Total Dietary Calories and Calories from Major Commodities (kcal Per Capita Per Day) in China, India and South Asia.

| *Country* | *Year* | *Total calories* | *% change between 1963 till 2011* | *Animal products* | *% change between 1963 till 2011* | *Sugar & sweeteners* | *% change between 1963 till 2011* | *Pulses* | *% change between 1963 till 2011* | *Starchy roots* | *% change between 1963 till 2011* | *Vegetable oils* | *% change between 1963 till 2011* | *Vegetables & Fruits* | *% change between 1963 till 2011* | *Cereals (excluding bear)* | *% change between 1963 till 2011* |
|---|---|---|---|---|---|---|---|---|---|---|---|---|---|---|---|---|---|
| Mainland China | 1963 | 1,594 | 93% | 86 | 701% | 19 | 247% | 106 | –91% | 256 | –39% | 34 | 456% | 52 | 508% | 981 | 48% |
| | 1973 | 1,897 | | 125 | | 29 | | 50 | | 318 | | 44 | | 41 | | 1,223 | |
| | 1983 | 2,399 | | 182 | | 55 | | 37 | | 224 | | 91 | | 55 | | 1,666 | |
| | 1993 | 2,538 | | 354 | | 50 | | 14 | | 173 | | 131 | | 109 | | 1,567 | |
| | 2003 | 2,831 | | 556 | | 62 | | 12 | | 184 | | 167 | | 228 | | 1,483 | |
| | 2011 | 3,075 | | 689 | | 66 | | 10 | | 155 | | 189 | | 316 | | 1,452 | |
| India | 1963 | 1,973 | 25% | 109 | 109% | 176 | 22% | 186 | –27% | 21 | 195% | 99 | 116% | 56 | 118% | 1,270 | 10% |
| | 1973 | 2,046 | | 106 | | 174 | | 141 | | 38 | | 110 | | 59 | | 1,362 | |
| | 1983 | 2,208 | | 138 | | 195 | | 132 | | 38 | | 126 | | 64 | | 1,457 | |
| | 1993 | 2,268 | | 162 | | 182 | | 111 | | 43 | | 145 | | 75 | | 1,473 | |
| | 2003 | 2,278 | | 183 | | 231 | | 105 | | 41 | | 188 | | 90 | | 1,361 | |
| | 2011 | 2,459 | | 228 | | 214 | | 135 | | 62 | | 214 | | 122 | | 1,394 | |

*Source:* All data has been obtained from food balance sheets available from FAOSTAT.

and the 90s needs to be examined more closely, because the figures in Table 2.13 obtained from the food balance sheets available from FAOSTAT clearly show a rise in per capita calorie consumption for both the decades.

There has been a massive diversification of diets of the Chinese with a 93% increase in the total calories consumed and a whopping 701% increase in per capita daily calories derived from animal products. According to FAO food balance sheets, for the same period India recorded a net increase of 25% in total calories and an increase of 109% in calories from animal products. What is most worrisome is that the contribution of calories from the main source of proteins in Indian diets i.e. pulses decreased by 27%. For the same period the increase in consumption of vegetable oils for China was a whopping 456%, while that for India was only 116%. The difference is even more remarkable with respect to consumption of vegetables and fruits. These differences also ring hollow in the context of the tall claims of differentiation of Indian diets that have been made by governments.

Deaton and Drèze assume that technological improvement necessarily leads to decreased dietary energy demand. For example they state, 'As the wage rises, and with less work being required to earn a given amount of income, there will be a downward shift in the calorie Engel curve. This may be accentuated by technological change . . . in the process calorie intake may decline as incomes rise, in contrast to calorie intake increasing with income in the cross-section at a given point of time' (Deaton and Drèze, 2009).

This however need not necessarily be true and the results could be just the opposite. Take the example of a fully automated assembly line of a modern car plant where the dictum is to produce a car a minute, a worker at his/her work station has only a few seconds to do his/her small bit in every car, for eight hours a day with limited breaks and a coercive supervisory mechanism (Sethi, 2011). In spite of the fact that newer technology facilitates production of same number of cars in much lesser time, the workers still have to put in 8 hrs of work. Just how much reduction in dietary energy needs does such automation bring about?

This however is not to deny the evidence from across the world that with technological change there has been an accompanying shift towards physically less active lifestyles, but this has invariably been accompanied with rise in obesity (Popkin, 2001, Popkin and Larsen, 2004) which could not have come about with falling calorie consumption. In case of India as well the National Family Health Surveys (NFHS) have provided evidence of rising obesity, but among the rich. The declining trend in calorie consumption in NSSO data however hardly betrays a possibility of rise in obesity. To reconcile these findings we shall have to accept that the NSSO data somehow does not capture the consumption patterns of the really rich.

We need also bear in mind the possibility that with time saved from the sundry activities of life due to increasing mechanisation, people may take to more rigorous, but enjoyable passtimes like sports or other outdoor activities, something that has been termed as a behavioural change state of 'nutrition transition' (Popkin and Larsen, 2004). The need therefore remains to undertake detailed time use studies to have a better understanding of how the activity pattern changes with increased mechanisation.

## The Need to Introspect Deeper

Going by the discussion till now, it would appear logical to explain the declining dietary energy consumption of the overwhelming majority of our population in terms of its declining purchasing power, especially because of the policies pursued during the neoliberal economic reforms. However, the need is to have a more comprehensive theorisation which would present a more composite picture of the entire population. This mandates a deeper reasoning and understanding of the problem to place the whole issue in the perspective of the stage of nutrition transition in India.

Nutrition transition is a cycle of changes in the structure of diets of the population that accompany changes associated with a number of factors like growth in income, urbanisation, changes in activity patterns, demographic structure, religious and cultural factors etc, and has implications for the health of the people. A nutrition transition is effected either simultaneously with, or is preceded by a demographic and epidemiological transition (Popkin, 2002). This situation is only complicated by the fact that India has neither fully undergone the demographic nor the epidemiological transition.

While on the one hand, as we have already seen, there continues to be a high burden of infectious diseases and on the other there is a considerable section of population that has come to be a repository of the lifestyle or non-communicable diseases. Likewise, different sections of our population are at different stages of nutritional transition.

The overwhelmingly dominant section, one whose consumption is mainly represented by the NSSO data and which constitutes more than 95% of the population is largely caught in what is described as the 'Receding Famine' stage of nutrition transition, characterised by staple starchy diets of high fibre content with little variety and lifestyles characterised by hard physical labour. Most of the rural population and a considerable section of the urban poor would fit this description. There have however been eminent signs of change and onward movement like the increase in consumption of beverages and processed foods and dietary fat among the lower expenditure classes and of course modern amenities like motorised transport, television, etc.

The other section, comprising 4 to 5% of the population, the ones who represent the 'new rich' and the traditional upper class, whose consumption is not reflected in the NSSO data, has graduated to what is described as the 'Degenerative Disease' stage of nutrition transition, or even the 'Behavioural Change' stage as is reflected in the 'fitness consciousness' of a section of the population. The former is characterised by 'increased consumption of dietary fat, sugar and processed foods and a shift in technology of work and leisure', while the latter signals a return to healthier diets and lifestyles of 'reduced fat, increased fruit, vegetables, carbohydrates and fiber along with replacing sedentarianism with purposeful changes in recreation' (Popkin and Larsen, 2004). This complexity is described by Popkin and Larsen in following words, 'The patterns (of different stages) can be thought of as historical developments, however, 'earlier' patterns are not restricted to the periods in which they first arose, but continue to characterize certain geographic and socio-economic subpopulations' (Popkin and Larsen, 2004).

The period of continuous decline in the consumption of dietary calories encompasses the period of neoliberal reforms, and to this extent it becomes important to study in detail the role of important drivers of dietary change vise trade liberalisation, transnational food corporations, changes in retailing and food industry marketing (Kearney, 2010) in order to have a fuller understanding of 'the puzzle' of declining dietary energy consumption of a majority of Indians.

Even as we emphasize the need to study the role of all these factors, it needs to be stated emphatically that the abysmal state of poverty of India's working masses is crucial to understanding the declining trend in dietary calories.

## Dietary Calories, Poverty Lines and Implications for Policy

Neither hunger nor the immense human suffering that comes in the wake of it is new to India and yet the falling dietary energy consumption has been at the centre of a highly contested debate. The debate itself has engaged those who are charged with taking care of the poor i.e. the government and the official policy establishment and those who are genuinely concerned about what happens to the poor. The later segment includes political activists, the members of the civil society and academics. But the anxieties of the official establishment are what have fuelled the debate in the main. The reasons for this are twofold:

- One, as has already been mentioned, the period of the decline in dietary energy consumption concerns the period of neoliberal economic reforms in the country. There has been a broad consensus on the desirability of these reforms between all the parties of the establishment. Thus any evidence that reflects poorly on these reforms becomes a matter of concern for the establishment.
- Secondly, poverty lines in India have always been pegged to per capita per day calorie consumption. Hence, declining calorie intake means that a greater proportion of population goes below the poverty line and more the resources required being committed towards welfare subsides for the poor. For an establishment obsessed with fiscal deficits and fiscal prudence this spells a nightmare and hence the efforts to normalise the falling calorie consumption.

Needless, to say such goals cannot be achieved through a fait accompli as these are bound to be challenged, so an effort is made to construct a wider consensus through debate. We cannot but welcome this debate, for issues of poverty and hunger at least gain visibility in the public domain rather than being taken as sundry realities. Our intent here is not to go into the debate itself but only to demonstrate its impact on welfare policy. Those interested in the detailed debate may refer to Patnaik 2007, 2010a, 2010b, Deaton and Drèze 2009, 2010 and GOI, 2009 among others.

In poorer countries like India where a high proportion of population lives in abject poverty and the poor spend a large proportion (often up to two-third) of their income on food, concerns regarding poverty have been conjoint with concerns regarding nutrition, food being the most basic requirement for subsistence. Little wonder then that food and nutritional requirements have traditionally been used as an anchor for deriving poverty lines in the context of poor countries by pegging these lines to normative benchmarks in terms of daily calorie intake. We have already mentioned that in India's case, these benchmarks were 2400 and 2100 kcal per capita per day for the rural and urban areas. Weakening the relationship between calorie intake and nutritional outcomes and thereby unpegging the poverty lines from the normative calorie norms has been central to this debate.

Deaton and Drèze stress that, 'Average calorie intake per se is a poor indicator of the nutritional status of the population' (Deaton and Drèze, 2009). Further, 'Calorie requirements seem to be highly context-specific, depending on activity levels, the epidemiological environment, the composition of the population, and other factors . . . Indeed, average calorie intake in India is lower today than it was 20 years ago, yet the nutritional status of the population has improved (Deaton and Drèze, 2009). To support their submissions they present two maps of India in Figure 2.12 (reproduced here as Figure 2.6) of their paper 'Nutrition in India: Facts and Interpretations.' The map on the left is of districts with varying proportions of underweight children and the one on right is of NSSO region wise per capita calorie consumption in 2004-05. Comparing the two maps they find that the, 'Correlation between average calorie intake and, say, the nutrition status of children is negative . . . child nutrition is worse in regions with higher levels of per capita calorie intake' (Deaton and Drèze, 2009). We shall return to the maps in a little while.

They have subsequently argued that, 'There are, in fact, very good reasons not to treat calorie intake as an 'anchor' for setting or adjusting poverty lines. Indeed, calorie requirements are known to vary between regions, between persons, over time, and so on' (Deaton and Drèze, 2010).

It can be no one's case that nutritional outcomes in a population can be judged by the average daily per capita calorie consumption. Indeed there are well defined nutritional parameters for the same. Further, even though factors like epidemiological environment, activity levels etc. play an important role in utilisation and assimilation of dietary energy intake, it is not as though this renders dietary energy intake secondary for nutritional well-being of the people. A more nuanced position would be that, 'Adequate dietary intake is a necessary condition for good nutritional outcomes, however, this by itself is not a sufficient condition to ensure good nutritional outcomes ensuring which would also require other sufficient conditions such as good sanitary conditions, safe drinking water, availability of effective healthcare facilities, proper housing, education etc.' Further, even optimal availability of sufficient conditions can be expected to make up for the deficiency of dietary calories only to a limited extent. Moreover, describing the 'Current Diet and Nutrition Scenario', authors of the latest NIN/ICMR (National Institute of Nutrition/Indian Council of Medical Research) guidelines state, 'The proportion of households with energy inadequacy was about 70%, while that with protein inadequacy was about 27%. Thus, in the cereal/millet based Indian diets the primary bottleneck is energy inadequacy and not protein, as was earlier believed' (NIN, 2011: 6.). It is further stated that, 'The most rational, sustainable and long term solution to the problem of malnutrition is ensuring availability, access and consumption of adequate amounts of foods' (Ibid: 7). The fact that there can be an additional case for setting similar normative standards for the persistently high levels of food inflation since 2008 would only lend further credence to this perception.

It follows then that in the context of countries like India with high levels of poverty and hunger, consumption of normative dietary energy continues to serve as an important anchor for poverty.

We come back to the maps presented above in Figure 2.6. For the purpose of a clearer comparison, we have presented the same data with slight variation in Figures 2.7a, 2.7b, 2.8a and 2.8b. While Figure 2.7a presents the classification of NSSO regions by calorie consumption, Figure 2.7b presents the classification of NSSO regions by prevalence of child malnutrition. Both the maps (Figures 2.7a and 2.7b) have been divided into five classes of calorie consumption and child malnutrition respectively beginning from the lowest to the highest. Maps in Figures 2.8a and 2.8b separately present respective data for Gujarat for reasons explained in the notes to the figures.

Table 2.14 gives the expected comparison between per capita calorie consumption classes and the malnutrition prevalence classes for respective maps in Figures 2.7 and 2.8. In Figure 2.7a and 2.7b out of a total of 73 NSSO regions there is prefect match between per capita calorie consumption classes and prevalence of child malnutrition classes for 12 NSSO regions while in 31 there is a mismatch of just one class and in 30 NSSO regions we have gross mismatches. Such a correspondence between per capita calorie consumption and

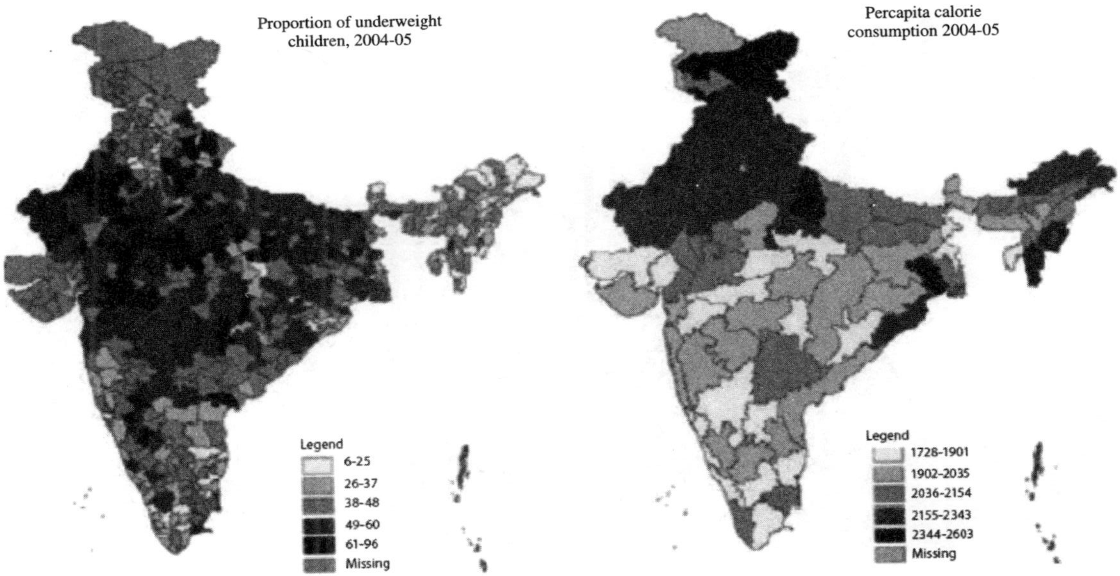


Figure 2.6 Comparison of districts by proportion of underweight children and per capita calorie consumption.

*Note:* Figure 2.6 has been reproduced here with permission from the authors. Figure above juxtaposes region-level NSS data on calorie intake in 2004-05 with district-level child nutrition data in 2002-04 from the second round of the Reproductive and Child Health (RCH) survey, also known as District Level Household Survey (DLHS).

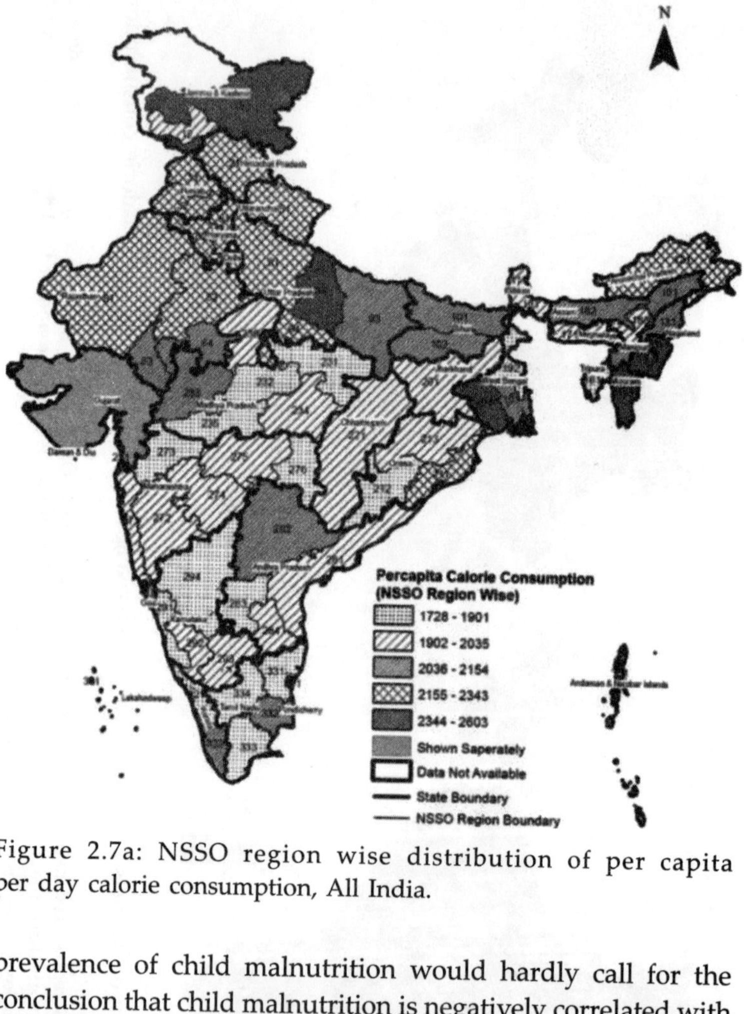


Figure 2.7a: NSSO region wise distribution of per capita per day calorie consumption, All India.

prevalence of child malnutrition would hardly call for the conclusion that child malnutrition is negatively correlated with calorie consumption. The correspondence between the two could have been closer to the expected if instead of per capita calorie consumption we had the figures for per capita calorie consumption for the age group of 0 to 6 years. A similar mixed picture is visible in the case of Gujarat as well. This however is not to ignore the fact that there are important regions of

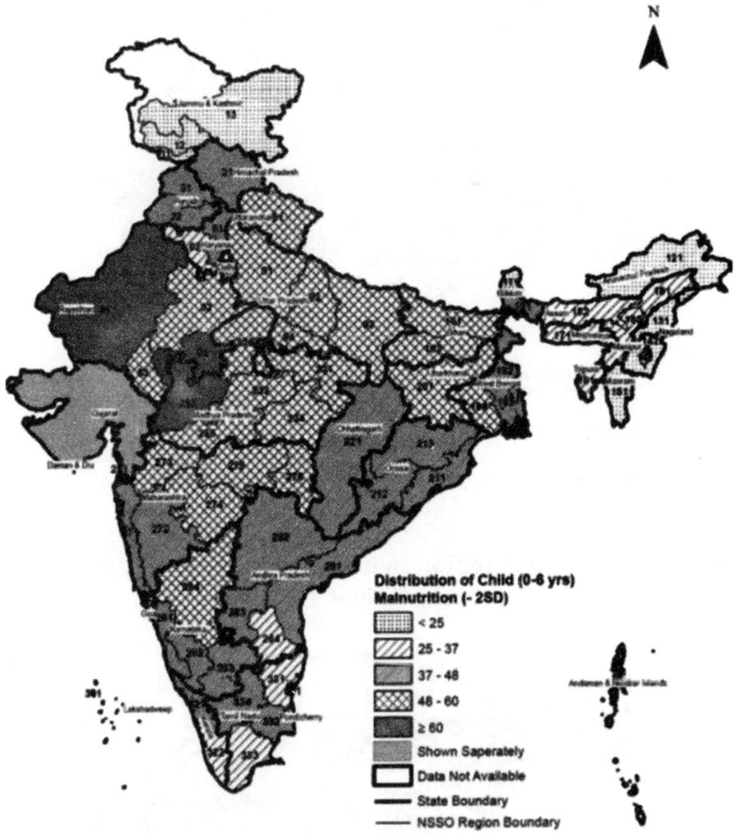


Figure 2.7b: NSSO region wise distribution of childhood malnutrition, All India.

gross mismatch between the two parameters. Our limited contention here is that on the overall balance, per capita dietary energy consumption does serve as an important indicator of well-being of the poor and thereby its continued relevance as an anchor for poverty lines until hunger and malnutrition have been overcome as major public health problems.

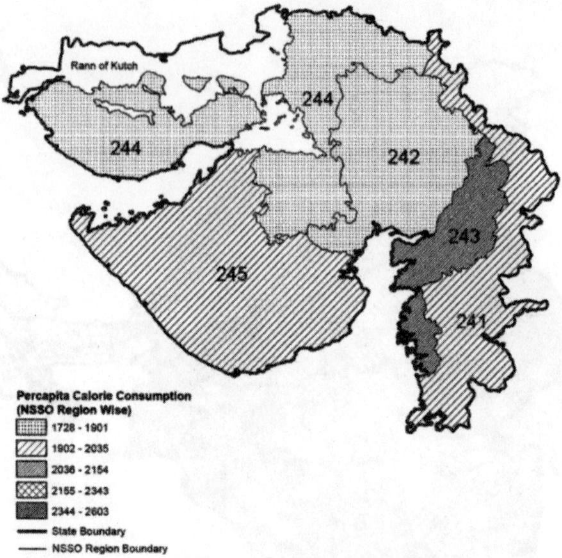


Figure 2.8a: NSSO region wise distribution of per capita per day calorie consumption, Gujarat.

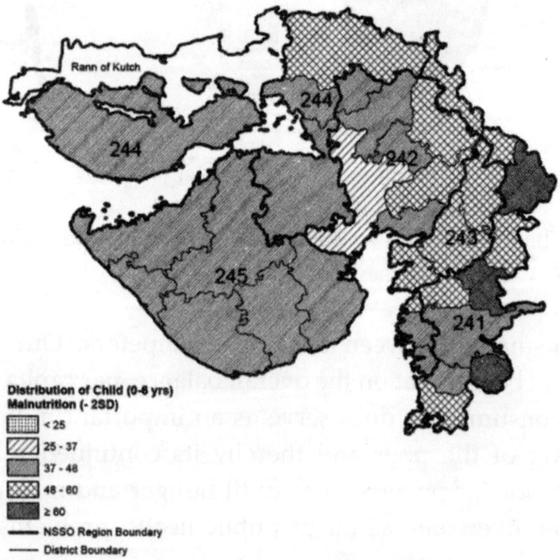


Figure 2.8b: District wise distribution of child malnutrition, Gujarat.

Notes for Figures 2.7a to 2.8b: Figure 2.7a presents per capita per day calorie consumption across NSSO regions in exactly the same way as in the right hand side map in Figure 2.6. Each NSSO region (except those in Gujarat) conforms to a group of districts; hence in Figure 2.7b we have mapped the weighted average of child malnutrition of all the districts comprising an NSSO region such that there is easy comparability between NSSO region-wise distribution of calorie consumption and child malnutrition. It need be noted that for some 20 districts, most of them in the North Eastern states, the district-wise child malnutrition data was not available. Data for such districts has been substituted with the state average in order to calculate the weighted average child malnutrition for respective NSSO regions.

The maps of Gujarat have been shown separately because in Gujarat boundaries of some of the NSSO regions conform to sub-district boundaries, however, the data of child malnutrition is available only for the districts. Hence, prevalence of child malnutrition for Gujarat has been mapped district-wise.

In all the maps the break points for different classes of calorie consumption and child malnutrition are the same as respective break points used in Figure 2.12 of Deaton and Drèze, 2009.

Table 2.14: Expected Correspondence between Per Capita Calorie Consumption and Prevalence of Child Malnutrition Classes in Figures 2.7 and 2.8

| *Per capita calorie consumption class (kcal)* | *Expected corresponding child malnutrition class (%)* |
|---|---|
| 1,728-1,901 | ≥ 60 |
| 1,902-2,035 | 48-60 |
| 2,036-2,154 | 37-48 |
| 2,155-2,343 | 25-37 |
| 2,344-2,603 | < 25 |

## Tendulkar Committee Recommendations—A Regressive Turnaround for Welfare Policy

Given the fact that its official poverty estimates had come under severe criticism, the Planning Commission set up an expert group under the chairmanship of Professor Suresh Tendulkar to review the methodology for estimation of poverty and suggest a new poverty line and estimates (GOI, 2009).

Even though the Tendulkar Committee formally recognised the multi-dimensional nature of poverty, for all practical purposes it did away with the concern for the falling calorie consumption and thereby the increase in the headcount of poor in India.

The Committee stated that:

'A conscious decision was taken by the Expert Group to move away from anchoring the PL (poverty line) in calorie norm as in the past because (a) there is overwhelming evidence of a downward shift in calorie Engel curves over time and (b) calorie consumption intake calculated by converting the consumed quantities in the last 30 days as collected by NSS has not been found to be well correlated either over time or across states with the nutritional outcomes observed in other specialised nutrition outcome surveys such as the National Family Health Surveys (NFHS)' GOI, 2009.

They further stated, 'Although those near the poverty line in urban areas continue to afford the original calorie norm of 2,100 calories per capita per day, their actual observed calorie intake from 61st Round of NSS is 1,776 calories per capita. This actual intake is very close to the revised calorie intake norm of 1,770 calories per capita per day currently recommended for India by the Food and Agriculture Organisation (FAO) (emphasis ours)[1]. Actual observed calorie intake of those near the new poverty line in rural areas (1,999 calories per capita) is higher than the FAO norm' GOI, 2009.

The Committee's contention also was:

'The new poverty lines have been arrived at after assessing the adequacy of private household expenditure on education and health, the earlier calorie-anchored poverty lines did not explicitly account for these. The proposed poverty lines are in that sense broader in scope' GOI, 2009.

So in one stroke two objectives were achieved (a) the calorie consumption at poverty line was rationalised at a

Table 2.15: Comparison of Poverty Lines (Rural and Urban) at Normative Calorie Consumption and those Prescribed by the Tendulkar Committee's Methodology

| *Year* | *Rural* | | | | *Urban* | | | |
|---|---|---|---|---|---|---|---|---|
| | *Normative calories* | *MPCE at normative calories (₹/mt)* | *OPL-T* | *Calories affordable at OPL-T* | *Normative calories* | *MPCE at normative calories (₹/ mt)* | *OPL-T* | *Calories affordable at OPL-T* |
| 2004-05 | 2400 | 814.73 (27) | 446.68 (14.9) | 1962 | 2100 | 997 (33.23) | 578.8 (19.29) | 1833 |
| 2009-10 | 2400 | 1580 (52.7) | 672.8 (22.4) | 1870 | 2100 | 2120 (70.7) | 859.6 (28.65) | 1720 |

*Notes:* MPCE = Monthly per capita expenditure, OPL-T = Official Poverty Line (Tendulkar). The figures in parenthesis are per day MPCE/PL. The figures for 2004-05 were taken/derived from Tables—Sector wise MPCE classes, Table 3R and Table 3U in NSSO, 2007. Figurs for 2009-10 were obtained from Patnaik, 2013.

level much below the earlier normative norms and (b) the claim that the new poverty lines provided for adequacy of household expenditure on education and health. The reality however is better reflected in Table 2.15.

One would expect that poverty lines providing for expenditure on education and health along with adequate dietary energy consumption would be far more liberal than the ones which only followed normative calorie norms without 'explicitly accounting' for expenditure on education and health. In this respect one has to admit that the Tendulkar Committee's poverty lines prove to be far too parsimonious and therein lies their significance for the policy establishment. Little wonder then that there was a huge public outcry when the Planning Commission filed an affidavit in the Supreme Court of India testifying to the new poverty lines (Parsai, 2011).

## Conclusion

To say that there is 'hunger amidst plenty' is to further sully the tragedy of millions who go hungry in India. Food security cannot be judged by the demand for food grains, as there will be little demand from those who have been reduced to possessing nothing more than their malnourished bodies. Food security ought to be judged against the benchmark of what people rightfully deserve to have. They deserve at least as much as many other countries, not necessarily very rich, have been able to provide to their citizens. There is hardly any contradiction in stating that the problem is not just of equitably distributing the plenty, but that there has actually been an acute dearth of food in the country if the genuine demands of the people were to be met in earnest. The plenty is created only by the lack of purchasing power of the people.

The situation is particularly worrisome as the agricultural sector of the economy has been in the throes of an enduring stagnation. Just a few years back some newspapers ran editorials ridiculing those who expressed concern for the country's food security, by saying that there was enough to buy from the international food grain market. No sooner did they say so, a massive food crisis burst on the face of the world with food riots taking place in many parts of the world in 2007-08, leading many countries to impose a ban on food grain exports. If food security becomes vulnerable, political and economic vulnerability can hardly be left far behind.

It is also apparent that the much talked of 'Green Revolution' hardly ensured an adequate supply of food grains to meet the optimal energy needs of the people, though it did result in an increased production of food grains to enable the Government to tide over the kind of acute shortages that existed hitherto and thereby avoid any major famines. The continued propaganda however remains that 'Green Revolution' made India self-sufficient in food and that the present problems in meeting the nutritional needs of the people require newer technological interventions, this time in the form of genetically modified food crops, to launch what has been described by M.S. Swaminathan, the country's much acclaimed agricultural scientist, as the 'evergreen revolution'.

Adequacy of dietary consumption lies at the very core of human subsistence, especially in countries like India with a huge burden of poverty and hunger. In the given context, the declining dietary energy consumption across different expenditure classes over the last two decades is a socially, economically and politically sensitive issue that has attracted much attention among policy circles and the academia. The analysis of these trends presented above not only exposes the spurious claims presented by the policy establishment to rationalise the observed trends but strongly points to the deepening crisis regarding food security of the people, especially the working masses.

The dietary energy insufficiency is also the biggest challenge facing the country on the malnutrition front. Under the circumstances suggestions to unpeg the poverty lines from the normative calorie anchor spells further disaster for welfare policy especially as alternative normative standards remain vague and little understood. The new official poverty lines derived as per Tendulkar Committee guidelines are but one example of this disaster. The challenge however is to strengthen the ways and means of making the ruling elite to take cognisance of the rising suffering of the people.

Even as the country is in the throes of an agricultural crisis with hundreds of thousands of farmers committing suicides and reports of widespread hunger from different parts of the country are commonplace, the well-to-do sections of the society and a large section of the intelligentsia, are taken in by the official 'myths'. To say the least, these myths confound reality and misdirect policy, they serve as diversionary tactics hopelessly seeking to provide legitimacy to the system.

## Endnotes

1. The FAO norm is meant to define 'total energy expenditure corresponding to the minimum acceptable limit of the range of body-weight for attained-height and the light physical activity norm' (FAO, 2008). Further, 'the FAO indicator (norm) is designed to capture a clearly—and narrowly—defined concept of undernourishment, namely a state of energy deprivation lasting over a year' (FAO, 2012).

## References

Bajaj J.K. and M.D. Srinivas (2002): 'Annam Bahu Kurvita: The Indian Discipline of Growing and Sharing Food in Plenty', in *Sustainable Agriculture and Food Security: The Impact of Globalisation,* Vandana Shiva and Gitanjali Bedi (eds.), Sage Publications, New Delhi, 2002.

Bennett M.K. (1954): *The World's Food: A Study of the Inter-relations of World Populations, National Diets and Food Potentials,* Harper and Brothers, New York.

Chandra Mohan N. (2010): 'The paradox of hunger amidst potential plenty', *Business Standard*, 18 April, Viewed on 23 June 2010 from http://www.business-standard.com/india/news/n-chandra-mohanparadoxhunger-amidst-potential-plenty/392228/.

Commissioners of the Supreme Court of India (2001): *Commissioners to the Supreme Court on the Right to Food: A Brief Introduction*, Centre for Equity Studies, New Delhi.

Deaton A. and Drèze J. (2010): 'Nutrition, poverty and calorie fundamentalism: response to utsa patnaik.' *EPW*, Vol. 45 (14): 78-80.

Deaton A. and Jean Drèze, 2009: 'Nutrition in India: Facts and Interpretation', *Economic & Political Weekly*, Vol. 44 (7):42-65.

Dhawan, Himanshi (2010): 'Hunger back to 1990 levels in South Asia: UN Report', *The Times of India*, 23 June, Viewed on 23 June 2010 from http://timesofindia.indiatimes.com/india/Hunger-back-to-1990-levels-in-South-Asia-UN-report/articleshow/6080627.cms.

Drèze, Jean (2003): 'Hunger amidst plenty'. Indiatogether.com, December 2003, Viewed on 23 June 2010 from http://www.indiatogether.org/2003/dec/pov-foodsec.htm.

FAO (2008): 'Food Security Statistics, Food consumption: Dietary Energy Consumption (kcal/person/day)', Viewed 23 June 2010, from http://www.fao.org/economic/ess/food-security-statistics/en/.

FAO (2011): 'Food Balance Sheet for India for the year 2005'. Available from http://faostat.fao.org/site/368/default.aspx#ancor on 3rd October.

FAO (1999): Prospects for the future: nutritional, environmental and sustainable food production considerations—changes in cultural and consumer habits by W. Bruce Traill, Professor of Food Management and Marketing, University of Reading, UK Conference on International Food Trade Beyond 2000: Science-Based Decisions, Harmonisation, Equivalence and Mutual Recognition Melbourne, Australia, 11-15 October.

FAO (2006): 'The State of Food Insecurity in the World', Rome.

FAO (2008): 'The State of Food Insecurity in the World', Rome.

Gopalan C. et. al. (1989): *Nutritive value of Indian foods*, National Institute of Nutrition, Hyderabad.

Ibid., (2004).

Government of India (2009a): 'Towards new poverty lines for India', Planning Commission, November. Available from http://planningcommission.nic.in/eg_poverty.htm on 20 September, 2011.

Government of India (2009b): 'Report of the expert group to review the methodology for estimation of poverty'. Planning Commission, November.

Ibid., 'Age group wise% distribution of estimated population by sex and residence in India'. Viewed on 2nd June 2010 from http://www.indiastat.com/demographics/7/moreoncensus/12977/stats.aspx.

Ibid., 'Per Capita Net Availability of Food grains (Per Annum) in India (1951 to 2007)'. Viewed 23 May 2010 from http://www.indiastat.com/table/percapitaavailability/24/fooditems/103/6368/data.aspx.

Ibid., 'Projected Total Population by Sex in India (As on 1st March, 2001 to 2026)' and 'Projected Urban Population by Sex in India (As on 1st March, 2001 to 2026).'

Ibid., p. 6.

Ibid., p. 7.

ICMR (1990): 'Average height and weight of boys at different ages', In *Nutrient Requirements and Recommended Dietary Allowances for Indians,* New Delhi.

ICMR (Indian Council for Medical Research) 1990: *Recommended dietary intakes for Indians,* New Delhi.

Indiastat.com: *Revealing India Statistically*. 'Projected Sex Ratio (India) (1996-2016)'. Viewed on 2 June 2010 from http://www.indiastat.com/demographics/7/sexratio/251/stats.aspx on 2 June 2010.

Kearney J. (2010): 'Food Consumption Trends and Drivers'. Phil. Trans. R. Soc. B, 365: 2793-2807.

Meenakshi J.V. (2000): 'Food Consumption Trends in India, A Regional Analysis, in *Public Support for Food Security, The Public Distribution System in India,* N. Krishnaji and T.N. Krishnan (eds.), Sage Publications, New Delhi.

Ministry of Rural Development (MRD) (2009): 'Report of the Expert Group to advise the Ministry of Rural Development on methodology for conducting the Below Poverty Line (BPL) Census for the 11th Five Year Plan.'

Morris S.S., Robert E. Black, Lana Tomaskovic (2003): 'Predicting the distribution of under-five deaths by cause in countries without adequate vital registration systems.' *International Journal of Epidemiology,* 32:1041-1051.

National Institute of Nutrition (2011): *Dietary Guidelines for Indians, A Manual,* Hyderabad.

National Sample NSSO 62nd Round (2008): *Household Consumer Expenditure in India, 2005-06,* Report No. 523, Ministry of Statistics and Programme Implementation, Government of India.

NCEUS (National Commission For Enterprises on Unorganised Sector) (2007): 'Report on Conditions of Work and Promotion of Livelihoods in the Unorganised Sector', New Delhi, Viewed 6 June 2010 from http://nceus.gov.in/Condition_of_workers_sep_2007.pdf.

NSSO 50th Round (1996): 'Key Results on Household Consumer Expenditure, 1993-94', Report No. 401, Ministry of Statistics and Programme Implementation, Government of India.

NSSO 53rd Round (1998): 'Household Consumer Expenditure and Employment Situation in India, 1997', Report No. 442, Ministry of Statistics and Programme Implementation, Government of India.

NSSO 56th Round (2002): 'Household Consumer Expenditure and Employment—Unemployment Situation in India, 2000-01', Report No. 476, Ministry of Statistics and Programme Implementation, Government of India.

NSSO 59th Round (2005): Household Consumer Expenditure and Employment-Unemployment Situation in India, 2003', Report No. 490, Ministry of Statistics and Programme Implementation, Government of India.

NSSO 61st Round (2006): 'Level and Pattern of Consumer Expenditure, 2004-05', Report No. 508, Ministry of Statistics and Programme Implementation, Government of India.

NSSO 64th Round (2010): 'Household Consumer Expenditure in India, 2007-08', Report No. 530, Ministry of Statistics and Programme Implementation, Government of India.

NSSO 66th Round: 'Key Indicators of Household Consumer Expenditure in India, 2009-10', NSS KI (66/1.0).

Park K. (2007): 'WHO Technical Report, Serial No. 522, 1973', quoted in *Nutrition and Health, Park's Textbook of Preventive and Social Medicine,* 19th edition, Jabalpur: Banarsidas Bhanot Publishers, 502.

Patnaik Utsa (2003): 'Food Stocks and Hunger: The Causes of Agrarian Distress', *Social Scientist,* Vol. 31(7/8): 15-41.

Patnaik Utsa (2006): 'Increasing hunger amongst relative plenty', Infochange Agenda, October, Viewed on 23 June 2010 from http://infochangeindia.org/200610015680/Agenda/Hunger-Has-Fallen-Off-The-Map/Increasing-hunger-amongst-relative-plenty.html).

Patnaik Utsa (2007): 'Neoliberalism and rural poverty in India', *EPW,* Vol. 42 (30): 3132-3150.

Patnaik Utsa (2009): 'Origins of the Food Crisis in India and Developing Countries', *Monthly Review,* Vol 61(3), Viewed 13 May 2010 from http://monthlyreview.org/090727patnaik.php.

Patnaik Utsa (2010a): 'Trends in Urban Poverty under economic reforms: 1993-94 to 2004-05', *EPW,* Vol. 45 (4): 42-53.

Patnaik, Utsa (2010b): 'A Critical Look at Some Propositions on Consumption and Poverty.' *EPW,* Vol. 45 (6): 74-80.

Poleman, Thomas T. (1981): 'Quantifying the Nutrition Situation in Developing Countries', *Food Research Institute Studies,* XVIII (I): 1-58.

Popkin B.M. (2001): 'The Nutrition and Obesity in the Developing World'. *Journal of Nutrition*, 131: 871S-873S.

Popkin B.M. (2002): 'An Overview on the Nutrition Transition and its Health Implications: The Bellagio Meeting', *Public Health Nutrition*, 5(1A): 93-103.

Popkin B.M. and P.G. Larsen (2004): 'The Nutrition Transition: worldwide obesity dynamics and their determinants.' *International Journal of Obesity*, 28: S2-S9.

Regmi Anita, M.S. Deepak, James L. Seale , Jason Bernstein (2001): 'Cross-Country Analysis of Food Consumption Patterns', in Changing Structure of Global Food Consumption and Trade, United States Department of Agriculture Economic Research Service.

Sethi A. (2011): 'Gone in 50 seconds'. *The Hindu*, 6th November, New Delhi.

Subramanian S.V., J.M. Perkins and K.T. Khan (2009): 'Do Burdens of Underweight and Overweight Coexist Among Lower Socio-economic Groups in India?', *American Journal of Clnical Nutrition*, 90: 369-76.

Subramanyam M.A. and S.V. Subramanian (2011): 'Low Socio-economic Groups are not Overweight in India', *Indian Journal of Medical Research*, 133: pp. 119-120.

Suryanarayana M.H. (2009): 'Nutritional Norms for Poverty: Issues and Implications', Concept paper prepared for the Expert Group to Review the Methodology for Estimation of Poverty. Indira Gandhi Institute of Development Research, Mumbai, Viewed 28 May 2010 from http://planningcommission.nic.in/reports/genrep/surya.pdf.

Suryanarayana M.H. (1995): 'Growth, Poverty and Levels of Living: Hypotheses, Methods and Policies', *Journal of Indian School of Political Economy*, Vol. (7) 2: 203-255.

United States Department of Agriculture (2011): 'Budget shares for broad aggregates and conditional budget shares for food categories', in 'International Food Consumption Patterns', Available from http://www.ers.usda.gov/Data/InternationalFoodDemand/ on 12th Sept. 2011.

WHO (2010): 'Global and Regional Food Consumption Patterns and Trends, WHO', Viewed 23 June 2010 from http://www.who.int/nutrition/topics/3_foodconsumption/en/print.html.

Zimmerman Carle C. (1932): 'Ernst Engel's Law of Expenditures for Food', *The Quarterly Journal of Economics*, Vol. 47 (1): pp. 78-101.

# Appendix 1

Table 2.5: Calculation of Average Per Capita Calorie Requirements for Rural and Urban Areas based on the ICMR Recommendations.

| 1 *Age group* | 2 *Projected sex ratio by age for 2006 (males per 100 females)* | 3 *Proportion of rural population in different age groups by sex and BPL/APL ratio* | | | 4 *Mean recommended daily energy requirement (rural) (kcal) According to APL/ BPL status and sex* | | | | 5 *Proportion of urban population in different age groups by sex and BPL/APL ratio* | | | 6 *Mean recommended daily energy requirement (urban) kcal by poverty ratio and sex* | | | |
|---|---|---|---|---|---|---|---|---|---|---|---|---|---|---|---|
| | | | | | BPL | | APL | | | | | BPL | | APL | |
| | | T | M | F | M | F | M | F | T | M | F | M | F | M | F |
| 0-4 | 105.7 | 10.4 | – | – | 1,125.0 | | | | 8.7 | – | – | 1,125.0 | | | |
| 5-9 | 105.4 | 11.9 | – | – | 1,820.0 | | | | 9.5 | – | – | 1,820.0 | | | |
| 10-14 | 104.0 | 11.4 | – | – | 2,307.0 | | | | 9.6 | – | – | 2,307.0 | | | |
| 15-19 | 107.1 | 10.6 | 11 | 10.2 | 2640 (M)/2060 (F) | | | | 10.0 | 10.1 | 9.8 | 2640 (M)/2060 (F) | | | |
| 20-24 | 112.2 | 9.2 | 9.1 (7.9/1.2) | 9.4 (8.2/1.2) | 3,800 | 2,925 | 2,875 | 2,225 | 10.3 | 10.0 (6.5/3.5) | 10.5 (6./3.7) | 3,800 | 2,925 | 2,425 | 1,875 |
| 25-29 | 112.3 | 8.4 | 8.3 (7.2/1.1) | 8.4 (7.3/1.1) | 3,800 | 2,925 | 2,875 | 2,225 | 9.6 | 9.5 (6.2/3.3) | 9.7 (6.4/3.3) | 3,800 | 2,925 | 2,425 | 1,875 |
| 30-34 | 103.2 | 7.1 | 6.9 (6/.9) | 7.4 (6.4/1) | 3,800 | 2,925 | 2,875 | 2,225 | 8.2 | 8.2 (5.4/2.8) | 8.3 (5.4/2.9) | 3,800 | 2,925 | 2,425 | 1,875 |
| 35-39 | 99.3 | 6.7 | 6.7 (5.8/.9) | 6.6 (5.7/.9) | 3,800 | 2,925 | 2,875 | 2,225 | 7.6 | 7.6 (5/2.6) | 7.6 (5/2.6) | 3,800 | 2,925 | 2,425 | 1,875 |
| 40-44 | 103.8 | 5.5 | 5.4 (4.7/.7) | 5.5 (4.8/.7) | 3,610 | 2,779 | 2,731 | 2,114 | 6.4 | 6.3 (4.1/2.2) | 6.5 (4.2/2.25) | 3,610 | 2,779 | 2,305 | 1,782 |
| 45-49 | 110.0 | 4.3 | 4.6 (4/.6) | 4.0 (3.5/.5) | 3,610 | 2,779 | 2,731 | 2,114 | 5.4 | 5.6 (3.7/1.9) | 5.0 (3.3/1.7) | 3,610 | 2,779 | 2,305 | 1,782 |

| 1 Age group | 2 Projected sex ratio by age for 2006 (males per 100 females) | 3 Proportion of rural population in different age groups by sex and BPL/APL ratio | | | 4 Mean recommended daily energy requirement (rural) (kcal) According to APL/BPL status and sex | | | | 5 Proportion of urban population in different age groups by sex and BPL/APL ratio | | | 6 Mean recommended daily energy requirement (urban) kcal by poverty ratio and sex | | | |
|---|---|---|---|---|---|---|---|---|---|---|---|---|---|---|---|
| | | T | M | F | BPL | | APL | | T | M | F | BPL | | APL | |
| | | | | | M | F | M | F | | | | M | F | M | F |
| 50-54 | 111.9 | 3.9 | 3.3 (2.9/.4 | 4.5 (3.9/.6) | 3,430 | 2,640 | 2,595 | 2,008 | 4.4 | 4.2 (2.7/1.5) | 4.6 (3/1.6) | 3,420 | 2,640 | 2,190 | 1,693 |
| 55-59 | 110.7 | 3.4 | 3.5 (3/.5) | 3.3 (2.9/.4) | 3,430 | 2,640 | 2,595 | 2,008 | 3.5 | 3.6 (2.4/1.2) | 3.4 (2.2/1.2) | 3,420 | 2,640 | 2,190 | 1,693 |
| 60-64 | 109.7 | 2.6 | 2.5 (2.2/.3) | 2.7 (2.3/.4) | 3,087 | 2,376 | 2,336 | 1,808 | 2.5 | 2.5 (1.6/.9) | 2.6 (1.7/.9) | 3,078 | 2,376 | 1,971 | 1,524 |
| 65-69 | 103.7 | 2.0 | 1.9 (1.6/.3) | 2.1 (1.8/.3) | 3,087 | 2,376 | 2,336 | 1,808 | 1.9 | 1.8 (1.18/.62) | 2.0 (1.3/.7) | 3,078 | 2,376 | 1,971 | 1,524 |
| 70-74 | 99.0 | 1.4 | 1.3 (1.1/.2) | 1.4 (1.2/.2) | 2,778 | 2,139 | 2,103 | 1,628 | 1.2 | 1.1 (.7/.4) | 1.3 (.85/.45) | 2,771 | 2,139 | 1,774 | 1,372 |
| 75-79 | 98.7 | 0.7 | 0.7 (.6/.1) | 0.7 (.6/.1) | 2,778 | 2,139 | 2,103 | 1,628 | 0.7 | 0.6 (.4/.2) | 0.7 (.45/.24) | 2,771 | 2,139 | 1,774 | 1,372 |
| 80-84 | 107.8 | 0.4 | 0.3 (.26/.04) | 0.4 (.34/.06) | 2,500 | 1,926 | 1,893 | 1,466 | 0.3 | 0.3 (.2/.1) | 0.4 (.3/.1) | 2,494 | 1,926 | 1,597 | 1,235 |
| 85 + | 107.8 | 0.2 | 0.2 (.17/.03) | 0.2 (.17/.03) | 2,500 | 1,926 | 1,893 | 1,466 | 0.2 | 0.2 (.13/.07) | 0.3 (.2/.1) | 2,494 | 1,926 | 1,597 | 1,235 |
| All ages | Average per capita per day total calorie requirement (rural) = 2,554 kcal | | | | | | | | Average per capita per day total calorie requirement (urban) = 2,487 kcal | | | | | | |

Notes for Table 2.5: Age specific sex ratio of the entire population in different age groups is obtained from the table, 'Projected Sex Ratio (India) (1996-2016)' available from Indiastat.com. Figures in columns 3 and 5 have been taken from the table, 'Age group wise% distribution of estimated population by sex and residence in India', available from indiastat.com. Figures in the parentheses are the ratios of BPL/APL population in each age group separately for males and females in rural and urban areas calculated on the basis of overall BPL/APL ratio for the rural and the urban areas. The per day calorie consumption for different age groups was calculated as under:

The calculations of dietary energy requirement are based on recommendations given in Table 2.1. For calculating the dietary energy requirement of the 0-4 year age group we have to first calculate energy requirements of < 1 year and 0-3 year children (from Table 2.1).

Further, to calculate the average energy requirement of children below 1 year of age we need to multiply their average weight with the average per kg calorie requirement values given in Table 2.1. The average weight was calculated by taking the average of desirable weight of an Indian child at birth, at 6 months and at one year of age, which comes out to be 6.9 kg (ICMR 1990, average height and weight of boys at different ages). Weighted average was then calculated for the children in 0-4 yr age group by taking daily energy requirements of < 1 year age group and 0-3 yrs. in the ratio of 1:3.

For the 5-9 year age group daily energy requirement was arrived at by taking the average of daily calorie requirement of 4-6 and 7-9 year age groups given in Table 2.1.

The per day calorie requirement for males in the 10-14 year age group was taken as the average of the daily calorie requirement for males in 10-12 and 13-15 year age groups given in Table 2.1 and likewise for females. Weighted average of the daily calorie requirement for males and females in this group is calculated using the age specific sex ratio in the 10-14 year age group, which is 104 males to 100 females.

For the 15-19 yr age group the calorie requirement for males and females in the 16-18 yr age group in Table 2.1 is taken to hold good and then weighted average is calculated as per the age specific sex ratio.

The calorie requirements for adult age groups are calculated as explained in section on recommended calorie norms. Finally a weighted average of daily calorie requirement for all age groups is calculated separately for rural and urban areas using the respective proportion of each age group in the rural and urban population to arrive at average daily calorie requirement for rural and urban areas.

# Appendix 2

Table 2.6a Cereal Calories for Different Age Groups Deduced from Recommended Calories.

| 1 Age group | 2 Projected sex ratio by age for 2006 (males per 100 females) | 3 BPL/APL proportion of rural population in each age group by sex | | | 4 Mean calories derived from food grains per capita per day (rural) kcal | | | | 5 BPL/APL proportion of urban population in each age group by sex | | | 6 Mean calories derived from food grains per capita per day (urban) kcal | | | |
|---|---|---|---|---|---|---|---|---|---|---|---|---|---|---|---|
| | | | | | BPL | | APL | | | | | BPL | | APL | |
| | | T | M | F | M | F | M | F | T | M | F | M | F | M | F |
| 0-4 | 105.7 | 10.4 | — | — | 765 | | | | 8.7 | — | — | 641 | | | |
| 5-9 | 105.4 | 11.9 | — | — | 1,238 | | | | 9.5 | — | — | 1,037 | | | |
| 10-14 | 104.0 | 11.4 | — | — | 1,569 | | | | 9.6 | — | — | 1,315 | | | |
| 15-19 | 107.1 | 10.6 | — | — | 1795 (M)/1401 (F) | | | | 10.0 | — | — | 1505 (M)/1174 (F) | | | |
| 20-24 | 112.2 | 9.2 | 9.1 (7.9/1.2) | 9.4 (8.2/1.2) | 2,926 | 2,252 | 1,668 | 1,291 | 10.3 | 10.0 (6.5/ 3.5) | 10.5 (6./3.7) | 2,166 | 1,667 | 1,382 | 1,069 |
| 25-29 | 112.3 | 8.4 | 8.3 (7.2/1.1) | 8.4 (7.3/1.1) | 2,926 | 2,252 | 1,668 | 1,291 | 9.6 | 9.5 (6.2/3.3) | 9.7 (6.4/3.3) | 2,166 | 1,667 | 1,382 | 1,069 |
| 30-34 | 103.2 | 7.1 | 6.9 (6/.9) | 7.4 (6.4/1) | 2,926 | 2,252 | 1,668 | 1,291 | 8.2 | 8.2 (5.4/2.8) | 8.3 (5.4/2.9) | 2,166 | 1,667 | 1,382 | 1,069 |
| 35-39 | 99.3 | 6.7 | 6.7 (5.8/.9) | 6.6 (5.7/.9) | 2,926 | 2,252 | 1,668 | 1,291 | 7.6 | 7.6 (5/2.6) | 7.6 (5/2.6) | 2,166 | 1,667 | 1,382 | 1,069 |
| 40-44 | 103.8 | 5.5 | 5.4 4.7/.7) | 5.5 (4.8/.7) | 2,780 | 2,140 | 1,584 | 1,226 | 6.4 | 6.3 (4.1/2.2) | 6.5 (4.2/2.25) | 2,058 | 1,584 | 1,314 | 1,016 |
| 45-49 | 110.0 | 4.3 | 4.6 (4/.6) | 4.0 (3.5/.5) | 2,780 | 2,140 | 1,584 | 1,226 | 5.4 | 5.6 (3.7/1.9) | 5.0 (3.3/1.7) | 2,058 | 1,584 | 1,314 | 1,016 |

| 1 Age group | 2 Projected sex ratio by age for 2006 (males per 100 females) | 3 BPL/APL proportion of rural population in each age group by sex | | | 4 Mean calories derived from food grains per capita per day (rural) kcal | | | | 5 BPL/APL proportion of urban population in each age group by sex | | | 6 Mean calories derived from food grains per capita per day (urban) kcal | | | |
|---|---|---|---|---|---|---|---|---|---|---|---|---|---|---|---|
| | | | | | BPL | | APL | | | | | BPL | | APL | |
| | | T | M | F | M | F | M | F | T | M | F | M | F | M | F |
| 50-54 | 111.9 | 3.9 | 3.3 (2.9/.4 | 4.5 (3.9/.6) | 2,641 | 2,033 | 1,505 | 1,165 | 4.4 | 4.2 (2.7/1.5) | 4.6 (3/1.6) | 1,949 | 1,505 | 1,248 | 965 |
| 55-59 | 110.7 | 3.4 | 3.5 (3/.5) | 3.3 (2.9/.4) | 2,641 | 2,033 | 1,505 | 1,165 | 3.5 | 3.6 (2.4/1.2) | 3.4 (2.2/1.2) | 1,949 | 1,505 | 1,248 | 965 |
| 60-64 | 109.7 | 2.6 | 2.5 (2.2/.3) | 2.7 (2.3/.4) | 2,377 | 1,830 | 1,355 | 1,049 | 2.5 | 2.5 (1.6/.9) | 2.6 (1.7/.9) | 1,754 | 1,354 | 1,123 | 869 |
| 65-69 | 103.7 | 2.0 | 1.9 (1.6/.3) | 2.1 (1.8/.3) | 2<377 | 1,830 | 1,355 | 1,049 | 1.9 | 1.8 (1.18/.62) | 2.0 (1.3/.7) | 1,754 | 1,354 | 1,123 | 869 |
| 70-74 | 99.0 | 1.4 | 1.3 (1.1/.2) | 1.4 (1.2/.2) | 2<139 | 1,647 | 1,220 | 944 | 1.2 | 1.1 (.7/.4) | 1.3 (.85/.45) | 1,579 | 1,219 | 1,011 | 782 |
| 75-79 | 98.7 | 0.7 | 0.7 (.6/.1) | 0.7 (.6/.1) | 2<139 | 1,647 | 1,220 | 944 | 0.7 | 0.6 (.4/.2) | 0.7 (.45/.24) | 1,579 | 1,219 | 1,011 | 782 |
| 80-84 | 107.8 | 0.4 | 0.3 (.26/.04) | 0.4 (.34/.06) | 1,925 | 1,483 | 1,098 | 850 | 0.3 | 0.3 (.2/.1) | 0.4 (.3/.1) | 1,422 | 1,098 | 910 | 704 |
| 85 + | 107.8 | 0.2 | 0.2 (.17/.03) | 0.2 (.17/.03) | 1,925 | 1,483 | 1,098 | 850 | 0.2 | 0.2 (.13/.07) | 0.3 (.2/.1) | 1,422 | 1,098 | 910 | 704 |

Notes for Table 2.6a: Age specific sex ratio of the entire population is obtained from the table, 'Projected Sex Ratio (India) (1996-2016)' available from Indiastat. com. Figures in columns 3 and 5 have been taken from the table, 'Age group wise% distribution of estimated population by sex and residence in India', available from indiastat.com. Figures in the parentheses are the ratios of BPL/APL population separately for males and females in rural and urban areas calculated on the basis of overall BPL/APL ratio for the rural and the urban areas.

The rural BPL population derives, on an average 77% their calories from cereals, while the same figure for the rural APL population is 58% (calculated from figures given in Table 2.2, lower three quartiles (for BPL) and upper quartile (for APL).) For the 0 to 19 yrs age group in rural areas the calories from cereals have been arrived at the rate of 68% of total recommended calories (see Table 2.3), as there is no BPL/APL demarcation for this group.

For the urban population the calories derived from cereals were not available separately for the BPL and the APL groups. However, on an average 57% of the calories are derived from cereals in the urban areas (Table 2.3 above) and this proportion has been used to calculate direct calories for both the BPL and the APL population in each age group. The direct calories in columns 4 & 6 of table 6a have been accordingly calculated from the figures for total calories given in columns 4 & 6 of Table 2.5.

Table 2.6b: Derivation of Total Cereal Calories by Taking Weighted Averages of Cereal Calories for BPL and APL Categories, for Males and Females and for Age Groups.

| 1 Age group | 2 Projected sex ratio by age for 2006 (males per 100 females) | 3 Proportion of rural population | 4 Weighted average calories (BPL & APL) by sex, rural kcal | | 5 Weighted average (male and female combined) of calories from food grains, using the sex ratio (rural) kcal | 6 Proportion of urban population | 7 Weighted average calories (BPL & APL) by sex, rural kcal | | 8 Weighted average (male and female combined) of calories from food grains, using the sex ratio (urban) kcal |
|---|---|---|---|---|---|---|---|---|---|
| | | | M | F | | | M | F | |
| 0-4 | 105.7 | 10.4 | 765 | | 765 | 8.7 | 641 | | 541 |
| 5-9 | 105.4 | 11.9 | 1238 | | 1,238 | 9.5 | 1037 | | 1,037 |
| 10-14 | 104.0 | 11.4 | 1569 | | 1,569 | 9.6 | 1315 | | 1,315 |
| 15-19 | 107.1 | 10.6 | 1795 (M)/1401(F) | | 1,605 | 10.0 | 1505(M)/1174(F) | | 1,345 |
| 20-24 | 112.2 | 9.2 | 2,760 | 2,129 | 2,463 | 10.3 | 1,892 | 1,329 | 1,627 |
| 25-29 | 112.3 | 8.4 | 2,759 | 2,126 | 2,461 | 9.6 | 1,894 | 1,464 | 1,691 |
| 30-34 | 103.2 | 7.1 | 2,762 | 2,122 | 2,447 | 8.2 | 1,898 | 1,458 | 1,681 |
| 35-39 | 99.3 | 6.7 | 2,757 | 2,121 | 2,438 | 7.6 | 1,898 | 1,462 | 1,679 |
| 40-44 | 103.8 | 5.5 | 2,625 | 2,061 | 2,348 | 6.4 | 1,798 | 1,375 | 1,590 |
| 45-49 | 110.0 | 4.3 | 2,624 | 2,026 | 2,339 | 5.4 | 1,806 | 1,391 | 1,608 |
| 50-54 | 111.9 | 3.9 | 2,503 | 1,917 | 2,226 | 4.4 | 1,699 | 1,317 | 1,519 |
| 55-59 | 110.7 | 3.4 | 2,479 | 1,928 | 2,217 | 3.5 | 1,715 | 1,314 | 1,525 |

(Contd.)

Table 2.6b: Derivation of Total Cereal Calories by Taking Weighted Averages of Cereal Calories for BPL and APL Categories, for Males and Females and for Age Groups (*Contd.*)

| 1<br>*Age group* | 2<br>*Projected sex ratio by age for 2006 (males per 100 females)* | 3<br>*Proportion of rural population* | 4<br>*Weighted average calories (BPL & APL) by sex, rural kcal* | | 5<br>*Weighted average (male and female combined) of calories from food grains, using the sex ratio (rural) kcal* | 6<br>*Proportion of urban population* | 7<br>*Weighted average calories (BPL & APL) by sex, rural kcal* | | 8<br>*Weighted average (male and female combined) of calories from food grains, using the sex ratio (urban) kcal* |
|---|---|---|---|---|---|---|---|---|---|
| | | | *M* | *F* | | | *M* | *F* | |
| 60-64 | 109.7 | 2.6 | 2,254 | 1,714 | 1,996 | 2.5 | 1,527 | 1,186 | 1,364 |
| 65-69 | 103.7 | 2.0 | 2,216 | 1,718 | 1,972 | 1.9 | 1,537 | 1,184 | 1,364 |
| 70-74 | 99.0 | 1.4 | 1,998 | 1,479 | 1,737 | 1.2 | 1,372 | 1,067 | 1,219 |
| 75-79 | 98.7 | 0.7 | 2,007 | 1,546 | 1,775 | 0.7 | 1,390 | 1,052 | 1,220 |
| 80-84 | 107.8 | 0.4 | 1,815 | 1,388 | 1,610 | 0.3 | 1,251 | 1,000 | 1,130 |
| 85 + | 107.8 | 0.2 | 1,801 | 1,388 | 1,602 | 0.2 | 1,243 | 967 | 1,110 |
| Weighted avg. per day calories from food grains | | 100 | Rural India | | 1,874 | 100 | Urban India | | 1,399 |

# 3

# Food Security, Public Health, Poverty and the Unfinished Agenda of Land to the Tiller

Hosting nearly 50% of the world's hungry people, India is home to world's largest number of hungry people. Food insecurity defined as 'consuming less than 80% of the minimum energy requirements', is as high as 35% i.e. nearly 350 million people. The incidence of malnutrition and anaemia among pregnant women in the reproductive age group is as high as 90% (WFP, undated). In Global Hunger Index (GHI) 2009 India's score of 23.9, is lower than even some of the most impoverished countries of sub-Saharan Africa. Without doubt, our performance at reducing hunger can be mildly put as 'poor' (Grebmer et al., 2009). These figures certainly do not behove of a country that aspires to a world power status.

The issues concerning food security and its linkages with mass hunger and poverty have acquired a new urgency at a time when the world is passing through an acute food crisis and the poor in India are reeling under unprecedented rises in prices of food. These issues are of cardinal importance to public health. And yet, rather than addressing the issues in a comprehensive manner, the Government's response to the crisis has been more in the nature of half-hearted attempts under compulsion in the form of legislations like the 'Food Security Bill' (which had initially sought to provide for lesser food entitlement at a higher price than the ongoing schemes like 'Antyodaya Yojana') which effectively seeks to reduce the meaning of food security to providing subsidised food grains. The need instead is to address the structural constraints plaguing Indian agriculture, which have a bearing on the overall economic and social development and the food security of India's impoverished masses. In this respect the issue of genuine land reforms needs to be brought to the centre of the development agenda of the country.

This chapter looks at the linkages between food security, hunger, poverty and the centrality of land reforms as a key to ensure not only long term food security of India but also as a means to alleviate the poverty of its people that is at the root of mass hunger.

According to the projected population figures, released by the Census of India, as on 1 March, 2010 approximately 70.2% of India's population live in rural areas. Agriculture constitutes the core of the economy in rural areas. Agriculture and allied sectors contribute 15.7% of the total GDP. Employment in the agriculture sector as a share of total employment in 2004-05 was 52.1% (GOI, 2010). Highlighting the importance of agriculture to Indian economy the Planning Commission says, 'Agriculture is so much at the centre stage in the Indian economy that any situational change in this sector, positive or negative, has a multiplier effect on the entire economy. The largest industries of the country like sugar, jute, textiles, food processing, milk, etc. are dependent on agriculture for their raw materials. Besides, the agriculture sector and rural areas are the biggest markets for low priced and middle priced consumer goods, including durable use items' (GOI a, Undated).

Both production and distribution are shaped by the relations of production determined by the ownership of the means of production. Land is the principal means of production in agriculture and the production relations based on the ownership and utilisation of land have profound impact on this crucial sector. How land relations in agriculture are of crucial importance to securing the food security of the country and the well-being of the society at large is the central theme of this chapter and we shall dwell on this relationship in greater detail later.

The health of agriculture quite literally determines the health of the population because India with a huge population cannot depend on imports from the highly unstable international market for its food security. The dependence of vast sections of our population directly or indirectly on agriculture for their livelihood also has implications for the levels of poverty in the country.

It is therefore a two-way dependence. The food security of the people is dependent upon the output of food grains and the effective demand for food is created by possibilities of livelihood and employment opportunities in agriculture. The retrogressive relations of production in agriculture based on highly iniquitous ownership of land coupled with neoliberal economic policies characterised by low investment in rural infrastructure have put fetters on increasing the food grain output and have led to severe restrictions on employment opportunities. The result is massive rise in poverty levels during the reform years.

Decreased food grain output and increased poverty, in combination with inequitable distribution of food, have led to precarious conditions of food security in the country, that have grave implications for public health and thereby decreased productivity of the work force. Poverty, besides decreasing the access to healthcare also decreases the size of effective demand for not only food but also for other consumer items. High levels of rural poverty invariably spill over to the towns and cities directly visible in desperate migration from agriculture, and indirectly through a sluggish market for mass consumption items.

## Neoliberal Economic Policies and Food Security

The maze of pathways in which the neoliberal economic policies have impacted the food security of the country is far too complex, to be elucidated here in detail. Nevertheless, the undermentioned evidence is damning enough to implicate these policies as the bête noir of the hungry millions of India.

Cut backs on Central Government spending and credit facilities, reduction in budget deficit to GDP ratio in the name of sound public finance targeting primary healthcare, education and food subsidy, lack of old age security for the majority of the population, lowering and effective freezing of real wages for workers are some of the salient features of the liberalisation policies (Patnaik, 2007). The Government and the World Bank never tire of claiming decrease in poverty levels on paper over the reform years. These claims fly in face of official data showing deterioration in a number of indicators of rural well-being like the investment in agriculture (Table 3.1), falling growth rates of agricultural production, per capita availability of food (Table 3.2) and last but not the least, the suicides by nearly two lakh farmers in precisely the years when the reforms were rolled out (Indiastat.com. a, Undated; Kamat et al, 2007; Indiastat.com. a, Undated; Sainath, 2010). It would appear reasonable to presume that the farmers would not choose to commit suicides because they have never had it so good.

Table 3.1 shows a persistent decline in the public expenditure in agriculture as a percent of GDP right through the reform years. In fact, from 1997-98 onwards there is a stagnation in public investment in agriculture.

Table 3.1: Investment in Agriculture as a Percentage of GDP in India (1985-86 to 2001-02)

| *Year* | *Investment in agriculture (₹ in crores)* | *Investment in agriculture as percentage of GDP* |
|---|---|---|
| | *At 1993-94 prices* | *At 1993-94 prices* |
| 1985-86 | 13,086 | 2.3 |
| 1986-87 | 12,562 | 2.1 |
| 1987-88 | 13,101 | 2.1 |
| 1988-89 | 13,483 | 2.0 |
| 1989-90 | 11,988 | 1.6 |
| 1990-91 | 14,836 | 1.9 |
| 1991-92 | 13,389 | 1.7 |
| 1992-93 | 14,508 | 1.8 |
| 1993-94 | 13,523 | 1.6 |
| 1994-95 | 14,969 | 1.6 |
| 1995-96 | 15,690 | 1.6 |
| 1996-97 | 16,176 | 1.5 |
| 1997-98 | 15,942 | 1.4 |
| 1998-99 | 14,895 | 1.3 |
| 1999-00 | 17,304 | 1.4 |
| 2000-01 | 16,687 | 1.3 |
| 2001-02* | 18,057 | 1.3 |

*Source:* indiastat.com. Abbr. GDP: Gross Domestic Product.

*Note:* *Quick Estimates. Compiled from the statistics released by: Rajya Sabha Unstarred Question No. 562, dated 25.07.2003. Year: Period of fiscal year in India is April to March, e.g. year shown as 1990-91 relates to April 1990 to March 1991 (Indiastat.com. a, Undated).

In Table 3.2, the year-wise figures have been converted to five year averages of per capita availability of food grains from 1951 till 2007. The per capita, yearly availability of total food grains was the highest in 1991 at 186.2 kg. It is evident from Table 3.2 that there has been a halting decline in the per capita food grains availability during the period of the

Table 3.2: Per Capita Net Availability of Foodgrains Per Annum (5 year Average) in India (1951 to 2007) in kilo grams.

| *Five year period* | *Net food grains availability Kg per year* | *Five year period* | *Net food grains availability Kg per year* |
|---|---|---|---|
| 1951-55 | 152.9 | 1986-90 | 172.5 |
| 1956-60 | 161.1 | 1991-95 | 175.9 |
| 1961-65 | 168.4 | 1996-2000 | 171.2 |
| 1966-70 | 158.5 | 2001-05 | 163.0 |
| 1971-75 | 161.7 | 2006 | 162.5 |
| 1976-80 | 161.4 | 2007* | 160.4 |
| 1981-85 | 166.42 | | |

*Source:* Based on data of the Ministry of Agriculture, Govt. of India (Indiastat. com b, Undated).

Note: (1) The net availability of food grains is estimated to be Gross Production (–) seed, feed and wastage (–) exports (+) imports, (+/–) changes in stocks. The net availability of food grains divided by the population estimates for a particular year indicates per capita availability of food grains in terms of kg/ year. (2) Figurers in respect of per capita net availability given above are not strictly representative of actual level of consumption in the country especially as they do not take in to account any change in stocks in possession of traders, producers and consumers. (3) For calculation of per capita net availability the figures of net imports from 1981 to 1994 are based on imports and exports on Government of India account only. Net imports from 1995 onwards are based on the total exports and imports (on Government as well as private accounts). (4) Cereals includes rice, wheat and other cereals. (5) Pulses includes all kharif and rabi pulses. (6) Food grains includes rice, wheat other cereals and all pulses.

economic reforms. Our commitment to banish extreme poverty and hunger as enshrined in the Millennium Development Goals notwithstanding, at the beginning of the new millennium, per capita yearly availability of food was 150.9 kg i.e. equivalent to the levels seen in the 1950s. The average availability in the first decade of the 21st century has been at 162.6 kg, a level that is equal to the average availability in the decade of the sixties, which was indeed a decade of crisis for India on the food front.

Table 3.3 compares the rate of growth of food grains with the rate of growth of population. For the entire period of the reforms beginning from 1991 till 2011, the growth rate of food grain production persistently fell behind the population growth rate.

Table 3.3: Comparison of the Growth Rates of Population to those of Foodgrain Production*

| *Year* | *Population growth rate* | *Foodgrain growth rate #* |
|---|---|---|
| 1961-71 | 2.24 | 2.83 |
| 1971-81 | 2.23 | 1.8 |
| 1981-91 | 2.16 | 3.13 |
| 1991-01 | 1.95 | 1.1 |
| 2001-11 | 1.65 | 1.03** |

*Source:* Sainath, 2012

* 1961-2011 in percent per annum, based on data derived from 'Census of India, Economic survey and agriculture ministry data.

# in calculating growth rates actual values are taken into account.

** For food grain in the last decade, the calculations are for the period up to 2009-10 as the final numbers available for 2010-11 were only advance estimates.

What these figures imply for our failure in food grain production becomes even more emphatic by making comparisons with the availability in British India. At the beginning of the twentieth century (1897-1902) the per capita availability of food grains was 199 kg, which was reduced to 136.8 kg during 1945-46 under the impact of colonial policies. The State-led capitalism pursued by Indian rulers in the wake of independence in 1947 reversed the legacy of colonial policies in agriculture only partially and now the corporate-led policies being pursued are resulting in even these gains being washed out (Patnaik, 2003). Evidence of fall in growth rate of food grain production is provided from a study by Kamat et al. (Table 3.4) (Kamat et al, 2007).

Table 3.4: Annual Growth in Foodgrain Production Before and After Economic Reforms. (in Percentage)

| *Crops* | *Before economic reforms* | *After economic reforms* |
|---|---|---|
| | *1981-82 to 1992-93* | *1993-94 to 2004-05* |
| Rice | 0.37 | – 2.38 |
| Wheat | 4.33 | 1.37 |
| Coarse cereals | 1.64 | 0.75 |
| Pulses | 0.65 | – 0.2 |
| Annual growth rate in food grain production | 3.00 | 0.67 |

*Source:* Kamat et al., 2007.

Table 3.5: Decline in Growth Rates of Agricultural Output during Nineties to Below Population Growth Rate

| *Period* | *Foodgrains growth rate* | *Non-food grains growth rate* | *All crops* | *Population growth rate* |
|---|---|---|---|---|
| 1980-81 to 1989-90 | 2.85 | 3.77 | 3.19 | 2.1 |
| 1990-91 to 2000-01 | 1.66 | 1.86 | 1.73 | 1.9 |

*Source:* Patnaik, 2003.

There is a naive perception that all gains are simply being washed away by the uncontrolled increase in population. Nothing could be farther from the truth. Table 3.4 shows the decline in the growth rates of food grain production has nothing to do with increase in population, but everything to do with public investment in the development of agriculture, rural infrastructure, diversion of agricultural land for cash crops and non-agricultural purposes. As a matter of fact the growth rate of food grain production has fallen below the population growth rate which itself is falling as is evident from Table 3.5 (Patnaik, 2003). The falling investment in agriculture has decreased productivity and increased the scale of rural poverty during the reform years, thereby reducing the access to food due to decreased purchasing power.

## Displacement Policies and Food Security

The neoliberal economic reforms have been characterised by a missionary zeal to implement a development paradigm based on exploitation of vast areas of the country rich in primary resources. Besides the redoubtable economic merit of these development projects, they have displaced or threaten to displace people from their land in many parts of the country, thereby threatening the security of their livelihoods based on land and agriculture. The intense resistance, armed or unarmed, by the people in different parts of the country is a dramatic manifestation of the consequences of the development paradigm being pursued by the Government.

According to one estimate, between 1951 and 2005, as many as 55 million people were forcibly evicted from their land through land acquisition processes. These numbers far surpass the population of many member countries of the United Nations (Fernandes, 1998). The overwhelming majority of them are tribal people. A draft report prepared by the Ministry of Rural Development has described the dispossession of the tribal lands in the State of Chhattisgarh as the 'biggest land grab of tribal lands after Columbus.' Describing the use of tribal people to abet the dispossession of other tribal people, the report says that 'the armed tribal fighters of the Salwa Judum created and encouraged by the Government and supported with the firepower and organisation of the central police forces . . . The drama is being scripted by Tata Steel and Essar Steel who wanted seven villages or thereabouts, each to mine the richest lode of iron ore available in India' (GOI b, Undated). The impact of such development policies on the health of agriculture and the food security of the people has been calamitous to say the least.

## Linkages between Hunger and Health

The relationship between hunger and increased susceptibility to disease is well documented. And yet, lack of food is a causal factor that invariably fails to register on the radar of our policy makers while formulating disease control programmes and health policies. It is the most badly kept secret of our democracy. The emphasis invariably is on the narrow medical model of improving health while something as basic as adequate nutrition that has the potential to dramatically alter the health outcomes in the population is ignored. It would suffice here to exhibit this relationship between hunger and health by examining how health parameters in different Indian states vary in relation to the State Hunger Index. Figures 3.1 to 3.6 show the variation of certain health indicators with the State Hunger index of different states in India. Except for the life expectancy at birth where the correlation with state hunger index is not very strong, a definite correlation in seen with infant mortality rate, maternal mortality rate, crude death rate, under five mortality rate and anaemia levels in different states.

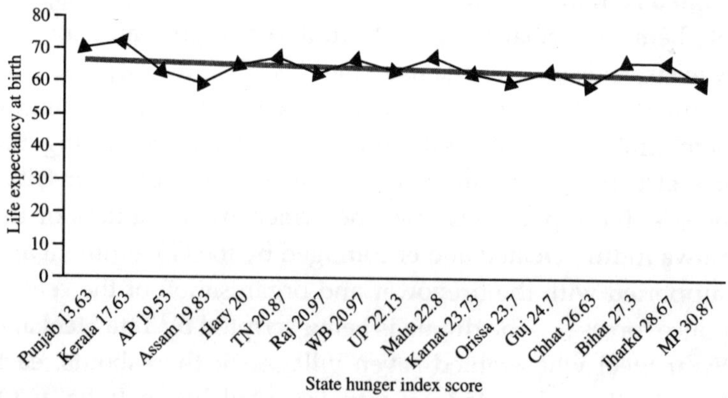


Figure 3.1: Variation of life expectancy at birth with state-wise hunger index.

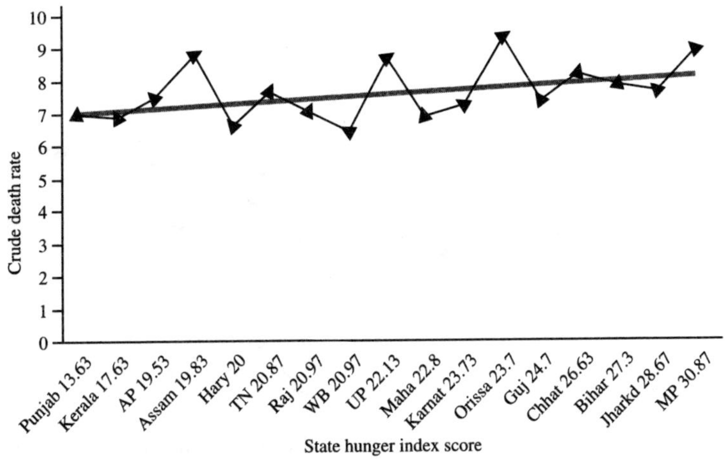


Figure 3.2: Variation of crude death rates (all deaths per 1,000), 2006 with state hunger index.

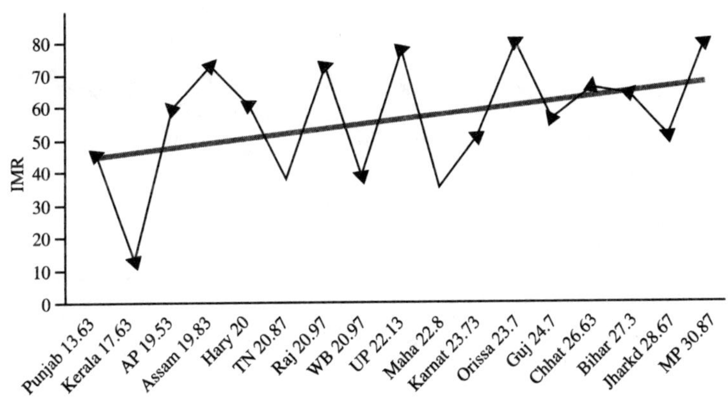


Figure 3.3: Variation of infant mortality rates with their state specific hunger index et. al.

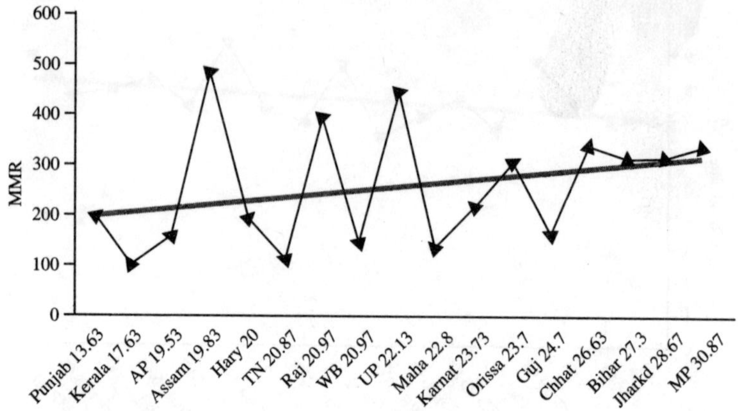


Figure 3.4: Variation of maternal mortality rate with the state specific hunger index.

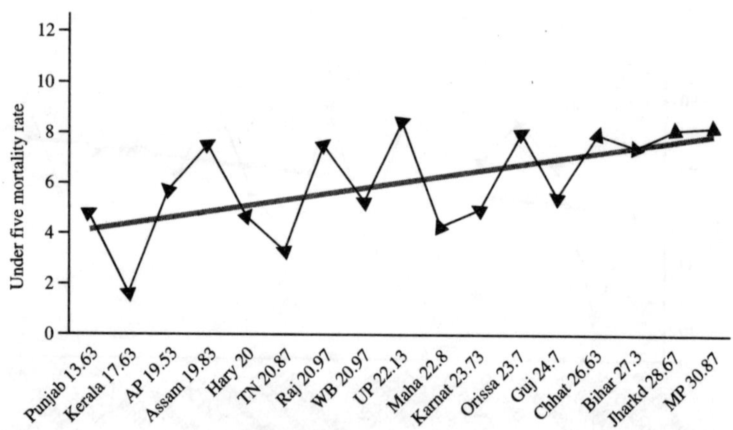


Figure 3.5: Variation of under five mortality rate with state specific hunger index.

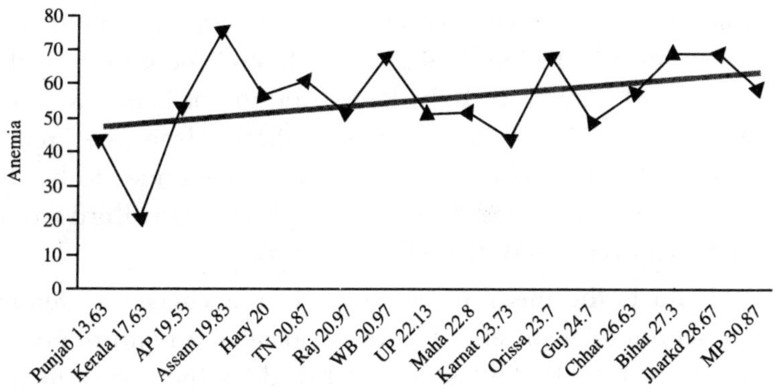


Figure 3.6: Variation of any anaemia with state specific hunger index.

Notes for Figures 3.2 to 3.7: The State Hunger Index Score is for the year 2008, while rest of the indices are for varying years ranging between 1997-98 to 2006. For life expectancy at birth for males and anaemia of all kinds in women, corresponding figures for Jharkhand could not be found; hence the corresponding figures for Bihar from the same data set were used for Jharkhand as well, as the state was carved out from Bihar. *Source:* Made by authors using primary data from the mentioned references (Menon et al, 2009; Indiastat.com c; d; e; f; g, all undated).

## The All Important Question of Land

'At his heart is his daughter's wedding,
in his eye foreknowledged of debt.
He eats and hath indigestion,
he toils and he may not stop;
His life is a long-drawn question,
between a crop and a crop.'

(Rudyard Kipling, Undated)

These lines of Kipling about the misery of Indian peasantry, written towards the end of the 19th century, ring true even today. Against this background we need to place the question of ownership of land—what has and has not changed.

Since time immemorial, land has captivated a peasant's imagination in his flight for freedom. The idea of 'land reforms' can be traced back to the times of the Roman aristocrat, Tiberius

Gracchus (163-133 B.C.) who thought of a programme of land ownership for the landless as a key to end the misery of the pauperised farmers of Italy. Redistribution of Land has been in the centre of the agenda of revolutions—from the French to the Bolshevik, to Chinese and indeed continues to be the 'whetstone' of the revolutionary struggles in many third world countries even today (Ladejinsky, 1964).

Land is the measure of power in the villages in feudal and semi-feudal societies like ours. Social and political power determined by the access to land decides the access to the 'Common Public Resources' (CPR) in the villages and the fortuitous arrangements made by the governments from time to time to improve the lot of the villages. It is instructive to remember that all the techno-economic solutions that are propagated as a solution to the problems of Indian agriculture, can't help but further widen the inequity unless the rural power structure is democratised. The entire experience of 'Green Revolution' bears testimony to this fundamental truth (George, 1977). The importance of the land reforms over other inputs was emphasised by Wolf Ladejinski—the American agricultural economist—who is considered as the father of land reforms in post-war Japan, Taiwan and Korea. In his words, 'Important though the other ingredients are, unless those who work the land own it, or are at least secure on the land as tenants, all the rest is likely to be writ in water' (Ladejinsky, 1964).

This is the fundamental truth and it has to be recognised that extreme rural poverty in India is rooted in massive landlessness. While 58% of India's population is dependent on agriculture for livelihood, about 63% of this population has land holdings of less than a hectare, while large farms of 10 hectares or more belong to less than 2% of this population. About 43% of the total peasant households are either absolutely landless or nearly landless i.e. own less than 0.2 hectares of land (Sethi, 2006). Between 1993-94 itself the proportion of landless rural households in India has increased by 10.6% (Bakshi, 2008).

National Sample Survey Organisation's (NSSO's) survey of land ownership patterns in 2003 also shows extremely skewed landholding patterns. At the all-India level, marginal and small owners constituted 90.40% of the total number of owners. But they owned only 43.43% of land, whereas medium and large farmers who constituted only 9.60% of landowners owned as much as 56.21% of land (Bandyopadhyay, 2008). Earlier government-led land reforms were motivated by altruistic notions of social justice, but with the advent of 'market-led land reforms' as part of neoliberal economic agenda, the objective is 'increasing GDP regardless of any externalities or costs associated with the process' (Sethi, 2006). As Manpreet Sethi writes, 'Promoted and guided by various international financial institutions (IFIs) such as the World Bank and the International Monetary Fund (IMF), government emphasis on land reform since the 1990s reflects and seeks to fulfil the macroeconomic objectives of these multilateral economic institutions' (Sethi, 2006). Neither social justice nor land reform has a place in this neoliberal agenda.

Statistics bear testimony to the little effort that has been made to correct such a skewed distribution of land. All the homilies paid by the country's ruling elite to implement land reforms have resulted in the vesting of 7.43 million acres of land over the last five decades of ceiling law application in the country. This amounts to less than 1% of the total area of 812.63 million acres in the country, barely 2% of the arable land area. Only 5.70 million acres of the vested land were actually taken over and 4.34 million acres distributed among roughly 5 million beneficiaries (Bandyopadhyay, 2008). There is hardly a comparison between this and the figures for Japan and Taiwan. Whereas in Japan, 54% of the land was owner operated, after the reforms it increased to 96% and the change in Taiwan was from 60% to 85% (Ladejinsky, 1964).

## Marginalisation of the Peasant and Inefficiency of

## Agricultural Production

With so many in the agricultural workforce literally being on the margins of the production process, owning little or no land, even subsistence has become difficult. For a landless labourer or a tenant farmer tilling other persons land under exploitative rent conditions, there is little motivation to work the land intensively for maximising production. Under the conditions there is also little incentive to invest and innovate. And yet, both are necessary conditions for increasing production. With the peasant having 'little to sell and pretty much little to buy', he is being pushed to the margins of the money economy leading to the declining domestic market size for mass consumption goods for the poor.

In contrast, land reforms resulting in peasants owning their own land would give them an incentive to maximise the produce. There is ample evidence now to show that small farms have a higher productivity than large industrial farms, and invariably contribute to the food security of communities much more as their produce is the one that finds its way to the local markets unlike that of the industrial farms where the production is mostly for export or now even for production of bio-fuels (Ladejinsky, 1964; Sobhan, 1993; Rosset, 2009; Altieiri, 2009). This is widely recognised by agricultural economists as the 'inverse relationship between farm size and output' (Rosset, 1999; Tomich, 1995). Table 3.7 shows that even in the U.S., the Mecca of the agribusiness and industrial farming, it is the small farms that score over the large farms in productivity.

Geovanni Andrea Cornea carried out a study for UNICEF in which he analyzed the 'relationship between factor inputs, land yield and labour productivity for farms of different sizes based on FAO farm management data for fifteen developing countries.' Besides elaborating on the various factors for higher productivity of small farms, an important observation is that 'where conspicuous labor surpluses exist, the superiority of small farming provides solid arguments in favor of land redistribution. Such an agrarian reform would determine higher output, higher labor absorption and a more equitable income distribution, thus contributing in a decisive manner to the alleviation of rural poverty' (Geovanni, 1985).

Table 3.7: Farm Size versus Output in the United States, 1992

| *Median Farm Size Category (Acres)* | *Average Gross Output ($/Acre)* | *Average Net Output **($/Acre)*** |
|---|---|---|
| 4 | 7424 | 1400 |
| 27 | 1050 | 139 |
| 58 | 552 | 82 |
| 82 | 396 | 60 |
| 116 | 322 | 53 |
| 158 | 299 | 55 |
| 198 | 269 | 53 |
| 238 | 274 | 56 |
| 259 | 270 | 54 |
| 694 | 249 | 51 |
| 1364 | 191 | 39 |
| 6709 | 63 | 12 |

Note: Figures are from U.S. Agricultural Census, Vol. 1, Part 51, pp. 89-96, 1992.
*Source:* Rosset M. Peter. Institute for Food and Development Policy.

However, the fixity of ideas with the policy establishment often leads to positions that are contrary to empirical evidence. The most popular perception is that there are far too many people dependent on agriculture in India than can be supported by it. Further, the decreasing size of operational holdings in the country is a drag on increasing the farm productivity as it prevents application of modern technology which can be applicable on large farms and prevents capital investment in agriculture as the capital (of the agribusiness) needs access to large enough farms. So the policy establishment comes up with a new variety of land reforms. The 'National Agriculture Policy, 2000' states, 'Development of lease market for increasing the size of the holdings by making legal provisions for giving private lands on lease for cultivation and agri-business . . . private sector participation will be promoted through contract farming and land leasing arrangements to allow accelerated technology transfer, capital inflow and assured markets for crop production, especially of oilseeds, cotton and horticultural crops' (GOI, 2000). These policy prescriptions are not just naive presumptions but are a move towards corporatisation of Indian agriculture. Viability and productivity of agriculture are being associated with large farm size and capital investments purely on the basis of presumed efficacy of such measures. However, what needs to be borne in mind is that the problem is not just of increasing production but also of strengthening the livelihoods of the people in rural areas. Viability of agriculture that rests upon active involvement of the peasantry in increasing production is the only way for sustainable agriculture in this country. Contrary to this, the proposed measures can prove to be cataclysmic for the lives and livelihoods of our people by turning on its head even a limited acknowledgement of the need for land and tenancy reforms. Apart from the flawed assumptions regarding increasing productivity in agriculture by promoting corporate farming, these policies are likely to carry with them seeds of further impoverishment of Indian agriculture (Saxena, undated). It would be instructive to have a hard look at the empirical facts with regard to farm size and productivity in the case of two most populous countries China and India.

The limited purpose of Table 3.8 is to show that there has been an increase in marginal and small holdings in the country both in terms of the number of holdings and the share in operational area. This implies that the productivity as also the use of higher technology by small farms should have further declined in the period between 1970-71 and 2005-06.

Tables 3.9 and 3.10 clearly show that in spite of farm size

having further reduced between 1970-71 and 2005-06, the small farms have maintained their edge over the large farms both in terms of productivity and in harnessing inputs of modern technology as reflected in use of higher amounts of fertilisers per hectare and the sowing of high yielding varieties. In terms of output value per hectare, the output of the smallest farm size is 3.26 times the similar value for the highest farm size. Likewise the smaller farms have outdone the larger farms in terms of irrigated area, fertiliser consumption, area under high

Table 3.8: Changes in Share of Small Holders in Number and Area of Operational Holdings at all India Level (%)

| *Year* | *Share in number of holdings* | | | *Share in operational area* | | |
|---|---|---|---|---|---|---|
| | *Marginal (<1 ha)* | *Small (1-2 ha)* | *Sub-total (<2 ha)* | *Marginal (<1 ha)* | *Small (1-2 ha)* | *Sub-total (<2 ha)* |
| 1970 –71 | 51 | 19 | 70 | 9 | 12 | 21 |
| 2005-06 | 65 | 19 | 83 | 21 | 21 | 42 |

*Source:* Agriculture census 2000-01 and 2005-06, available from the website of the Department of Agriculture and Cooperation, Government of India.

Table 3.9: Agricultural Output Per Household, Per Hectare and Per Capita in Different Farm Size Categories

| *Farm size (ha)* | *Per capita land (ha)* | *Output value (₹)* | | |
|---|---|---|---|---|
| | | *Per household* | *Per capita* | *Per ha* |
| 0.01-0.4 | 0.04 | 4,783 | 965 | 25,173 (3.26) |
| 0.4-1 | 0.12 | 12,563 | 2,364 | 18,921 |
| 1.01-2 | 0.24 | 23,292 | 3,801 | 16,780 |
| 2.01-4 | 0.43 | 40,403 | 6,734 | 15,091 |
| 4.01-10 | 0.82 | 77,120 | 10,588 | 13,564 |
| > 10 | 2.20 | 1,37,473 | 16,782 | 7,722 |
| All | 0.22 | 18,858 | 3,143 | 15,426 |

*Source:* Situation Assessment Survey, NSSO 59th Round, Report No. 497. The figure in parentheses is the ratio of output value for the smallest farm size divided by the output value for the largest farm size.

yielding varieties and crop intensity. In fact, the proportionate increase in the use of fertilisers and area under high-yielding varieties is far greater for smaller farms than large farms for the given time period.

Table 3.10: Variation in Area under Irrigation, Fertiliser Consumption, Area under HYV (High Yielding Varieties) and Cropping Intensity on Farms by Farm Size Categories

| *Year* | *Marginal* | *Small* | *Semi-medium* | *Medium* | *Large* | *All categories* |
|---|---|---|---|---|---|---|
| Extent of area under irrigation in different farm size categories (%)[1] | | | | | | |
| 1980-81 | 40 (2.5) | 33 | 29 | 24 | 16 | 27 |
| 2000-01 | 51 (1.6)<br>[27.5%] | 39 | 37 | 36 | 31<br>[93.8%] | 39 |
| Fertiliser consumption per ha of net sown area according to farm size categories (kg)[2] | | | | | | |
| 1981-82 | 55<br>(2.04) | 48 | 42 | 36 | 27 | 40 |
| 2001-02 | 175<br>(2.6)<br>[218.2%] | 129 | 112 | 95 | 68<br>[152%] | 119 |
| Share of area under HYV in different categories of farms (%)[3] | | | | | | |
| 1996-97 | 59 (1.4) | 55 | 54 | 53 | 42 | 54 |
| 2001-02 | 72 (1.5)<br>[22%] | 68 | 65 | 61 | 47<br>[12%] | 64 |
| Cropping intensity on farms of different size categories (%)[2] | | | | | | |
| 1981-82 | 134<br>(1.2) | 128 | 125 | 120 | 116 | 124 |
| 2001-02 | 139<br>(1.15)<br>[3.7%] | 128 | 126 | 125 | 121<br>[4.3%] | 128 |

*Source:* 1. Agricultural census 1980-81 2. Input survey of 1981-82 and 2001-02, Ministry of agriculture, GOI. 3. Input survey of 1996-97 and 2001-02, Ministry of Agriculture, GOI. The figures in parentheses under the marginal category is the ratio of marginal/large for the given year. Figures in square brackets is the% increase in the same category between the base year and the later year.

However, the small farms fare very poorly in terms of output value per household, which is on account of the fact that the per capita land is the minimum for these households. This in turn points to the need for land reforms to improve the endowments of productive assets for the smaller farms, both for increasing the productivity and as a measure to decrease the poverty of these households.

Further light is thrown on the relationship between farm size and productivity by comparing the relevant data for China and India. Table 3.11 gives a comparison for arable area, farm size, productivity, agricultural growth rate and poverty reduction for China and India. In spite of average farm size in China being half of that in India, the productivity of Chinese farms is far higher than the Indian farms. Another important point to notice is that China's net arable area is considerably smaller, both in absolute terms and in proportionate terms, as compared to that of India.

These figures should put in their right place the arguments supporting corporate framing on the plea that small farms are a hindrance to increasing agricultural productivity. Agriculture still employs more than 50% workforce of the country. The neoliberal economic policies pursued over the last two decades have hardly created job opportunities that could absorb this workforce in any significant manner by increasing migration from rural areas to the urban areas. The likelihood of this happening anytime in near future is also negligible. The solution lies in improving the productive asset endowment of the small and marginal farm households as well as those of the landless agricultural labourers through implementation of progressive land reforms and by generating off-farm rural employment opportunities (Chand et al., 2011).

Most importantly redistributive land reforms fulfil an important historical prerequisite for further development of productive forces in agriculture i.e. satisfying the land hunger

Table 3.11: Arable Land, Farm Size, Productivity (kg/ha), Agricultural Growth and Poverty in China and India

| *Parameter* | *China* | *India* |
|---|---|---|
| Arable land[1] | 109,999 1,000 ha (11.9%) | 157,923 1,000 ha (53.12) |
| Average farm size[2] | 0.6 ha | 1.21 ha |
| Productivity of main crops in kg / ha:[1] | | |
| • Paddy | 6,548.23 | 3,264.41 |
| • Wheat | 4,748.51 | 2,829.95 |
| • Maize | 5,459.79 | 1,958.22 |
| • Groundnut | 3,454.12 | 1,144.02 |
| • Sugarcane | 65,745.94 | 66,130.95 |
| • Soyabean | 1,771.14 | 1,065.15 |
| Share of people living on less than 2005 ppp $1.25 a day (%):[3] | | |
| • 1981 | 84% | 59.8% |
| • 2008 | 13% | 37.4% |
| Average annual agricultural growth rate (%):[4] | | |
| • 1989-99 | 4.3 | 3.3 |
| • 1999-2009 | 4.2 | 2.7 |

*Source:* 1. FAOSTAT, 2. Chand R et al., 2011, 3. Table 2.8, *World Development Indicators 2012*, 4. *Selected Indicators of Food & Agricultural Development in the Asia-Pacific Region 2000-2010*, RAP Publication 2011/21.

of the peasant, without fulfilling which there can be no further advancement. Realisation of peasant empowerment through redistribution of land and the resultant economic prosperity creates the material basis for industrial development based on development of agro-based industries and increasing the consumer base of the industry in general (Brigham, 2000). It gives rise to assertiveness of the hitherto oppressed peasants for equitable implementation of government schemes, sharing of resources like water, electricity, fertilisers etc. which otherwise are cornered by the more affluent sections.

The question may be asked that why small farms, and why not collectivisation as done in the erstwhile socialist countries? It is important to bear in mind that people can understand and will accept a higher form of development only when they have passed and tested all the preceding stages. Promising cake to the hungry when they can envision only bread will only lead to guillotining of even the best-intentioned redistributive programmes. Peasants' hunger today is for land and that must be assuaged first.

Development of the economy on the foundation of redistributive land reforms has implications for poverty reduction. Japan, Taiwan, South Korea as well as the immediate post-revolution Soviet Union, China and Vietnam to mention a few are shining examples of this. Even from India where the implementation of land reforms has otherwise been minimal, wherever these have been implemented with any measure of sincerity, their econometric analysis shows that they have had a positive impact on decreasing poverty (Sethi, 2006; Besly and Burgess, 1998; Deininger, 2007). Increased productivity, poverty reduction and economic growth, all have implications for enhancing the food security of the populations across the globe.

## References

Altieiri M.A. (2009): 'Agroecology, small farms, and food sovereignty.' *Monthly Review*, Vol. 61 (3).

Bakshi A. (2008): Social inequality in land ownership in India: a study with particular reference to West Bengal. *Social Scientist*, Vol. 36 (9/10): pp. 95-116.

Bandyopadhyay D. (2008): 'The Relevance of Land Reform in Post-liberalisation India.' Infochange—News and analysis on social justice and development issues in India. Accessed on 15th March, 2010 from.

Besley T and Robin Burgess (1998): 'Land reform, poverty reduction and growth: evidence from India.' Draft paper, The Development Economics Discussion Paper Series. London School of Economics, September. Accessed on 2 April from http://sticerd.lse.ac.uk/dps/de/dedps13.pdf.

Brigham A.M. (2000): 'Land Reform: A Foundation For Industrial Growth in developing countries?' *Sociological Research Online*, Vol. 5, No. 3, Accessed on 4 April, 2010 from http://www.socresonline.org.uk/5/3/brigham.html.

Chand R., P.A. Lakshmi Prasanna, Aruna Singh (2011): 'Farm size and productivity: understanding the strengths of smallholders and improving their livelihoods.' *Economic and Political Weekly*, Vol. 46 (26 & 27): 5-11.

Deininger K., Songqing Jin, Hari K. Nagarajan (2007): 'Land reforms, poverty reduction, and economic growth: evidence from India', Policy Research Working Paper 4448. The World Bank Development Research Group, Sustainable Rural and Urban Development Team, December 2007.

Fernandes W. (1998): 'Land Acquisition (Amendment) Bill, 1998: Rights of Project-Affected People Ignored.' *Economic and Political Weekly*, Vol. 33 (42/43): pp. 2703-2706.

George Susan (1977): 'The green revolution.' In: *How the Other Half Dies, The Real Reasons for World Hunger*. Penguin Books, London 1977, pp. 113-132.

Geovanni A.C. (1985): 'Farm Size, Land Yields and the Agricultural Production Function: An Analysis for Fifteen Developing Countries. *World Development*, Vol. 13, No. 4, pp. 513-534.

Government of India (2000): 'National agriculture policy'. Department of Agriculture and Co-operation.

Government of India (2010): 'Chapter 8, Agriculture and food management', *Economic Survey 2009-10*, Ministry of Finance.

Government of India a (Undated): 'Working Group Report on Agriculture and Allied Sector.' Planning Commission. Accessed on 1st April, 2010 on http://planningcommission.nic.in/aboutus/committee/wrkgrp/agriallied.pdf.

Government of India b (Undated): 'Chapter IV. Committee On State Agrarian Relations and Unfinished Task of Land Reforms.' VOL. I Draft Report. Ministry of Rural Development, Government of India, New Delhi. Accessed on 12th of March, 2010 from http://southasia.oneworld.net/Files/MRD%20Commitee%20Report.pdf.

Grebmer K.V., Bella Nestorova, Agnes Quisumbing et al. (2009): *Global Hunger Index 2009*. International Food Policy Research Institute, Bonn, Washington D.C., Dublin, October.

Ibid b (Undated): 'Per capita net availability of food grains (Per Annum) in India (1990 to 2007) in Kilo grams (Kgs).' Available from http://www.indiastat.com/table/percapitaavailability/24/fooditems/103/6368/data.aspxaccessed on 2 April 2010.

Ibid c (Undated): 'Major state-wise crude death rates (CDR) by sex in India (2006).' Accessed on 2 April, 2010 from http://www.indiastat.com/table/health/16/deathrate/17792/440998/data.aspx.

Ibid d (Undated): 'Major state-wise maternal mortality rate (MMR) in India (2007).' Accessed on 2 April, 2010 from http://www.indiastat.com/Health/16/MortalityRate/17796/461504/data.aspx.

Ibid e (Undated): 'State-wise women with any anaemia (1998-99).' Accessed on 2 April, 2010 from http://www.indiastat.com/table/economy/8/indicatorsonhealthattainmentanddemography/32211/32902/data.aspx.

Ibid f (Undated): 'State-wise infant mortality rate in India (1990 to 2006).' Accessed on 2 April, 2010 from http://www.indiastat.com/table/health/16/infantmortalityrate/17794/27445/data.aspx

Ibid g (Undated): 'State-wise life expectancy at birth by sex in India (1991-1996, 1992-1996, 1993-1997, 1994-1998, 1995-1999, 1996-2001 and 2001-2006).' Accessed on 2 April, 2010 from http://www.indiastat.com/table/health/16/lifeexpectancy/17797/7698/data.aspx.

Indiastat.com. a (Undated): 'Investment in agriculture as a percentage of GDP in India (1985-1986 to 2001-2002).' Accessed on 2 April, 2010 at http://www.indiastat.com/table/economy/8/agriculture/17943/107992/data.aspx.

Kamat M.S., Sanjay N. Tupe, Manasvi M. Kamat (2007): 'Indian agriculture in the new economic regime, 1971-2003: Empirics based on the Cobb Douglas Production Function.' MPRA Paper No. 6150, posted 07. December. Munich Personal RePEc Archive. Accessed on 2 April, 2010 from http://mpra.ub.uni-muenchen.de/6150/1/MPRA_paper_6150.pdf.

Kipling R. (Undated): 'The masque of plenty.' PoemHunter.com Accessed at http://www.poemhunter.com/best-poems/rudyard-kipling/the-masque-of-plenty/ on 30th April, 2010.

Ladejinsky W. (1964): 'Agrarian Reform in Asia.' *Foreign Affairs*, April, Vol. 42 (3): pp. 445-460.

Menon P., Anil Deolalikar, Anjor Bhaskar (2009): *India state hunger index, comparisons of hunger across states*. International Food Policy Research Institute. Washington, D.C., Bonn, and Riverside, February.

Patnaik U. (2003): 'Food stocks and hunger: the causes of agrarian distress'. *Social Scientist*, Vol. 32 (7-8).

Patnaik U. (2007): 'Theorizing food security and poverty in the era of economic reforms'. In *The Republic of Hunger and Other Essays*. Ed.

Utsa Patnaik, First Edition, March 2007. Three Essays Collective, Gurgaon, p. 154.

Rosset P.M. (1999): 'The multiple functions and benefits of small farm agriculture in the context of global trade negotiations'. Institute for Food and Development Policy, Food First Policy Brief No. 4, September.

Rosset P.M. (2009): 'Fixing our global food system food sovereignty and redistributive land reform.' *Monthly Review*, Vol. 61 (3).

Sainath P. (2010): 'Agricultural Crisis. Nearly 2 Lakh Farm Suicides since 1997.' Indiatogether.org. Accessed on 3 April, 2010 from http://www.indiatogether.org/2010/jan/psa-suicides.htm.

Sainath P. (2012): 'The Food, the Bad and the Ugly'. *The Hindu*, March 22nd.

Saxena N.C. (undated): 'Tenancy Reforms vs Open Market Leasing—What Would Serve the Poor Better?' Planning Commission, Government of India. Available from http://planningcommission.nic.in/reports/articles/ncsxna/index.php?repts=leasing.htm#top on 13th August, 2012.

Sethi M. (2006): 'Land Reform in India: Issues and Challenges'. In *Promised Land: Competing Visions of Agrarian Reform*, Rosset P., Patel R., Courville, M. (eds.), Food First Books, USA, Nov. 2006: 73-92.

Sobhan R. (1993): 'The Economic Impact of Agrarian Reform'. In: *Agrarian Reform and Social Transformation—Preconditions for Development*. Zed Books, London, 1993: pp. 83-100.

Tomich, Thomas P., Peter Kilby, and Bruce F. Johnston (1995): *Transforming Agrarian Economies: Opportunities Seised, Opportunities Missed*. Cornell University Press, Ithaca.

World Food Program (undated): 'Country Profile India'. Accessed on 1st April, 2010 at http://www.wfp.org/countries/india.

# 4

# The Pathology of Food Security

## From False to Correct Diagnosis

### Introduction

It was in 1990-91 that the Manmohan Singh, P. Chidambaram and Montek Singh combine launched the accelerated phase of neo-imperialist globalisation in India, which has been euphemistically called implementation of the new economic policies. The apprehensions regarding the adverse impact of these policies on the overwhelmingly impoverished working masses of India that were echoed from the very beginning, have now come into their full bloom. There is much disquiet about these policies in the country today resulting in dogged resistance by the people in different parts of the country. Acknowledgement of this disquiet as a result of widening inequities and hardships of the people came by in the form of post-haste programmes launched by the UPA Government since its first term in office, for example the National Rural Health Mission (NRHM), Mahatma Gandhi National Rural Employment Guarantee Act (MNREGA) and the much debated 'Food Security Act'. Even the Modi government after having described NREGA as a program designed to dig holes and then filling them, had to beat a retreat post haste. Even as the implementation of these programmes betrays a lack of seriousness of purpose on the part of the Government, the moot point remains that, even if these programmes were to be implemented in right earnest would they rectify the structural factors at the root of the deprivation that pervades our people or would it only amount to applying balm over the festering wounds without even wanting to cure the pathology per se?

The very fact that there is a remarkable unanimity over the development policy paradigm among the different parties of the ruling classes wherever they are in government bears testimony to their wilful omission of the need to understand the 'pathology' beyond the superficial critique of the economic policies to suit their political convenience. Talking of the inequities and imbalances that have arisen as a result of the 'neoliberal' policies, the starkest is the one between 'urban India' and 'rural India'. Even though discussion about it has largely been subdued in the policy circles and certainly in popular public debate, the one factor to which we can attribute the deprivation of our villages, in spite of the booming growth rates of the economy witnessed not so long back , is the deep seated agrarian crisis that stalks rural India today. Not just that the public debate over the agrarian crisis is subdued, but even the debates that we have had on this issue fail to go beyond implicating the 'new economic policies' perfunctorily, while bypassing the crux of the matter.

Understanding the crux of the agrarian distress is essential to any meaningful discussion on the present disquiet over development issues in the country. We argue here to bring forth the centrality of land reforms in resolving the country's agrarian crisis. In the wake of the neoliberal reforms, not only has the trend in implementing land reforms been reversed, but there is sophisticated theorisation around this issue that seeks to make the question of 'land to the tiller' secondary without admitting as much and we feel it is important to effectively counter such attempts. This paper attempts to examine the question of land reforms in the context of the agrarian crisis, as also to thoroughly rebut the theoretical attempts to marginalise the land reforms.

## Agrarian Crisis; Diagnosing the Disease

Tragic though it is, one important result of nearly three lakh farmer suicides in the country over two and a half and a half decades of 'neoliberal' economic reforms is, that it has obviated the need to prove the existence of a massive agrarian crisis in the country. The debate now is about what constitutes the agrarian crisis and what is the way out? To the ruling establishment the real crisis of Indian agriculture is the 'Deceleration in Agricultural Growth' and 'Technology Generation and Dissemination' (Planning Commission, Agriculture Strategy for the 11th Plan). A second view from within the establishment, that of the Parliamentary Left is that the present agrarian crisis is essentially the result of policies of 'economic reforms' that have dominated the discourse in much of the last two decades. The second view emphasises the role of Government's fiscal policies affecting the agricultural sector, cutting back of rural development expenditure, opening up of the agricultural sector to international trade, the drying up of institutional credit to agriculture, increasing inviability of agriculture and the resultant loss of jobs in the agricultural sector and policy initiatives inviting the corporate sector to take up farming in a big way through contract farming (Pillai, 2007; Patnaik, 2007a). The rest of the voices from within the establishment vary between relative mixtures of these two views.

The question of land reforms, i.e. land to the tiller, while being obsolete to the former view, has become nothing more than a footnote for the Parliamentary Left—a footnote because of the way it is prioritised in their discourse and emphasised in their policy prescriptions (Ibid). Their talking of the issue of land reforms appears more as an apology for their claim to being 'Left' than being a matter of commitment to be pursued in the form of mass mobilisation of the small, marginal and the landless peasantry. In fact in 2006, the CPM-led West

Bengal Government brought the Land Reforms Amendment Bill to the State Assembly to relax the land ceiling provisions for the industries (*Express News Service*, 2010). The bill was withdrawn post-haste owing to opposition from the Left block MLAs which seemed more in keeping with the consideration for the assembly elections due in 2011 than any kind of ideological opposition.

The developments in Nandigram and Singur, where prime agricultural land was forcibly acquired to subserve the business interests of the corporate houses, resulting in much violence and loss of lives, exposed the truth of their frustration with slogans of the past only too well. What made these events appear so stark is the fact that with the passage of time perhaps the Parliamentary Left itself feels less constrained by the ideological pretences of the past, even though the people outside West Bengal who were untouched by the experience of the 'Left Front' rule in Bengal, looked at this 'Left' with some hope from amongst all other parliamentary political parties. The subsequent developments in Lalgarh have only served to undo any such expectations that may still have been left of them.

These events were no misguided policy adventures of the 'Left Front' Government that ruled West Bengal for over 30 years but a logical culmination of ideological deviation aimed at adjusting to parliamentary politics. The exigencies of parliamentary politics have made the mainstream Left place the issue of land reforms also purely within the framework of bourgeois reform, i.e. bereft of militant mobilisation of peasantry that the implementation of any meaningful land reforms necessarily entails.

The theoretical formulations postulated by the ideologues of this Left also meander around the issue of land reforms in a manner as to bring forth an action programme that is in conformity with the parliamentary process of government formation. Unlike the mainstream ruling establishment, to which the slogan of 'land to the tiller' is an outdated idea, the mainstream Left still theorises the need for redistributive land reforms while doing exactly what other bourgeois parties do. This sophisticated duality in words and deeds tends to create confusion over the relevance of 'land reforms' and makes it incumbent upon us to have a closer look at some of their theoretical formulations in the next section of this paper.

Meanwhile, talking of the political economy of the agrarian crisis and keeping the question of land reforms subdued, is like cutting on the margins of the crisis while keeping the core intact. So what really is the core and why does it need to be kept intact?

The answer to this question brings us to the third view of the agrarian crisis. This view holds the structural imbalances in Indian agriculture categorised by the skewed distribution of land in the main and the additional infirmities created by the imposition of neoliberal economic policies on this substratum as being central to understanding the political economy of agrarian distress in India. Though a minority view, this is a view that is central to the ideology of the revolutionary or non-mainstream or extreme Left and has gained some ascendency of late with a rising tide of people's resistance against the neoliberal development paradigm that has increasingly sought to displace the people from their land.

## A Closer Look at the Theorisation of the Agrarian Crisis and Land Reforms by the Mainstream Left

We draw here on the opinions expressed by S. Ramachandran Pillai, President of the Communist Party of India (Marxist) (CPM)-led All India Kisan Sabha and member of the polit bureau of the CPM and by Utsa Patnaik, who is widely recognised as an authority on the issues of 'agrarian crisis', 'food security' and 'poverty' and closely identifies with the CPM.

Both the authors have forcefully argued that the aforementioned neoliberal policies of different governments at the Centre are central to the present agrarian crisis. Both have also conceded the importance of implementing land reforms in alleviating the hardships of the small and marginal peasants. However, it is in the manner in which 'land reforms' are leveraged vis-à-vis the imperative for rolling back of the neoliberal policies that the crucial difference is made, and to justify this difference an analysis of principal societal contradictions in India is presented which needs to be mentioned here in some detail.

Patnaik has argued that while during the colonial period the principal contradiction was between 'the Indian people as a whole, and imperialism and its local comprador allies' (Patnaik, 2007a: 208), after independence, the principal contradiction came about to be 'between the mass of the working peasantry and labourers on the one hand, and the minority of landlords, traders and moneylenders on the other who monopolised control over land and money-capital', in the background of imperialism's retreat internationally (Ibid: 209). Independence is said to have afforded an opportunity for 'development of capitalism in agriculture' due to 'expansionary policies of autonomous national development' that 'were followed during 1950 to 1990 in India' which were 'geared to the expanding internal market.' This is said to have led to 'some prosperity, though very unequally shared, in the agrarian sphere' (Ibid: 228).

However, in the context of the implementation of neoliberal economic reforms the principal contradiction is once again said to be rapidly shifting towards that between 'the mass of Indian people, and the new imperialism' (Ibid: 226). In the agrarian sphere the fast emerging principal contradiction is 'between all the peasant classes in rural areas on the one hand, and imperialism with its local landed collaborators on the other.' (Ibid). Patnaik adds that, 'This does not mean that earlier contradictions have ceased to be important but only that they have begun to move to a subordinate or secondary position, in the sense that the nature of the emerging new contradiction determines the nature and path of the land question, and all other contradictions' (Ibid).

The author says further that this does not amount to the land question 'being put on the back burner' (Ibid: 227). It is stated that, 'Not only can it (land question) never be separated from the fight against imperialist globalisation, this fight is a necessary condition for any advance on the land question.'

Before we progress any further, it is important to absorb the implications of these profound statements. The question that need be asked here is, who were imperialism's 'local comprador allies' during the colonial period and what happened to them after independence. They could not have disappeared or changed character overnight. It appears from the slant of the formulations presented above that the indigenous industrial houses (the Tatas, Birlas, Singhanias and Bajajs) who had prospered under the tutelage of the British and the Congress Party that was financed by these houses, were beyond the pale of the term 'local comprador allies' of the British, in spite of the fact that distinguished members of the inudstrial houses and the congress party served on the Viceroy's Executive Council at different points in time. This mantle seems to have fallen on a 'minority of landlords, traders and moneylenders who monopolised control over land and money-capital', while the former ushered in 'development of capitalism in agriculture' and 'expansionary policies of autonomous national development' between 1950 to 1990. If this indeed is true then they can without any hesitation be categorised as 'Nationalist Bourgeoisie.'

Such a formulation provided the mainstream Left parties the ideological rationale to compete and collaborate with the parties of the 'national bourgeoisie' for capturing state power through parliamentary means. This had an important bearing on the most burning question of agrarian India, 'the question of land'. As a first step, the central leadership of the then united Communist Party of India betrayed the 'Telengana Armed Peasant Uprising' (1946-51) that was led by the regional leadership of the Party (Ram, 1973). The Telengana Peasant Uprising represented the first independent revolutionary trend in the Indian Communist movement that had a long term vision and strategy. More importantly, it presented a revolutionary alternative for resolving the land question before the toiling peasantry in the rest of newly independent India. After the Telengana uprising there was a pressing imperative for the ruling classes of the country to bring the question of 'land' within the safe confines of bourgeois reform. Little wonder then that Vinoba Bhave launched his 'Bhoodan Andolan' form Pochampalli village in Telengana in 1951 after the 'Police Action' by the Indian State had drowned the uprising in a blood bath.

With their new found 'pragmatism' leading the Communists to ally with the system, the land question was forfeited to the realm of 'land reform laws' that were to be framed and implemented by the feudal landlords and bureaucratic bourgeoisie well entrenched in the legislature and the State machinery. Little wonder then that their fate has been as we know it, 'dismal'. The saga of betrayal of the revolutionary peasantry by the Parliamentary Left was once again to be repeated in 1967 during the Naxalbari peasant uprising, by which time the Left had already tasted state power in Kerala and was a coalition partner in the 'United Front Government' in West Bengal.

It should be recalled here that from the point of Marxist phraseology 'land reform' is essentially a 'bourgeois democratic reform' which was accomplished in the advanced capitalist countries by the nationalist bourgeoisie. In the context of the developing countries like India it has been argued that since the local bureaucratic bourgeoisie rules in alliance with the feudal class, both of which are comprador in character, it is incapable of carrying out this democratic reform. However, rationalising the dominant section of the Indian bourgeoisie as nationalist, that has largely been committed to capitalist development of agriculture in India creates the scope, at least in theory, of peacefully cooperating or contesting with it, within the confines of a parliamentary system to bring about greater democratisation of agrarian relations. The aberrations of such a 'capitalist development', however glaring, can then be projected as a rectifiable aspect of agrarian development without entailing any radical upheaval. Likewise, the minority of 'landlords, traders and moneylenders' can be handled if state power can be captured through electoral mobilisation of the oppressed masses; agitational mobilisation of the same can come in as occasional fillers towards the same end. But then the history of parliamentary deviation of the Left from across the world is replete with fantastic illusions and even greater liquidation of the revolutionary potential of the masses.

## The Change of 'Principal Contradiction'?

The question that arises naturally as a corollary to the above conclusions is that if the ruling alliance in India brought about 'development of capitalism in agriculture' in the mode of 'autonomous national development' then whose responsibility is it to implement of the 'neoliberal economic reforms'? These reforms have once again brought about a shift in the principal contradiction wherein imperialism once again has become the main enemy of the Indian people, pushing the question of 'land reforms' to the status of a secondary contradiction. To this the answer that is presented is that 'imperialist globalisation of our agriculture' has been aided by 'the comprador elements in government placed in key decision-making positions and they have the support of comprador elements of the domestic landlords (emphasis ours)' (Ibid: 230).

We need to mark the words; it is only *'comprador elements'* in the government and domestic landlords and not comprador classes. Even the earlier 'minority of landlords, traders and moneylenders' that existed after independence, has got reduced to just 'comprador elements', perhaps as a result of the 'capitalist development of agriculture'. If this is indeed true, then we shall also have to presume that the bulk of the 'nationalist bourgeoisie' and landlord classes (now transformed into capitalist farmers) abdicated their authority to 'comprador elements' that came to occupy important positions in government. It allowed these elements to tear down the 'autonomous national development' so painstakingly built by them, bringing the country so close to imperialist subjugation and that too at an enormous cost to the toiling masses of the country (with more than 200,000 farmers having directly committed suicide owing to the agrarian crisis in the country). The million dollar question is—is this feasible?

Our understanding is that it will be simplistic to presume so. The fact is that India's ruling classes have had a comprador character in the main. So long as there was the 'Soviet Social Imperialist' camp in world politics as a countervailing force to the US led Western imperialism, it enabled the comprador ruling classes of India to play one against the other in order to win favours and concessions weaving illusions of 'autonomy' in the process. The demise of 'Soviet Social Imperialism' afforded the more reactionary segment of our ruling classes the opplortunity to openly align themselves with the US led imperialism. With the growing emergence of multipolarity in world politics, these alignments are bound to change again.

However, the insistence of our friends from the mainstream Left on the existence of only 'comprador elements' while denying the comprador nature of the ruling classes per se, is designed to a purpose. If the task at hand is only of defeating the 'comprador elements', then one can always align with the 'nationalist section' of the ruling classes, which leaves ample scope for various kinds of electoral alliances with different parties of the ruling classes, in an attempt at government formation, seemingly to reverse the current policy paradigm. This however is a tall order. Since 1990, the year since when neoliberal policies started undermining India's 'autonomous capitalist development', different coalitions involving almost all the parliamentary parties have come to power at the Centre, including coalitions in which the Parliamentary Left was prominently involved. Not even one of these governments differed from the other in its commitment to implementing the neoliberal policies. The track records of the Left Front Government in West Bengal and the Left Democratic Front Governments in Kerala have also been much the same. The fact is that the Parliamentary Left now is very much a part of the ruling class, its protestations notwithstanding.

The principal contradiction of the Indian people with imperialism post-1947 is not new; rather for much of the post-war history, both the US led Western imperialism and the 'Soviet Social Imperialism' vied with each other for domination over the developing World, India included, in collaboration with the comprador ruling classes of these countries. The areas in which the dominance of these imperialisms got reflected may have been different; while the Soviet Social imperialism had a major presence in the development of heavy industries and defence, US led imperialism dominated in private industry and agriculture, besides having a pervasive influence in technical higher education.

The entire 'Green Revolution' was inspired by the private US foundations and the US agribusiness corporations backed and supported by the US Government (George, 1977). More than develop 'capitalism in agriculture' in India, it led to far more disproportionate and pervasive controls for the Western transnational corporations in the rural economy of India, than bolstering our food security. Besides worsening the land relations in rural India, including the agriculturally more prosperous areas of Punjab, Haryana and Western Uttar Pradesh, it led to the perpetual dependence of our farmers for seeds, fertilisers, insecticides and technological support on the Western transnationals through agricultural extension services guided by their experts (Chakravarti, 1973; Cleaver, 1972). Much of the research agenda of Indian agricultural universities came to be dictated by them to support the cultivation of the new hybrid varieties, instead of developing the indigenous varieties of seeds better suited to the local agro-climatic conditions. If anything, the 'Green Revolution' led to growth of simple commodity production over the prevailing semi-feudal relations of production in agriculture, barring of course the growth of some capitalist farmers in agriculturally better suited regions of primarily Punjab, Haryana and Western Uttar Pradesh (Sarkar, 2008).

Any shift in the principal contradiction notwithstanding, the fact is that land still is the main rallying point for the small and marginal farmers and the landless agricultural labourers who constitute the overwhelming bulk of the peasantry. No doubt that the neoliberal policies have spelt doom for agriculture in the country, and to the extent diminished productivity reduces employment opportunities in agriculture, they have affected the lot of the small and marginal farmers and the agricultural workers; however they have spelt doom for the middle and a section of the rich peasantry in the main that produce for the market. For subsistence farmers, it is the security over land that still is the main issue. Fierce resistance to eviction from their land by the people in POSCO, Kalinganagar, Niyamgiri, Nandigram and Singur in West Bengal, parts of Central India, Jharkhand, Raigad and Jaitapur in Maharashtra bear testimony to this. Under the circumstances, making the question of land 'secondary' amounts to precisely what Patnaik tries to preempt, i.e. land struggles being 'put on the back burner.'

## Policy Implications of Different Views on the Agrarian Crisis

It is only natural that the solution to the agrarian crisis will emerge from the way it is conceptualised. These above mentioned three views of the way agrarian crisis is viewed in India have led to different set of solutions for it.

### Implications of 'Productivity' Centred View of Agrarian Crisis

According to the view of the ruling establishment that prioritises the question of 'productivity' and 'technological inputs', the logical answers lie in encouraging the corporate sector in different segments of agricultural activity to increase productivity by investing capital in technology-intensive cultivation on land acquired either directly or indirectly through an agency of the government or contracted from peasants. Restructuring the research priorities and the agricultural research institutes to invent and innovate technology geared to achieve higher productivity, disseminating this technology among the farmers, implementing various irrigation projects including mega dams, rationalising subsidies in agriculture and improving agricultural support services are some other measures that are often discussed. The main thrust however appears to be towards corporate takeover of agriculture that is viewed as the all encompassing panacea that will result in radical transformation of Indian agriculture. If the experience of the 'Green Revolution' and the general industrial development of the country, especially during the years of neoliberal reforms is anything to go by, this strategy would result in importing Western technology and methods of farming lock, stock and barrel without contextualising them to the social, economic and political conditions in our country. In fact, in February 2010, the Congress led UPA government at the Centre quietly paved the way for the signing of the Memorandum of Understanding with the US Government on 'Agriculture Cooperation and Food Security' aimed at promoting the privatisation of agricultural extension services and facilitating collaboration between American agribusiness and the Indian farm sector (Parsai, 2010).

As to placating the distressed farmers, announcements of loan waivers and the public relations exercise in the form of visiting the distressed farm households by the leaders of the ruling alliance at the Centre are considered sufficient. What remains unsaid, but very much implied in policy is that peasant agriculture is an outmoded fetter to increasing productivity and the ruination of peasant households may well be an unavoidable price of progress. Nothing else would explain the profound apathy of the establishment that has been reserved for the nearly three lakh farm suicides in the country. According to the National Crime Records Bureau in 2008, the year the first UPA government at the centre declared its farm loan waiver scheme, 16,196 farmers committed suicide in the country. The pogrom against peasant agriculture is progressing well indeed. Between just the census of 1991 and that of 2001, nearly 8 million cultivators quit farming (Sainath, 2010) and at the time of writing 2011 Census was slated to show that this figure has only got much more inflated over the last decade. Talking to newspersons at his residence on September 6, 2010, the then Prime Minister Dr. Manmohan Singh said that, 'The only way we can raise our heads above poverty is for more people to be taken out of agriculture' (Varadharajan, 2010).

Needless to say that this is a deeply flawed strategy, for alleviating the agrarian crisis is more than merely increasing the productivity; it is about alleviating the lot of the people dependent on agriculture which in 2004-05 amounted to 52.1% of our workforce (GOI, 2009-10). Given the extent of unemployment, any sizable displacement of workforce from agriculture is unlikely to be absorbed by the non-agricultural sectors of the economy. There are other constraints too. With nearly 70% of our population still living in the rural areas there is no alternative to adopting a strategy for rejuvenating agriculture that first and foremost takes into consideration the material well-being of the people dependent on it. Their decimation would effectively mean the decimation of the market for our industrial production. What will increased productivity of agriculture mean if ultimately the consumers do not have the power to purchase either the food or the products of the industries supplied by agriculture?

As to the question of increasing productivity, it need not necessarily be viewed as conflicting with the well-being of the farmers and the outmoded means of production in agriculture when there is a solution to both. Table 4.1 below shows the area sown more than once as a proportion of the total cropped area from 2000-01 to 2006-07. It can be seen that only about a fourth of the total cropped area in the country is sown more than once. If the average duration of one crop is taken to be four months, then nearly three-fourths of our total cropped land goes waste for nearly eight months in a year. Such a colossal waste of the land resource is possible only in a semi-feudal agrarian economy like ours. Further, only about 32.3% of India's agricultural land had access to irrigation in 2001 (IFFCO, 2004). This clearly shows the tremendous potential of increasing the productivity of our total agricultural land without having the need to 'take people out of agriculture' to 'raise our heads above poverty'. But of course this will entail on the part of the government the resolve to give the kind of attention for the development of agriculture that it deserves.

Simultaneously, we need to develop our industrial base, especially the industries that will be able to consume raw materials supplied by agriculture such that there is little conflict between industrialisation and agricultural development and the farmers producing cash crops are not rendered vulnerable to the vagaries of international price fluctuations.

Table 4.1: Area Sown More than Once as a Proportion of Total Cropped Area ('000 hectares)

| *Year* | *Area sown more than once* | *Total cropped area* | *Proportion of area sown more than once to total cropped area (%).* |
|---|---|---|---|
| 2000-01 | 43,980 | 185,344 | 23.7 |
| 2001-02 | 48,268 | 189,680 | 25.44 |
| 2002-03 | 42,939 | 175,530 | 24.5 |
| 2003-04 | 49,137 | 190,082 | 25.8 |
| 2004-05 | 50,090 | 191,164 | 26.2 |
| 2005-06 | 50,800 | 192,611 | 26.4 |
| 2006-07 | 53,425 | 193,723 | 27.6 |

*Source:* Pattern of land utilisation—All India, Data Bank on Agriculture and Allied Sectors, Planning Commission, Government of India.

## Implications of 'Neoliberal' Reforms-Oriented View of Agrarian Crisis

The policy implications of the view propounded by the Parliamentary Left are, that the neoliberal reforms in the agricultural sector be rolled back, there should be increased budgetary support for agriculture and rural infrastructure development to make peasant agriculture viable, easier 'institutional credit facilities for the small and marginal farmers, remunerative prices for agricultural produce, protecting the farmers from unfair competition from the highly subsidised agricultural produce from the West, prioritising agricultural research to meet the needs of the peasant agriculture, launching of massive employment generation schemes in the rural areas and strengthening of the public distribution system to secure the food security of the poor. These above measures besides being within the scheme of the liberal parliamentary democracy would avoid inconvenient stirring up of any major or fundamental shift in the balance of class forces in the society.

Apart from these measures there are some other important suggestions that are made by those subscribing to primacy of 'neoliberal' reforms in the creation of the agrarian crisis. These are:

- Forming associations of small agricultural producers to reap the benefits of 'large scale production' and to make agriculture viable and profitable (Patnaik, 2007a: 231). What is being suggested is the formation of production collectives of small peasants.
- Formation of associations of agricultural labourers which can 'jointly take land on lease from large owners who are increasingly finding it unprofitable to cultivate directly' (Ibid).
- Measures such as the State contracting for three to five-year periods with farmers' groups and associations where the State provides security for produce against market price fluctuations in return for the peasants undertaking to sell a predetermined quantum of their produce to the State (Ibid: 232).
- Ensuring implementation of minimum wages for the agricultural labourers and various social security measures (Pillai, 2007).
- 'Most importantly, the unfinished tasks of land reforms in most states should be taken ahead by breaking land monopoly, vesting ceiling surplus land and redistribution of land among the landless households' (Ibid).
- Ushering in rapid industrialisation wherein surplus labour from agriculture can be absorbed (Ibid).

The important thing to bear in mind is that implementing solutions for as vexed a crisis as the present agrarian distress is not just a technical issue of policy formulation, but is tempered in the harsh realities of the power relations in the society. Empowering the dispossessed essentially entails disempowering the powerful, to ensure that they are not able to expropriate the dispossessed. In a nutshell, it means, changing the power relations in the society. We have seen form experience over the years that it is the powerful that corner the fruits of even the most magnanimous of the policy initiatives.

In agrarian India, the one thing that defines social power is the ownership of land, and this makes it incumbent upon us to register here the arrangement of forces in agrarian India vis-à-vis ownership of land. Table 4.2 below gives the number and the area operated by the size of operational holdings for the year 2000-01. It can be seen from the Table that the small and marginal holdings constitute 81.8% of the total holdings while accounting for only 40% of the area, while the rest account for 18.2% of the holdings and corner 61.1% of the area. Of this also the top 6.5% occupy 37% of land (Planning Commission, Agricultural data bank). Further, from 1971-72 to 1991-92 the percentage of landless rural households increased

Table 4.2: Number and the Area Operated by the Size of Operational Holdings

| *Category of holding* | *Number of operational holdings (`000 Number)* | *Area operated (`000 hectares)* |
|---|---|---|
| Marginal (< 1 hectare) | 75,390 (62.9) | 29,807 (18.7) |
| Small (1.0 to 2.0 hectares) | 22,687 (18.9) | 32,128 (20.2) |
| Semi-medium (2-4 hectares) | 14,014 (11.7) | 38,174 (23.9) |
| Medium (4 to 10 hectares) | 6,573 (05.5) | 38,194 (24.0) |
| Large ( > 10 hectares) | 1,230 (01.0) | 21,092 (13.2) |

*Source:* Distribution of Operational Holdings—All India, Agricultural data bank, Planning Commission of India, Government of India. The figures in parentheses are percentages.

from 9.6 to 11.3 while that of near landless households (operational holding < 1 hectare) increased from 45.8% to 62.8%. If anything, this situation has only worsened since the initiation of macroeconomic policy changes since 1991, which according to a report of the Planning Commission, has been directly responsible for 'increasing rural unrest and 'extremist' violence in 220 districts of the country' (GoI, Ministry of Rural Development).

This highly skewed distribution of land, coupled with continuing direct/indirect dependence of nearly two-third of the population on agriculture and poor development of the means of production have ensured continuance of semi-feudal relations of production in agriculture (Sarkar, 2008). The given milieu ensures the economic dependence of the small and marginal farmers and the landless on landlords, rich peasants and moneylending traders. Landed gentry ensures its affluence not by enhancing the productivity of its land resource as much, as by extracting usurious surplus by exploiting the labour of the dependent sections. Economic dominance automatically ensures social, political and cultural domination as well. This section also has its representatives in the government bureaucracy and police. It is in the interest of the landed class to ensure conditions that perpetuate their domination and as such it is highly intolerant of any political organisation of the dispossessed (formation of collectives is a political process) that may challenge or erode their authority. The alliance of this class with the bureaucratic bourgeoisie and imperialism further strengthen its advantaged social, economic and political position.

Formation of small producer and landless labourer associations is easier said than done. Conceiving themselves as a collective requires a much higher level of political consciousness, the foundation for which cannot be laid till the land hunger of the small and marginal peasant and the landless is satisfied. Even if this consciousness were to materialise somehow, to what extent formation of collectives of small producers and agricultural labourers, without breaking the monopoly of the landlords on land, will succeed in changing the power relations in agrarian India? Can the disempowered peasantry ensure that the policy initiatives being so enthusiastically propagated by the Parliamentary Left will have their desired effect? The fate of the Mahatma Gandhi National Rural Employment Guarantee Act and the watering down of the 'Food Security Act' are there before us as examples.

Even as to the suggestion that the 'unfinished tasks of land reforms be taken ahead', can this suggestion be left at just this much without discussing the reasons as to why they have not been implemented in the years of history of independent India's 'democratic' polity. What is it that is new in our 'so-called' democratic system which should give the hope to the 'land hungry' that this time around their demands will be met? If at all, the situation is far worse than ever before with even the So to say 'progressive' state governments like the erstwhile Left Front government of West Bengal which tried to reverse the land ceiling laws and the ruling combine at the Centre launching 'Operation Green Hunt' against the sons of the soil to vacate their lands for corporate loot of their resources.

We can take some lessons from the implementation of the Constitutional provision for giving 'reservations' to the oppressed castes. Constitutional reservations are quintessentially a reform aimed at co-opting the better off sections of the oppressed castes into the ruling elite while leaving the traditional power structure untouched, yet they have remained woefully unfulfilled till date. Land reforms strike at the very root of the traditional power structure of our society; they entail overthrowing the present power structure and substituting it with that controlled by the labouring masses. Can such a change be conceived merely through the power of the vote, that too in a country of more than a billion people?

## Rationale of Land Reforms Being at the Core of the Agrarian Crisis

The proposition of the revolutionary/non-mainstream/extreme Left, which holds the unfinished task of the land reforms to be at the centre of the agrarian crisis, though still not part of the dominant discourse, is increasingly creating a wider space for itself. It has indeed been pushed to the centre stage as a result of numerous struggles by the peasantry in different parts of the country against the development policies of the government that have threatened to displace the people from their lands and livelihood. This view holds that one sided emphasis on 'neoliberal reforms' without emphasising the preeminence of 'land reforms' amounts to merely treating the symptoms of the agrarian crisis without addressing the principal cause of the overall stagnation in agriculture. Even though the phenomenon of peasant suicides is something that is the peculiar result of the reform policies affecting the agriculture, the crisis of the agrarian sector goes much beyond farmer suicides alone.

Without wanting to diminish the significance of the neoliberal reforms in aggravating the agrarian crisis in the country in any way, one needs to nevertheless answer the question—was there no crisis in the farm sector before the era of neoliberal reforms or is it that the neoliberal reforms only added insult to injury by further sharpening the class divide in the production base of agriculture in the country, which was anyway heavily tilted in favour of the big landholders?

To answer this, we need to look at what was happening to the rural economy before the reforms. Even before the reforms were launched, poverty in rural India, as found in the data collected in the various rounds of the NSSO, had already been rising and had assumed massive proportions. Between 1973 and 1993-94, calculating by direct method, the proportion of rural population living below the poverty line first dipped from 72% in 1973-74 to 65.5% in 1977-78, but then again increased sharply to 70% in 1983. This trend continued to register a high of 74.5% in 1993-94 (Table 4.3) (Patnaik, 2007b).

Table 4.3: The Rural Poor as Percentage of Rural Population in India

| *Round No.* | *28 (1973-74)* | *32 (1977-78)* | *38 (1983)* | *50 (1993-94)* | *55 (1999-00)* | *61 (2004-05)* |
|---|---|---|---|---|---|---|
| Direct method MPCE giving 2,400 kcal, ₹ (poverty line) | 56* | 67 | 120 | 325 | 565 | 790 |
| Percent below poverty line | 72* | 65.5 | 70 | 74.5 | 74.5 (77.5) | 87.0 |

*Source:* Utsa Patnaik (2007). Note: 2200 calories was the actual norm accessible with ₹ 49 MPCE, that was set as the poverty line in 1973-74. For the 2,400 calorie norm ₹ 56 was required as the poverty line, and about 72% of persons were below this.

Table 4.4 shows the per capita net output and availability of food grains in India in the pre-reform years (Patnaik, 2003). Not only are these levels much below the levels of output and availability in British India at the turn of the 20th century (201.1 and 199 kgs respectively in 1897-1902), but are not even sufficient to sustain a poverty line level consumption of calories (2,400 for rural and 2,100 for urban areas) for all Indians. It needs to be emphasised here that the figures of 2,400 and 2,100 calories are only averages. It is obviously not true that all Indians consumed just this much.

While the small percentage of the affluent had consumption levels matching those of the West, the poor consumed even less than the levels at poverty line, which has been correctly described as destitution line by some authors. These facts make the situation really precarious.

Table 4.4: Annual Per Capita Output, Imports and Availability of Foodgrains 1950-51 to 1989-90 in Kilograms

| *Period* | *Net cereals output* | *Net import* | *Change in stocks* | *Net annual availability of food grains per capita* | | | |
|---|---|---|---|---|---|---|---|
| | | | | *Cereals* | *Pulses* | *Total* | *Pulses/ Total, %* |
| 1951-55 | 122.74 | 6.06 | –0.33 | 129.13 | 23.59 | 152.72 | 15.4 |
| 1956-60 | 121.81 | 8.30 | –5.82 | 135.93 | 24.84 | 160.77 | 15.5 |
| 1961-65 | 135.02 | 10.99 | –0.31 | 146.32 | 22.12 | 168.44 | 13.1 |
| 1966-70 | 129.83 | 12.45 | 1.34 | 140.94 | 17.78 | 158.72 | 11.2 |
| 1971-75 | 135.48 | 6.17 | 1.11 | 140.54 | 15.47 | 156.01 | 9.9 |
| 1976-80 | 147.13 | –0.77 | 0.57 | 145.79 | 15.63 | 161.42 | 9.7 |
| 1981-85 | 153.18 | 2.30 | 3.54 | 151.95 | 14.34 | 166.29 | 8.6 |
| 1986-90 | 155.95 | 0.65 | –1.56 | 158.16 | 14.61 | 172.77 | 8.5 |
| Change in per capita availability, percent | | | | | | | |
| 1951-55 to 1971-75 | | | 2.15 | | | | |
| 1971-75 to 1986-90 | | | 10.74 | | | | |
| Total change 1951-55 to 1986-90 | | | 13.12 | | | | |

*Source:* Utsa Patnaik (2003).

In fact, for Indian agriculture, the entire period before the commencement of the reforms was nothing short of a battle extending from one crisis to another. Not only that the whole 'Green Revolution' was set in the face of an acute food crisis, but also it ended up fuelling the present one as well. In 1965-66, India was in the throes of yet another famine after a period of drought and dependent on the US Food for Peace shipments. As already mentioned, rather than being an indigenous solution to the backwardness of agriculture in India, the 'Green Revolution' was a western export tempered in the conditions attached to the aid (George, 1977: 118). Contextualising the import of 'Green Revolution', Susan George writes, 'There seems little doubt, however, that aside from its contributions to the profit side of MNC business ledgers, it has also been viewed by the various American interests pushing it as an alternative to land reform and to the social change reform would require. Since land reform is the only other way to increase food production, these experts are willing to settle for the lesser of the two evils' (Ibid: 125). So much then for the 'autonomous national development'.

Further, some of the leading protagonists of the 'Green Revolution' recognised that 'the dramatic gains in income being realised by farmers who are able to use the new seeds abruptly widens the gap in living standards, and the consequent conflicts, between them and those who are still tied to traditional husbandry practices.' What was left unexplained was 'why only a few had been able to use the new seeds?' (Ibid)

From Tables 4.4 and 4.5 it can be seen that the 'Green Revolution' hardly solved India's food crisis, which was rooted in the more fundamental issues of structural imbalances like the 'skewed ownership of land.' Instead, all that the 'Green Revolution' succeeded in achieving was tiding over the precipitous crisis in food production by bringing about a shift from 'hunger in the midst of absolute scarcity of food' to 'hunger in the midst of relatively better food production' consequent upon the introduction of high yielding varieties of cereals. However, the kind of input intensive (high use of fertilisers, irrigation and pesticides) cultivation that these seeds required, soon led to the plateauing and decline in the growth rates of agricultural production in the country in the absence of desired development in rural infrastructure.

Table 4.5: Growth Rate in Output of Various Crop Categories of Agriculture (Gross Value of Output at 1999-2000 Price)

| *Period* | *Cereals* | *Pulses and oil seeds* | *Fruits and vegetables* | *Other crops* | *All crops* |
|---|---|---|---|---|---|
| 1951-52 to 1967-68 (Pre-Green Revolution period) | 4.19 | 2.98 | 2.67 | 2.42 | 3.00 |
| 1968-69 to 1980-81 (Green Revolution period) | 3.43 | 0.97 | 4.82 | 2.98 | 3.00 |
| 1981-81 to 1990-91 (Wider technology dissemination period) | 3.52 | 5.41 | 2.84 | 1.71 | 2.97 |
| 1991-92 to 1996-97 (Early reforms period) | 2.36 | 2.92 | 6.07 | 2.18 | 3.09 |
| 1997-98 to 2001-02 (Ninth Plan period) | 1.49 | –1.43 | 4.11 | 3.82 | 2.25 |
| 2002-03 to 2006-07 (Tenth plan period) | 1.28 | 4.29 | 2.97 | 3.58 | 2.46 |

*Source:* Dhas Albert Christopher (2009).

In fact, as can be seen from Table 4.5, the growth rate in the production of cereals in the country was lower in the Green Revolution period and the wider technology dissemination period of the 1980s than even the pre-Green Revolution period. Towards the end of the 20th century and the beginning of the 21st century the fall in growth rates of cereals is precipitous indeed falling even below the population growth rates. Apart from the cereals there is also a decline in the production of fruits and vegetables as well (Christopher, 2009).

Another factor that makes us believe that the present agrarian crisis is a continuation of the earlier crisis in agriculture prevalent before the reform years is the fact that the investment in agriculture and spending in rural development is a phenomenon identifiable with the policy establishment in the country since 1947 itself and not necessarily a contribution of the economic reforms. In a country where 80% of the people still derived their income from agriculture, the First Five Year Plan devoted barely 17% of the outlay for agriculture (Sanyal, 1983). Table 4.6 clearly shows that the decline in investment in agriculture had started from much earlier on (Christopher, 2009).

Table 4.6: Trends in Share of Agriculture and Allied Sectors in India's GDP

| *Period* | *1950/ 51* | *1960/ 61* | *1970/ 71* | *1980/ 81* | *1990/ 91* | *2000/ 01* | *2005/ 06* | *2007/ 08* |
|---|---|---|---|---|---|---|---|---|
| % share | 56.60 | 52.48 | 46.00 | 39.93 | 34.04 | 26.18 | 21.65 | 17.8 |

*Source:* Dhas Albert Christopher (2009).

The pervasiveness of international agribusiness in Indian agriculture may have qualitatively increased with the commencement of the neoliberal reforms, but certainly did not start from this time on. Susan George writes, in 1965-66 'the US and the World Bank did indeed put a great deal of pressure on India'. *The New York Times* reported that you could 'call them strings, call them conditions' or anything else, India had no choice but to accept America's terms for resuming the Food for Peace programme. These conditions consisted largely in greater freedom for US private investment in general and for the American management of India's fertiliser industry in particular... American businessmen insisted on importing all the necessary machines and equipment for fertiliser plants under construction, even though India could have provided some of them' (George, 1977: 118). Besides fertilisers, the high yielding varieties increased India's dependence on the international agribusiness for pesticides, high-pressure sprayers, mechanical dryers for crops and motorised equipment, etc. all of which were necessary adjuncts for the cultivation of the high yielding varieties (Ibid: 118). Is it not reasonable to presume then that the earlier phase of imperialist inroads had only laid the foundation for the present accelerated phase of imperialist encroachment, rather than it being a de-novo phenomenon post-1990?

India's ruling elite, beholden as they are to the technological superiority of their western role models have tried to tide over the agricultural crisis by resorting to borrowed technology in the past and the same is at the root of the renewed calls for a 'second Green Revolution' (*Business Standard*, 2006; Dorin, 2000; Subramanian, 2010; FAO, 2006). All that can be said of such ill-conceived initiatives is that they are likely to fail again, as they did in the past as long as the structural constraints due to iniquitous ownership of land continue to sustain semi-feudal relations of production in agriculture in India. Modern agricultural outputs cannot be obtained from outmoded relations in production merely by superimposing modern techniques of production—this is a fundamental political economic understanding of the production process.

Any subjective application of technological solutions in violation of this understanding was bound to result in failure. In the villages, land means power, the ones who own more agricultural land are the ones who are more powerful and it is the powerful who appropriate all resources. Before the Green Revolution, the small and marginal farmers who could not obtain livelihood from their own land alone and therefore were forced to work as labourers to supplement their income comprised 40 to 50% of the rural sector. Wage labourers who had no access to land and whose income depended entirely on wages comprised 25 to 30% of the agricultural sector while middle-size farmers with sufficient land to enable them to produce enough for their subsistence, and perhaps even a small surplus were to the tune of 5 to 7%. Large landowners and moneylenders, comprised 7 to 10% of the agricultural sector (Griffin, 1974), The large proprietors, vested with political power and influence, appropriated unto themselves all the inputs in terms of technical assistance, credits by different government agencies and subsidies on fertilisers, electricity, etc. Some of these benefits also went to a section of middle peasantry. Nevertheless, the grain output still remained well below the level of self-sufficiency that the Green Revolution was expected to have facilitated (George, 1977: 125-126).

The Green Revolution helped further accentuate the inter-regional and the intra-regional imbalances in agriculture. In Punjab, the index of income inequality had increased as a result of the Green Revolution (ILO, 1977). A sample survey of 67,800 large farms conducted in Punjab in 1968-69 indicated that large landowners were increasing the average size of their holdings (Rudra, Majid and Talib, 1969). Most of the land that was added to the large farms came primarily from small farmers and peasants, who were forced to become agricultural labourers. The evidence from other states of India also indicated similar tendencies (Krishnamurthy, 1972).

Introduction of high yielding varieties of crops resulted in sudden increases in the outputs and profits from agriculture in some areas endowed with better irrigation and higher purchasing power of the peasants enabling them to make initial investments in fertilisers, pesticides and implements. This led many absentee landowners to get back to self-operation of their lands by evicting their tenants in order to retain the maximum share of the profit. This while swelling the ranks of the agricultural labourers forced many to work on their previous farms on much more exploitative terms. Increases in the market price of agricultural land furthermore worked towards the same end (Sanyal, 1983).

On the one hand, the Green Revolution thus gave rise to a bigger, more powerful and assertive rural class of rich peasants which was to become an ally of the ruling elite based in cities and the main bulwark against the more restive small and marginal peasants and the landless labourers. On the other hand, there was destruction of the productive potential of the small farms and small and marginal farmers and the landless agricultural labourers. This class of the rich peasants with a vested interest in the given distribution of landholdings also tenaciously fought back all attempts at implementing the land reforms.

## What Holds Back the Land Reforms?

If land reforms are so crucial to putting Indian agriculture back on its feet, then why have they not been implemented? It certainly is not a matter of oversight. Soon after independence, the All India Congress Committee (AICC) set up the Congress Agrarian Reform Committee, commonly known as the Kumarappa Committee. Among other measures the Kumarappa Committee proposed a fairly radical ceiling on land (Bandyopadhyaya, D.). Land was an important issue even in the international political milieu as obtaining in the immediate post-war era. The Americans realised the attraction that land held for the impoverished masses, so much so that they made implementation of throughgoing land reforms their top priority agenda in the post-war Japan, South Korea and Taiwan (Ladejinsky, 1964)—the three countries surrounding Socialist China that had already held out its radical land reforms as an ideal to be emulated in the eyes of the peasant masses in the rest of Asia. In these countries, which occupied a strategic geopolitical position in the then prevailing political atmosphere in Asia, besides preempting a revolutionary upheaval implementation of radical land reforms, by alleviating the poverty of the masses ensured the expansion of the market that was so essential for the development of the industrial base in these countries.

The historical circumstances in India were different. The two supporting pillars of British imperialism in India had been the comprador bourgeoisie that had grown under the patronage of the British and the landowning feudal class (Ghosh, 1988). With the imposition of the Permanent Settlement Act 1793 the British introduced taxation on land and established the exploitative Zamindari system as the revenue collection mechanism. The Indian bourgeoisie continued to maintain umbilical linkages with their foreign masters in myriad ways even after the transfer of power in 1947 (Ghosh, 1985a). Both the Indian bourgeoisie and the feudal class exercised considerable influence in the Congress Party (Mundargi, 1990), which instead of calling for a radical departure from colonialism, pursued a collaborationist line with the colonial masters.

Dr. Rajendra Prasad, President of the Indian Constituent Assembly, described the transfer of power as 'the consummation and fulfilment of the historic tradition and democratic ideals of the British race' (Ghosh, 1985b). Instances of such outpourings of affection for the British from the Congress leaders are many.

As a result of this course of events, in 1947 the British rule in India was replaced with the rule of the Indian elite as concentrated in the leadership of the Congress Party, without there being any change in the social, economic and political order of the day unlike the developments in China, Korea, Japan or Taiwan and later in Vietnam where the break from imperialism was accompanied with radical changes in the social, economic and political structure of the society. The former props of the British rule in India—the big bourgeoisie and the feudal class were seamlessly incorporated into the ruling elite post-1947.

Writing in the *Social Scientist* in 1974, V.C. Koshy says, 'An analysis of Congress agrarian legislations during the last twenty-three years of Indian economic planning reveals that the aim of government policy has not been to abolish landlordism; on the contrary, it has led to the transformation of feudal landlords into semi-feudal and capitalist landlords and created a stratum of rich peasants with the hope that they would rally around the ruling class' (Koshy, 1974).

Rehman Sobhan writes, 'the limited impact of the agrarian reforms in India reflects the new configurations in the social balance of power in the country once the feudal rent receiving interests created by the British Raj were eliminated. The new, more numerous class of middle and large farmers is well entrenched in the hierarchy of power in the local community and effectively constitutes the bridge between the tillers of the soil, be they minifundist farmers, sharecroppers or agricultural labourers, and the machinery of the State' (Sobhan, 1993).

Feudal relations of production in agriculture continue to exist in large parts of the country along with the growth of capitalist methods in agriculture in some parts. Even in these parts where there is a greater prevalence of capitalist means of production, the widespread indebtedness of the peasants to moneylenders gives a usurious character to the agrarian economy. Thus the overall picture of agrarian relations that emerges in the country can be characterised as a semi-feudal one. These semi-feudal relations are maintained through the alliance of the big landlords, rich peasantry and the comprador bourgeoisie with imperialism.

The task of taking the agricultural production to a higher level entails breaking the semi-feudal relations of production in agriculture, and implementation of thoroughgoing land reforms is the way to do so. This however, is easier said than done. Implementation of land reforms is not any technical issue, but entails radical realignment of political, social and economic power in the society, something which the system is hardly willing to let happen voluntarily.

## Conclusions

A well-reasoned understanding of the political economy of the agrarian crisis in the country has immense implications for the future of the country as a whole and the well-being of the agricultural economy and peasants in particular. It is central to achieving a more equitable growth of the people as also for ensuring the food security of the country and hence the health of its people.

Those who have developed vested interests in the system and have got used to making political alliances with the very forces that stand opposed to the implementation of land reforms, will naturally avoid getting to the core of the agrarian crisis in the country by emphasising the aspects that might be more acceptable within a liberal bourgeoisie framework. Their eulogising land reforms in subdued undertones in theory and negating them altogether in current practice, besides being designed to ward off any ideological critique of their policy, seeks to create confusion over the relevance of land reforms in the current economic and political milieu.

Those obsessed with increasing productivity through wider dissemination of technological inputs and envisaging a direct role for the corporate sector in food grain production through contract farming have got on to an entirely different kind of land reform—what has been described as the market-led land reform as theorised and propagated by the World Bank. While seeking to blunt the edge of the peasant struggles for land and livelihoods in different parts of the world, market-led land reforms seek to establish the role of market mechanisms in resolving land issues, e.g. setting up of land banks in some countries. The idea however is to facilitate easier takeover of land to further private profit, be it for agribusinesses or other corporate sectors.

Market-led land reforms have invaded different parts of the world including India. This has given rise to a sharp conflict between the State and the corporate alliance on the one hand and the working people on the other. The attempts in different parts of India to usurp people's land and livelihood in furtherance of corporate profits, is being resisted by militant opposition of the masses. An important thing to point out here is that none of these struggles is being led by any of the ruling classes and allied parliamentary parties. The fact that all these parties, irrespective of their ideological persuasion are one on the implementation of the pro-reform policies, has pushed the question of land reform out of the parliamentary arena. The ruling classes will try to keep up their guile on the question of land and may yet pretend to consider seriously the question of redistribution of land. In the wake of the Naxalbari peasant uprising in the late 1960s and early 1970s, the Planning Commission admitted that the programmes of land reform adopted since independence have failed to bring about the required changes in the agrarian structure. It says, 'In no sphere of public activity in our country since independence has the hiatus between the precept and practice, between policy-pronouncements and actual execution, been as great as in the domain of land reform' (Planning Commission, 1973). The gulf between people and parties is dangerous and yet pregnant with the possibilities of a breakthrough to take the society to a higher stage of social, economic and political development.

## References

Badyopadhyaya, D., 'Does Land Still Matter', Accessed on 21 April, 2010, URL: http://infochangeindia.org/200804047062/Agenda/Battles-Over-Land/Therelevance-of-land-reform-in-post-liberalisation-India.html.

*Business Standard* (2006), 'PM calls for second green revolution', regional bureau, Hyderabad, January 04, URL: http://www.business-standard.com/india/news/ pm-calls-for-second-green-revolution/229136/.

Chakravarti, A.K. (1973), 'Green Revolution in India', *Annals of the Association of American Geographers*, Vol. 63 (3): pp. 319-330.

Cleaver, Jr., Harry M. (1972), 'The contradictions of the green revolution', *The American Economic Review*, Vol. 62 (1/2): pp. 177-186.

Dhas Albert Christopher (2009), 'Agricultural Crisis in India: The Root Cause and Consequences', The American College, Madurai, MPRA Paper No. 18930, 30th November.

Dorin, Bruno (2000), 'For a Second Green Revolution: A Seminar Report', *Economic and Political Weekly*, Jun. 3-9, Vol. 35 (23): pp. 1893-1895.

*Express News Service* (2010), '2011 Polls Looming, Buddha Government Scraps Land Reforms Bill', Tuesday, 9 March, Kolkata, accessed on 23 April, 2010, URL: http://www.indianexpress.com/news/2011-polls-looming-buddha-govt-scrapsland/ 588560/.

FAO, 2006: 'FAO Director-General Appeals for Second Green Revolution. Vast Effort Needed to Feed Billions and Safeguard Environment', September 13, Rome/San Francisco, FAO News room, accessed on 23 April, 2010, URL: http:// www.fao.org/newsroom/EN/news/2006/1000392/index.html.

George, Susan (1977), 'The Green Revolution', in *How the Other Half Dies*, New York: Penguin Books.

Ghosh, S.K. (1985a), *The Indian Big Bourgeoisie; Its Genesis, Growth, and Character*, Calcutta: Subarnarekha.

Ghosh, S.K. (1985b), 'On the Transfer of Power in India', *Bulletin of Concerned Asian Scholars*, Vol. 17 (3): pp. 30.

Ghosh, S.K. (1988), 'Indian Bourgeoisie and Imperialism', *Economic and Political Weekly*, Vol. 23 (45/47): pp. 2445-2447, 2449-2458.

Government of India, 2009-10: Chapter 8, Agriculture and Food Management, *Economic Survey 2009-10*, Ministry of Finance.

Griffin, K. (1974), *The Political Economy of Agrarian Change*, London: MacMillan Press.

IFFCO (2004), 'Selected indicators of agriculture development in India, Asia—Pacific region and the world, 1991 and 2001', in *Agricultural Statistics at a Glance*, New Delhi.

International Labour Office (1977), *Poverty and Landlessness in Rural Asia*, Geneva: ILO.

Koshy, V.C. (1974), 'Land Reforms in India under the Plans', *Social Scientist*, Vol. 2 (12): pp. 43-61.

Krishnamurthy, J. (1972), 'Working force in the 1971 census: some exercises on provisional results', *Economic and Political Weekly*, 8 (3), January.

Ladejinsky, Wolf (1964), 'Agrarian Reform in Asia', *Foreign Affairs*, Vol. 42 (3): pp.445-460.

Mundargi, Tirumal (19900, 'Congress and Zamindars: Collaboration and Consultation in Bihar, 1915-36', *Economic and Political Weekly*, Vol. 25 (22): pp. 1217-1222.

Parsai, Gargi (2010), 'Below the radar, a new agribusiness pact with the US', *The Hindu*, Wednesday, February 24.

Patnaik, Utsa (2003), 'Food Stocks and Hunger: The Causes of Agrarian Distress', *Social Scientist*, Vol. 31, No. 7-8, pp. 15-41.

Patnaik, Utsa (2007a), 'Agrarian Crisis in the Era of the New Imperialism and the Role of Peasant Resistance', in *The Republic of Hunger and Other Essays*, First Edition, Gurgaon: Three Essays Collective.

Patnaik, Utsa (2007b), 'Neo-liberalism and Rural Poverty in India', *Economic and Political Weekly*, Vol. 42(30): pp. 3132-3150.

Pillai, S. Ramachandran (2007), 'Agrarian Crisis and the Way Out', *The Marxist*, July to September, Vol. XXIII, No. 3: pp. 1-18.

Planning Commission (1973), Report of the task force on agrarian relations Rudra, Majid and Talib (1969), 'Big Farmers of Punjab', *Economic and Political Weekly*, 25 December; Volume IV, Number 39: p. A-143.

Planning Commission of India, 'Distribution of Operational Holdings—All India' in 'Agricultural Data Bank', Government of India.

Planning Commission, Government of India, New Delhi, 'Agriculture Strategy for Eleventh Plan: Some Critical Issues.'

Ram, Mohan (1973), 'The Telengana peasant armed struggle, 1946-51', *Economic and Political Weekly*, Vol. 8(23): pp. 1025-1032.

Rudra A., A. Majid and B.D. Talib (1969), 'Big Farmers of Punjab: Some Preliminary Findings of a Small Survey', *Economic and Political Weekly*, Vol. 4, No. 39, September.

Sainath, P. (2010), 'Between just the Census of 1991 and that of 2001, nearly 8 million cultivators quit farming. A year from now, the 2011 Census will tell us how many more quit in this decade. India Together', 3 February, accessed on 20 April, URL: http://www.indiatogether.org/2010/feb/psa-suicides.htm.

Sanyal, Biswapriya (1983), 'How Revolutionary Was India's Green Revolution?' *South Asia Bulletin*, Vol. III (2): pp. 31-44.

Sarkar, Abhijan (2008), *Class Analysis of Indian Agriculture: Towards a New Dawn*, Vol. 1 (2): 13-17.

Sobhan, Rehman (1993), 'Non-Egalitarian Agrarian Reforms without a Social Transition', in *Agrarian Reform and Social Transformation; Preconditions for Development*, Dhaka: The University Press Limited.

Subrahmaniam, Vidya (2010), 'President Calls for Second Green Revolution', *The Hindu*, accessed on 24 April, URL: http://www.thehindu.com/2010/01/26/ stories/2010012654871000.htm.

Varadarajan, Siddharth (2010), 'Order on Free Grain to Poor Can't be Executed: Manmohan Singh', *The Hindu*, New Delhi, September 7.

# 5

# Food Security
## The Gaffes of the Past and the Options for the Future (Part I)

### Introduction

As the difficulties in ensuring food for the people have increased over the past decade, anxious calls for a 'second Green Revolution' (SGR) have gained stridency (*Business Standard*, 2006, Dorin, 2000, Subrahmaniam, 2010, FAO, 2006). It leaves an impression that everything else possible under the sun to resolve the worsening crisis in food security has already been done. The crucial question however is: is the present crisis of food security inevitable in the dearth of further technological advancement or is it the result of the policies pursued by the governments over the years? Answering this calls for a scrutiny of trends and issues related to food security in India.

### Conceptual Framework

According to FAO, food security is said to exist when 'all people, at all times, have physical and economic access to sufficient, safe and nutritious food that meets their dietary needs and food preferences for an active and healthy life' (FAO, 2008). As per this definition there are four aspects of food security—food availability, food access and food utilisation and the fourth aspect is the stability of the first three aspects in perpetuity. Accordingly, policies directed at ensuring food security ought to be designed to impact favourably on all these aspects.

This chapter is organized in two parts. The first part examines the impact of Government's policies, especially since the beginning of the neoliberal economic reforms, on the aforementioned aspects of food security with the purpose of judging whether they have succeeded in ensuring even minimal dietary requirements of the people. We have examined the following trends: the per capita yearly net food grain output and availability in India before and after independence,* variation in food grain stocks in the country over the years, trends in food grain exports, trends in rural and urban poverty and the impact of targeting in the Public Distribution System, trends in financial outlay for the rural sector and last but not the least, the consequences that have followed the fabled First Green Revolution (FGR). The logical sequence drawn here from should enable us to decipher the real causes of food insecurity and thereby the possible solutions.

The second part deals within the next chapter deals with the policy initiatives that are being put in place by the Government to meet the food policy challenges before the country. The different steps initiated for rolling out SGR have been discussed as an integral part of these policy initiatives. Drawing from the discussion on the aforementioned aspects a broad framework of alternative approaches has then been suggested for securing food security of the vulnerable masses in the second part.

* These have been mentioned and discussed variably in earlier chapters as well, but are being brought up here again to wholesomely present the arguments given here without the reader having to incur the inconvenience of referring to the foregone pages.

## Per Capita Yearly Net Food grain Output and Availability in India

By now the facts regarding net per capita food output and availability in the country as obtaining in the available literature on the subject have adequately settled that food grains available for per capita consumption in the country has been declining over the years. In fact the highest per capita food grain output and availability in the country were observed in the period 1897-1902 at 201.1 and 199 kg respectively (Patnaik, 2003). This achievement was inspite of the British exporting 475 thousand tons of food grain from India during this period. After 1947 the highest triennial average per capita availability of food grains was reached in 1990-91 at 176.6 kg i.e. on the anvil of the neoliberal economic reforms. Since the beginning of the economic reforms, there has been a halting slide down the slope. According to the figures available from indiastat.com at the beginning of the new millennium, even as the Government committed itself to achieving the Millennium Development Goal of banishing extreme poverty and hunger from the country, the net per capita yearly food grain availability touched 151.9 kg in 2001, equivalent to the levels seen in early fifties. Average food grain availability in the first decade of the 21st century has been 162.6 kg, equal to the average availability in the sixties, which was a decade of perpetual food crisis. Again these figures are only availability and not actual consumption, for indeed there has been a growing divergence between availability and the purchasing power of the people which has been falling over the years.

Only to bring out the gravity of the situation it needs reiterating that even the Famine Commission appointed by the British administration in 1880 held the per capita yearly availability of 200 kg of food grains to be the minimum required for staving off famines (Bajaj and Srinivas, 2002).

Alongside declining food grain production, the agricultural sector has been starved of investments. Investment in agriculture and allied services (at current prices) as a percentage of GDP (at factor cost at current prices) declined from 0.6% in 1990-91 to 0.4% in 2000-01 and was only 0.5% in 2009-10 (calculations based on figures in tables 1 and 107 in *Handbook of Statistics of Indian Economy*, Reserve Bank of India, 2011-12), whereas the agriculture's contribution to India's GDP has been much higher, varying from more than 50% during the First Five Year Plan period to about 20% during the Eleventh Plan period. Besides, agriculture forms a firm foundation for growth in other sectors of the economy. The share of public sector in capital formation (such as expansion in the irrigation systems, seed production and research and development facilities, etc.) in agriculture, declined from 33% at the beginning of 1990s to a mere 24.2% in 2000-01 and 17.1% in 2009-10. The Gross Capital Formation in agriculture as a proportion of overall GDP (at factor cost at current prices) stagnated to around 2.5 to 3% between 2004-05 and 2009-10 (GOI, 2010-11). These statistics show that agriculture is receiving back just a tiny proportion of what it has contributed to the country's growth. Such nihilism in government policy towards agriculture is inexplicable in a country where more than 50% of the work force is still engaged in agriculture and allied sectors. The ensuing crisis in agriculture is reflected in the unprecedented rise in farm suicides. During the period of economic reforms, as per an earlier estimate, more than two lakh (0.2 million) farmers have taken their lives under duress (Sainath 2010 a)—a protracted human tragedy that is little talked of either in the media or among policy circles, despite the suicides rising by the day.

## Hungry Masses and the Burgeoning Food Grain Stocks

Figure 5.1 shows the situation of buffer stocks of food grain from 1982 till 2008. The situation of the food stocks has in general been good even as the people perpetually consumed food grains at much below the poverty line level. Beginning from 1998 there is a sharp increase in the stocks which peak at close to 60 million tonnes around 2002-2003, while the per capita food grain availability during this period dipped from 173.5 kg per year in 1996-98 to 162.6 kg per year in 1999-01 before recovering to a level of 169.7 kg per year in 2002-04 (calculations based on figures available from indiastat.com). In fact, 2003 was one of the worst drought years in recent memory with per capita food grain availability of only 159.7 kg.

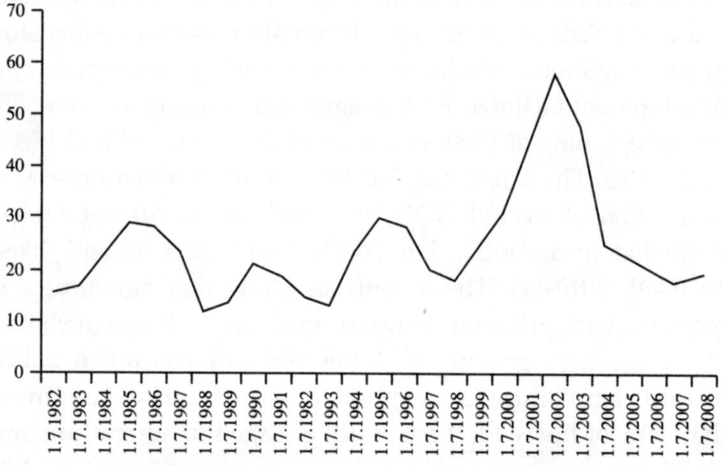


Figure 5.1: Buffer Stock of Food Grains (Central and State Governments) in India (01.07.1982 to 01.01.2008) in million tons.

*Source:* Indiastat.com: Buffer stock of food grains.

There have been attempts by the Government to explain this through bunkum theories of 'diversification of diets' and 'voluntary choice' of the people to move away from consumption of food grains (Government of India, 2001-02). The simple fact of the matter however has been the inability of the people to buy enough food and the government's lack of willingness to provide cheap food to as many who required it. For a more detailed discussion on the subject people can refer to Patnaik, 2005.

## Continuing Exports of Food Grains

A tendency has been visible to privilege trade in food over using it to satiate people's hunger. As is evident from Figure 5.2 food grain exports picked up during the reform years beginning from 1994-95 and reached their peak in 2003 (Figure 5.2)—the drought year that was particularly harsh on the hunger front.

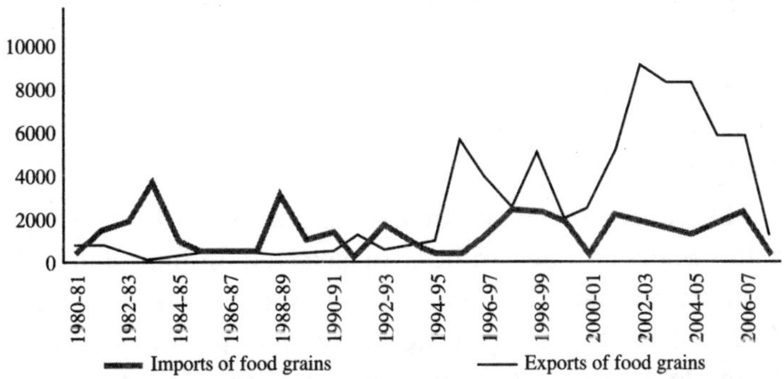


Figure 5.2: Export and import of Food grains from India in thousand tones. (1980-1981 to 2007-2008)

*Source:* Data based on which this graph was drawn is available from indiastat.com.

There has even been export of pulses, a variety of food grains that has been among the biggest loser in 'Green Revolution' driven expansion in acreage of High Yielding Varieties of wheat and rice. The saddest part of the food grain export is that the Government chose to heavily subsidize the exports rather than make it available to the poor who went hungry (Damodaran, 2001, World Bank, 2005, Gaiha and Kulkarni, 2005).

## Increasing Poverty and the Declining Demand for Food Grains

We have already indicated the relationship between rising food grain stocks and the decline in peoples' purchasing power due to the phenomenal increase in poverty during the years of neoliberal reforms. The increasing levels of poverty in India during the period of neoliberal reforms have been attested to by a number of academics and government committees (GOI, 2009, Deaton and Drèze, 2009, NCEUS, 2007, Mehta, 2005). By the time of 61st NSSO Round, 87% of the rural population was living below poverty line calculated by direct method[1] of taking the MPCE (monthly per capita expenditure) class that afforded a calorie consumption of 2,400 kcal (Patnaik, 2007). The corresponding figure for urban poverty was 64.5% by 2004-05 (Patnaik, 2010).

The consequences of this were borne out by the report on the State Hunger Indices of selected Indian states. The report stated that 'All 17 states have India State Hunger Index (ISHI) scores that are significantly worse than the 'low' and 'moderate' hunger categories. Twelve of the 17 states fall into the 'alarming' category, and one—Madhya Pradesh, falls into the 'extremely alarming' category. Punjab, the State with the best hunger score at 13.6, falls in the serious category of hunger index' (Menon et al., 2009).

## Impact of Targeting in PDS

In 1998, the Government of India resorted to targeting in the Public Distribution System (TPDS) with the objective of directing the food subsidies only to the poor. One crucial objective of the TPDS was to keep the 'budgetary food subsidies under control to the desired extent' (UNESCR, 2008).

In all talk of 'mounting food subsidy bill', the need for 'fiscal prudence' or diversion of wasteful food subsidies to 'productivity enhancing investments', what is deliberately not mentioned is the meagre proportion of subsidies compared to country's GDP.

It can be seen from Figure 5.3 that India's food subsidy bill has consistently been much below 1% of the GDP for the better part, it touched a maximum of around 1% of GDP only in three years—2002-03, 2003-04 and 2004-05. Moreover, in proportionate terms the food subsidy bill has actually increased after introduction of targeting in 1997. These figures belie the claims of 'huge subsidy bill' and distortion of 'fiscal health', neither has targeting improved the efficiency of subsidies in providing relief to the poor. A much clearer, albeit subtly put intent behind targeting is to gradually phase out food subsidies to prepare the ground for opening up food procurement, storage, distribution and retail to the private sector. This

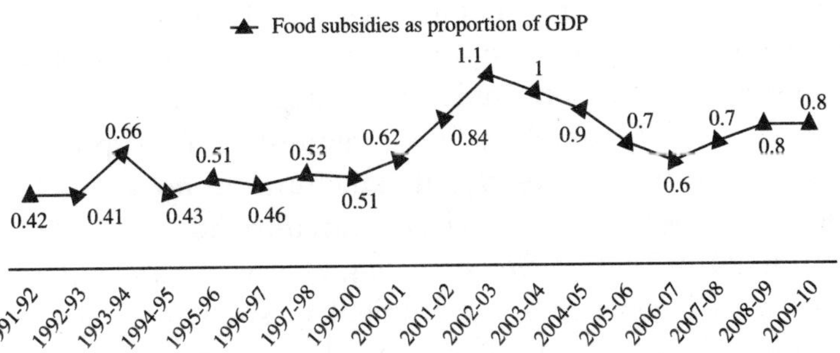


Figure 5.3: Trends in Central food subsidy bill as a proportion of GDP.

*Source:* To make the figure, figures for GDP have been taken from Table 5.1: Macro-economic aggregates (at current prices) in 'Handbook of Statistics of Indian Economy, 2010. Figures for food subsidies have been acquired from the table on Food and Fertiliser Subsidies in India (1976-2010), available from indiastat.com on 29 July 2011.

*Note:* Components of food subsidies comprise: acquisition costs (these include cost of grains, statutory taxes, storage and interest charges etc. at acquisition stage.)—sales realisation, distribution costs, and carryover charges paid to state agencies. Dsitribution costs include: freight charges, handling charges, storage and interest charges, transit and storage shortages and administrative overheads. (*Source:* Table on Major Components of Food Subsidy in India (1999-2000 to 2003-04.), available from indiastat.com.)

cannot be done in one go for obvious political reasons, and hence the intermediary stage of targeting.

It is interesting to note that among those asking for universal PDS today is the Parliamentary Left which promptly shifted to targeted PDS in 1997 in the states ruled by it—Kerala, Tripura and West Bengal. This was so even when so to say 'non-progressive' rulers of neighbouring Tamil Nadu chose to get back to universal PDS under public pressure. It is a tribute to the people of the State that PDS system in Tamil Nadu is among the best in the country (RTF, 2007).

Industry has been swift in its follow-through of the Government's overtures. The Federation of Indian Chambers of Commerce and Industry came up with a report on the restructuring of PDS that calls upon the Government to privatise the procurement, storage and distribution of food. FICCI released its report on 23 May 2010 and on 26 May 2010 in the first meeting of the then newly constituted 'Prime Minister's Council on Trade and Industry', the then Prime Minister, Dr. Manmohan Singh requested the captains of Indian industry to 'to reach out to the rural economy and help the government on food security and affirmative action' (The Hindu, 2010).These developments give rise to serious doubts over the Government's commitment to strengthening social security measures to alleviate the food insecurity of the people.

## Just How Much of a Priority Has Agriculture Been?

We have already pointed out above to the neglect and stagnation that bedevil Indian agriculture, here we wish to elaborate just a little more on this.

The country's political leadership often resorts to rhetoric like 'India's development is the development of her villages' or that 'India lives in its villages', however, this has failed to make a dent in the more concrete development policies pursued by the political leadership. 'Nehru's vision of 'modern India' was anchored around heavy investment in industrial production in centrally located urban centres' (Sanyal, 1983). In a country where more than 80% of the people lived in villages and derived their income primarily from agriculture and allied activities, the First Five Year Plan devoted only 32.1% of the outlay for rural development (here is meant to include 'Agriculture and Community Development, Irrigation and Flood Control'). This trend continued subsequently. Table 5.1 clearly shows that in proportional terms this outlay got further constricted over the subsequent Five Year Plans. In fact, it can be seen from Table 5.2 that rural development expenditures have remained consistently below 1% of GDP from the 1990s and the following decade, with this dipping to as low as 0.48% in 2004-05. For a country where 70% of the population live in rural areas this is indeed surprising. As a proportion of the total budget it has barely managed to hover around 10%.

While it is true that there are non-industrialised developing countries with even less proportion of their national budgets devoted to the development of their agriculture sector, as for example in Africa, it needs to be borne in mind that neglect of rural and agricultural development in a country of India's size and population can have potentially destabilising impacts on food security not only in India but also in other countries dependent on imports of food to feed their populations. If India imports food, the quantities involved are invariably so huge that international prices of food grains become unaffordable for smaller countries.

Between 2000-01 and 2006-07 only about a fourth of the total cropped area in the country is sown more than once (Planning Commission, Undated a). If the average duration of one crop is taken to be 4 months, then nearly three-fourth of our total cropped land goes waste for nearly eight months in a year and the main reason for such a colossal waste of India's

Table 5.1: Decline in Public Development Expenditures in Rural Areas through different plan periods. (As percentage of GDP)

| *Five Year Plan* | *1st Plan (1951-56)* | *2nd Plan (1956-61)* | *3rd Plan (1961-66)* | *4th Plan (1969-74)* | *5th Plan (1974-79)* | *6th Plan (1980-85)* |
|---|---|---|---|---|---|---|
| Rural development expenditure (RDE) | ₹ 758 crores (32.1%) | ₹ 950 crores (20%) | ₹ 1,718 crores (23%) | ₹ 3,815 crores (23.9%) | ₹ 7,616 crores (20.4%) | ₹ 23,218.8 crores (22.5) |
| Five Year Plan | 7th Plan (1985-90) | 8th Plan (1992-97) | 9th Plan (1997-02) | 10th Plan (2002-07) | 11th Plan (2007-12) | |
| Rural development expenditure | ₹ 44,629 crores (18.8%) | ₹ 89,418 crores (20.6%) | ₹ 172,568 crores (20.1) | ₹ 284,176 crores (18.7%) | ₹ 647,776 crores (17.8) | |

*Source:* Figures for GDP at Factor cost are from Table 5.1, Handbook of Statistics of Indian Economy, Reserve Bank of India, 2011-12. For RDE outlay from 1st Five Year Plan to the 5th Plan was obtained from Plan documents available from Planning Commission of India website at http://planningcommission.nic.in/plans/planrel/fiveyr/welcome.html on 31 August 2013. For 6th to the 11th Plan the figures for RDE were calculated from Table 2.5 to Table 2.10 in the Economic Survey 2011-12.

Note: RDE includes expenditure on Agriculture and Community Development/allied sectors, Irrigation and Flood control. Figures in parentheses are percentages of the total Plan outlay.

Table 5.2: Rural Development Expenditures through the Decade of 2000s

| *Year* | *1996-97* | *1998-99* | *2000-01* | *2002-03* | *2004-05* | *2006-07* | *2008-09* | *2010-11* | *2011-12* |
|---|---|---|---|---|---|---|---|---|---|
| GDP (₹ in crores)* | 1,301,788 | 1,668,739 | 1,991,982 | 2,338,200 | 2,971,464 | 3,953,276 | 5,303,567 | 7,157,412 | 8,232,652 |
| RDE** as% of GDP | .73 | .74 | .6 | .52 | .48 | .66 | .65 | .95 | .86 |
| Total budget*** | 87,086 | 105,187 | 117,334 | 144,038 | 163,720 | 254,041 | 375,485 | 534,484 | 592,457 |
| RDE as% of budget | 10.9 | 11.8 | 10.2 | 8.4 | 8.8 | 10.3 | 9.1 | 13 | 11.9 |

* GDP at factor cost at current prices, **RDE = Rural Development—includes Agriculture and Allied activities, Rural Development schemes, Irrigation and Flood Control. Note: Figures for GDP are from Table 1, Handbook of Statistics of Indian Economy, Reserve Bank of India, 2011-12. Total outlay and allocation for Rural Development Expenditures were obtained from the 'sectorwise outlay' in budgets of respective years available from the Ministry of Finance website.

arable land mass is the lack of irrigation which stood at only 31.41% (net area under irrigation by all sources) of the total cropped area in 2006-07 (Planning Commission, Undated b). This amounts to an increase of just 1% since 2000-01.

It is really remarkable that while the multilateral donor agencies like the World Bank and the IMF have proactively advocated withdrawal of subsidies for agriculture in developing countries, subsidies for agriculture in the OECD countries remain much higher. Compared to many developed countries where agriculture is a much smaller sector of the economy, the government support that agriculture receives in India is woeful. Figure 5.4 gives a comparison of the subsidies given to agriculture in some countries as a proportion of agricultural GDP, which is the lowest in case of India.

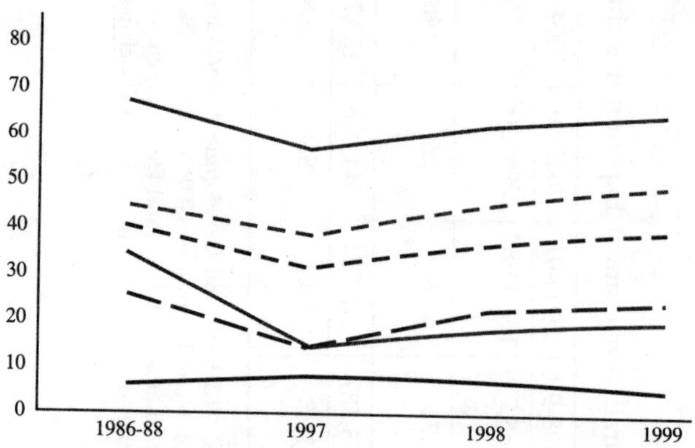


Figure 5.4: Agricultural Subsidy in Selected Countries and India {Base Year (1986-1988)}(1997 to 1999) as percentage of agricultural GDP.
*Source:* Based on data available from Indiastat.com.

Low investment in agriculture and rural development is coupled with the number of people dependent on agriculture increasing all through since independence. Table 5.3 gives decadal trends in employment in agriculture since 1951 census. With productivity in agriculture declining, this increase in labour force dependent on agriculture means concentration of unproductive labour in agriculture which directly feeds into the vicious cycle of poverty in rural India and thereby undermining the food security of the people.

However, there are further ominous signs, for the first time since independence the number of cultivators decreased in 2011. It is ominous because this first time decrease has come about because of prevalent agrarian distress in the country that forced the cultivators to give up agriculture even as the picture on employment front is not very rosy in other sectors of the economy either.

Table 5.3: Employment in Agriculture Sector in Millions

| Agricultural workers/year | *1951* | *1961* | *1971* | *1981* | *1991* | *2001* | *2011* |
|---|---|---|---|---|---|---|---|
| Cultivators | 69.9 | 99.6 | 78.2 | 92.5 | 110.7 | 127.3 | 118.7 |
| Agricultural laborers | 27.3 | 31.5 | 47.5 | 55.5 | 74.6 | 106.8 | 144.3 |
| Total | 97.2 | 131.1 | 125.7 | 148.0 | 185.3 | 234.1 | 263.0 |

*Source:* Swati Dhoot (2006) Note: The corresponding figures for 2011 census have not been released yet, however, a 2009-10 survey with a smaller sample size shows that the share of agriculture in total employment has come down to 45.5% of total employment from 52.1 in 2001 census (GOI, 2010). Figures for 2011 are from the corresponding census.

## Green Revolution: A Panacea or a Pandora's Box

An entire generation in India has come up being fed on the folklore of India having become self-sufficient in food due to the 'Green Revolution' unleashed by the leadership of the Congress Party. And yet within the same generation we are now hearing that the 'Green Revolution' has run out of steam. The very areas to which 'Green Revolution' was largely limited—i.e. Punjab, Haryana and Western Uttar Pradesh are now witnessing declining output in food grains (Kumar and Mittal, 2006, Dutta, 2012). It is being increasingly acknowledged that cereal based, input intensive mono-crop farming model has already led to deterioration in soil quality, depletion of water table and other ecological consequences, and as such is no more sustainable (Datta, 2012).

Food systems are supposed to last for generations, but here we are confronted with a situation where it has run out of steam within a generation. Even at its peak 'in Punjab (including Haryana)—the throbbing heartland of the 'Green Revolution'—the percentage of the rural population below the minimum level of living nearly quadrupled between 1960-61 and 1967-68' (Bardhan, 1970). In as much as the impact of technology is mediated through the existing social, political and economic structures of inequity and power, there remains a possibility of technology having quite the opposite of its anticipated effect. In the case of 'Green Revolution' it was one of increasing rather than decreasing poverty. With respect to the First Green Revolution (FGR) of the 1960s and the 70s this possibility has been attested to by a number of authors (Ladejinsky, 1969, 1970, Wharton Jr, 1969, Sanyal, 1983, Shiva, 1991). Even when Green Revolution percolated to smaller farms, the proportional gains for them were minimal compared those of the richer farmers (Beck, 1995). FGR led to considerable inter-regional disparities which need to be accounted for in its final assessment (Chakraborty, 1973).

The FGR led to the creation of a class of rich peasants who monopolised the resources pumped into 'Green Revolution' areas and led on to cement the social, economic and political power structure in the rural society in alliance with the urban based bourgeoisie and political class.

In the realm of production, supported by a system of both supply and demand side incentives it led to a vast expansion in the acreage under wheat and paddy. This was to the accompaniment of the shrinking crop area devoted to coarse grains (Figure 5.5) and decline of coarse cereals in the diets in different parts of the country.

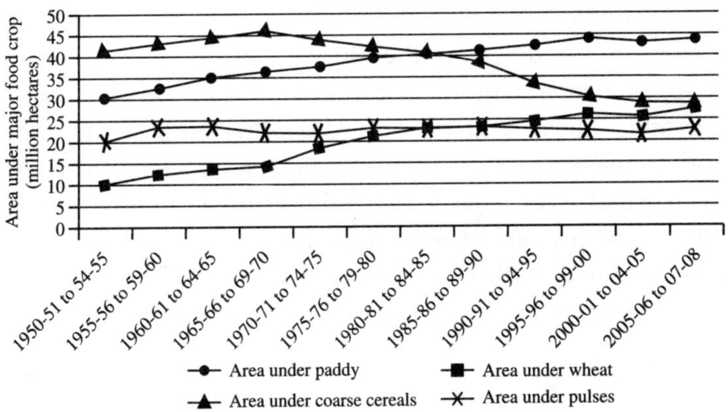


Figure 5.5: Changes in area under different food crops since 1950s.

*Source:* Based on calculations made from figures in Table 1.12: Area under principal crops—All India, Data Bank on Agriculture and Allied Sectors, Planning Commission, Government of India. Available from http://planningcommission.nic.in/sectors/agri_html/selagri/T%201.12.xls on 13 June, 2013.

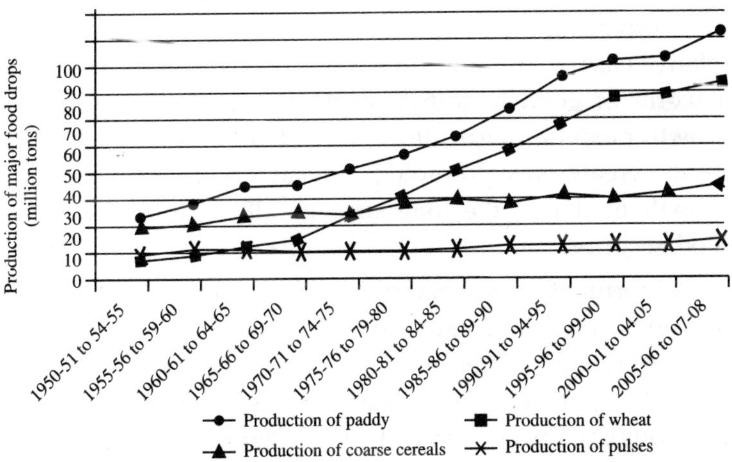


Figure 5.6: Trends in production of principal food crops.

*Source:* Based on calculations made from figures in Table 1.11: Production of major crops—All India, Data Bank on Agriculture & Allied Sectors, Planning Commission, Government of India. Available from http://planningcommission.nic.in/sectors/agri_html/selagri/T%201.11.xls on 13 June, 2013.

The single most important lesson of FGR is that while on the one hand it was the story of high yields of wheat and paddy monoculture in a limited region of the country (Haryana, Punjab and Western Uttar Pradesh), on the other hand it was also the story of neglect of agriculture and the livestock economy in the rainfed areas of the country which constitute about 68% of the arable area. The approach paper to the Twelfth Five Year Plan in a way admits this by acknowledging that of the total subsidy on irrigation, fuel and fertiliser, the rainfed areas have been receiving only about 6 to 8% (CSSP-ERU, 2012).

Figure 5.6 shows the trends in the production of major food crops in the country. While production of rice and wheat has registered considerable increases, that of coarse cereals registered only a marginal increase and the production of pulses has remained virtually stagnant. The coarse cereals are now being rediscovered as 'nutri-cereals.' Given the fact that these cereals are less input intensive and can be grown with relative ease in arid and semi-arid areas, it would have done a world of good to India's food security if an appropriate growth model for agriculture in rainfed areas that privileged these cereals was promoted instead of projecting the GR growth model as the 'one size fits all' solution for India's food security.

Unfortunately, the planners seldom take into account the insidious and less tangible costs involved in the introduction of a technology. Water table depletion, soil degradation, loss of biodiversity and environmental costs are only some of the insidious costs associated with FGR technologies that are being acknowledged now. However, what is not acknowledged upfront is the long term impact that FGR has had on the diets of the people.

Besides diminishing the consumption of 'nutritious cereals' (the erstwhile coarse cereals) FGR may also have been responsible for reducing protein consumption in the diets of most Indian families. Pulses are the most common source of proteins in Indian diets. Between 1950-51 and 2005, while the country's population increased three times, the production of pulses barely increased one and a half times. Between the same period the production of 'nutri-cereals' (coarse cereals) increased only two times. This thereby indicates a net decline in consumption of pulses and 'nutri-cereals' in the diets of an average Indian family. In contrast to this the production of rice and wheat in the referred period increased by four and ten times respectively.

Higher yield of the hybrid varieties of wheat and rice in the presence of irrigation and high fertiliser inputs has been only one of the factors in giving high yields of these crops. More than this, an incentive structure comprising public investments made available in certain irrigated regions of the country, setting of agricultural prices, considerable fertiliser subsidy, using Public Distribution System to generate massive demand for rice, wheat and sugar, and tying up of agricultural credit with adoption of specific varieties of wheat and rice were some of the more important structures deployed to make FGR a success (CSSP-ERU, 2012).

FGR thus created a model of agricultural growth that has so imbued the agriculture policy establishment as to make it inimical to the alternative strategies for agricultural growth suited for non-FGR areas of the country (CSSP-ERU, 2012). The tragedy of the situation is that in spite of the consequences of the FGR technologies showing up, the refrain continues to be—'extend the Green Revolution to Eastern India' or as already noted above—'the second Green Revolution'. These are nothing but efforts to extend the prevailing model of agricultural development to the rainfed areas (Raina and Shankar, 2011). The need clearly is for developing sustainable agriculture in line with the requirements of regional agro-ecology. The potential for agricultural growth thus remains untapped in much of the country.

The FGR revolution strategy stood in negation of the fact that 'backwardness of Indian agrarian systems is not simply a result of low productivity but also it is due to factors like caste, patriarchy etc. that prevail to deepen exploitation and inequality. Hence, technological frontiers as well as social barriers have combined to result in the continuance of agrarian backwardness and poverty' (CSSP-ERU, 2012). Keeping this cardinal truth in mind, a meaningful agrarian change can only be consummated through a change in both the forces of production (technology, skilled human resources) as also a change in production relations.

Though not by way of acknowledgement by the country's planners, a profound requiem to the FGR is being written in the villages of India, that too in the very heart of 'Green Revolution'. Driven by agrarian distress, a non-descript village, Harkishanpura in the Bhatinda district of the food bowl of the country, Punjab, attracted much attention for itself by passing a dramatic resolution in the 'Village Panchayat' (Village Council) to put itself up for sale in 2001. Similarly placed Bhuttal Kalan and Bhuttal Khurd in the Sangrur district of Punjab followed suit—up to 80% of the villages being mortgaged to private money lenders and commission agents (Sharma, 2006).

In July 2005, the 150 year old Malsinghwala village in Mansa district of Punjab put itself up for sale. 'Lack of food, water, loss of soil fertility, incidence of diseases, deaths, huge debts, poverty and indifference of the concerned authorities' are said to be the reasons. 50% of the agricultural land in the village has been left barren. As per the statement of a villager, 'Earlier, when we had water, we had enough to eat. Now we are totally finished and are ready to leave the village' (Bhattacharya, 2007).

Elsewhere, outside Punjab, the condition is all the more pathetic. Unable to pay their mounting debts, the residents of Chingapur village in Yeotmal region of the State of

Maharashtra decided to sell off their kidneys in 2005 and invited the then President of the country, Dr. A.P.J. Abdul Kalam and the Prime Minister, Dr. Manmohan Singh to preside over a 'Human Market' organised for sale (Sharma, 2006).

Nothing exemplifies the nihilism of the establishment towards this deeply entrenched agrarian distress better than the following statement of the country's erstwhile Prime Minister. Commenting on the situation of a debt ridden farmer in a Bollywood film, who migrated to the city, he said, 'There is no such thing as a free lunch . . . The only way we can raise our heads above poverty is for more people to be taken out of agriculture' (Varadharajan, 2010).

## Conclusion

The foregoing discussion on the food policies that have been pursued by the governments over the years, especially since the beginning of the neoliberal economic reforms clearly show that many of these policies have had a role in undermining the food security of the country both in the short and the longer terms. The few positive steps like assuring the minimum support prices for various crops have also been used selectively to largely enhance the production of the Green Revolution crops overlooking the desirability of such crops for the vast rainfed areas of the country. Given the present grim situation on the food security and nutrition front in the country it would be reasonable to expect that the policy makers revisit these policies to draw appropriate lessons for future policy.

However, there seems to be an assumption of infallibility on the part of the food policy establishment. In the seeming absence of any visible efforts to learn from the mistakes of the past, one gets an impression that probably the prevailing thinking is that this is about the best that could be achieved under the circumstances. The only lessons that seem to have been learnt are directed at gradually withdrawing the few concessions that had been granted to the poor and the vulnerable.

It is least surprising then that, what is being offered as a solution in the name of 'Second Green Revolution' is more of the same that was done in the past, as the things stand today, the SGR holds out the thrent of being an even bigger Pandora's Box than the FGR. Some of the other measures like 'going hunting for farmland in Africa' are outrightly regressive and abominable. In the second part of the paper we shall discuss the solutions to India's food security being proposed by the ruling class along with suggestions for the desirable solutions of our own.

## Endnote

1. Direct method of poverty line estimation entails reading directly from the various NSSO Rounds data the MPCE class that is able to afford consumption of 2400 and 2100 calories per day in the rural and the urban areas respectively. As opposed to this, indirect method entails deriving the new poverty line by adjusting the original direct poverty line deciphered initially in 1973-74 (NSSO 28th Round) with price indices for the agricultural labourers and the urban unorganised sector workers to derive the poverty lines for the rural and the urban areas respectively. The latter however does not give a correct estimate of the rise in poverty line for a variety of reasons such as increasing monetisation of the economy, especially the rural economy and progressive reduction in access to the common property resources for the poor has meant that the non-formal sources (i.e. without having to purchase) of arranging food and other utilities of life with which the poor could support themselves have decreased over the years and they are increasingly having to directly purchase their necessities including food. This means that while earlier prices of commodities were only partially relevant in fulfilling the daily needs of life for the poor, their relevance has progressively increased over the years with the poor having to directly purchase a larger share of their needs. This reality is not adequately captured in adjusting poverty lines with price indices.

   For further discussion on the topic one can refer to the following works of Utsa Patnaik 'Poverty and Neoliberalism in India', 'Trends in Urban Poverty under Economic Reforms: 1993-94 to 2004-05' and 'Neoliberalism and Rural Poverty in India.'

## References

Bajaj J.K. and M.D. Srinivas (2002): Annam Bahu Kurvita: The Indian discipline of growing and sharing food in plenty. In *Sustainable Agriculture and Food Security, The Impact of Globalisation* (Vandana Shiva, Gitanjali Bedi eds.), Sage Publications, New Delhi.

Bardhan P. (1970): 'Green Revolution and Agricuitural Labourers', *EPW*, Vol. 5 (29/31): pp. 1239-1241+1243-1246.

Beck T. (1995): The Green Revolution and Poverty in India: A Case Study of West Bengal, *Applied Geography*, Vol. 15 (2): pp. 161-181.

Bhattacharya Tamosi (2007): 'Violation of Human Right to Water: A Case Study of Malsinghwala, The 'Village for Sale in Punjab', Janhit Foundation, July.

*Business Standard* (2006): PM calls for second Green Revolution. Regional Bureau, Hyderabad 4 January, Accessed at http://www.business-standard.com/india/news/pm-calls-for-second-green-revolution/229136/.

Centre for Studies in Science Policy—Economic Research Unit (CSSP-ERU) (2012): 'Rainfed Area Atlas of India', Working Paper Series 9, Jawaharlal Nehru University, New Delhi.

Chakraborty A.K. (1973): 'Green Revolution in India', *Annals of the Association of American Geographers*, Vol. 63, No. 3 (Sep., 1973): pp. 319-330.

Damodaran H. (2001): 'Food grains exports from FCI stocks—the billion dollar game', *Business Line*, June 15. Available from: http://www.hindu.com/businessline/2001/06/15/stories/041520mn.htm on 12 June 2013.

Deaton A. and J. Drèze (2009): 'Nutrition in India: facts and interpretation. *Economic and Political Weekly*, 14 February, Vol. 44 (7).

Dhoot S. (2006): National Agriculture Policy–A critical Evaluation, Briefing paper published by CUTS Centre for International Trade, Economics and environment.

Dorin B (2000): 'For a second green revolution: a seminar report'. *Economic and Political Weekly*, Jun. 3-9, Vol. 35 (23): pp. 1893-1895.

Dutta S (2012): 'Green Revolution Revisited: The Contemporary Agrarian Situation in Punjab, India'. *Social Change*, Vol. (42): 229-247.

FAO (2006): AO Director-General appeals for second Green Revolution. Vast effort needed to feed billions and safeguard environment. 13 September, Rome/San Francisco, FAO Newsroom. Accessed on 23rd April, 2010 from http://www.fao.org/newsroom/EN/news/2006/1000392/index.html.

FAO (2008): 'What is food security? Food security concepts and frameworks', EC-FAO Food Security Information for Action Programme, p. 3.

Gaiha, R. and Kulkarni, V.S. (2005): 'Food grain surpluses, yields and prices in India', Draft paper presented at 'Global Forum for Agriculture: Policy Coherence for Development', 30 November to 1 December 2005, Paris, France.

Government of India (2000): *National Agriculture Policy, 2000,* Department of Agriculture and Cooperation, Ministry of Agriculture.

Government of India (2001-02): *Economic Survey 2001-02,* Ministry of Finance

Government of India (2009): 'Report of the Expert Group to advise the Ministry of Rural Development on methodology for conducting the Below Poverty Line (BPL) Census for the 11th Five Year Plan'. Ministry of Rural Development, New Delhi, Aug, p. 9.

Government of India (2010): *Report on Employment & Unemployment Survey, Ministry of Labour& Employment,* Labour Bureau, Chandigarh, October.

Government of India, 2010-11: *Economic Survey 2010-11,* Ministry of Finance.

Kumar P. and Mittal S. (2006): 'Agricultural Productivity Trends in India: Sustainability Issues'. *Agricultural Economics Research Review,* Vol. 19, 2006, pp. 71-88.

Ladejinsky Wolf (1969): 'The Green Revolution in Punjab: a field trip', *Economic and Political Weekly,* Vol. 4 (26): pp. A73-A75, A77-A79,A81-A82.

Ladejinsky Wolf (1970): 'Ironies of India's Green Revolution', *Foreign Affairs,* Vol. 48 (4):, pp. 758-768.

Mehta J. (2005): Poverty in India. *Revolutionary Democracy,* Vol. 11(1).

Menon P., A. Deolalikar, A. Bhaskar (2009): 'India State Hunger Index. Comparisons of Hunger Across States'. International Food Policy Research Institute. Washington, D.C., Bonn, and Riverside February.

National Commission for Enterprises on Unorganized Sector (NCEUS) (2007): 'Preface of the report on conditions of work and promotion of livelihoods in the unorganized sector', New Delhi. Available from http://nceus.gov.in/Condition_of_workers_sep_2007.pdf on 6th June, 2010.

Patnaik U. (2003): 'Food stocks and hunger: the causes of agrarian distress'. *Social Scientist,* Jul.–Aug., Vol. 31(7/8): pp. 15-41.

Patnaik U. (2005): 'Theorizing food security and poverty in the era of economic reforms'. *Social Scientist,* Vol. 33 (7/8): 50-81.

Patnaik U. (2007): 'Neoliberalism and rural poverty in India'. *EPW*, Vol. 42 (30): 3132-3150.

Patnaik U. (2010): 'Trends in urban poverty under economic reforms: 1993-94 to 2004-05'. *EPW*, Vol. 55(4): 42-53.

Planning Commission (Undated a): Table on 'Pattern of land utilisation—All India', Data Bank on Agriculture and Allied Sectors, Planning Commission, Government of India. Available from http://planningcommission.nic.in/sectors/agri_html/selagri/T1.4.xls on 14th June, 2013.

Planning Commission (Undated b): 'Net Area Under Irrigation by Sources—All India', Data Bank on Agriculture & Allied Sectors, Planning Commission, Government of India. Available from http://planningcommission.nic.in/sectors/agri_html/selagri/T%201.6.xls on 14th June, 2013.

Raina R.S. and P.S.V. Shankar (2011): 'Rainfed Agriculture: Enabling New Rules of the Game.' Systems of Innovation for Inclusive Development (SIID) Policy Options, No 1.

Right to Food Campaign (RTF) (2007): 'Report of the Consultation Held on the Public Distribution System in Chennai', Tamil Nadu, 10 July.

Sainath P. (2010): 'Agricultural Crisis'. Nearly 2 lakh farm suicides since 1997. Indiatogether.org., 25 Jan. Accessed on 3 April, 2010 from http://www.indiatogether.org/2010/jan/psa-suicides.htm.

Sanyal B. (1983): 'How revolutionary was India's Green Revolution?' *South Asia Bulletin*, Vol. III (2): pp. 31-44.

Sharma D. (2006): 'Indian Villages for Sale', Countercurrents.org, 13 February. Available from http://www.countercurrents.org/gl-sharma130206.htm on 14 June, 2013.

Shiva V. (1991): 'The Green Revolution in the Punjab, *The Ecologist*, Vol. 21 (2).

Subrahmaniam V. (2010): 'President calls for second Green Revolution'. *The Hindu*, dated 26 January. Accessed on 24 April, 2010 from http://www.thehindu.com/2010/01/26/stories/201001265487 1000.htm.

Swati Dhoot (2006): 'National Agriculture Policy—A Critical Evaluation', Briefing Paper is published by CUTS Centre for International Trade, Economics & Environment.

*The Hindu* (2010): Manmohan asks corporates to reach out to rural economy, 27 May, viewed on 5 June, 2010 at http://thehindu.com/business/Industry/article439110.ece.

UN Committee on Economic, Social and Cultural Rights (UNESCR) (2008): 'The problems of non-implementation of ESCR rights in India: The tribal dimension', National Committee for Human Rights Treaty Monitoring in India, New Delhi.

Varadharajan S. (2010): 'Order on free grain to poor can't be executed: Manmohan Singh', *The Hindu*, 7 September. Available from http://hindu.com/thehindu/thscrip/print.pl?file=2010090759590100.htm&date=2010/09/07/&prd=th& on 14 June, 2013.

Wharton C.R. Jr. (1969): 'The Green Revolution: Cornucopia or Pandora's Box?' *Foreign Affairs*, Vol. 47 (3): pp. 464-476.

World Bank (2005): *India: Re-energizing the Agricultural Sector to Sustain Growth and Reduce Poverty*, New Delhi, Oxford University Press.

# 6

# Food Security

## The Gaffes of the Past and the Options for the Future (Part II)

In the previous chapter with reference to various causes being made from different quarters for a Second Green Revolution, we carried out a broad overview of the food security policies that have been pursued by the Indian ruling classes, especially since the beginning of the neoliberal economic reforms in 1990. To put it mildly, these policies have singularly failed to address the challenge of ensuring the food security of the people of the country. The apparently overflowing food stocks of the Government are more a consequence of the falling purchasing power of the people due to their rising impoverishment rather than an excess left after satisfying their dietary needs. Even the greenery of the most treasured achievement of India's rulers on the food security front—the 'Green Revolution' appears illusionary with its adverse effects on food production, environment, health and prosperity of the people showing up in the very heart of the 'Green Revolution' belt—in Punjab.

Chapter 5 lays down the context in which to examine the new policies that are being proposed towards addressing India's food security needs, among which the policies for ushering in the 'Second Green Revolution' (SGR)are the most prominent. This part of the paper discusses these policies as also what we think should be at the centre of policies directed at ensuring India's food security.

## What does the 'Second Green Revolution' (SGR) Mean?

Most of us in the developing world have got used to the 'made in the West, only for the Third World' kind of solutions to a wide range of problems from population, to health, to economic growth and hunger. Till the demise of Soviet Union, countries like India had the relative comfort of manipulating between one of the two super powers with regard to help at resolving different problems, but post-cold war US has been the undisputed beacon light of our policy establishment.

The concern for restraining the spread of communism may have lent a sense of welfare concerns to the efforts of USAID and foundations like the Ford and Rockefeller to export the First Green Revolution (FGR) to the developing world. Under the changed political and economic circumstances, the SGR is an outright commercial enterprise of the Western agribusiness corporations to comprehensively dominate the Third World food chains—from farm to plate, of course with the active collabouration of their Third World acolytes.

The broad contours of the SGR were laid down in the National Agriculture Policy declared on 28 July 2000. Among the various propositions of the policy, the following directly prepared the ground for greater role of corporate sector in agricultural growth (GOI, 2000):

- An agricultural growth rate more than 4 per cent per annum.
- Accelerate the growth of agrobusiness in the country.
- Growth of agriculture that 'maximizes benefits from exports of agricultural products in the face of the challenges arising from economic liberalisation and globalisation.'

- 'Quality consciousness amongst farmers and agro-processors will be created. Grading and standardi-sation of agricultural products will be promoted for export enhancement.'
- It sought to promote the use of bio-technology in evolving new species of food crops.
- Development of marketing infrastructure and setting up of agro-processing units in rural areas to reduce post-harvest losses, value addition to the produce and generate employment.
- It promised institutional reforms to support the above policy measures for achieving higher productivity.

The policy does not even mention protecting the interests of small and marginal farmers who constitute the overwhelming majority of India's peasantry, let alone those of landless agricultural labourers. The process of deepening the reach of markets in agriculture was later taken further through the following measures (Gurung and Gilmour, 2008):

- Restrictions on contract farming inherent in the 'Agricultural Produce Market Committee Act' were revised.
- Food processing sector which was hither to the reserve of small sector was opened up for big business.
- Many more commodities were opened up for futures trading.
- Many agribusiness sectors, except some kinds of retail trade and primary production, were opened up for 100% foreign ownership.

Interestingly, many of these policy initiatives are in conformity with the World Bank directives which identified following priority areas (among others) for its support (World Bank, Undated):

- 'Shift in public expenditures away from subsidies towards productivity enhancing investments.'
- 'Agricultural diversification to higher value products . . . creating the enabling environment for private sector participation and competition for agribusiness' for growth in rural non-farm sector.
- Reforms in land policy, especially tenancy policies to facilitate access to land (read for the corporate sector).

The soul and the body of the SGR however is constituted in the Indo-US Agriculture Knowledge Initiative (AKI) that was signed on the 18 July 2005 between the two governments in Washington D.C. during the visit of the Indian Prime Minister Dr Manmohan Singh. Addressing the US Congress the Prime Minister said (*The Economic Times*, 2005):

> 'The Green Revolution lifted countless millions above poverty . . . I am very happy to say that US President George Bush and I have decided to launch a second generation of India-US collaboration in agriculture.'

The pact targets four areas for cooperation (Majumdar et al., 2010):

1. Agricultural education, syllabus formulation, research and training
2. Food processing and the utilisation of fossil fuels
3. Biotechnology and
4. Irrigation methods

Of the ₹ 350 crore (US $ 3.5 billion) to be spent by India on AKI, ₹ 65 crore (0.65 billion $) shall be spent on human resource development, ₹ 45 crore (0.45 billion $) are to be spent on agroprocessing and bio-fuels, ₹ 25 crore (0.25 billion $) on water management and the bulk ₹ 214 crore ($ 2.14 billion) on biotechnology (Goswami, 2006).

As regards agricultural education, research and training, if the general scheme of things and experience of FGR is anything to go by, there need not be any illusion about who will teach and who will be the taught. The important thing to note is that the American agribusiness corporations and their scientists in American universities shall leverage their role in AKI to cultivate generations of agricultural scientists in India who would be seeped in the value system of American industrial agriculture and shall be an instrument to safeguard the interests of American agribusiness in India. Moreover, the starting premise of initiatives like AKI, as indeed was the case with FGR, is that the peasants themselves are an ignorant lot, there is no place in this schema for the traditional knowledge of the local farming communities who have maintained, nurtured and enriched the biodiversity of food crops in India over the centuries. Rather than enrich and develop their traditional knowledge and practice and be enriched in return, the underlying zeal is that of improving the farming practices of the backward peasants to modernise agriculture.

Biotechnology clearly is the priority. Representatives of Monsanto, which seeds three-quarters of World's farm lands growing genetically modified crops (Goswami, 2006), are there on the board of AKI. It is not difficult to know exactly who would be calling the shots. Most importantly, Government shall brook no resistance to its designs. The Draft National Biotechnology Regulatory Bill lays the ground for gagging dissent by proposing that any person 'who provides any information or produces any document that he knows is false or misleading' shall be penalised under the provisions of the Act (GOI, 2008).

Besides Monsanto, the presence of the representatives of Walmart, (world's number one retailer) and Archers Daniel Midlands (world's largest food trader) on the board of AKI rounds up the design to dominate every aspect of food chain from the farm to plate (Goswami, 2006).

For the Indian corporate, AKI is 'the opportunity' to rake in windfall profits. They have already forayed into areas like direct buying and selling of agricultural produce, production of gherkins and other horticultural produce for export, animal feed, and sale of agricultural inputs—all of little significance to the problem of hunger in the country (Mukhopadhyaya, 2010). Meanwhile different multinational agribusinesses have already established strong presence in the country. There has been a creeping Monsanto-isation of agriculture in India (Kuruganti and Madineni, 2010).

Other companies like DuPont, BASF, DOW, Dean Foods, Bayer and Syngenta which provide genetically modified seeds, pesticides, herbicides etc. have already established their presence in the agribusiness of the country. There is presence of farm equipment manufacturers—John Deere and CNH's New Holland. US based companies like ePlanet Ventures and Blakcstone Group have made an entry into Indian agribusiness by buying stakes in Indian companies. Private equity firms like Morgan Stanley, The Netherlands Development Finance Company (FMO) and Rabobank are all there, probably to help develop the futures trading component of ensuring food security (Mukhopadhaya, 2010). It was not long back that the then ruling coalition at the Centre led by the Congress Party ran into rough weather over its proposal to allow 100% foreign equity in multi-brand retail trade. We have already noted in Part 1, the Indian companies that have forayed into agribusiness sector. Hence we have a transnational and their Indian partner ready to pitch in at every step of the food chain involving every step of the crop cycle, food processing, packaging and retailing.

This scheme of things was given a formal shape by the Government of India in its 'Framework for Supporting Public Private Partnerships for Integrated Agricultural Development (PPPIAD) under Rashtriya Krishi Vikas Yojana (RKVY).' The Framework is described upfront as (GOI, 2012):

> A Scheme for facilitating large scale integrated projects, led by private sector players in the agriculture and allied sectors, with a view to aggregating farmers, and integrating the agricultural supply chain, with financial assistance through RKVY, under the direct supervision of State Governments, supported by National Level Agencies.

As to the industry's influence in designing these schemes we need not draw inferences when we can have it from the horse's mouth. The 'Overview' statement of the 'Agriculture Sector' of FICCI (Federation of Indian Chambers of Commerce and Industry) as accessed on the FICCI website states:

> Over the years, through its long standing collaboration with the Ministry of Agriculture, Government of India, the Agriculture desk has worked assiduously to promote public-private partnership in various parts of agriculture value chain including agri-warehousing, farm mechanisation, extension, secondary agriculture, risk management and agri-marketing reforms (FICCI, 2013).

Entailing all of this could still be considered provided we had any reason to believe that this would deliver for the Indian people, especially its poor, most of whom are directly involved in farming. But then we need to be wiser by the experience—both our own as also that of others. We have mentioned, albeit briefly, regarding the effects of the FGR in its very heartland in Part I. The acclaimed success of the FGR notwithstanding, no one can say that it is an experience worth repeating in the areas where SGR is proposed to be staged.

As to the agribusiness-led model of the SGR that is on the anvil, the question is not just of its within country operations, this means that not only is there going to be greater industrialisation of food chains within the country but also that India's food economy shall be in an ever increasing embrace of the world food economy and thus liable to be impacted by it. Many authors have commented on the increasing influence of the western food transnationals on the food markets in the developing world (Wilkinson, 2009, Benjamin and Venturini, 2005). This interlinking means that much of the food production in the developing countries starts gearing to cater to the markets of the developed world (Rae and Josling, 2003) even as conditions of deficient food consumption remain in these countries. Simultaneously, there could be dumping of cheap food from the developed countries in the developing world markets, thus adversely affecting local food producers.

Simultaneously, notwithstanding the spirited arguments of the policy planners favouring greater industrialisation of food chains in the name of getting new technology to help preserve and process food better and thereby reduce food wastages, the available evidence suggests that food wastage is a direct function of industrialisation of food chains (Goswami, 2011, Competition Commission, 2000, Kantor et al., 1997). Let alone food wastage at farm level and retail, the consumer level food wastages in Europe and North America amount to around 222 million tons which almost equals the net food production of Sub-Saharan Africa at 230 million tons (Goswami, 2011). One can only imagine the extent to which this corporate-led model of SGR can undermine India's food security. And given the size of India's population, India's food insecurity cannot but imperil the food security of other food deficient countries in the developing world.

## Extending Green Revolution to Eastern India

In the 2010 budget, the then Finance Minister, Pranab Mukerjee announced an allocation of ₹ 400 crore under the 'Rashtriya Krishi Vikas Yojana' (National Agriculture Development Scheme) towards furthering efforts at extending the Green Revolution to the eastern Indian states of Bihar, Jharkhand, Eastern UP, Chhattisgarh, Odisha and West Bengal (GOI, 2010).

We have already sketched the broad contours of the proposed Second Green Revolution and this gives little reason for us to hope for success in this endeavour. This still leaves for us the task of fathoming what lies in store for the people of the country as a consequence of these efforts.

To answer this question, we would like to begin by delineating our analytical framework. To put it simply, it is—'Increasing production is not a function of advancement in forces of production alone insofar as forces of production operate in the context of given relations of production. Hence, advancing production entails progressively changing the relations of production through the due social, economic and political processes to create new relations of production that are in tandem with the advanced forces of production. Disjunction between the two can be socially and economically disruptive resulting in huge costs to human welfare. Further, the people involved in production are the most invaluable among the forces of production.

The strategy to unleash 'Second Green Revolution' (SGR) seeks to detach the advancement of 'forces of production' (read technology controlled by agro-corporations and only the rich peasantry) from the 'context of production' i.e. the semi-feudal relations of production that bedevil Indian agriculture. Without affording the risk of delving into the larger debate on the mode of production in Indian agriculture over here, we would nonetheless like to trace certain developments over the years in the seven states where Green Revolution is sought to be extended, as also in the states of Punjab and Haryana which hosted the first Green Revolution. These developments shall serve as a pointer to the nature of the relations of production in Indian agriculture. What this means as to the ability of the proposed technological interventions to enhance agricultural production and food security and the consequences to human welfare in these states would remain to be seen.

## Changes in the Operational Holdings

Figure 6.1 below gives the changes in the Gini coefficient of concentration of size distribution of operational holdings in

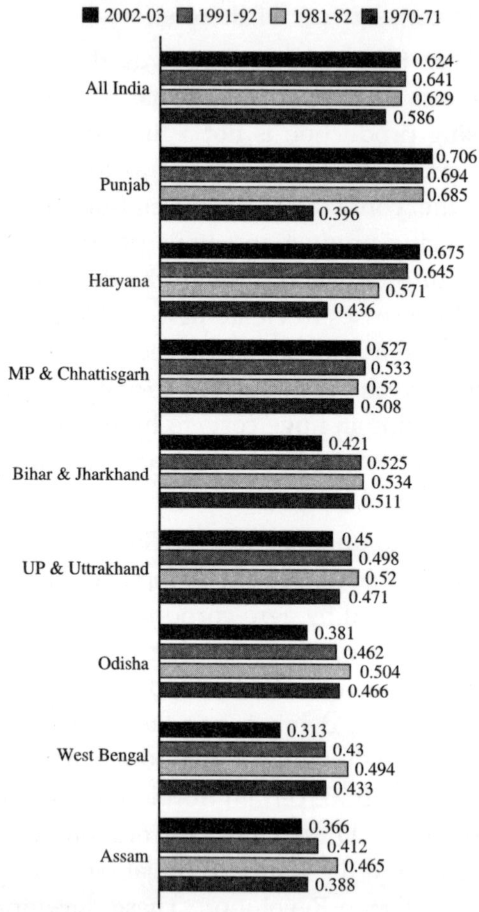


Figure 6.1: Trends in inequality in the distribution of operational holdings—All India, Punjab, Haryana and the targeted Second Green Revolution states.

*Source:* Table 2.4.3 in NSSO, 2006, p. 25.

*Note:* Since separate Gini coefficient for all the years is not available for Jharkhand, Chattisgarh and UP excluding Uttrakhand, the Gini coefficients used are those for the earlier unified states. For the year 2002-03 the Gini coefficient is arrived at by taking average of the parent state and the new state.

Table 6.1: Proportions of Number and Area Operated for Operational Holdings of Different Sizes

| *India/State* | *Size of land holding* | *1970-71* | | *1981-82* | | *1991-92* | | *2002-03* | |
|---|---|---|---|---|---|---|---|---|---|
| | | *% of holdings* | *% area operated* | *% of holdings* | *% area operated* | *% of holdings* | *% area operated* | *% of holdings* | *% area operated* |
| All India | Large | 03.1 | 23.0 | 01.9 | 18.2 | 01.3 | 15.2 | 00.8 | 11.8 |
| | Medium | 11.1 | 30.5 | 08.6 | 30.2 | 06.1 | 26.4 | 04.2 | 22.2 |
| | Semi-medium | 17.7 | 22.5 | 14.2 | 23.6 | 12.0 | 24.1 | 09.0 | 22.5 |
| | Small | 22.4 | 14.8 | 19.3 | 16.6 | 17.8 | 18.7 | 16.2 | 20.9 |
| | Marginal | 45.8 | 09.2 | 56.0 | 11.5 | 62.8 | 15.6 | 69.8 | 22.6 |
| Assam | Large | 0.01 | 0.70 | 0.01 | 01.4 | 0.02 | 02.6 | 0.00 | 0.00 |
| | Medium | 03.0 | 12.2 | 02.7 | 13.7 | 01.5 | 09.1 | 0.60 | 04.9 |
| | Semi-medium | 14.3 | 30.5 | 11.3 | 29.3 | 07.5 | 22.9 | 04.7 | 17.1 |
| | Small | 30.2 | 34.9 | 24.3 | 33.5 | 20.0 | 31.2 | 18.4 | 36.0 |
| | Marginal | 52.4 | 21.6 | 61.6 | 22.1 | 70.8 | 34.2 | 76.2 | 42.0 |
| Bihar and Jharkhand | Large | 00.5 | 05.7 | 00.4 | 05.9 | 00.2 | 03.9 | 00.2 | 03.2 |
| | Medium | 04.5 | 21.0 | 03.4 | 18.8 | 02.5 | 18.2 | 01.0 | 08.7 |
| | Semi-medium | 12.9 | 28.9 | 09.9 | 27.1 | 06.9 | 23.7 | 4.00 | 17.6 |
| | Small | 23.3 | 26.2 | 17.6 | 25.9 | 13.7 | 25.1 | 12.2 | 27.4 |
| | Marginal | 58.9 | 18.1 | 68.7 | 22.4 | 76.8 | 29.0 | 82.6 | 43.0 |

(*Contd.*)

Table 6.1: Proportions of Number and Area Operated for Operational Holdings of Different Sizes (*Contd.*)

| *India/State* | *Size of land holding* | *1970-71* | | *1981-82* | | *1991-92* | | *2002-03* | |
|---|---|---|---|---|---|---|---|---|---|
| | | *% of holdings* | *% area operated* | *% of holdings* | *% area operated* | *% of holdings* | *% area operated* | *% of holdings* | *% area operated* |
| Haryana | Large | 05.6 | 21.8 | 03.4 | 17.9 | 04.0 | 31.0 | 00.9 | 15.1 |
| | Medium | 31.1 | 49.2 | 18.8 | 45.6 | 11.5 | 29.4 | 07.8 | 35.0 |
| | Semi-medium | 28.3 | 19.9 | 22.9 | 25.6 | 20.3 | 25.5 | 12.3 | 26.0 |
| | Small | 17.5 | 06.5 | 12.7 | 07.3 | 13.5 | 08.8 | 12.8 | 13.5 |
| | Marginal | 17.5 | 02.5 | 42.2 | 03.7 | 50.7 | 05.3 | 66.3 | 10.4 |
| MP and Chhattisgrah | Large | 06.2 | 28.6 | 03.6 | 20.2 | 02.5 | 16.4 | 01.2 | 11.2 |
| | Medium | 21.6 | 38.0 | 17.9 | 38.6 | 13.5 | 35.9 | 07.7 | 27.0 |
| | Semi-medium | 25.8 | 21.2 | 23.1 | 24.2 | 20.9 | 25.5 | 16.7 | 28.5 |
| | Small | 20.3 | 08.9 | 22.5 | 12.3 | 24.4 | 15.6 | 23.3 | 20.3 |
| | Marginal | 26.1 | 03.4 | 32.9 | 04.7 | 38.7 | 06.7 | 51.2 | 13.1 |
| Odisha | Large | 00.6 | 05.5 | 00.7 | 12.5 | 00.3 | 03.7 | 0.10 | 0.90 |
| | Medium | 05.3 | 21.6 | 04.6 | 17.8 | 03.4 | 16.2 | 01.1 | 08.6 |
| | Semi-medium | 13.9 | 27.1 | 14.1 | 26.2 | 12.0 | 27.9 | 05.2 | 18.8 |
| | Small | 25.8 | 27.3 | 26.1 | 26.5 | 24.3 | 30.2 | 15.2 | 28.7 |
| | Marginal | 54.5 | 18.6 | 54.5 | 17.0 | 60.0 | 22.1 | 78.4 | 43.0 |

(*Contd.*)

Table 6.1: Proportions of Number and Area Operated for Operational Holdings of Different Sizes (*Contd.*)

| *India/State* | *Size of land holding* | *1970-71* | | *1981-82* | | *1991-92* | | *2002-03* | |
|---|---|---|---|---|---|---|---|---|---|
| | | *% of holdings* | *% area operated* | *% of holdings* | *% area operated* | *% of holdings* | *% area operated* | *% of holdings* | *% area operated* |
| Punjab | Large | 06.0 | 22.1 | 02.5 | 19.6 | 01.7 | 15.8 | 01.9 | 18.5 |
| | Medium | 30.5 | 45.1 | 14.2 | 45.9 | 09.8 | 40.6 | 07.8 | 36.4 |
| | Semi-medium | 32.7 | 24.3 | 14.0 | 21.8 | 13.9 | 26.7 | 12.9 | 26.2 |
| | Small | 19.1 | 07.1 | 10.4 | 08.9 | 11.4 | 10.7 | 11.2 | 11.7 |
| | Marginal | 11.7 | 01.5 | 59.0 | 03.9 | 63.2 | 06.2 | 66.3 | 07.3 |
| UP and Uttrakhand | Large | 0.70 | 06.0 | 0.50 | 06.5 | 0.30 | 03.7 | 00.1 | 00.9 |
| | Medium | 06.2 | 23.3 | 05.4 | 23.6 | 03.4 | 16.2 | 01.1 | 08.6 |
| | Semi-medium | 16.5 | 29.8 | 12.9 | 28.0 | 12.0 | 27.9 | 05.2 | 18.8 |
| | Small | 26.9 | 25.3 | 21.6 | 23.8 | 24.3 | 30.2 | 15.2 | 28.7 |
| | Marginal | 49.8 | 15.6 | 59.6 | 18.1 | 60.0 | 22.1 | 78.4 | 43.0 |
| West Bengal | Large | 00.1 | 00.6 | 00.5 | 06.5 | 00.3 | 04.3 | 00.1 | 02.8 |
| | Medium | 3.00 | 23.3 | 05.4 | 23.6 | 03.3 | 18.2 | 01.7 | 12.5 |
| | Semi-medium | 12.9 | 29.8 | 12.9 | 28.0 | 09.9 | 26.3 | 05.6 | 19.8 |
| | Small | 22.8 | 25.3 | 21.6 | 23.8 | 18.5 | 26.3 | 15.9 | 29.2 |
| | Marginal | 61.2 | 15.6 | 59.6 | 18.1 | 68.0 | 25.0 | 76.7 | 35.7 |

*Source:* Table 3.6, NSSO, 2006. Note: Large land holding (>10 hectares), Medium (4-10 hectares), Semi-medium (2-4 hectares), Small (1-2 hectares) and Marginal (<1 hectare).

the seven eastern states and Punjab, Haryana and All India. It can be seen from the figure that while inequity in the distribution of operational holdings has increased for the country as a whole, it has increased rather sharply in the two FGR states of Punjab and Haryana, meaning thereby that land has progressively got concentrated in the hands of fewer big landowners while the proportion of land in control of small and marginal farmers has decreased.

With the exception of Madhya Pradesh and Chhattisgarh where there has been a marginal increase in the inequity of the distribution of operational holdings, in all the other states this inequity has decreased. However, to be able to get the full import of these changes we have to look at Table 6.1 and Figures 6.2a to 6.2d which record the changes in the number and area of operational holdings of different sizes in the aforementioned states along with the all India picture.

From the Figures 6.2a and 6.2b we can see that for the country as a whole there was a six times increase in the number of marginal operational holdings per large holding between 1970-71 and 2002-03, while similar increase in case of FGR states of Punjab and Haryana has been 17.9 and 23.5 times respectively. On the other hand, size of an average

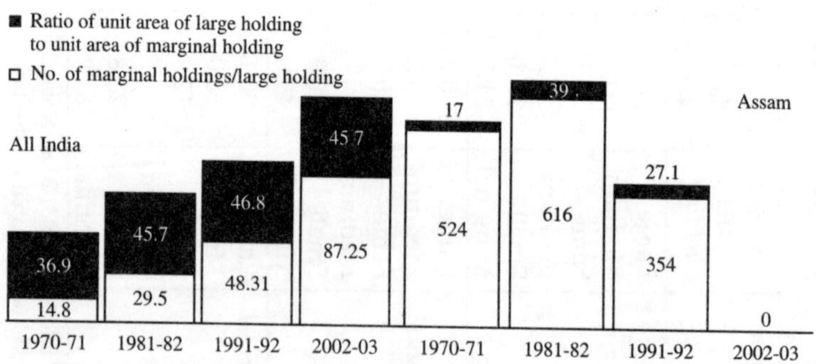


Figure 6.2a: Changes in numbers and area of marginal as compared to large operational holdings: All India and Assam.

*Source:* Based on calculations made from figures given in Table 6.1.

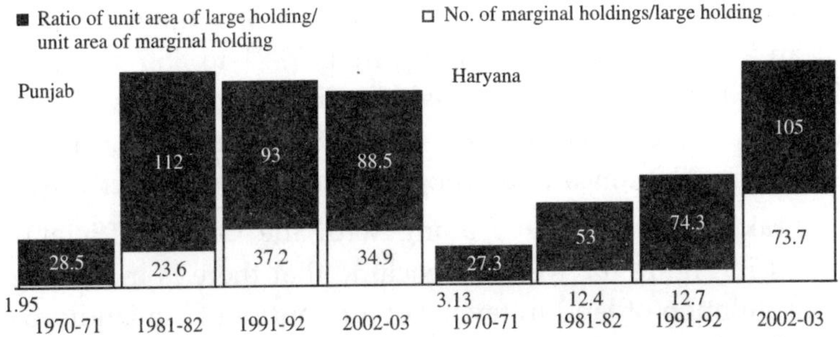


Figure 6.2b: Changes in numbers and area of marginal to large operational holdings: Punjab and Haryana.

*Source:* Based on calculations made from figures given in Table 6.1.

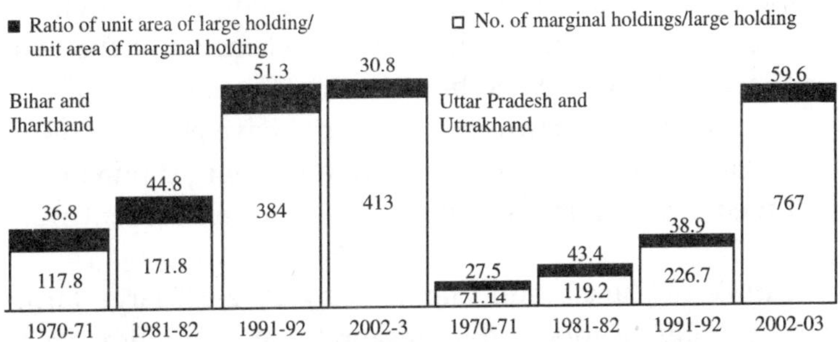


Figure 6.2c: Changes in numbers and area of marginal to large operational holdings: Bihar and Jharkhand and UP and Uttrakhand.

*Source:* Based on calculations made from figures given in Table 6.1.

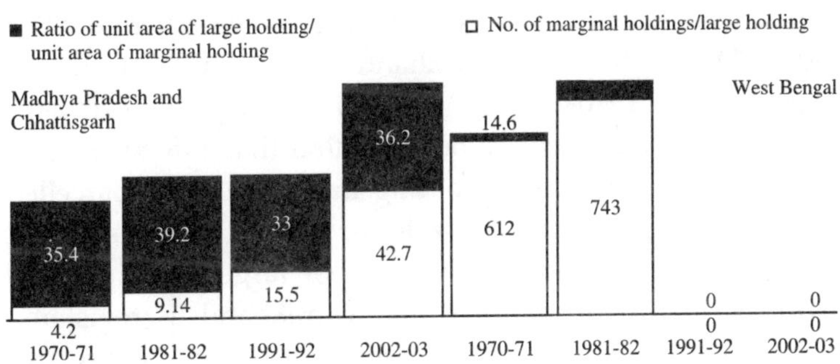


Figure 6.2d: Changes in numbers and area of marginal to large operational holdings: Madhya Pradesh and Chhattisgarh and West Bengal.

*Source:* Based on calculations made from figures given in Table 6.1.

large operational holding increased from 36.9 times the size of an average marginal holding in 1970-71 to 45.7 times in 2002-03 for the country as a whole. Similar increases in case of Punjab and Haryana were from 28.5 times to 88.5 times and from 27.3 times to a whopping 105 times respectively.

Taking these figures along with the Gini coefficients given in Figure 6.1 we can conclude that there is increasing consolidation of land in favour of a minority of big landlords even as the number of marginal farmers has seen a quantum jump in the country as a whole and particularly in the FGR states of Punjab and Haryana. This also indicates that the technological interventions—hybrid seeds and chemical fertilisers that constituted the essential elements of the FGR have largely benefited the big farmers. The increases in the number of marginal farms could not but have been the result of marginalisation of some medium and a larger number of semi-medium and small farmers as is so well evident from Table 6.1.

Unlike in Punjab and Haryana, by 2002-03, large farms have virtually disappeared in Assam. What is significant here is the huge numbers of marginal farms. Likewise, in case of Bihar, Jharkhand, UP and Uttrakhand (Figure 6.2c) the number of large operational holdings is miniscule while the number of marginal farms per large farm has increased from 117.8 and 71.14 for Bihar and Jharkhand and UP and Uttrakhand respectively in 1970-71 to 413 and 767 respectively in 2002-03.

However, one needs to bear in mind that a de facto large or very large operational holding may de jure be parcelled out into smaller holdings in order to avoid land ceiling laws. To this extent, the low proportion of large land holdings in Bihar, Jharkhand and UP and Uttrakhand as registered in NSSO data may be an underestimate. Nonetheless, this does not deviate from the significance of the overwhelming existence of marginal farms in these states. We can further note from Figure 2d that the situation in West Bengal is almost the same as in case of Assam with the exception that the number of marginal farms is much more. The development in case of MP and Chhattisgarh again shows that the number of marginal farms has been increasing even as there has not been an appreciable increase in the further concentration of land into large farms.

## Some Features of Tenancy in the Second Green Revolution Target States

Tenancy relations in agriculture production can be a very good measure of the relations of production in agriculture in the country—who leases out to whom and at what terms. Tables 6.2 and 6.3 bring out these aspects to some extent.

Table 6.2: Share of Landless and Semi-landless Households to Total Households Leasing in Land (2002-03)

| *State/India* | *Landless* | *Less than 0.5 ha* | *0.5 to 1 ha* | *Total* |
|---|---|---|---|---|
| Punjab | 23.8 | 31.9 | 13.0 | 68.7 |
| Haryana | 24.0 | 45.4 | 8.90 | 78.3 |
| Assam | 34.7 | 43.6 | 11.3 | 89.6 |
| Bihar | 5.80 | 87.0 | 6.00 | 98.8 |
| Chhattisgarh | 26.9 | 43.5 | 18.6 | 89.0 |
| Odisha | 17.3 | 71.8 | 7.90 | 97.0 |
| Uttar Pradesh | 7.80 | 69.5 | 13.2 | 90.5 |
| West Bengal | 14.1 | 75.1 | 8.40 | 97.6 |
| Jharkhand | 45.0 | 42.9 | 8.10 | 96.0 |
| All India | 35.8 | 47.5 | 8.20 | 91.5 |

*Source:* Table 2.5 in GOI, undated.

Combining the findings of Table 6.2 and 6.3 gives a fairly good idea of the semi-feudal relations of production that are entrenched in Indian agriculture including in states like Punjab and Haryana where it is contended that capitalism in agriculture is developed maximally. With the exception of

Punjab and Haryana, where the proportion is a little lower, in the rest of the states, the landless and marginal farmers constitute 90% or more of the households leasing in land. Since agriculture is far more developed in Punjab and Haryana and much of the production takes place for selling, it is possible that some land is leased in by bigger farmers to produce greater marketable surplus.

Table 6.3: Percentage Distribution of Area Leased Out by Terms of Lease for the SGR States, Punjab, Haryana and All India

| *State/India* (*a*) | *For fixed money* (*b*) | *For fixed produce* (*c*) | *For share of produce* (*d*) | *Other terms* (*e*) | (*b*) + (*c*) |
|---|---|---|---|---|---|
| All India | 31.04 | 15.30 | 39.55 | 14.11 | 46.34 |
| Punjab | 91.69 | 01.73 | 01.98 | 04.60 | 93.42 |
| Haryana | 84.95 | 02.10 | 12.75 | 00.20 | 87.05 |
| Bihar | 08.89 | 20.90 | 59.90 | 10.20 | 29.79 |
| Chhattisgarh | 07.29 | 44.36 | 45.95 | 02.40 | 51.65 |
| Jharkhand | 00.53 | 00.00 | 99.47 | 00.00 | 00.53 |
| Odisha | 11.52 | 10.65 | 71.13 | 06.70 | 22.17 |
| Uttar Pradesh | 14.84 | 21.18 | 51.98 | 12.00 | 36.02 |
| West Bengal | 29.38 | 48.79 | 10.55 | 11.28 | 78.17 |

*Source:* Table 2.4 in GOI, undated. Draft Report of the 'Committee on State Agrarian Relations and the Unfinished Agenda of Land Reforms', Vol. 1, Ministry of Rural Development, Government of India.

That the majority of marginal and landless peasants who lease in land have to do so on exploitative terms is clear from Table 6.3. The terms are the most exploitative in Punjab and Haryana where agriculture is maximally developed, with close to 90% of the farmers paying rent in the form of fixed money or fixed produce, that is, all risk goes to the tenant while the landlord's fixed compensation is ensured. This could be attributed to the fact that production takes place for selling,

Table 6.4: Procurement of Rice and Wheat from States Targeted for Second Green Revolution, Punjab, Haryana and All India.

| *Crop* | *State* | *2007-08* | *2008-09* | *2009-10* | *2010-11* | *2011-12* |
|---|---|---|---|---|---|---|
| Rice (Lakh Tonnes) | Assam | 0.00 (0.00) | 0.03 (.009) | 0.08 (.03) | 0.16 (0.05) | 0.23 (0.07) |
| | Bihar | 05.55 (1.9) | 10.83 (3.2) | 08.9 (2.8) | 8.83 (2.58) | 15.34 (4.4) |
| | Chhattisgarh | 27.43 (9.5) | 28.48 (8.4) | 33.6 (10.5) | 37.5 (10.9) | 41.2 (11.7) |
| | Haryana | 15.74 (5.5) | 14.25 (4.2) | 18.19 (5.7) | 16.87 (4.9) | 20.07 (5.7) |
| | Jharkhand | 00.19 (.07) | 1.43 (0.42) | 0.23 (.07) | 0.00 (0.00) | 2.75 (0.78) |
| | Odisha | 23.57 (8.2) | 28.01 (8.2) | 24.9 (7.8) | 24.65 (7.2) | 28.66 (8.2) |
| | Punjab | 79.8 (27.8) | 85.5 (25.1) | 92.8 (29) | 86.4 (25.3) | 77.3 (22.1) |
| | Uttar Pradesh | 28.91 (10) | 40.1 (11.8) | 29.01 (9.1) | 25.54 (7.5) | 33.57 (9.6) |
| | West Bengal | 14.29 (4.9) | 17.43 (5.1) | 12.4 (3.9) | 13.1 (3.83) | 20.4 (5.82) |
| | All India Total | 287.36 (100) | 341.02 (100) | 320.34 (100) | 341.98 (100) | 350.60 (100) |

(*Contd.*)

Table 6.4: Procurement of Rice and Wheat from States Targeted for Second Green Revolution, Punjab, Haryana and All India (*Contd.*)

| *Crop* | *State* | *2007-08* | *2008-09* | *2009-10* | *2010-11* | *2011-12* |
|---|---|---|---|---|---|---|
| Wheat (Lakh MT) | Assam | 0.00 (0.00) | 0.00 (0.00) | 0.00 (0.00) | 0.00 (0.00) | 0.00 (0.00) |
| | Bihar | 0.08 (0.07) | 05.00 (2.2) | 4.97 (1.96) | 1.83 (0.81) | 5.56 (1.96) |
| | Chhattisgarh | 0.00 (0.00) | 0.00 (0.00) | 0.00 (0.00) | 0.00 (0.00) | 0.00 (0.00) |
| | Haryana | 33.5 (30.1) | 52.4 (23.1) | 69.2 (27.3) | 63.5 (28.2) | 69.3 (24.5) |
| | Jharkhand | 0.00 (0.00) | 0.02 (.009) | 0.00 (0.00) | 0.00 (0.00) | 0.00 (0.00) |
| | Odisha | 0.00 (0.00) | 0.00 (0.00) | 0.00 (0.00) | 0.00 (0.00) | 0.00 (0.00) |
| | Punjab | 67.8 (60.9) | 99.4 (43.8) | 107.3 (42.3) | 102.1 (45.4) | 109.6 (38.7) |
| | Uttar Pradesh | 5.46 (4.90) | 31.4 (13.8) | 38.8 (15.3) | 16.5 (7.31) | 34.6 (12.2) |
| | West Bengal | 0.00 (0.00) | 0.00 (0.00) | 0.00 (0.00) | 0.09 (0.04) | 0.00 (0.00) |
| | All India Total | 111.28 (100) | 226.89 (100) | 253.82 (100) | 225.04 (100) | 283.34 (100) |

*Source:* Data obtained from Planning and Research Division, Food Corporation of India Headquarters, New Delhi.

Note: It ought to be noticed that the procurement in UP is mainly from the western region of the state that forms part of the First Green Revolution areas. Procurement from eastern region of the state would at best be about the same as in case of Bihar.

however, we need bear in mind that the majority of these farmers leasing in land are landless and marginal farmers who anyway are hard pressed for resources and inputs and a good proportion of their produce is for self-consumption.

For the country as a whole, fixed rent is the condition for leasing in land in close to 50% of the tenancies. Same is the case in Chhattisgarh, and in West Bengal it is as high as 78%. The proportion remains high for Bihar and Uttar Pradesh. It is surprising that in spite of its much trumpeted tenancy reforms during the Left Front rule in West Bengal the terms of tenancy remain so exploitative for the small and marginal peasants. Such exploitative tenancy arrangements serve as a disincentive for the farmers and are a drag on increasing production.

## Production for Self-consumption

Using the data of 59th Round of National Sample Survey, De Janvry and Sadoulet (2008) estimated that in India 74 and 53.7% of marginal and small farmers respectively, and a higher proportion of landless peasants are net purchasers of food (De Janvry and Sadoulet, 2008). In a scenario where not even the small, but it is the marginal and landless peasants who constitute the overwhelming majority of farmers, the implications of these findings are quite apparent. This further brings forth the exploitative character of tenancy arrangements in Indian agriculture in general and the SGR targeted states in particular.

Barring parts of Western Uttar Pradesh, in most of the states where Green Revolution is sought to be extended production primarily takes place for self-consumption with very little marketable surplus as is evident from Table 6.4 and Figures 6.3a and 6.3b which give the procurement of wheat and rice in these states as a proportion of total rice and wheat procurement for central pool in the country.

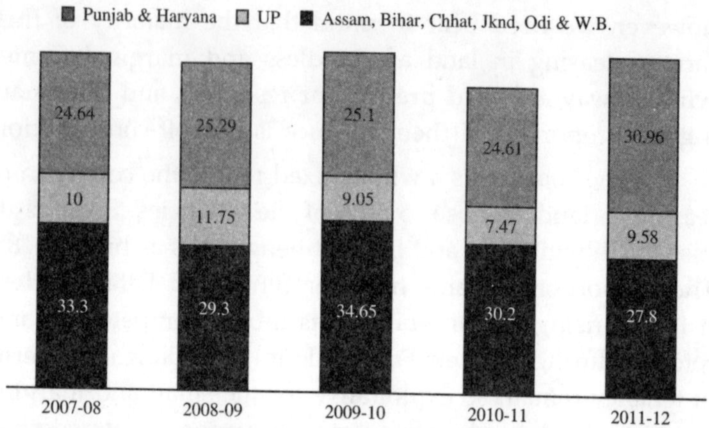


Figure 6.3a: Share of different states in the procurement of rice for central pool.

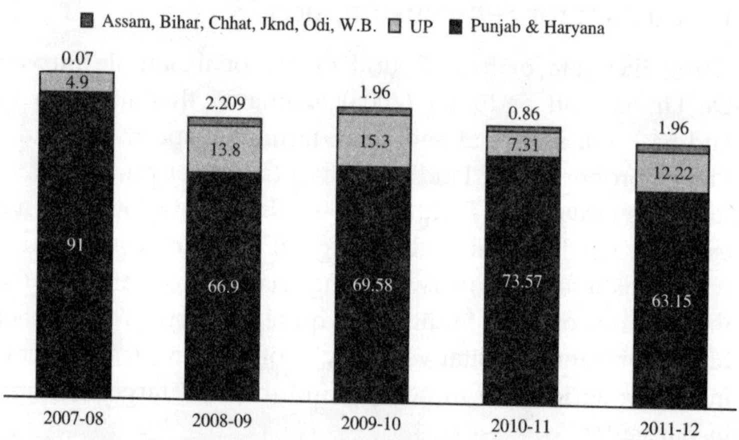


Figure 6.3b: Share of different states in the procurement of wheat for central pool.

*Source:* Both Figures 6.3a and 6.3b are based on data obtained from Planning and Research Division, Food Corporation of India Headquarters, New Delhi. Again UP has been shown separately from other Second Green Revolution (SGR) states as most of the food grain procurement in UP is from western region of the state rather than the eastern region which is the target area for SGR.

As regards the procurement of rice, Punjab and Haryana alone account for 31.05% of the procurement, the six states barring UP targeted for SGR account for 26.12%, in which also only two states—Chhattisgarh and Odisha account for more than half. In the procurement of wheat, the contribution of the six targeted states is virtually negligible at an average of 1.41%, and all of this comes almost from one state only—Bihar.

We have mentioned UP separately in Figures 6.3a and 6.3b because virtually entire procurement of rice and wheat in UP comes from the western part of the state. Eastern part of UP which is targeted for SGR contributes minimally. The substantive contribution of Punjab and Haryana to rice and wheat procurement need not be taken as an ode to Green Revolution. The reasons for this have already been discussed in Part I of the paper. Besides, the yield in Punjab and Haryana still remains lower than small farms in countries like China, Japan and many others. Higher contribution of Punjab and Haryana does not go to prove that similar or even higher productivity could not have been achieved with more sustainable methods in agriculture.

## Indebtedness in the SGR Targeted States

In the era of country's entrenched agrarian crisis no description of peasantry can be complete without discussing the issue of indebtedness. In this regard, the findings of the 59th Round of NSSO survey on the 'Indebtedness of Farmer Households' are very illustrative. The data of this survey is about a decade old (January to December 2003) and in that sense, is relatively dated. In view of this, the following findings are sufficient to bring out the gravity of the situation as might exist today. Table 6.5 gives the incidence of indebtedness of farm households in the SGR targeted states, Punjab, Haryana and the All India figures.

Table 6.5: Estimated Number of Rural Households and Total and Indebted Farmer Households in Different States

| *State* | *Estimated number of rural HH ('00)* | *Estimated number of farmer HH ('00)* | *Estimated number of indebted farmer HH ('00)* | *Percentage of indebted farmer HH* |
|---|---|---|---|---|
| Punjab | 29,847 | 18,442 | 12,069 | 65.4 |
| Haryana | 31,474 | 19,445 | 10,330 | 53.1 |
| West Bengal | 121,667 | 69,226 | 34,696 | 50.1 |
| Odisha | 66,199 | 42,341 | 20,250 | 47.8 |
| Uttar Pradesh | 221,499 | 171,575 | 69,199 | 40.3 |
| Chhattisgarh | 36,316 | 27,598 | 11,092 | 40.2 |
| Bihar | 116,853 | 70,804 | 23,383 | 33.0 |
| Jharkhand | 36,930 | 28,238 | 5,893 | 20.9 |
| Assam | 41,525 | 25,040 | 4,536 | 18.1 |
| All India | 1,478,988 | 893,504 | 434,242 | 48.6 |

*Source:* Statement 1 in GOI, 2005.

It is noteworthy from the Table above that close to 50% of the peasants in India were indebted in 2003. Further, the incidence of indebtedness is the highest in the states that hosted the FGR i.e. Punjab and Haryana. We do not have the disaggregated figure for the western region of UP which was also covered by FGR, but the 40% indebtedness for the whole state does point to the probability that indebtedness could be closer to that observed in Punjab and Haryana, in the western region of the State. That indebtedness is less in other SGR targeted states does not leave the farmers in these states far behind in the misery lane as is evident from Tables 6.6 and 6.7.

In West Bengal, it was already above the national average. Table 6.6 gives the average amount of outstanding loan in rupees per farmer household in different states. Again the pattern is the same as in case of incidence of indebtedness with the highest outstanding loans per farm household in Punjab followed by Haryana and then UP.

Table 6.6: Average Amount of Outstanding Loan in Rupees Per Farmer Household (of All Social Groups Combined) in Different States

| *State* | *Average loan per farmer household (All social groups)* |
|---|---|
| Punjab | 41,576 |
| Haryana | 26,007 |
| Uttar Pradesh | 7,425 |
| Odisha | 5,871 |
| West Bengal | 5,237 |
| Bihar | 4,476 |
| Chhattisgarh | 4,122 |
| Jharkhand | 2,205 |
| Assam | 813 |
| All India | 12,585 |

*Source:* Statement 14 in GOI, 2005.

Table 6.7 on the other hand shows that maximum indebtedness is seen among the marginal and small peasant households. Of the 9 states mentioned in the Table, in 5 SGR targeted states, farm households with landholdings less than 2 hectares constituted more than 90% of the indebted households. In UP it was only 1.3% less than the 90% mark. The proportion of small and marginal farmers among indebted households is slightly less in states like Punjab and Haryana probably because in these agriculturally more productive states the large and middle peasants could also be availing of loans for investments to further increase the marketable surplus produce. However, they are better placed to avail of the formal sector loans at more convenient terms. Moreover,

Table 6.7: Per 1000 Distribution of Indebted Farmer Households by Size Class of Land Possessed in Different States

| *State* | *Size class of land processed (in ha)* | | | | | | | | | |
|---|---|---|---|---|---|---|---|---|---|---|
| | *0.01* | *0.01-0.04* | *0.041-1.00* | *1.01-2.00* | *2.01-4.00* | *4.01-10.00* | *10.0 +* | *All sizes* | *< 1.00 (%)* | *< 2.00 (%)* |
| Assam | 3 | 332 | 371 | 208 | 81 | 5 | 0 | 1,000 | 706 (70.6) | 914 (91.4) |
| Bihar | 18 | 580 | 271 | 92 | 28 | 7 | 6 | 1,000 | 869 (86.9) | 961 (96.1) |
| Chhattisgarh | 1 | 114 | 331 | 306 | 169 | 75 | 4 | 1,000 | 446 (44.6) | 752 (75.2) |
| Haryana | 38 | 305 | 180 | 183 | 197 | 88 | 9 | 1,000 | 523 (52.3) | 706 (70.6) |
| Jharkhand | 8 | 506 | 281 | 156 | 27 | 9 | 12 | 1,000 | 795 (79.5) | 951 (95.1) |
| Odisha | 3 | 235 | 465 | 206 | 73 | 17 | 0 | 1,000 | 703 (70.3) | 909 (90.9) |
| Punjab | 27 | 398 | 108 | 158 | 170 | 118 | 22 | 1,000 | 533 (53.3) | 691 (69.1) |
| Uttar Pradesh | 25 | 399 | 289 | 174 | 78 | 34 | 3 | 1,000 | 713 (71.3) | 887 (88.7) |
| West Bengal | 7 | 582 | 298 | 85 | 24 | 4 | 0 | 1,000 | 887 (88.7) | 972 (97.2) |
| All India | 13 | 299 | 298 | 189 | 125 | 64 | 12 | 1,000 | 610 (61.0) | 799 (79.9) |

*Source:* Statement 6 in GOI, 2005.

areas where the feudal mode of production is more overt in agriculture, the big landlords characteristically tend to maximise gains from usurious labour through rent seeking on land, for example through exploitative tenancy arrangements, rather than themselves invest in land to increase production.

## Problems of Budgetary Support for Agriculture in SGR Targeted States

Table 6.8 below gives the trends in total budgetary expenditure to support rural economy in the SGR targeted states in eastern India. Without exception, the budgetary allocation (as a proportion of the net State Domestic Product) for each one of the states for each year is lower than the average for all states and union territories. What is more, the purportedly progressive and pro-poor Left Front Government of West

Table 6.8: Trends in Budgetary Support for Overall Rural Economy as a Proportion of Net State Domestic Product

| *State* | *2005-06* | *2006-07* | *2007-08* | *2008-09* | *2009-10* | *Average annual share (2005-06 to 2009-10)* |
|---|---|---|---|---|---|---|
| Assam | 2.36 | 2.78 | 3.13 | 3.29 | 3.85 | 3.08 |
| Bihar | 4.11 | 4.90 | 4.99 | 4.93 | 4.70 | 4.73 |
| Chhattisgarh | 4.53 | 3.93 | 5.09 | 4.81 | 5.29 | 4.73 |
| Jharkhand | 3.48 | 2.98 | 3.36 | 2.84 | 2.54 | 3.04 |
| Odisha | 2.35 | 2.57 | 3.22 | 4.13 | 4.03 | 3.26 |
| Uttar Pradesh | 4.18 | 2.82 | 3.48 | 4.11 | 3.98 | 3.71 |
| West Bengal | 1.35 | 1.24 | 1.42 | 1.32 | 1.58 | 1.38 |
| All States and UTs | 4.92 | 5.39 | 5.31 | 7.28 | 6.01 | 5.78 |

*Source:* (Acharya and Das, 2012) Note: Net State Domestic Product of respective states are at factor costs and at current prices.

Bengal that ruled the state for 32 years by enchasing primarily rural votes starved the rural economy in the State worst of all.

Table 6.8 still does not convey the full picture of the neglect of rural economy in these states. Table 6.9 shows that as a proportion of aggregate expenditures by these state governments, the expenditure on rural economy stood much reduced at the end of 2009-10 as compared to that in 1990-91. The worst performer in this respect is again West Bengal, which attests as much to the pro-poor credentials of the Parliamentary Left in India.

As already mentioned, the first time ever central grant of ₹ 400 crore for extending Green Revolution to eastern India was announced in 2010-11. This amounted to a mere ₹ 123 per annum per farm household in the targeted states (Acharya and Das, 2012). For the next financial year, the situation

Table 6.9: Declines in Expenditure on Rural Economies (RE) in SGR Targeted States

| *State* | *Percentage difference of average share of expenditure on RE between 1990s and 2000s* | *Percentage difference of average share of expenditure on RE between 1990-91 and 2001 to 2009-10* |
|---|---|---|
| Assam | –16.3 | –40.3 |
| Bihar | –10.9 | –21.8 |
| Haryana | –20.4 | –63.4 |
| Madhya Pradesh | –19.9 | –66.9 |
| Odisha | –48.8 | –88.2 |
| Punjab | –58.2 | –85.1 |
| Uttar Pradesh | –44.8 | –83.9 |
| West Bengal | –80.2 | –113.8 |
| All States | –30.0 | –47.3 |

*Source:* Jha and Acharya, 2011 (Compiled by authors from data provided in the *Handbook of Statistics on State Government Finances, 2010*, RBI).

Table 6.10: Budgetary Allocation for the Department for Land Resources Since 2006-07

| *Parameter* | *2006-07* | *2007-08* | *2008-09* | *2009-10* | *2010-11* | *2011-12* | *2012-13 (RE)* | *2013-14 (BE)* |
|---|---|---|---|---|---|---|---|---|
| Total expenditure under Department of Land Resources (₹ crore) | 1,411 | 1,406 | 1,793 | 2,025 | 2,618 | 2,419 | 3,000 | 5,765 |
| As% of total union government expenditure | 0.24 | 0.20 | 0.20 | 0.20 | 0.22 | 0.18 | 0.21 | 0.35 |
| As% of GDP at market prices | 0.03 | 0.03 | 0.03 | 0.03 | 0.03 | 0.03 | 0.03 | 0.06 |

*Source*: Compiled from budget statements for respective years and economic surveys available from Ministry of Finance, Government of India website. Note: RE is revised estimate and BE is budget estimate.

remained the same. In 2012-13 however this amount was raised to ₹ 1,000 crore and has been maintained at the same level in the budget of 2013-14. Assuming that the number of farm households has remained the same as in 2010-11, this would amount to a sum of ₹ 307.50 per farm household per annum. To judge the adequacy of these allocations we need only see Table 6.6 once again which tells us that the minimum debt on the head of a farm household was in Assam at ₹ 813.

One of the main reasons for the backwardness of agriculture in the SGR targeted states is that agriculture in these states is dependent on rain, as indeed is nearly two thirds of cultivated land in the country. All the programmes meant for improvement of dryland/rainfed agriculture in the country are implemented through the 'Department for Land Resources' of the 'Ministry for Rural Development' (Acharya and Das, 2012). The priority accorded to this crucial department in the union budget over the years is reflected in Table 6.10.

The paltry allocation for dryland/rainfed agriculture development reflects a lack of clear strategy and well thought out programmes towards this end. With so little state support or even intent to help the peasants overcome their enormous difficulties in the path of increasing agriculture productivity, it is always easy and convenient to declare small peasant agriculture backward and a drag on productivity only to pave the way for corporate agriculture.

## What Do We Surmise?

There are important take-home messages that arise from the foregoing discussion and which need to be made explicit here.

1. That throughout the country, agriculture is dominated by small and marginal farms is very well known, however, what is more important is that in the states that had been witness to FGR have also witnessed maximum concentration of land into large farms along with increase

in the numbers of marginal farmers. This has resulted in sharp inequity in the ownership of land as is also evident from the high Gini coefficient for Punjab and Haryana.

In the FGR, the role of agribusiness was confined to being the suppliers of inputs—seeds, fertilisers, insecticides and weedicides etc. Agribusiness corporations were not directly involved in cultivation. SGR seeks to pave the way for their direct entry in cultivation in a big way through programmes like PPPIAD which will make the peasants as subsidiaries and appendages to the corporations. If increasing concentration of land in FGR areas in favour of the big landlords is anything to go by, this could easily mean that the agribusiness corporations may become the biggest owners of agricultural land in times to come, further robbing the peasants of the principal means of production and their livelihood. It would be especially so as much of the economic growth witnessed in the country has been a jobless growth accompanied by greater informalisation of the work force (Mehrotra et al., 2012).

2. The prevalent semi-feudal relations of production in agriculture, including in areas where there has been considerable growth of capitalist methods of production in agriculture, emphasises the task of breaking these backward relations of production as a precondition to increasing agricultural productivity. Further expropriation of land from small and marginal peasants by corporations and imposition of mechanised agriculture, when their hunger for land remains insatiate can prove to be socially and politically highly disruptive and perilous for the food security of the country.
3. Small and marginal peasants are not just producers of food, but also its biggest consumers. Under circumstances

where the overwhelming majority of farmers are net buyers of food, they also constitute the biggest chunk of food-insecure population in the country. Further alienation of small and marginal farmers as also the landless peasants from land will directly undermine the food security of hundreds of millions of people in the country.

4. The Government has been much less enthusiastic in its efforts to make investments in improving the lot of rainfed area agriculture in general and the farmers in all the SGR targeted states specifically. This in fact is the biggest reason for the poor agricultural productivity in these states.
5. Rather than seeing them as a drag on increasing agricultural productivity, the solution for increasing food production in a sustainable manner lies in making the small and the marginal farms economically viable through suitable policy instruments while banking on the proven greater productivity of the small family farms.

   In spite of a huge body of evidence from across the world that shows that small and marginal farms are much more productive than large farms, Indian Government remains skeptical of their ability to rise to the challenge of meeting India's food security needs. The framework document of PPPIAD states (GOI, 2012) lays down:

   However, several hurdles need to be overcome to reach these highly desirable goals. For one, 83% of land holdings in the country are now marginal or small and unless there is urgent intervention in aggregating producers through farmers' institutions, we are unlikely to achieve scale in production and leverage it to the advantage of all stakeholders, especially primary producers.

However, such is the method in the madness that intuitively speaking, many a wise man may fall for the Government's line. Such are the notions of science, scientific thinking, modernity and progress that technology as dished out by the western agribusiness corporations in the main has come to command the blind faith of policy makers and the mainstream scientific community that was groomed in such a concept of science. It is not easy to even suggest alternatives let alone convince people of their potential. Nonetheless, we shall make an attempt to do so in the following section.

## Possible Solutions and the Centrality of Agrarian Question

In this section, we are attempting to establish a case for a logical approach to pertinent issues concerning India's food security. The possible solutions can only emerge from such an approach.

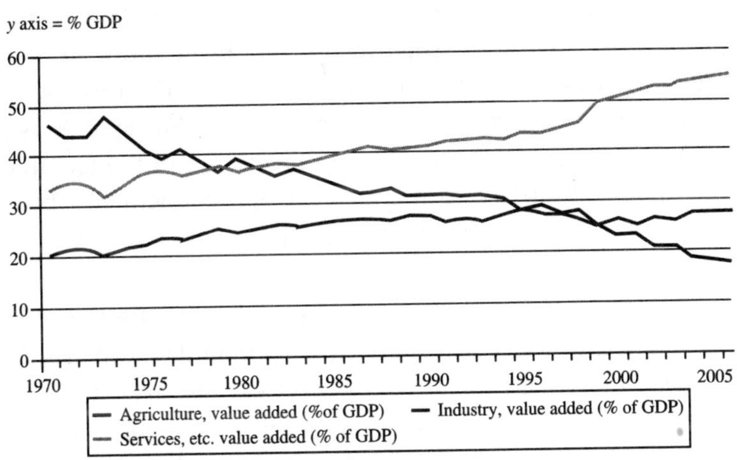


Figure 6.4: Trends in growth of different sectors of Indian economy.

*Source:* European Commission, 2007.

Figure 6.4 gives the trends of growth in different sectors of the Indian economy. Table 6.11 gives sector-wise variations in total employment in different sectors of the economy during the years of new economic policies. It is evident that the share of agriculture in the GDP declined by 12.5% from 30% in the mid-nineties to reach 17.5% in 2006. However, agriculture continues to play a significant role in the economy because it still supports the largest segment of the workforce which is about 53% as per the current estimates. This estimate is still larger than 44% in 2002 and 21% in 2004 for China and Brazil respectively. Secondly, even though its share in employment is declining, there is a net increase in the number of people employed in agriculture. Thirdly, nearly 70% of country's population continues to live in rural areas and is directly or indirectly dependent on agriculture for subsistence.

What is noteworthy is that the maximum growth has been observed in the services sector of the economy, with the rate of growth picking up with the onset of the economic reforms, in 1990. During the entire period of the neoliberal economic reforms the manufacturing sector has been more or less stagnant, except for some blips here and there. The increase in share of employment in industry and manufacturing observed in 2011-12 (Table 6.11) seems to be on account of the fact that construction industry as a source of employment has been included under this head as against the services sector in the previous years.

There is a symbiotic relationship between the manufacturing sector and the services sector. A growing manufacturing sector creates the demand for different services, and availability of services in itself helps grow industrial production. 'Among service inputs to manufacturing, the parallel development of the producer services becomes essential to increasing productivity and competitiveness of the manufacturing sector' (Park S.H., 1994). However, in India's case, the entire economic growth seems to be fuelled by extraordinary growth

Table 6.11: Distribution of Workforce in Different Sectors of the Indian Economy

| *Sector of the economy* | *Total Employment UPS* (millions)* | | | |
|---|---|---|---|---|
| | *1993-94* | *1999-2000* | *2004-05* | *2011-12* |
| Agriculture | 206.0 (61.7%) | 214.8 (58.6%) | 225.0 (54%) | 52.9% |
| Industry (Mining, Manufacturing, Electricity, Water) | 40.6 (5.2%) | 44.1 (12.1%) | 55.3 (13.3%) | 19.3 (including construction) |
| Services (Construction, Trade, Hotel & Rest, Transportation, Storage & Communication, Finance, Insurance, Real estate, Community Social & Personal Services.) | 87.6 (26.2%) | 107.9 (29.4%) | 136.2 (32.7%) | 27.8 (excluding construction) |
| Total | 334.0 (100%) | 366.8 (100%) | 416.5 (100%) | 100% |

*Source:* Calculated from the data given in the table 'Sectoral Break-up of Employment & Value Added per Worker (93-94, 99-00 & 04-05)' given as table number 48 in Indian Economy related data tables available from Planning Commission website at http://planningcommission.nic.in/data/datatable/index.php?data=datatab on 19 August 2012.

Figures for 2011-12 are from GOI, 2011-12.

* Usual Principal Status. A person is considered unemployed according to this concept if available for but without work for major part of the year.

in services sector, even as the growth in manufacturing sector has been minimal.

In the three sectors of economy comprising agriculture, industry/manufacturing and services, the growth of services sector is contingent upon the output of the earlier two sectors. But this obviously does not seem to have been the case in India. Growth in services sector has not happened to the accompaniment of the quantitative jump in employment opportunities (Banga, 2005, Jain 2011), neither is it that the growth in services has been largely for the consumption of the domestic industry or agriculture. Much of the growth in services sector is on account of the growth in rising export of these services. Table 6.12 clearly shows that an overwhelming proportion of services exported from India is constituted of IT (software services) and IT enabled services (business services, communication services) which have resulted in the growth of a few highly paying jobs for some professionals even as the majority of jobs, even in the IT sector have come up in the non-formal sector. This has been said to be due to the poor performance of industry (Jain, 2011). Even if the services sector were to rely primarily on the home market, the pattern of growth of services is such that it would cater to the needs of a very small segment of the population.

Table 6.12: Composition of the services exported in 2008-09

| *Services* | *Proportion (%)* |
|---|---|
| Software services | 47 |
| Business services | 16 |
| Travel | 11 |
| Transportation | 11 |
| Financial services | 4 |
| Communication services | 2 |
| Insurance | 1 |
| Other services | 8 |

*Source:* Banga and Kumar, 2011.

From the foregoing discussion in this section, the following conclusions can be drawn:

- Unlike the developed West, the growth of services sector in India has happened in the absence of growing output in the industrial and agriculture sector.

- This growth of Indian economy largely obtained through export oriented growth in services sector can be maintained only so long as there is a demand for these services in the developed countries of the West.
- The service-sector-led growth of the economy remains tenuous in the light of growing and entrenched economic crisis in the West. There are already ominous signs of considerable slowing down of India's economy.
- To make the economy stand erect without the crutches of western markets, there has to be growth in industry and services sector spurred by enlarging the domestic market beyond the present affluent sections of the country which constitute only a very small proportion of India's population.
- 70% of India's population still relies on agriculture directly or indirectly. There appears little scope of this proportion coming down substantially anytime soon. The majority of small, marginal and landless peasants constitute the vast majority of the poor in this country. The only way in which the domestic market for indigenous industrial produce can be vastly expanded is by improving the lives and livelihoods of this segment of the population, which can come from revitalising of agriculture sector alone, rather than pinning hopes on the jobless growth of the services sector.
- Words of our erstwhile Prime Minister Dr. Manmohan Singh, need be recalled once again. He said regarding the agrarian distress in the country that, 'The only way we can raise our heads above poverty is for more people to be taken out of agriculture' (emphasis ours) (Varadarajan, 2010). As opposed to this opinion, our opinion is that, to raise our heads above poverty, we need to increase the productivity in agriculture by initiating the much required agrarian reform centred on the principle of

'land to the tiller.' This alone can usher in a measure of prosperity in the lives of the small and marginal farmers and the landless agricultural labourers.

As opposed to this, India's ruling elite are only attempting to adjust and readjust the present economic order on the back of the prevalent political consensus over the policy paradigm among all the ruling class parties, including the Parliamentary Left. Such a tubular vision is bound to make the country prone to the immediate and long term economic and political turbulence.

## In Agriculture-Led Growth, What should be the Premise?

On the face of it, there can hardly be a division of opinion regarding the please all phrases like 'agricultural growth should be the priority in India' and that 'the poorest of the poor should benefit from it.' However, there is a huge difference over how this ought to be achieved. As already mentioned, there is one perspective that talks of 'taking people out of agriculture' to facilitate leasing out of land to the agribusiness for industrial farming. Towards this end, it argues for abolition of land ceiling laws. Perhaps with the presumption that private corporations can invest the capital and the latest technology—both of which are considered necessary for the growth of agriculture and food production. The general prosperity of agriculture, it is presumed, will percolate down to alleviate the sufferings of people from 7. In a nutshell, such a strategy argues for lock, stock and barrel adoption of the western model of agricultural growth.

It is not always that these formulations are stated very clearly. Articulation of these arguments follows as a natural corollary from the reading of the provisions of the National Agricultural Policy, 2000 and the draft of the Indo-US deal on agriculture signed in 2005. Such a policy direction fails to acknowledge that every growth strategy operates in its given socio-economic context and as such may not be transplantable in an entirely different context, except of course at considerable human cost.

## The Food Systems in the West

The agricultural and food systems in countries like US and 7 developed in the historical circumstances where land was aplenty, but the people to work it were few. An important corollary of this has been that, in the US agricultural productivity has always been measured in terms of output per worker and not per unit of land (George, 1979). Maximisation of such an output of necessity entails that various inputs like seeds, fertilisers, pesticides and equipment for sowing, harvesting and post-harvest storage and processing etc be readily available for use on large farms. Such processes may not be possible through family labour alone and it created the need for mechanisation and large scale production of inputs like synthetic fertilisers, pesticides and seeds, besides farm equipment. This is where industry stepped in to provide for every segment of food chain, banks stepped in to provide loans to the farmers to purchase the inputs and equipment. The agribusiness itself facilitated loans for the farmers. Over the years there was vertical integration of the entire food chain by individual companies. Increasing confluence of interests between the agribusiness and the banks led to their total domination of family farms, so much so that these were either forced out of business, or were forced to produce crops in line with the business decisions of the corporations and banks (Ibid).

Though their trajectories may have been somewhat different, in the present time the domination of food systems in Europe may only be different from that in US in terms of the turnovers of the agribusinesses. Many a scientific critique of the food systems in the developed countries is available that argues the unviability of these systems in the long run on various counts. The rapid development of the sectors of the economies other than agriculture in the capitalist countries has ensured that increasingly less and less of their population is involved in agriculture. This process could only have been aided by outward emigration from Europe to the newfound lands in America, Australia and New Zealand. Suffice it to say here that in spite of the control the western agribusinesses exercise over the world food system, they have failed to ensure the food security of all the citizens in their own countries.

As per the 2010 report of 'Feeding America' (FA) just one of the hunger charity organisations in the United States, the charity's network 'served an estimated 37 million different people annually, an increase of 46% since 2005' and 'about 5.7 million different people, or 1 in 50 Americans, receives emergency food assistance from the FA system in any given week, an increase of 27% since 2005.' An increasing number of the charity's clients reported having to choose between paying for food or utilities like heating fuel and paying for their mortgages (Mabli et al., 2010).

## Why Must We Reject the Corporate Model of Agricultural Growth?

Contrary to the conditions that defined the growth of agriculture in the American continent, the conditions in which the agricultural systems of much of the developing world have been tempered were entirely different. There has been a high dependence of an overwhelming segment of the population on land. Agricultural productivity always came to be defined in terms of output per unit of land.

In populous countries like India, where agriculture directly engages well over half of the workforce and sustains nearly 70% of the population, the adoption of industrial farming would lead to loss of livelihood for an overwhelming section of population. Before propagating market oriented, technology guided industrial farming as the panacea for agricultural growth in India, it should be borne in mind that all farmer suicides in India have occurred in areas where agricultural technology and markets were rather well developed.

There cannot be an equal relationship between big agricultural corporations and the individual farmers, especially the small and the marginal farmers, who are being shown a mirage that they can sit pretty on the assured returns from leasing out their land to the corporations or the big farmers. So the country can now have a new rentier class whatever may be its social consequences. The landless agricultural labour might as well pack their bags, and be ready to be 'taken out of agriculture,' for they are not likely to find work in the large farms worked by a small skilled staff with machines.

Handing over the farms to the corporations would mean that decisions about the use of farm land will be dictated by what is expedient for profit maximisation of the agribusiness, rather than what is expedient for securing food security of the people. The question of the government being able to exercise enough regulation of agribusiness to make them comply with its policies for ensuring the food security of the people simply does not arise when those who are supposed to regulate are only too willing to be regulated by the corporations.

At present, the small and marginal farmers are able to make a very important contribution to the country's food security through subsistence farming which may take care of their family needs to a large extent. If given the required support, they may even be able to produce marketable surplus as has happened in case of China in spite of the fact that the average farm size in China is almost the half of that in India. However, having rented out their land to the agribusinesses, they would stand to lose even the relative comfort of self-provisioning agriculture as the foremost concern of the agribusiness would not be to provide for the food security of the rural households but to produce for maximising their profits.

Another important factor to note is that when production is guided by effective market demand, then it is automatically privileged to fulfil the needs of those who have the purchasing power. Society's productive resources are directed towards fulfilling the needs of the rich and the production processes become totally divorced from the needs of the poor, who in India's case could constitute close to 80% of the population. So, even as the production grows and profits from it rise, the condition of the poor deteriorates. This has been described by Bhaduri as 'Predatory Growth' (Bhaduri, 2010).

In the agriculture sector it could mean that satisfying the western taste for exotic fruits of the tropics or flowers for decoration could be more important for the agribusiness, rather than catering to the nutritional requirements of the poor in India. This is not mere speculation. The term 'Banana Republic' bears testimony to the loot and plunder of Central America by the American agribusinesses (Newby, 2012).

Another important question that needs be looked into in the context of the attempted corporate takeover of Indian agriculture is the security of India's biodiversity in the variety of crops, weeds, insects, farm animals and a number of other organisms that constitute the varied agro-ecology of the country. One has only to remember the patent granted to the US company RiceTec for basmati rice, which has been developed by Indian farmers over centuries (Browne, 2000). In another instance, the 'National Biodiversity Authority of India' found the US multinational giant Monsanto to be in violation of the country's biodiversity law in a genetically-modified food project funded by the US Agency for International Development (Gunion, 2011).

## Question of Technology in Agricultural Growth

To begin with, let this be stated unambiguously—the question that needs to be answered with respect to technology is that of 'appropriate' and 'inappropriate' technology, rather than modern and traditional/backward technology. This implies that what is 'modern' may be entirely 'inappropriate' and what is old may be required to be rejuvenated to suit the needs of modern agriculture. Unfortunately, in the eyes of the third world policy makers, what is 'modern' automatically becomes more suitable, especially if the technology has originated from Western labs irrespective of the way newer technologies come about and whose interest they serve in the main.

For example, the whole structure of agricultural research in the United States is controlled by the agribusiness either by virtue of research being carried out by the corporations themselves or by universities which may be contracted by United States Department of Agriculture (George, 1979). This arrangement is further cemented by the fact that often the government officials are appointed on the boards of these companies, or company officials go on to occupy important positions in the government. Many of the big names in agricultural research are on the payrolls of the companies either directly or indirectly.

It is worth pondering, whether Monsanto, a company that provides from genetically modified seeds, to fertilisers, to pesticides and other inputs would undertake research to develop systems for biological control of pests or fertilising the soil? In other words would it allow research that can possibly render its inputs redundant in the market? Obviously not! To the contrary, it would develop seeds that would require higher levels of fertilisers and pesticides marketed by the company in return for higher yields. The hybrid varieties of wheat and rice that ushered in the Green Revolution in many countries of the developing world were one such invention of modern agricultural science.

Contrary to this, let us consider the following example of scientific traditional agriculture practised by Kikuyu farmers in the Kilimanjaro region of Kenya:

> The Kikuyu system is multi-faceted, and includes various tree crops, bushes, standing crops, and 'weeds' (which play a positive protective role): a system characterized by high species diversity, stability, and complexity able to withstand the particular hazards of the local environment. The Kikuyu peasants exhibit great skill in arranging the species so that they interact with one another, they have also perfected anti-erosion and waste-using techniques demonstrating a high level of scientific sophistication (George, 1986).

Just compare this complex open field labouratory of the African farmers with hectares of mono-crop fields in the US or large acreage devoted to wheat and paddy in India's agriculturally most prosperous state of Punjab. We leave it to the readers to decide which agriculture is more modern and more scientific.

It is pertinent here to consider one more example of what happens when modernity visits the practices of traditional peasants. In the francophone Sahelian colonies of West Africa, well managed granaries were the cornerstone of the rural food security systems until these societies came under colonial rule. The following note with reference to the alleged careless attitude of farmers in storing their grain and preventing it from pest, communicated forthrightly by one French Colonial Inspector in Upper Volta during the famine year 1932, says volumes about the science inherent in the traditional food systems:

> One can only wonder how it happens that populations . . . who always had on hand three harvests in reserve

> and to whom it was socially unacceptable to eat grain that had spent less than three years in the granary have suddenly become improvident. They managed to get through the terrible famine of 1914 without difficulty . . . (However, since the late 1920s) these populations, once rich in food reserves are now living from hand to mouth . . . (Egg J. et al., 1975).

The inspector presented the diagnosis of the problem in the form of enforced cash crop production that drastically reduced the food crop reserves. However, the point to be noted is that the 'backward' peasants had developed a grain storage system that was both efficient and scientific to keep their grain reserves edible for at least three years (Ibid). Meanwhile in the neo-imperialist world order, the World Bank and the International Monetary Fund continue to force many developing countries to make a shift from food grain crops to cash crops for export.

The tension here is not between science and tradition. The tension actually is between 'science for development of the people' or 'science for corporations and their profits?' For science to become relevant to the needs of the people, the scientists have to recognise that their knowledge stands where it is because the basis for it was prepared by millions of unnamed and unrecognized human beings who crystallised the knowledge developed through ages and passed it on to their succeeding generations. Technology per se is not to be blamed. But it becomes a powerful negative force if it is wielded for parochial gains of a few or as a tool to reinforce the coercive superiority of the powerful.

The confrontation between science for the people and science for serving the parochial interests of a few, can be resolved only if the modern science and scientists adopt an attitude of give and take of learning from and contributing to the traditional knowledge and value systems of the people.

Given such an attitude, the wisdom inherent in the traditional farming practices ought to be recognised as the basic building block for any growth trajectory coupled with inputs that modern science can provide.

The pre-condition for technology is that it should develop and strengthen the livelihoods rather than diminish and destroy livelihoods. This implies that in situations where human labour is aplenty, labour displacing technologies shall have a negative impact on agriculture unless of course there is simultaneous development of alternate livelihoods to absorb surplus labour from agriculture. Secondly, the notion of technology should move away from the popular western conceptualisation of the term. This implies that the non-formal, non-theorised traditional agricultural knowledge of the peasants should be taken as a worthy complement to and an important source of developing lab- grown technology using all the sophisticated techniques that modern science has to offer.

The 'Western Industrial Farming Model' which is sought to be imposed on the country in the garb of SGR has a proven track record of finishing off the family farms and deepening the schism between practice of agriculture and the society it is meant to feed. The record of agribusinesses and multinational food retailers in wasting precious food post-harvest on the farms and in the stores is equally distressing. Neither is this model particularly energy efficient. The Government's intentions of promoting agri-business for efficient utilisation of food and preventing post-harvests losses is aimed at deception so long it allows thousands of tons of food grain to rot in its godowns year after year even as millions go to bed hungry.

The FGR is running aground in its heartland, in the States of Punjab and Haryana. It is remarkable how the ruling elite are intent upon ignoring these lessons in thrusting SGR upon the people. Perhaps SGR is required only to take the initiative of FGR to its logical conclusion, as one of the critiques has remarked, 'Second Green Revolution is aimed at preparing ground for large-scale industrial farming and final takeover of Indian agriculture by TNCs like Monsanto, Syngenta and Cargill. To do so, it is important to first create a debilitating farm crisis by decimating the dryland farms owned by small and marginal farmers and declare the entire agriculture sector as 'sick and unviable' so that these farms could be auctioned to agribusiness companies and big agri-multinationals for large scale industrial farming' (Mukhopadhyaya, 2010).

For the Indian ruling elite educated, trained and nurtured in the western value system, exemplar of the West is the epitome of modernity. They obviously see little contradiction in the policies they pursue and in the impact on the people that are just a little cost that ought to be paid. It would be prudent here to reproduce verbatim Dr. Manmohan Singh's quote on India's experience of British colonialism that he articulated on a visit to his alma mater, Oxford University, during his first tenure as India's Prime Minister. He said:

> 'Today, with the balance and perspective offered by the passage of time and the benefit of hindsight, *it is possible for an Indian Prime Minister to assert* that India's experience with Britain had its beneficial consequences too. Our notions of the rule of law, of a constitutional government, of a free press, of a professional civil service, of modern universities and research labouratories have all been fashioned in the crucible where an age-old civilisation met the dominant Empire of the day. These are all elements which we still value and cherish. Our judiciary, our legal system, our bureaucracy, and our police are all great institutions derived from British-Indian administration and they have served the country well' (Singh Manmohan, 2005). Without offering any comments of our own, Dr. Singh does seem to suggest that independent India's administration is about as good as the colonial British administration in its overall moorings.

## Conclusion

India's agricultural economy continues to be riddled with poor yields and a political economy that results in highly iniquitous distribution of food. The fact that our highest per capita food grain availability till date remains at a level that was achieved at the turn of the 20th century, reflects on the nature of advancement Indian agriculture has undergone. Calls for a second 'Green Revolution' are being made feverously, when there is all evidence to show how even the objectives of the first one have not been achieved till date.

There is little inclination on the part of the ruling establishment to analyse the actions of the past and draw lessons for the future. The Government has responded instead by lowering the standards to improve the performance e.g. lowering of the calorie norms to 1800 calories per day in order to decrease the levels of poverty because the poor must subsist within the fiscal limits for food security subsidy prescribed by the Government.

The role of technology as an essential input in advancing the productive forces of our agricultural economy cannot be denied, but technology has to be conducive to the societal conditions and human needs, rather than the profit motive. Calls for reliance on technology without addressing the structural constraints like skewed distribution of land, iniquitous access to agricultural resources, stagnation in the development of irrigation and agricultural research directed at the needs of the small farms, boils down to detracting from the system's failure in tackling these core issues.

We had talked in the beginning of how the 'forces of production' are sought to be separated from the context of production i.e. the 'relations of production' and at the end we find just how this is coming into its own with peasants being rendered surplus to production even as technology gets more and more narrowly defined. In a semi-feudal agrarian economy that is already reeling under crisis, the bulk of the peasantry—the marginal, small and landless peasants are sought to be pushed to the stage of utter destitution and decimation. This cannot but have immense social consequences. The only ray of hope can come from a rising tide of progressive peasant movement in the country dutifully supported by the intelligentsia and the scientific community.

## References

Acharya Nilanchana and Subrat Das (2012): 'Revitalising agriculture in eastern India: investment and policy priorities.' *IDS Bulletin,* Vol. 43 Number S1: 104-112.

Banga R. (2005): 'Critical issues in india's service led growth.' ICRIER, Working Paper No. 171, October.

Banga R. and Kumar D. (2011): 'India's exports of software services: role of external demand and productivity.' *Science, Technology, Society,* Vol. 16 (3): 285-307.

Benjamin S. and Venturini L. (2005): 'The globalisation of food systems, a conceptual framework and empirical patterns', Working Paper 05-01, The Food Industry Center, University of Minnesota.

Bhaduri A. (2010): 'Predatory growth: the face we are afraid to see.' *Think India Quarterly,* Vol. 13(3): 26-36.

Competition Commission (2000): 'Supermarkets: a report on the supply of groceries from multiple stores in the United Kingdom', Cm 4842 October 2000.

De Janvry A., Sadoulet E. (2008). How to manage a quick response to the food crisis in poor countries with weak policy instruments? Unpublished paper, University of California at Berkeley. Quoted in Pica-Ciamarra U. and J. Otte Poultry (2009): 'Food Security and Poverty in India: Looking Beyond the Farm-Gate', Research Report No. 09-02, Pro Poor Livestock Policy Initiative, February. Available from http://www.fao.org/ag/againfo/programmes/en/pplpi/docarc/rep-0902_indiapoultry.pdf on 21st July 2013.

Egg J., F. Lerin, M. Venin (1975): 'Analyse Descriptive de la Fmine des Annees 1931 au Niger, Institut Natoinal de la Recherche Agronomique (INRA) Paris, p. 28 & p. 52. Quoted in Susan George (1979): *Feeding the Few: Corporate Control of Food.* Institute of Policy Studies, Washington D.C., 1979, p. 60.

European Commission (2007): World Development Indicators, quoted in: *Monitoring Agri-trade Policy: India's Role in World Agriculture,* Directorate-General for Agriculture and Rural Development.

FICCI. 'Overview' in 'Agriculture Sector', FICCI website. Available from http://www.ficci.com/sector.asp?secid=1 on 21 July, 2013.

Goswami R. (2006): A bargain-basement knowledge 'mandi', *InfoChange News & Features*, August.

Goswami R. (2011): 'Industrialising India's Food Flows: An analysis of the food waste argument', MACROSCAN: An Alternative Economics Website, 23 May. Available from http://www.macroscan.com/anl/may11/anl230511Food_Flows.htm on 23 Nov, 2012.

Government of India (2000): *National Agriculture Policy, 2000*, Department of Agriculture and Cooperation, Ministry of Agriculture.

Government of India (2005): Statement 1 in 'Situation Assessment Survey of Farmers—Indebtedness of Farmer Households, NSS 59th Round (January-December, 2003),' Report No. 498, National Sample Survey Organisation, Ministry of Statistics and Programme Implementation, Government of India, May.

Government of India (2008): Draft National Biotechnology Regulatory Bill, 2008, Department of Biotechnology, Ministry of Science and Technology.

Government of India (2010): 'Extending Green Revolution to Eastern India', Ministry of Agriculture, Press Information Bureau, 1 June. Available from http://www.pib.nic.in/newsite/erelease.aspx?relid=62229 on 6 July 2013.

Government of India (2011-12): Report on Second Annual Employment & Unemployment Survey, (2011-12), Ministry of Labor and Employment, Labour Bureau, Chandigarh.

Government of India (2012). 'Framework for supporting public private partnerships for integrated agricultural development (PPPIAD) under Rashtriya Krishi Vikas Yojana (RKVY).', Ministry of Agriculture, March.

Government of India (Undated): Draft Report of the 'Committee on State Agrarian Relations and the Unfinished Agenda of Land Reforms', Vol. 1, Ministry of Rural Development.

Gunion B. (2011): 'USAID programme charged with seed theft in India.' *One World*, 16 August.

Jain M. (2011): 'Asymmetrical Growth Pattern in Service Sector in India.' *The Alternative*, Department of Management, *B.I.T. Mesra Journal*, Vol. 10 (2): 5-28.

Jha P. and Nilanchana Acharya (2011): 'Expenditure on the rural economy in India's budgets since the 1950s: an assessment.' *Review of Agrarian Studies*, Vol. 1 (2): 134-156.

Kantor L.S., Kathryn Lipton, Alden Manchester, and Victor Oliveira (1997): 'Estimating and Addressing America's Food Losses', *Food Review*, January-April: 2-12.

Kuruganti K. and Madineni A. (2010): 'Monsanto-ising Indian Agriculture: A Paper on Giving Away Indian Agriculture on a Platter to Monsanto Through Public—Private Partnerships', Booklet printed for private circulation by Living Farms, Bhubaneswar, November.

Mabli J., Cohen R., Potter F. and Zhao Z. (2010): 'Hunger in America 2010 National Report Prepared for Feeding America.' Prepared by Mathematica Policy Research, Inc. Mathematica Reference No.: 06251-600.

Majumdar A.D., Siddharta Gupta, Parthasarathi Dasgupta (2010): 'The Second Green Revolution: A Blue-Print to Control India's Agriculture—Indo-US Treaty, New Seed Act'. Published by Published by Lokayata Sahitya Chakra, August. Available from http://sanhati.com/excerpted/2698/ on 28 June, 2011.

Mehrotra S., Ankita Gandhi, Partha Saha, Bimal Kishore Sahoo (2012): 'Joblessness and Informalisation: Challenges to Inclusive Growth in India', IAMR Occasional Paper No. 9/2012, Institute of Applied Manpower Research, Planning Commission, Government of India, December.

Mukhopadhyay S. (2010): '2nd Green Revolution and Agribusiness in Emerging India—Policies, Strategies and Future', 5 August. Available at SSRN: http://ssrn.com/abstract=1656472.

National Sample Survey Organisation (2006): Table 3.6 in NSSO Report No. 492, 'Some Aspects of Operational Land Holdings in India, 2002-03', NSS 59th Round, Ministry of Statistics & Programme Implementation, Government of India, August, pp. 23-24.

Newby F.C. (2012): 'Banana Republic—The Rape of Central America.' Published by Frank C. Newby, 284 pages. Available from http://www.amazon.com/Banana-Republic-Central-America-ebook/dp/B006V56I4K on 21 August 2012.

Park S.H. (1994): 'Intersectoral Relationships between Manufacturing and Services: New Evidence from Selected Pacific Basin Countries.' *ASEAN Economic Bulletin*, Vol. 10 (3): 245-263.

Rae A. and Josling T. (2003): 'Processed Food Trade and Developing Countries: Protection and Trade Liberalisation.' *Food Policy*, Vol. 28: 147-166.

Singh Manmohan (2005): 'Of Oxford, Economics, Empire, and Freedom'. *The Hindu*, online edition dated Sunday, 10 July. Accessed from http://www.hindu.com/2005/07/10/stories/2005071002301000.htm on 28 July 2011.

Susan George (1979): 'Feeding the Few: Corporate Control of Food.' Institute of Policy Studies, Washington D.C., 1979.

Susan George (1986): 'Dimensions and Rationale of the Food Problem' in *Ill Fares the Land: Essays on Food, Hunger, and Power*. Institute for Policy Studies, Washington D.C., p. 67.

*The Economic Times* (2005): 'India, US team up for 2nd green rev', 19 July. Available from http://economictimes.indiatimes.com/india-us-team-up-for-2nd-green-rev/articleshow/1175995.cms on 28 May, 2011.

Varadarajan S. (2010): Order on Free Grain to Poor Can't be Executed: Manmohan Singh, *The Hindu*, New Delhi, 7 September.

Wilkinson J., (2009): 'Globalisation of Agribusiness and developing world food systems', *Monthly Review*, Vol. 61 (4).

World Bank (Undated): 'India: Priorities for Agriculture and Rural Development' In 'Agriculture in South Asia.' Available from: http://go.worldbank.org/8EFXZBL3Y0, on 2 Nov 2012.

# 7

# Hunger and Food Insecurity
## Structural Causes and their Remedies
## (Part I)

This chapter is organised in two parts as two separate chapters. In the first part here we have traced the entire debate around food security in India that preceded the passage of the 'National Food Security Act' in 2013, with an intent to bring out the political positions of different actors party to this debate and the inadequacy of their positions in bringing out the transition of 'strengthening the weak, and weakening the strong' that is so very central to resolving the problem of food insecurity of the poor in this country. Later in Part I we have further traced the ideological roots of the so called 'inclusive growth' and politics of its leading proponents to make explicit the options they present before the people. Part II of the paper deals with the possible remedies.

## Introduction

The 'Great Indian Food Security Debate' reminds one of the story in which five blind men exploring an elephant came up with different perceptions of the beast depending upon the part of the elephant's body they explored while totally missing its composite form. Likewise, the different sides to this debate in India have been articulating different views as per their convenience while missing the single most important point which to put in the words of Susan George is 'overcoming hunger' is to 'strengthen the weak' and 'weaken the strong' (George, 1984). Unlike the original story, different actors in the food security debate have deliberately chosen to be blind to the main issue.

Through this apparently animated debate, a magnificent illusion is woven in which the Government now and then reiterated its commitment to ensure people's food security on the one hand while doing much the reverse through its policies. The erstwhile 'National Advisory Council' (NAC) that was headed by the leader of the then principal ruling party, pretended to act as an opposition to its own Government. Nestled within the NAC and enjoying official patronage was the civil society, a section of which performed the role akin to 'Her Majesty's Loyal Opposition'. The Supreme Court was the third important player, which through its various orders sought to appropriate the role of the nation's conscience keeper on issues of hunger and poverty. Together the combine manufactured the grand illusion of progress towards food security with the help of a corporate controlled media.

As to the role of the political parties, most of them continue to be disinterested in the issue beyond pinpricking the Government of the day to score political debating points. The Parliamentary Left seems to have outsourced food security issues and dispossession of land from the peasantry to the civil society, with occasional demonstrations when the Parliament session is on to prove their credentials. The all important question, 'how to weaken the few to strengthen the weak for overcoming mass hunger' remained outside parliamentary discourse.

Even though poverty and hunger are very much to be found in the developed world as well, and in increasing numbers of late, in terms of mass affliction these primarily remain Third World phenomena. The ruling elite in developed capitalist countries are able to ensure the food security of their poor largely through effective social security nets, facilitated through enormous resources, much of which are obtained through the exploitation of the Third World. However, for the working masses in the Third World, the question is primarily of altering the power relations in the society that are structured around antiquated relations of production and gross inequality in access to society's productive resources. These relations are perpetuated and maintained by the subservience of the ruling elite in these countries to the western imperialist powers in the exploitation of the resources and working masses in their own countries. This makes the rulers in the majority of the Third World countries incapable of independently developing the productive capabilities and effective demand of their populations. Hence the task of mitigating hunger from the Third World necessitates the weakening of the dominant sections of the society to 'strengthen the weak.' We shall dwell on the need for this in the specific context of India in a later section.

## Food Security: Tracking the Developments

The World Food Summit at Rome in 1996, attended by the highest representatives of the Governments of 186 countries, defined 'Food Security' as a multidimensional concept which implies that, 'All people, at all times, have physical and economic access to sufficient, safe and nutritious food that meets their dietary needs and food preferences for an active and healthy life' (FAO, 2008). It is only natural then that all measures directed at food security, nationally or internationally, should be judged against this gold standard.

With regard to eradicating hunger in the country, much hope had been generated by the Food Security Act (FSA) enacted by the second UPA Government at the Centre. Enactment of FSA was preceded by a raging debate over its enactment, with the National Advisory Council (NAC), the empowered group of ministers and the NGOs setting the pace. The debate was given a wide coverage coupled with the time to time pronouncements of the Supreme Court on the issue of food security. Given the background that India is home to the highest number of hungry people in the world, both in absolute and proportional terms, the FSA could have scripted a new story.

The story however went awry even before completion. After months of high decibel debate, the National Advisory Council (NAC) passed a much watered down proposal for a Food Security Bill (FSB) that legally entitled 75% of the population in the country to subsidized food grains. This 75% population was to be further divided into 'priority households' entitled to ₹ 1/kg of millets, ₹ 2/kg of wheat and ₹ 3/kg of rice, and 'general households' entitled to 20 kg of food grains every month at a price that was not to exceed 50% of the minimum support price (*The Hindu*, 2010 a). Even before the ink of its recommendations had dried, Government appointed Rangarajan Panel declared NAC's recommendations 'unfeasible' on account of 'supply side constraints' (*Indian Express*, 2010). The Government draft of the FSB prepared by the Ministry of Food and Consumer Affairs (GOI, 2011) undermined much of the little potential for public good that was left in the already watered down draft of the NAC.

This debacle was not entirely unexpected. The seeds of FSA's failure had been sown in the very conceptualisation of food security in the Bill. The entire debate on food security overwhelmingly focused on two issues—the quantum of monthly food grain entitlement to a family and the 'Universalisation of PDS.'

To begin with, the United Progressive Alliance (UPA) manifesto had promised 25 kgs of grain at ₹ 3/kg for BPL households (Right to Food Campaign). Later, citing paucity of funds and food grain, the Empowered Group of Ministers on food security that was constituted by the Government not only opposed the demand for a universal Public Distribution System (PDS) but also wanted that the FSB should be restricted to giving 25 kg of food grains to those living below the poverty line (Gupta, 2010a). This was a total negation of demand for raising the food grain limit and inclusion of many more items to be supplied through the PDS. The fact that the Government got mired in huge corruption charges and its largesse to the tune of lakhs of crores to the corporate sector in every year's budget only betrayed a lack of political will to act in favour of people rather than a paucity of resources.

## A Number Game without People

Any attempt at addressing the issues of poverty and hunger by its very nature gets linked up with a numbers game, for one has to know how many poor and hungry are there before one can plan or make policies for them. The problem however is that the game has become more about suppressing the truth rather than knowing it, especially since the advent of the 'economic reforms' in 1990. In 1993-94, the Planning Commission pulled off the impossible by bringing the poverty down to 19% from 25.5% in 1987-88. 'The never-tell-a-lie Dr. Manmohan Singh' was then the country's finance minister. This extraordinary feat was knocked down in 1996 by the then Planning Commission Chief, the veritable Prof Madhu Dandavate. He said, 'Kill me, I say, I just doubled poverty in your country today' (Sainath, 2012).

In fact, the numbers game vis-à-vis poverty has a history. It started with Robert McNamara as the US defense secretary who wanted records of the number of dead bodies of US soldiers that arrived in bags to monitor the progress made in winning the war in Vietnam. US lost the war, but McNamara brought the tradition to the World Bank as its President—to body count the number of 'poor' in the world. As a young officer in the World Bank, Montek Singh Ahluwalia rose in rank as an enthusiast engaged in this number game and the game soon developed into a vast academic industry with a large consultancy fees and financial support from the Bank.

Dr. Singh as the Prime Minister and Montek Singh Ahluwalia as the Planning Commission chief, were once again at the helm of affairs in the country during the reign of the UPA Government. It is little surprising then that 'Planning Commission', the country's erstwhile topmost policy institution acquired less than an enviable reputation in making poverty disappear, at least on paper. There was widespread public outcry at the poverty line cut-offs of ₹ 32 and ₹ 26 per capita per day for the urban and the rural areas respectively given by the Planning Commission in an affidavit filed in the Supreme Court of India in September 2011. However, the Commission's response to the outcry was to further bring down the cut-offs to ₹ 28.35 and ₹ 22.42 per capita per day for the urban and rural areas respectively in March 2012 (*The Hindu*, 2012).

Planning Commission's position on the FSB flows from this mindset. Planning Commission's take on the Bill matched with the Government's position, albeit its argument was a little more sophisticated and came in a roundabout manner. Planning Commission's representative on NAC, Dr. Abhijit Sen struck a very progressive note, 'If you are taking the rights approach, the law must be universal in scope'. He even advocated that 'there should be one price, as the BPL (Below Poverty Line)/APL (Above Poverty Line) distinction divides society' (Gupta, 2010a). However, he added that 'providing grain at ₹ 3 is not economically viable' (Gupta, 2010). He suggested that the grain be provided 'at a price reasonably close to the minimum support price (MSP), for which a small subsidy would be required—rice, say at ₹ 12 a kg and wheat at ₹ 8/9' i.e. ₹ 420 and ₹ 315 for 35 kilograms of wheat and rice respectively per month. What he failed to reflect upon was just how much would this pricing mechanism leave from the overall poverty line level consumption expenditure, for the poor to meet expenditure on other necessities of life. Dr. Sen further premised that 'In a normal year, most people would not exercise their right to these food grains. Of course, in years when the market price shoots up for any unforeseeable reason, more people will avail themselves of the PDS and the Government must be prepared to meet that contingency' (Gupta, 2010a). This was the clearest indication that the Government had little intention of implementing whatever the NAC finalised, for when the hope is that people would 'normally' not use PDS, then where is the need to have an effectively functioning PDS in 'normal times', and if there is no effectively working PDS in normal times, then it is least likely to come alive in times of 'unforeseen' circumstances. So how does the Government propose to prepare itself for such 'unforeseen' circumstances?

To this the Planning Commission proposed that the concession of ₹ 3 a kg of food grains 'could be' extended to the poor only in such 'unforeseen years' when market prices shoot up and that too through 'smart cards' rather than the PDS network (Ibid)—a suggestion that has an uncanny concordance with the proposal of issuing 'food stamps' that has been so vigorously argued by FICCI (Federation of Indian Chambers of Commerce and Industry) in a report on restructuring of food procurement and distribution system. This only indicates that even as the NAC and the Government were seemingly exerting themselves to feed the poor, plans were already afoot to dismantle the PDS in due course.

## Civil Society's Take

For civil society groups like 'Right to Food Campaign', what was to be a *cause célèbre* became a 'cause turned sour'. In what they have described as addressing 'the structural roots of hunger', they demanded an Act that ensures 'a universal PDS (providing at least 50 kgs of grain per family with 5.25 kgs of pulses and 2.8 kgs of edible oils), special food entitlements for destitute households (including an expanded Antyodaya programme), consolidation of all entitlements created by recent Supreme Court orders (e.g. cooked mid-day meals in primary schools and universalisation of ICDS), support for effective breastfeeding (including maternity entitlements and crèches), safeguards against the invasion of corporate interests in food policy, and elimination of all social discrimination in food-related matters. Further, the Act must include strong accountability and grievance redressal provisions, including mandatory penalties for any violation of the Act and compensation for those whose entitlements have been denied' (Right to Food Campaign). They also emphasised that 'ensuring the right to food requires, economic access for people, involving for instance adequate employment and wage levels, the protection of existing livelihoods, and equitable rights over land, water and forests' (Right to Food Campaign, 2009). The demands of 'adequate employment', 'protection of livelihoods' and 'equitable rights over land, water and forests' appear only on the website of the Campaign, but have been notably absent from the actual debate during the formulation of the FSA, which as we have already mentioned, has largely been about 'universalisation of PDS' and the 'quantum of food grain' to be provided.

In a later open letter written to the Prime Minister and his Council of Ministers, the Campaign failed to mention employment, protection of livelihoods and land, water and forest rights in the list of demands mentioned in the letter (Right to Food Campaign, 2011a). The letter reflects in good measure the disillusionment of this section of the civil society with what the Government had proposed for mitigating hunger in the country.

It may be argued that at least the demand for adequate employment has been addressed to some extent by the passage of Mahatma Gandhi Rural Employment Guarantee Act (MNREGA), but the fact remains that to the best of our knowledge, not even once was the issue of plugging the loopholes in the implementation of MNREGA and further increasing its scope been raised while debating the Food Security Bill, even though ensuring food security was one of the express purposes of enacting MNREGA. Along with the absence of a proactive approach on the issues of equitable land, water and forest rights, this approach only underscores the myopia in the conceptualisation of food security while framing the FSB.

While it may be assumed that the later demands were dropped in order to focus on the more achievable ones, the question that still begets an answer is—do all of the above mentioned demands raised by the Campaign suffice to strike at all at 'the structural roots of hunger'. We shall assess this shortly.

## Alternative Opinion Within the Civil Society

To begin with, the NAC, led by the UPA Chairperson, Ms. Sonia Gandhi argued in farover of a fairly substantive opinion for making the Food Security Act all inclusive and comprehensive. However, it wasn't long before the establishment put its safety valves in operation to let off much steam. Ms. Gandhi remarked in one of the subsequent meetings that 'the poor might wonder why the rich were being given the same entitlements—a comment that paved the way for the view that there should be a system of two prices/differential entitlements' (Gupta, 2010b).

Anyhow, in its final assessment, the NAC quietly buried its initial proposal to begin implementing a universal PDS first in the 150 poorest districts of the country, followed by gradual implementation in the rest of the country (Gupta, 2010a).

The rest, as they say is history. With the NAC itself prepared to move two steps backward, the Government forced a couple more on it, and the final Government draft of FSB was only a pale shadow of what was promised by the NAC to begin with. This however did not mean that there were no takers for this version of the Bill. Indeed, there was a section of Civil Society within the NAC that found merit with the Bill as it stood at this stage. Their opinion was that the Bill would 'end indifference' and 'exile hunger' (Mander, 2011).

The arguments of this section of civil society within the NAC pulled off the impossible, they dexterously (tread) the paths of the supporters of 'universalisation' and those favouring a 'targeted' approach both at the same time. On the one hand they affirmed, 'Basic rights like to food, education, social security and healthcare must be guaranteed by Governments to all citizens, as universally state-supplied and common entitlements . . . It should be the choice of citizens whether or not they wish to use these public services, but none should be excluded by law'. On the other hand 'ethical grounds of opposition' were found to agree with the opinion, 'What is the justification to give you and me, and for that matter a rich rural landlord subsidized grain, and that too at the same levels and price, as a destitute rural landless widow, or a homeless disabled beggar' (Ibid) (the marked fidelity of this argument with Ms Gandhi's comment to same effect must be noted). They ultimately settled for a 'middle path' through an 'administratively complicated formula' in the draft presented by the Government. Solace was found in the fact that the sections of the Government that would earlier settle for nothing but the absolute minimum, ultimately conceded to 'the monthly entitlement to 35 kg, and the coverage of households to 46% of the rural and 28% of the urban households' (Ibid).

As to the more substantive demands raised by the 'Right to Food Campaign' vis-à-vis ensuring food security, their disarming reply was, 'There is no dispute that each of these is imperative, if malnutrition is to be fought. But how much can you load on to a single law?' (Ibid).

Anyhow, the final Food Security Act passed by the Parliament in 2013 is not universal in its scope and actually guarantees only 5 kg of food grains per person per month in the priority households as against the earlier stipulated amount of 7 kg per person per month.

## Coming Back to 'The Structural Roots of Hunger'

It is understandable that the 'Right to Food Campaign' activists criticised the Bill's recommendations as 'a minimalist proposal that missed many important elements of food security' and retained a PDS with a framework that is 'very fragmented and fails to abolish the artificial distinction between APL and BPL households' (Drèze, 2010). But suppose all the demands put up by the Campaign vis-à-vis the Act were accepted, would that have ensured food security in the sense of its definition that we began with?

Poverty is the biggest impediment in ensuring economic access to food even if we presume that physical access should not be a problem. However, in the debate summarised above, though there is mention of the poor, hardly has any emphasis been placed on poverty reduction. It must be mentioned though that in its critique of the NAC's final recommendations, the 'Right to Food Campaign' does talk of sustainable development process that protects people's livelihood and development of agriculture, albeit only in generalist terms, the thrust of their critique is on making the PDS more inclusive and comprehensive (Right to Food Campaign, 2011b).

Alleviating hunger would essentially require an all round attack on poverty of the people which is propagated by the social, economic and political structure of the society. In India, agriculture still forms the bedrock of rural economy. Talking of poverty reduction would necessarily entail far-reaching structural changes in agriculture that would make it not only economically gainful for those engaging in it, but also would increase its productivity which remains a lot poorer than many other countries at similar levels of development.

Since the importance of the following facts can hardly be over emphasized, we are once again repeating them here. Development of agriculture is a function of both the forces of production (technology and the peasantry) and the relations of production in agriculture which are determined by the ownership of the principal means of production—the land. While the forces of production are the key to increasing productivity, their impact is mediated in the context of the relations of production. Together they form the mode of production in the given phase of development of society. Applying advanced means of production e.g. advanced technologies, while the relations of production remain antiquated would only mean that the benefits of the advanced technologies by way of increased production shall be cornered by those who predominantly control the means of production. Besides, the production process provides little incentive for the majority who do not have sizeable ownership of means of production, thus imperilling sustainability of enhanced production. It is only through equitable control over the means of production that the benefits of increased production can be availed by the society at large.

The ruling classes in India have always placed one-sided emphasis on the development of 'forces of production' within which also the emphasis is on introduction of newer technologies, increasingly through industrial farming, at the cost of the small, marginal and the landless peasants who will simply be rendered surplus for agriculture and will have to join the reserve of poverty-stricken mass of unemployed as a source of cheap industrial labour.

The most important characteristic of Indian agriculture is the highly skewed ownership of land. The National Sample Survey Organisation (NSSO) survey for land holding patterns in 2003 showed that at the all-India level, marginal and small owners constituted 90.4% of the total number of owners. But they owned only 43.43% of land, whereas medium and large farmers who constituted only 9.60% of landowners owned as much as 56.21% of land (Bandyopadhyay, 2008). Besides this, there is a huge chunk of landless agricultural labourers, by far the largest and the poorest segment of the population in the country. Though landless, the land hunger of this segment remains unsatisfied.

Iniquitous relations of production in agriculture result in disproportionate appropriation of produce by a handful of the rich landowners, thereby disinsentivising agriculture for the majority who work in it. In this context, land reforms that transfer the ownership of land to the tiller are the most potent poverty alleviation programme which will unleash in its wake a productive potential that will ensure both 'physical and economic' access to food for an overwhelming majority of our population. Besides, land means power. You empower the people, they will themselves ensure that the Government cares for them.

Both the Government and the civil society activists, parties to the above debate know all this. It is surprising then, that the civil society chose to mention 'equitable rights over land' as less than a footnote in the whole scheme of the 'Food Security Act'. The problem actually is that what they describe as addressing 'the structural roots of hunger' is nothing more than a 'reformist policy orientation' to the immense structural problem of 'hunger' that afflicts millions of poor Indians.

The essence of this 'reformist policy orientation' is that it seeks to ameliorate the symptoms of food insecurity while avoiding redressal of the causes of food insecurity. The capitalist countries of the West were able to enormously develop their productive capabilities through the historical process of development of bourgeoisie democracies, wherein the revolutionary bourgeoisie uprooted all antiquated forces and relations of production through popular mobilisation of the hitherto oppressed masses. The bourgeoisie strived to develop production in their own countries and competed with the bourgeoisie of other countries for the expansion of the markets for its products.

Much different from this, the bourgeoisie and the big feudal classes were propped up as the supporting pillars of colonialism by imperialist powers in their erstwhile colonies in Asia and Africa. As colonialism receded, the political power in the newly independent colonies fell in the hands of this alliance between the comprador bourgeoisie and the big feudal class. Addressing the 'structural roots of hunger' would of necessity entail striking at the existing power structures in the society and a redistribution of its resources in order to develop the forces of production and improve the material conditions of the people. The comprador nature and subservience of the ruling alliance between the big bourgeoisie and the feudal class of the country to the imperialist powers renders it incapable of independently developing the productive forces in the country and the markets for its products. The ruling elite of India are content to play second fiddle to their imperialist masters and attempt to bargain for a higher share of the country's loot to the extent this is possible by using the contradictions between the imperialist powers. It is for this reason that combating food insecurity in the country is not possible while retaining its semi-feudal, semi-colonial social, economic and political structure.

Such change is a tall order to achieve through pleadings for some policy reforms from the very sections that benefit from the present unjust social, economic and political order. This is a political task requiring a much larger political mobilisation of the masses, and is certainly beyond the limited capabilities of the civil society. This is where the political parties need to step in.

It can be agreed that one cannot have two Acts in one—i.e. both a comprehensive land reforms Act and a PDS reforms Act. Nonetheless the following need to be acknowledged:

- That the concept of food security goes much beyond policy reforms directed at increasing the size of food subsidies and designing an appropriate mechanism for their distribution. To achieve a long term sustainable food security for the people, the problem is not how 'we' feed 'them', but how to 'make sure that the people can feed themselves. Given the opportunity, they would do just that, they will not need 'us' '(George, 1984). The 'moral question' here is—'not of 'charity' but of 'social justice'' (Ibid).

  It is most unfortunate that under the conditions as are increasingly obtaining in our country and around the world (including many parts of the developed world), an ever increasing number of people are finding it difficult to feed themselves for reasons that are beyond their control.
- Secondly, the FSB ought to be recognised for what it really is—a 'Public Distribution Reforms' Bill, which seeks to secure only one aspect of food security.
- Thirdly, the preamble and the provisions of the FSB, and subsequently the Food Security Act, ought to have reflected the comprehensive understanding of food security as outlined above, to serve as a guide to future action.

In the scheme of things as they stand at present, even a marvellously functioning PDS, providing all the commodities asked for and a universal coverage, will only lead to a mass of perpetually 'dependent people' rather than self-respecting people capable of feeding themselves with secure livelihoods.

Given the neoliberal development paradigm, the livelihoods of the poorest of the poor have come under increasing liquidation. The figures of the 2001 Census (which was during the erstwhile NDA regime) revealed that in the period between 1991 and 2001 Census as many as seven million people for whom agriculture was the primary means of subsistence left the field. The drastic increase in the growth rates of urban population as per the 2011 Census, which has overtaken the increase in rural population for the first time in last ninety years indicates a huge footloose migration from the villages to the urban areas in search of livelihoods. So, the ruination of the viability of agriculture for the hundreds of millions of the most impoverished of India's population is indeed progressing very well. The only problem is that rather than a decrease, the runaway footloose migration is an indication of a steep rise in rural distress, poverty and therefore hunger.

The lack of willingness of the civil society to look beyond the structural boundaries of the present social, economic and political system for empowering the poor and alleviating their poverty and hunger, has reduced them to the status of being hangers on to the system's coattails. It is least surprising that the Government is keeping two steps ahead of the samaritans of civil society. Even as they cried hoarse about the sham that NAC played on food security, at many places, the Government introduced 'smart cards' on a trial basis as a substitute to PDS. This will allow the beneficiaries to get rations for a given amount from designated shops rather than have a fixed quota of food grain through PDS irrespective of the fluctuations in the market price of food.

## Why must a Few be Weakened to Ensure Food Security for the Masses?

It is difficult to understand why a seemingly simple thing as reaching food to the people, especially as it is said to be available in plenty, cannot be achieved, unless we are willing to understand the class character of the ruling elite and the governance system built by them. We have already dwelt in brief on this aspect above. However, a discussion on such issues is either dismissed as political jargon by many or the illusions propagated regarding the present political system prevent the full meaning of these terms from sinking into the popular psyche. We try to present an answer to this question in a simpler form here.

Nearly seven decades after the 'transfer of power' and the transplanting of 'parliamentary democracy' from above by the colonial masters, the democratic credentials of the social, economic and political fabric in the country have come to be questioned as never before. To illustrate the point being raised here, we would like to add a few questions of our own:

- Since 1991, the year when the 'neoliberal' policies were launched, almost every ruling class party spanning the entire ideological spectrum from the far Right to the mainstream Left, have wielded power at the Centre and different states, yet, not only has there been continuity in economic policies but the neoliberal economics has gone from strength to strength. It is worth understanding, as to what explains this continuum.
- Even as purchasing power of the people is falling, making even the minimum required dietary calories inaccessible to them, Governments at the Centre have tried to paint a picture of 'Shining India.' Overflowing food stocks amidst hunger have been sought to be explained by spurious theories of diversification of diets. People were

said to be opting for high value foods at the cost of food grains (GOI, 2002)[1]—what explains such nihilism for people's plight?

- The country is in the throes of an agrarian crisis. A former chief minister of an otherwise affluent state which has witnessed the largest number of farm suicides in the country, mocked at the cotton farmers of the state as cheats (Sainath, 2007). What fuels such audacity with impunity?
- Even as millions go hungry in the country, the Parliamentary Standing Committee on Commerce remarked regarding the wastage of food grains in the godowns, 'Huge quantities of grains are being wasted and farmers are scarcely getting returns for their investments. The Committee expresses serious concern about the problem and is of the view that under favourable global market conditions, the question of permitting export of food grains should be considered as an option to save the farmers from this crisis, to earn valuable foreign exchange and to prevent the produce from going to waste' (Mehdudia, 2011). In the past, the Government made available food grains at less than the BPL prices to private exporters, thus enabling them to make huge profits.

The Government, the Supreme Court, the National Advisory Council, the civil society, all wished to wipe out hunger from the country, yet the food produced in the country goes waste than being fed to the people. This does not happen by providence but occurs regularly

1. Apart from chapter 2 of this book the spurious theory of 'voluntary choice' and 'diversification of diets' away from food grain consumption, in favour of high value foods, has been dealt with in detail by Utsa Patnaik in her essay 'Food Stocks and Hunger: The Causes of Agrarian Distress' published in *Social Scientist*, Vol. 31, No. 7/8 (Jul.–Aug., 2003), pp. 15-41.

year after year. What makes such criminal governance possible? Who benefits from this, and how do they manage to go scot free?

- In a country that is host to the largest number of hungry people on the globe, the precious food grain gets diverted for manufacturing alcohol (Tiwale, 2010). Whose interests does the Government serve through such decisions?
- According to an estimate, from 1951 to 2005, nearly 55 million people were forcibly evicted from their land for different projects (Fernandes, 1998) During the reform years, this process gained a lot more urgency with the might of the State's armed forces being openly used to dislocate the security of people's lives and livelihoods (MRD, Undated). That all the ruling class parties cutting across the political spectrum are united in the pursuit of such development policies is demonstrated by the fact that the inglorious 'Special Economic Zones Act, 2005' was unanimously passed by the Indian Parliament in May 2005 (Dohrman, 2008). What explains such remarkable unity of ostensibly disparate political forces in the pursuit of power?
- How come the Prime Minister of the country has the audacity to equate the subsidies for food security to the losses due to multi-billion dollar scams by his Government (Sainath, 2011 a), and has the gumption to tell the farmers that, 'There are no free lunches' (Varadarajan, 2010), for after all he still has to get their votes?
- While on the one hand, subsidies on health, education, food and agriculture are sought to be reduced in the name of resource crunch or for the sake of fiscal prudence, direct and indirect concessions worth lakhs of crores are doled out to the corporate sector year after year through budgetary provisions.

- We need to look at what explains the indifference with which the Government files an affidavit in the courts saying that a person earning more than 25 rupees a day cannot be considered to be poor (Parsai, 2011). Or for that matter why does the Government pursue policies which hit the poorest of the poor the most, a section which ought to be the valued vote bank of all the ruling class parties?

The answer to these questions is both simple and complex at the same time. It is simple because there is a straightforward answer in the fact that the poor have been totally marginalised in their ability to make an impact upon the dynamics of politics and State power in the country which has become the exclusive preserve of the wealthy and their managerial middle classes. A direct measure of this can be had from the number of billionaires in the Lok Sabha (Sainath, 2009) and the rates at which those in power have increased their financial worth (Sainath, 2011b).

Yet, the answer is complex because this loot by the rulers is maintained through the instrument of parliamentary democracy and regular elections are managed by a maze of money power, powerful propaganda machinery and the coercive might of the State. As for the ordinary mortals, they are free to vote for their favourite billionaire.

Many individuals, even among those who otherwise have genuine concern for India's working masses, harbour illusions about the 'right to vote' that is conferred by the country's Constitution. However, what needs be emphasised here is that the Indian 'parliamentary democracy' is not as much about the 'power of the vote', as much it is about undermining the interests of the oppressed masses by utilising the faultlines of region, religion, caste, ethnicity and nationality.

Presenting a much nuanced analysis of this, Atul Kohli has described this process as 'management of power conflicts' by the Indian State in dealing with a 'variety of politicized social groups—ethnic, caste, class or regional—that periodically demand a greater share of resources, autonomy and self-government' (Kohli, 2001). It is further stated, 'No electoral democracy can long survive without protecting the interests of the powerful . . . While the rhetoric of the Indian State has often been redistributive—socialism, abolition of traditional privileges, reform of caste system, and populism—political practice has been considerably more conservative eschewing any decisive redistribution . . . However, the political impact of these twin tendencies—radical in tone, conservative in practice—may well have been benign, strengthening democracy: the powerful in society feel well served by the system but the weaker groups do not feel totally excluded or hopeless, at least not so far' (Ibid: 2).

In fact, the real worth of India's democracy has been best articulated by the representatives of the system itself. Please refer in Chapter 6 to the address of the then Prime Minister, Dr. Manmohan Singh delivered at his alma mater, the Oxford University in 2005.

While those infamous words may have been said by one Prime Minister, the experience of governance that people have had throughout the country since 1947, would easily attest those in governments to be true specimens of the country's mainstream polity, bureaucracy, the police forces and the armed forces. In a nutshell, the State structure in the country continues to espouse the colonial legacy. The change from ruling in the name of the British Crown to ruling in the name of Indian people, only serves to confound its tyranny and the path to liberation from it.

So, while India's 'parliamentary democracy' may have effected changes from within the ruling class parties in the formation of Governments, or may even have delivered partial relief on some issues to the oppressed classes, their emancipation should entail a revolutionary upheaval. The system carefully ensures that the existing power relations in the society are not only maintained but are further strengthened. Resultantly, the interests of the oppressed masses can be ensured in this system only to the extent that doing so also favours the interests of the ruling classes or if a relative leveraging of the interests of the oppressed people can be achieved at no significant cost to the dominant classes.

Hence, while adjusting the amount of food subsidy is possible, even if only with a lot of pleading, equitable division of productive resources, of which land is the most important with respect to ensuring food security, is not permissible. Food subsidies distributed through PDS help project the ruling classes as the compassionate 'provider' for the poor. The poor must feel obliged to the ruling elite for these favours.

Secondly, subsidies do help the poor to tide over extreme depravation. However the cheap labour of the poor is exploited by those who own the means of production. Thirdly, subsidies are an instrument to buy social peace for the ruling elite in the face of the overall impact of their exploitative policies.

Another important point is that unlike the developed countries, where only a small minority is poor, in countries like India both the size and depth of poverty are huge. A number of Government committees themselves have acknowledged that nearly 80 per cent of the country's population consumed less than the minimum calories (2,400 and 2,100 calories for the rural and the urban areas respectively) designated for estimation of poverty. Deprivation on such a mass scale is built on the foundation of gross inequality in the ownership of productive resources and can hardly be remedied through the usual policy instruments of subsidies. Thus, inasmuch as the challenge remains to enable the people to feed themselves, this cannot be achieved without a redistribution of society's productive resources. Weakening of the strong is imperative for such redistribution.

## The Role of Political Parties

`We have mentioned above the essentially political nature of the task of upturning the existing power relations in the society to achieve long term gains in ensuring the food security of the oppressed masses.

However, all this debate for a just, humane, comprehensive PDS, seems to have done little to mobilise the poor themselves who ought to be the motive force for ensuring the success of any food security programme. Perhaps the poor realise how ephemeral this debate is to their real needs i.e. the need for economic security and freedom from dependence on the propertied classes.

We say this even as we are aware of the fact that numerous dharnas, rallies, demonstrations and other programmes have been organised by the different civil society organisations that are fighting for a comprehensive and meaningful 'Food Security Bill' to be enacted into law by the Parliament. There are inherent limitations when such efforts are left to the capabilities of the civil society organisations alone, and we shall come to that a while later. Here we deal with the role of the political parties.

Even though there is a consensus among the different political parties on the broad contours of the economic policy, they differ in the way they prioritise issues and articulate their stand depending on which side of the political spectrum they belong to. Further, the class character of different parties must be recognised not by what they say, but by what they do.

Generally speaking, in the economic sense, the mainstream political spectrum in India can be considered to be divided into the right wing and the left wing parties, with the centrist parties having all but disappeared. Outside of these there exists a revolutionary Left movement in the country, but it does not aspire for any stakes in the given State structure. When it comes to upholding the economic interests of the poor, little reliance is placed on the right wing parties like the BJP, Congress and other bourgeois parties even though they all depend on the vote bank of the poor for staking their claim to power. The poor are sought to be manipulated by these parties by stoking emotions around the numerous faultlines of religion, region, ethnicity or caste backed by the money bags of the propertied classes.

As opposed to this, the Parliamentary Left seeks to occupy a political space in the name of upholding the interests of the working class and the poorer peasantry. It is natural then that there is a greater expectation from these parties to provide leadership on issues that primarily affect these sections. In this respect a prominent role by the Left was desired in the struggle for ensuring the food security of the poor.

If we leave it to the Left parties themselves to describe their conduct on the issue of food security, they may cite the number of mass programmes undertaken by them in this regard. They may proclaim how their parliamentarians raised this issue in the Parliament or other forums that are suitable for raising such issues. However, to what effect actions are carried out and where they will lead, is decided by the politics that commands them, the true nature of politics is determined not by what is said but what is practically done.

There is accumulated experience from across the world that the Left parties have come to be accepted into the mainstream parliamentary framework only when they have tempered down the revolutionary content of their politics to suit the sensibilities of the dominant classes. As to the rest, with respect to the Third World, imperialist forces have moved with great alacrity and ruthlessness to cut short any possibility of a change that is perceived to be harmful to their interests. The overthrow of the Salvadore Allende regime in Chile on 11 Sepctember 1973 and the liquidation of the Indonesian Communist Party in the mid-sixties, both with the involvement of the CIA are two examples worth remembering.

The mainstream Indian Left has learnt its lessons well from such experiences. Indeed, its topmost leaders have demonstrated their ability to forthrightly articulate their liking for capitalism, even as they use the symbols and slogans of the oppressed classes to garner the support of these sections. In 2008, just days after the erstwhile Left Front Chief Minister of West Bengal, Buddhadeb Bhattacharjee advocated a capitalist course for the Left bastion, perhaps the tallest figure of the mainstream Left, the late Jyoti Basu said, 'We want capital, both foreign and domestic. After all we are working in a capitalist system. Socialism is not possible now . . . We had spoken about building up a classless society, but that was a long time ago . . . Socialism is our political agenda and was mentioned in our party document, but capitalism will continue to be the compulsion for the future' (*Indian Express*, 2008). Like every wise leader, he had his alibis for saying so. Pointing to the fact that CPM-led Governments were in power in only three states, he said, 'Can we say we will establish socialism on the basis of this?' (Ibid)

These were not one off comments of a tired and retired leader. It was indeed the prevalent view in the Party, as was affirmed by the comments of the then general secretary of CPM, Mr. Prakash Karat who articulated it while addressing the alumni meeting of the Madras Christian College in Chennai on 30 October, 2010. Elabourating on the ostensible contradiction in the positions Left took on the FDI and market economy at the national level and in the states where it was in power, Mr. Karat clarified that contrary to the misconception, 'Marxists are not against the market', or opposed to FDI. Based on CPM's experience of building socialism, he had words of wisdom to offer, that, 'market has a function even in a socialist order . . . and that if you eschew the market, or fail to integrate the market into a planned economy, as the Soviet Union did, you are in trouble' (*The Hindu*, 2010b).

It was perhaps an effort at integrating markets into their economic planning that the CPM daily in West Bengal, *Ganashakti* carried a full page Coca-Cola ad long ago (Vanguard, 1994). We have already pointed out their acquiescence in the passage of the 'Special Economic Zones Act.' The developments of Singur (TATA Nano car plant) and Nandigram (where land was forcibly acquired for the SEZ of the Abu-Salem group of Indonesia) bear further testimony to the results of this friendship between markets and CPM variety of socialism.

If one comes to collating the instances of acceptance of the role of markets there can be any number of them to cite such opportunism of the mainstream Left both in theory and in practice. This need not be by inference for we have it from the horse's mouth.

The roundabout manner of their confession notwithstanding, the Left parties statesmen have themselves agreed that for now their task is to build capitalism in the States where they rule. While much may be said or done for public consumption, it is this ideological position that defines and limits the scope of their agitational programmes and what is intended to be achieved through them. In respect of food security, this practically rules out the feasibility of taking up a revolutionary agenda like the land reforms. However, the tragedy is that the performance of the mainstream Left even with regard to partial measures like the PDS and their position on the FSB leave much to be desired.

While the Parliamentary Left may well have postponed the task of building socialism for now, a sincere attempt at implementing bourgeois reform in the arena of food security i.e. an efficient PDS, would not have gone against their principle of friendship with capitalism. This however has not been the case. We would like to dwell on this in some detail lest we are accused of assaulting the integrity and pro-people credentials of the Parliamentary Left with unfounded allegations.

Though the Left is now crying itself hoarse on making the PDS universal, the State Governments led by the Left i.e. the Left Democratic Front Government in Kerala and the Left Front Government in West Bengal were among the first Governments in the country to adopt the Targeted PDS (TPDS) when it was introduced in the country in 1997. While the State Government in Tamil Nadu, a neighbouring state of Kerala, chose to go back to universal PDS under public pressure, the same option however was not exercised by the Left ruled States. That Tamil Nadu did so at least shows that it could have been done by others as well if there was sufficient political will to leverage the welfare of the people.

Meanwhile, the functioning of PDS has steadily deteriorated in the States of West Bengal and Kerala. We shall take up here a detailed exposition of the PDS in West Bengal, as that is the State which has known a long unbroken stint of 'Communist' Government, which afforded all the time that could have been desired to streamline PDS in the State. The following discussion largely relies on the findings in the report of Justice Wadhwa Committee for the State of West Bengal (Justice Wadhwa, 2010) that was constituted by the Supreme Court to study the maladies afflicting the functioning of PDS in different states and suggest remedial measures.

Criticising the provisions of the FSB, the CPM Polit Bureau member Ms. Brinda Karat wrote in The Hindu that, 'The Bill shifts from the present quota of 35 kg per family to an individual based system fixed at a monthly quota of 7 kg per person for a BPL (below poverty line) family. While individual based quotas may appear to be reasonable, it will end up punishing poor families that have fewer children . . . For APL (above poverty line) sections it is even worse, with just a 3 kg quota per individual. Can 3 kg a month provide food security? This is an affront to human dignity and shows utter lack of social conscience' (Karat, 2011)

It must be appreciated that she has found such provisions to be 'an affront to human dignity' amounting to 'utter lack of social conscience', she somehow did not seem to know that her comrades in West Bengal translated these very provisions into policy. As to the 'individual based quotas' (Unit-based Ration Card Scheme)[2], the Justice Wadhwa Committee reports that, 'Ironically the State also projects itself as one of the examples so far as the implementation of the TPDS and Unit-based Ration Card Scheme is concerned.' Cautioning regarding the implementation of Unit based ration cards scheme, the Committee has cited Bengal as a model for studying the loopholes of the scheme (Justice Wadhwa, 2010).

It becomes evident from the report that this scheme has led to a rather serious situation wherein 'as a consequence of unit system and non-issuance of the ration cards to the minors, minors in many families do not get rations for themselves. Considering poor families like AAY (Antyodaya Anna Yojana the scheme which is for the poorest of the poor) families, such situation is alarming and needs immediate consideration and action from the Government in order to avoid cases of malnutrition among minor children both in tribal and non-tribal families' (Ibid).

The 'unit system of ration cards' has led to weird situations for many families all over West Bengal, if the husband has the AAY card, the wife and daughter have APL cards, while

2. In the 'Unit based Ration Card System' a separate card is made for each member of the family. As revealed in the Report of the Justice Wadhwa Committee, this has led to a number of anomalies wherein different cards under different categories have been made for members of the same family. Often new cards are difficult to get for newer additions to the family either by birth or by marriage of an offspring. As the knowledge regarding the provisions of the scheme is very poor among the beneficiaries, often the rations due for an adult are not obtained as the card made during childhood was never updated.

the grandchild has none even seven years after filing an application for him. The situation constrained the Committee to note that, 'If we compare the AAY family residing in other states which do not follow unit system, it appears that AAY families residing in those states enjoy better benefits than in Bengal' (Justice Wadhwa, 2010).

Through these pages we shall endeavour to tell Ms. Karat of another fact which her West Bengal comrades never cared to inform her about—that until September 2010 the Left Front Government in Bengal rubbed in 'affront to human dignity' with 'utter lack of social conscience' by earmarking exactly 3 kg of food grains (500 gm of wheat and 250 gm of rice every week) per adult in APL category per month. It was only from September 2010 onwards the burden of this 'affront' was lightened by 400 gm every month by increasing the wheat quota to 600 gm per week (Ibid).

The litany of complaints against the PDS in West Bengal is long and at least some more of them deserve mention here to drive home our case regarding the sincerity of mainstream Left in ensuring the food security of the people anymore than what other parties desire.

- The Committee report mentions that most of the rice that is procured locally is of an unacceptable quality for the consumers. As regards wheat, nearly 50% of the stock is usually found to be of an unacceptable quality for human consumption (Ibid).

  The following description of a grain storage facility in the Kashipur block of Purulia district completes the picture for us (Ibid):

  The sheds were in deplorable condition. They were poorly managed. The shed storing APL grain (shed No. 28) was even stinking. The sheds storing BPL grain (shed No. 13 and 9) were badly maintained and the grain stored there in was of inedible condition. In all the sheds, a large quantity of grain was scattered on the floor. It was dirty with rodent and bird faeces in it . . . The premises outside the shed were also poorly maintained. There were drains with stagnant water around the sheds which was seeping into the sheds and causing the sheds to emanate a foul smell.'

The godown premises were of State Government and FCI officials blame the State Government for the condition and claimed that the upkeep and maintenance of the godowns are responsibility of the department i.e. the State Government.

Contrary to this, on a visit to another godown owned by FCI, conditions were found to be satisfactory.

- The Parliamentary Left is never found tiring in their advocacy of the importance of public sector in the economy except of course in states where they themselves are in power. Even though the State Government has its 'West Bengal Essential Commodities Supply Corporation', it has not been allocated any role in the functioning of the PDS in the State, while reliance is placed on private distributors and wholesalers who act as middlemen in the system (Ibid).

The Chairman of the Corporation, Mr Rebati Bhattacharjee felt that given a chance, the Corporation was willing to perform its role in smooth functioning of PDS. He said that, 'The private wholesalers are unable to lift all commodities in prescribed time for want of capital. This can be done by the Corporation in a better way by enhancing the role of the Corporation in distribution' (Ibid).

Actually the distributors, wholesalers and fair price shop (FPS) owners are part of a system of political patronage that was built by the Left Front in general and CPM in particular throughout the State and the same is even reflected in the Report of the Committee.

- Vis-a-vis the appointments of dealers and middlemen the Committee notes, 'All appointments in the State are political at the State Government level. The appointments of FPS/MR dealers and distributors/wholesalers should be made apolitical for a fair and effective functioning of the PDS. The appointment process ought to be made transparent.'
- The patronage system extended even to the making of ration cards with a clear goal of increasing the influence of the Party. The report notes, 'It was also informed to the Committee that there was political influence when BPL and AAY cards were initially given to influence maximum families for vote bank. It was tried to distribute AAY and BPL cards to as many families as possible rather than covering all the members of a family. Focus was to cover maximum families rather than to cover the AAY families' (Ibid).

  Needless to say such practices have led to all sorts of anomalies in the making of ration cards in the State.
- In 2010, the State had more ration cards in circulation than its projected population for the year 2011. It was estimated that up to 20% to 30% cards in the State are bogus with there being widespread errors of inclusion and exclusion from the BPL list.
- With all these anomalies being rampant, it is of little surprise that massive pilferage and grain diversion was detected at all levels of the system.
- Complaints of under-weighment and forced sale of non-PDS items by the FPS owners were rampant throughout the State with the consumers having little recourse to any remedial action as the elaborate scheme of vigilance

committees at different levels remained only on paper in most parts of the State. 'Most of the beneficiaries were unaware of the authority which can address their complaints and grievances' (Ibid).

- Inspections of the FPS by any authority were few and far between sending the 'monitoring' mechanism for a toss.

With these being the results to show after 34 years of uninterrupted rule by the Left Front in the State, what measure of seriousness can be accorded to their objections to the FSB and an ostensible concern for ensuring the food security of the poor? These details also affirm that the move to outsource the fight for food security to the civil society is not a tactical error, but is a strategic shift that was initiated quite some time back when they joined forces with national and international NGOs and their funding agencies which in turn had links with imperialist powers, for organising the 'World Social Forum' jamboree at Mumbai in January 2004.

The near absence of any elaboration on the role of other ruling class parties over here is not to absolve them of their role in the present state of food security in the country, but only because of the fact that their self-professed political stand does not inspire any expectation from them insofar as the issues relating to the poor are concerned. These parties are obliged to talk of food security only because the responsibility of managing the ongoing food security schemes falls on them by default. We have no illusion that they would usher in any positive change in policy vis-à-vis food security of their own accord, the same will be possible only under the impact of powerful people's movements.

The emphasis on the role of the Parliamentary Left is required for another reason because it is the biggest obstacle in mounting determined class struggles of the section of oppressed people that is motivated and is willing to be mobilised under the revolutionary banner. Because of their history of militant struggles in the distant past and by virtue of the fact that they still remain the largest Left parties, they manage to diffuse the anger of a large section of working masses into safe channels of parliamentarism. Therein lies the challenge for the revolutionary Left to clearly expose the true character of the mainstream Left by launching widespread militant struggles of the working masses on various issues that impact on their existence.

## Potential of the Civil Society to Arouse Masses

There has been an extensive debate on the role of NGOs from the standpoint of bringing about a change in society. Without revisiting the debate per se over here, it may suffice to note that from the point of view of radical politics and a radical social transformation, an NGO instituted reform is a countervailing force that seeks to protect the given social, economic and political order of the day (Research Unit for Political Economy, 2004). Desrochers writes of NGOs, 'Most NGOs function to mediate and diffuse the enormous build-up of social and political tension, which is the outcome of iniquitous and highly destructive development' (Desrochers, 2006).

The decades of the 1980s and the 1990s were marked by a worldwide rise of NGOs, especially across developing countries. This also is the period when the process of 'globalisation' and neoliberal economic reforms were unrolled, most prominently in the developing world. The coinciding of the two processes is especially important. NGOs were the prop to mitigate the profound human suffering caused by 'globalisation' (Research Unit for Political Economy, 2004). NGOs have a specific political purpose, as opined by the World Bank, 'Social tensions and divisions can be eased by bringing political opponents together within the framework of formal and informal forums and by channelling their energies through political processes, rather than leaving confrontation as the only form of release' (World Development Report, 2000-01, quoted in Desrochers, 2006). Such a conceptualisation if taken to its logical conclusion would recognise the political processes acceptable to the system as the only 'legitimate' political processes, while political action that defies established authority becomes 'illegitimate'.

There are two other important issues regarding NGOs that have an immense bearing on the outcome of their action. The first is that they emphasise primacy of 'identity' (region, religion, caste, gender or ethnicity) over 'class', leading thereby to the negation of factors that can form the basis of a broader unity of the oppressed masses. In fact, the emphasis on identity may pitch one section of the oppressed people against another.

Secondly, there is the issue of funding, rarely is it that the NGOs depend for their day-to-day functioning and sustenance on the resources provided by the sections whose interests they claim to espouse. The issue of outside funding, including from foreign organisations, some of whom have had a very dubious record as to furthering the democratic aspirations of the people has been a big issue regarding NGOs (Research Unit for Political Economy, 2004, Biswas, 2006).The answerability of the NGOs to their funding agency is absolute, which effectively sets the limits as to which NGOs can afford to cross the establishment. As to the people, they can only be thankful for the selfless services of the NGOs rather than stake any claims as a matter of right.

Given this summarisation of the political character of NGOs, it becomes clear that taking up of equitable distribution of land as a measure for ensuring food security by the civil society is ruled out for this would necessarily entail intense confrontations with the dominant forces in the society. So, reforming the PDS becomes the only and the best way forward.

The 'Right to Food Campaign' (RTFC), which has been in the forefront of the debate on the 'Food Security Bill', describes itself as, 'An informal network of organisations and individuals committed to the realisation of the right to food in India'. Admittedly, its sustained focus has been on 'on legislation and schemes such as the Mahatma Gandhi National Rural Employment Guarantee Act (MNREGA), the Integrated Child Development Services (ICDS), Mid-day Meals (MDM) Scheme, and the Public Distribution System (PDS) and the Right to Food Campaign. While there is always scope and need for framing better laws and schemes, what needs to be realised here is that the lot of the poor in India is what it is, not due to a dearth of schemes or laws but because of the ruling elite to whom we entrust their implementation. Right to life is a fundamental right, protected under the Constitution, yet encounter killings, custodial deaths and wanton killing of people under draconian laws like the Armed Forces Special Powers Act by the security forces are widely prevalent in large parts of the country. It is always the powerful who commit these crimes against the powerless, highlighting again the fundamental issue of changing the power relations, empowering people vis-à-vis the rulers.

A militant mass mobilisation of the people is the only way to make this elite yield to the people's needs even as regards the policy reforms that are feasible within the system. The meaning of the word 'militant' becomes clearer form the discussion to follow.

It is with respect to building militant mass struggles that the campaigns such as the RTF hit the roof. Let alone the organisations working for the physically challenged, single women, Dalits and those promoting breast feeding, which are all part of the RTF and are not likely to have an appeal beyond their sectoral constituencies, even a trade union centre that is part of a Campaign talks of building a 'unity of the trade union movement on the basis of independence from Government, employers and political parties' (NTUI, 2009). Given the fact that the bulk of the organised working class in the country is with the trade union centres affiliated to political parties, not only such an orientation practically works at keeping the working masses divided over their bread and butter issues, but it also seeks to detach them from the rich ideological heritage of the working class movement in the country. Little wonder then that the major trade unions in the country have kept themselves aloof from the activities of the Right to Food Campaign.

Suffice it to say, such a coalition of forces can hardly challenge the establishment's apathy towards the plight of the people in any meaningful way, especially if its leading lights have been lending their credibility to the very establishment as members of the notable advisory committees.

Above all this, there is plenty of advice from them for the people. Even the 'what to do' portions of the primers on different food security schemes that are available at the RTF website are nothing but exhortations for what the people can do to make things run better for themselves: stuff like community organisation for action, community awareness regarding their entitlements or the courts' rulings, education about nutritive value of foods, health melas, having kitchen gardens, maintaining cleanliness and hygiene, and of course petitioning to the authorities about what might be lacking.

All of this is definitely important and helpful for the efficient implementation of different schemes, but the question is—is it for the lack of all this that India is home to the largest number of hungry people in the world? One has only to go to the people to know that it is the authorities that systematically and systemically fail these schemes. Few if any of the drawbacks of PDS mentioned in the report of the Justice Wadhwa Committee are amenable to these 'what to do' prescriptions. How would these prescriptions oblige the authorities to 'give me what is my right?'

We are likely to be challenged on this by citing the number of agitational programmes taken up by the Right to Food Campaign and its affiliate organisations to press for the various demands from the Government. Sure, but to what effect? There is no reason yet, to believe that any of these programmes have challenged the establishment to the detriment of its designs on tampering with food security of the people.

Meanwhile, the country has been witness to a number of other kinds of people's movements in the past few years, most of which can be categorized under the umbrella of 'anti-displacement struggles'. These struggles have effectively stalled the Government's policies of furthering the loot of country's resources or uprooting the livelihoods of the people in the name of so-called development. Examples are many: starting with Singur or Nandigram in West Bengal, anti-POSCO movement and the movement against the steel plant of the Tatas in Kalinganagar or the successful struggle against the mining of bauxite by Sterlite group in Niyamgiri, the movement of the tribal peasantry of Narayanpatna against the alienation from their lands, all in Odisha, the struggles against setting up of nuclear power plants at Jaitapur in Maharashtra and Koodankulam in Tamil Nadu or the struggle by tribals against State sponsored vigilante groups like Salwa Judum unleashed with the purpose of opening up the mineral resources in the forest area of central India. All of these movements have profound ramifications for food security of the people in the respective areas. These movements enjoy no formal recognition of the Governments they confront, none of their leaders share the high table with their tormentors and they are not the virtuous 'opposition within'. Rather some of these have been labelled as extremist-led or influenced.

The immediate demands in most of these aforementioned movements do not seek a radical transformation of the society. The people involved therein seem to be asking the Government to leave them in their present condition rather than impose on them its model of development. Yet, they have had to sacrifice lives to maintain the status-quo.

The Parliamentary Standing Committee on Commerce 'helplessly' pleaded that food grain be rather exported than let it rot in the godowns (Mehdudia, 2011). Ironically such recommendations come even as millions go hungry in the country. The sinister design is that most of the FCI godowns are located in areas with excess food grain production. Had these godowns been located in the pockets of hunger, the people would have readily spared the honourable Parliament members the helplessness of taking such unpleasant decisions by timely utilisation of this grain. In doing so they would only be implementing the Supreme Court orders to the effect that the grain be distributed free which the Government had refused to do.

## Putting Two and Two Together

We have deliberated in quite some detail on the stand and the roles of the different sides in the debate on food security in the foregoing sections. The question is how do we make sense of this debate?

Even as they prepare to sustain a high growth rate of the economy by intensifying the neoliberal economic policy, Governments have often expressed their commitment to an 'inclusive growth.' Though not in the actual life conditions of the people, one instnce in which the idea of inclusive growth was consummated was in the creation of the National Advisory Council (NAC) during the rule of erstwhile UPA Government which took on board civil society activists to give it the flavour of activism, action-oriented body seized with welfare of the people.

There were layers within layers in the above arrangement. The NAC acted as an opposition to the Government, placing its own demands on it and even managing a standoff of sorts before wilting under the spell of pragmatism and finally settling for much the same as what Government initially offered. This transition itself was played out over a long period and every stage of it hogged due media coverage, at least in the print media, until people were thoroughly confused over who was saying what and yet the impression carried through was that they were all concerned about removing hunger sooner than later.

A section of the civil society took on the mantle of opposing and critiquing the changing stance of the NAC as also the Government. It did its homework well and continues to be technically impeccable in its critique. It even backs its words with demonstrative actions—dharnas, demonstrations, conventions, academic consultations and the like.

The UPA Government, more often than not, did not decry the position of those opposed to its stand as being flawed, its stance invariably was that their propositions were not feasible for one reason or the other. Even after the change in guard of the Government at the Centre it is these actors only, who in varied ways and forms, continue to define the boundaries within which the great Indian food security debate revolves. The only difference is that with the far Right wing NDA (National Democratic Alliance) Government at the Centre, the battle for food security appears to be all the more a losing one. The report of the 'High Level Committee on Reorienting the Role and Restructuring of Food Corporation of India (FCI)', popularly known as the Shanta Kumar Committee Report, that came out in January 2015 has virtually written the prescription for relegating FCI to a marginal role and further watering down the implementation of the National Food Security Act, 2013 (Basu and Das, 2015).

Given the kind of acceptance this caucus has as 'thee credible authority' on issues of poverty, food security, employment and health in the academic institutions, both within and outside the country, in the academic journals, national and international donor agencies and technical bodies, in the media, among the judiciary and different executive arms of the Government, it becomes near impossible to penetrate the boundaries of the debate set by them. Worse still, within the caucus it is not the reform oriented civil society that sets the agenda for the debate, rather it is the Government which has kept two paces ahead of the rest. So when the rest are talking of 'universalisation' and 'increased quota' of food grain, the Government throws up the issue of 'cash transfer' which becomes the new talking point, an entire issue of a prestigious academic journal was devoted to this. Such a debate becomes the veritable rat race in which the real issues of the people are left far, far behind and are ultimately lost.

As someone has said that the 'opposite of love is not hate, it is indifference', this caucus maintains an eloquent indifference to the central question of the need for equal redistribution of society's resources as a precondition to eliminating poverty and hunger from the country. The din of partial demands for PDS reform is kept up in the policy circles, the corridors of power, among the academia and the public spaces in an effort to firmly establish that comprehensive PDS reform is equal to ensuring food security and conversely ensuring food security is to ask for implementation of comprehensive PDS reform. In the process, the question of broader societal change is sought to be sidelined.

Such tactics are nothing new and have been choreographed as and when the establishment has felt the need for regarding it as a high stakes issue. The last time that this was resorted to was during another highly contentious debate in the development sector, 'The Great Indian Poverty Debate' in the late 1990s and early 2000s. It would be worth quoting Utsa Patnaik on this:

> Many critical voices (Suryanarayana, 1996, Mehta and Venkataraman, 2000, Swaminathan, 1999, 2002) which had continued to draw attention to the high prevalence of under nutrition and malnutrition, to the secular decline in average rural calorie intake, to high direct poverty estimates using reasonable calorie norms and which criticized the indirect estimates, have been sought to be silenced by the pro-reform economists, by the simple expedient of ignoring them altogether. Not one critical author is referred to in the articles by those presenting their indirect estimates at a Conference and later collecting them in a special issue of 'The Economic and Political Weekly' tendentiously titled 'Poverty Reduction in the 1990s' (Deaton, 2003a and 2003b, Tendulkar and Sundaram, 2003 etc.) (emphasis ours) (Patnaik, 2007).

The readers should kindly take note of the names mentioned here. Outside of this elite food security caucus there are other actors who exert influence upon its actions—the Supreme Court and the political parties of the Opposition. The Supreme Court sought to occupy the high moral pedestal through its various pronouncements in the civil writ petition 196 of 2001 that seeks enforcement of the right to food. Not only have orders been passed that have converted the provisions of different food security schemes into legally enforceable rights for different sections of the population, but a new set-up has also been created in the form of Supreme Court's Commissioners on Food Security who assist the Court in the supervision of its orders. These Commissioners were also the members of the NAC.

There are numerous reports of the Commissioners on implementation of the Court's orders and investigations of hunger deaths, but unfortunately there is little data to show the extent to which this exercise has led to ensuring the food security of the people by any conventional measure of the term. In fact, one of the Commissioners to the Supreme Court while participating in the 'National Consultation on Developing Tools for Early Identification of Acute Hunger for Effective Administrative Action' organised at the Jawaharlal Nehru University on the 13 May 2010 even remarked that as and when a situation of hunger stalking the people in a given place is brought to the notice of the Government through the office of the Commissioners, subsequent visits to the place have only revealed a worsening of the situation.

The other element outside of this elite caucus is the political parties other than the ruling party, who largely satisfy themselves by scoring debating points against the Government and the ruling party while assiduously avoiding building any sustained and militant movement of the people against hunger, much less talk of bringing the core issue of 'weakening the few to empower masses' to the forefront.

This has been a long drawn out process and by the time of coming to its present stage, the original definition of food security, by which the world knows it has been completely lost in the public eye. It has been supplanted by a much dwarfed understanding that limits itself to asking for reforms in the PDS alone. Dwarfing of the 'concept' leads to dwarfing of people's expectations or their understanding of what is possible. People can hardly fight for achieving what they cannot even visualise.

This enables the establishment to manage people and their expectations with relative ease and even go two steps ahead to further restrict the public purse for the poor. The official scaling down of the poverty line by the Tendulkar Committee to a level of consumer expenditure that would enable the people to consume only 1,800 calories per day both in rural and urban areas, as against the previous cut off of 2,400 calories for rural and 2,100 calories for the urban areas, is a case in point.

All the exertions at fructifying even the partial demands notwithstanding, we are as yet nowhere near to achieving the universalisation of the PDS as it stood in 1997 before switching over to the targeted PDS. Further, in the meeting of the full Commission held on the 15 of September 2012, the then Deputy Chairman of the now dismantled Planning Commission, Montek Singh Ahluwalia expressed hope that 'the exercise of cash transfer of subsidies would be completed by March 2017' in line with 'Finance Minister P. Chidambaram's suggestion with regard to cash transfers pertaining to food, fuel and fertiliser subsidies' (*The Hindu*, 2012).

The Government clearly has gone from one step to another bigger step to implement its agenda, while those who have ostensibly been arguing the case of the poor and the hungry are still busy mobilising the people (which most of the time fails to go beyond a limited circle of NGO activists) for dharnas, demonstrations and other such programmes to ask for implementation of PDS reforms, and probably they will continue doing this until the last man interested in a fight with the rulers on the issue of food security leaves in frustration.

If at every stage, the Government has chosen to ignore the protestations of the civil society and goes ahead with its plans that are bound to put the people in greater distress should it not be expedient for those fighting on the side of the people, to take their movement also to the next higher stage? This would be the stage of letting the people know the true political character of their rulers and instead of being perpetual pleaders, of joining forces with other militant movements in the country that have been steadfastly opposing Government's development policies, all of which have immense bearing on the food security of the people. Idioms should be developed that help in aligning the fight for food security with the issues being articulated by different people's movements, among which the anti-displacement struggles are the foremost.

However, the disillusion woven by the NGO agenda is far more sinister and attempts to pre-empt any possibility of a real change that might put the system in crisis. The small, marginal or landless peasants by far constitute the largest section of the people in the country engaged not only in producing food but also of being among the worst sufferers of food insecurity. Militant mobilisation of this section of people in mass struggles on their core demand of land reform constitutes the axis of revolutionary change in the country. As and when such a mobilisation has happened in the country, the ruling classes have come down heavily on such struggles. Amongst them were the 'Telangana Peasants' Armed Struggle' between 1946-51 against the feudal forces in the Telangana region, the Naxalbari movement on the central demand of 'Land to the Tiller' or the ongoing 'Operation Green Hunt' and its variants in parts of central and eastern India against the mobilisation of the tribal peasantry under the leadership of communist revolutionaries. The repression unleashed on such struggles has cost thousands of lives as the ruling elite knows that these struggles can succeed only at the cost of undermining their social and political base in the country. Even as the restiveness among the peasantry in different regions of the country increases, the NGOs are rising to the occasion in defence of the system by trying to wean away the sections of the peasantry who constitute the core strength of the Indian revolution.

In October 2012, an NGO, 'Ekta Parishad', organised a 350 km long march of some 60 thousand landless peasants gathered from across the country, from Gwalior to Delhi. As per the Parishad's claims, some 1 lakh peasants would have entered Delhi on 28 October 2012 to press for their demands of homestead rights and fast track land tribunals for implementation of land reforms. Unlike the peasant struggles mentioned above, this struggle had the then Union Rural Development Minister, Mr Jairam Ramesh rushing to meet the leaders of the march at Agra while they were still more than half way from their destination (Jebaraj, 2012a).

A successful deal clinched between the Government and the march leaders through backroom negotiations enabled the minister to declare, 'The nation will get happy news from the city of the Taj Mahal', and indeed the next day's newspaper headlines declared victory for the marchers as an agreement was reached between the Government and the Ekta Paraishad leaders. Whatever, may well be the fate of this deal reached between these champions of landless peasants and the Government, it needs to be noted that, 'A similar padayatra (travel by foot) organised by Ekta Parishad five years earlier than the 2012 attempt, resulted in the setting up of a National Land Reforms Council. Headed by the Prime Minister, and including the state Chief Ministers; that eminent body had not met even once' (Ibid). Little wonder then that the representatives ranging from that of the Parliamentary Left to the Right wing parties, besides other NGO eminences were all eager to join the march. All of these are equally united in their opinion that the communist revolutionary movement in this country which has its mass base almost exclusively among the small, marginal and landless peasants, is the biggest internal security threat to the country.

As to the enthusiasm of many of the landless peasants who took part in the march with high hopes, the following comments by one participant from Tamil Nadu at the beginning and the end of the march convey much more than what the Ekta Parishad leadership would have liked to reveal. Malliga, a 35-year-old Paliyar tribal woman from Kodaikanal taluk in Tamil Nadu quoted a Tamil proverb at the beginning of the march:

> I may not have very much in common with people from Madhya Pradesh or the Northeast or Odisha, but I know that if one hand claps, it cannot be heard. But if many

> hands clap, if we all join together, they will have to hear us (Jebaraj, 2012b).

By the time an agreement was reached at Agra and the march called off, Malliga was a dejected woman. To the news of the agreement that promised 10 cents of land to the landless for a homestead, she responded thus:

> What will I do with one-tenth of an acre? What can I grow on it? If I throw my seeds on that land, can my children eat from it?

Even if we presume that all the rural homeless will be given a plot for homestead (which has not been possible till now) and land tribunals will be set up as promised in the agreement, does that amount to implementing land reforms? Landless peasants like Malliga know it does not. And yet demands like homestead and setting up of meaningless tribunals are fought under the banner of struggle for 'Land Reforms' while actually sidelining the real land reforms by generating false hopes through 'managed' struggles that seek to dissuade people from joining revolutionary struggles.

In this respect, the similarity between the NGO struggle for 'Food Security' and their struggle for 'Land Reforms' is not providential. Even as the march for the landless was being organised, the 'Right to Food Campaign' was busy organising marches in different states for the enactment of the 'Right to Food Bill.' Even as these marches were on, the Government pushed ahead with its agenda of opening up the economy to imperialist capital through two successive rounds of reforms that further undermined the livelihoods of the poor. It is undeterred by these marches and yet has granted them respectability by way of agreements and saying all the nice words that will help sustain the illusion woven by the NGOs/civil society in the service of the ruling classes.

## Making Sense of the Debate

We would like to start the food security debate by opening a broadside against neoliberal reforms that is to say that, 'Given the manner in which it has been conducted by different constituents, the food security debate has furthered the corporate agenda of controlling the food chains of the people in the country.'

If the first decade of the neoliberal economic reforms was about 'Poverty reduction by manipulation' (*EPW*, 1996) and the brazen 'Shining India' campaign to somehow prove the success of the reforms, the actual results of the reforms have obliged the ruling establishment to start talking of 'Inclusive Growth' during the second decade of the reforms, but without jettisoning the reforms per se. The more the people are uprooted by the reforms, the more will be the need for their inclusion.

The title of the 12$^{th}$ Plan approach paper reads, 'Faster, Sustainable and More Inclusive Growth' (Planning Commission, 2012). Actually, to maintain and increase their profits, even as one sector after another is becoming sick, it is imperative for the big capital to open up newer areas for loot of the country's resources. The country's natural resources are literally being given away to the corporate groups as was evidenced through the scams involving allocation of gas fields in the Godavari Basin to Reliance Group, the 2G scam and allocation of coal blocks to various industrial houses for free. With the coming of Modi government to power the government complicity with the corporate has scaled new heights. Only time will tell how much this bon-homie has costed to the public exchequre. The volley of reforms in the retail and aviation sectors and disinvestment in a number of public sector undertakings are steps in this direction only. The mandarins at the helm of affairs know very well that this will lead to pauperisation of more and more people for none other than the incumbent

President and not until long ago, the Finance Minister of the country, Pranab Mukherjee admitted that 'Trickle down' will not work in tackling poverty' (*The Telegraph*, 2012). Hence, there will be a greater need for handing out some relief/doles to the millions adversely affected by these policies. This relief is being euphemistically called 'inclusive growth.'

Hence the greater the depth and the expanse of neoliberal loot, the shriller are the voices calling for 'inclusive growth.' The dominance of the 'corporate media' as a means of reaching out information and moulding opinions in society at large, helps in projecting the slogan of 'inclusive growth' to the advantage of the ruling elite. While on the one hand it seeks to blunt the resentment against Government's policies, on the other, those who are pressing for more inclusive social sector policies from outside the Government, are portrayed as the champions of 'welfare state' in the interest of the oppressed masses. In the process however, the real solutions to the problems of the working masses are sought to be sidelined further.

### *The Ideological Roots of This Welfarism*

Beginning from the first tenure of the UPA Government at the Centre, starting in 2004, a few very high profile social sector programmes were launched viz the 'National Rural Health Mission', the 'Right to Information Act', the 'Mahatma Gandhi National Rural Employment Guarantee Act' and then the 'National Food Security Act.' There is a need to look closely at the genesis of these programmes. As is the wont of policy formulation in much of the Third World, our policies originate in the West, only their implementation is left to local Governments, of course with the able guidance of the western multilateral and bilateral agencies.

Before the aforementioned social sector initiatives were launched here, the need for 'welfare economics' in the development policy paradigm was first realised in the West. This change in the mood in the policy capitals of the world was signalled by bestowing Nobel Prize for economics, first on our own Amartya K. Sen in 1998 and then on Joseph Stiglitz in 2001, followed by Muhammad Yunus of Bangladesh in 2006 and Paul Krugman in 2008. These are very important names along with that of Jean Drèze with respect to the discussion in the following section.

Jean Drèze is a well known development economist and has co-authored books on issues of poverty and hunger with Amartya Sen. Drèze has been a member of Ms Sonia Gandhi led 'National Advisory Council' and is among the most acclaimed personalities in India in the fight against hunger. He has been closely associated in guiding the 'Right to Food Campaign' for legislation of a comprehensive 'Right to Food Bill.'

According to one account, less than two years before Amartya Sen was finally given the Nobel Prize for Economics, a Calcutta professor had quizzed Prof Asar Lindbeck of the Nobel Economic Committee in Stockholm regarding the reason for Amartya Sen being overlooked for Nobel Prize in Economics. Lindbeck's reply, after considering the question with due seriousness, was a rather derisive one. He said, 'Much of Sen's work was on the fringes of the subject called economics' (Sen, 1998). Yet the rapidly evolving economic crisis in the financial markets and the economic crisis in South Asia, Japan, China, South Korea and South East Asian economies in 1997-98 made Lindbek's of the West eat their own words. Voices from within the establishment in America decried IMF as 'ineffective, unnecessary and obsolete' (Passell, 1998). While the 1997 Nobel in economics was given to America's Robert Merton and Myron Scholes for devising techniques that facilitated scientific speculation in hedge fund markets, the meltdown in the world financial markets and several Asian economies with its attendant societal implications brought a shift in focus among the bourgeoisie think tanks in the West from 'market worship' to 'welfare economics' (Sen, 1998). Amartya Sen being the tallest figure in the field, then became a natural choice for the 1998 Nobel Prize in Economics. He was followed by the Nobel Prize in economics being awarded to the erstwhile chief economist of the World Bank, Joseph Stiglitz (author of the much acclaimed book, Globalisation and its Discontents) in 2001, then the Nobel Peace Prize to Bangladesh economist Muhammad Yunus (promoter of microcredit) in 2006 and another Keynesian economist (emphasising the welfare function of the State) Paul Krugman in 2008. All this happened even as the economic crisis of the mid and later 1990s fast developed to the unprecedented world economic crisis of 2008.

The important question to answer here is—did these luminaries represent an 'alternative economic paradigm' to the reigning 'economic philosophy' or did they represent more of a 'cautionary voice' within the reigning 'economic philosophy'? Our focus here will be on Amartya Sen whose pre-eminent stature as the 'Indian expert on poverty, hunger and famines' has had an overbearing influence on the recent welfare policy formulation in the country in collabouration with Jean Drèze.

It is important to note that the running thread in the economic and the political philosophy of all the aforementioned luminaries has been that none has actually repudiated the economic and political process of 'globalisation' that has dominated the world economic and political scene over more than last two decades. Broadly speaking, they consider 'globalisation' as unavoidable and indeed desirable for the betterment of the world, provided adequate measures are taken to shield the weaker sections of the society from its ill-effects, including the need to go beyond and proactively develop the economic, social, intellectual, cultural and political capabilities of all the citizens such that they can partake in the process of globalisation. There apparently is no contradiction in the fact that a person can be the Chief Economist of the World Bank (the organisation most often blamed for the devastating impact of the 'globalisation' policies across much of the world) and also be a critique of the 'globalisation' process.

Talking of 'globalisation' Amartya Sen takes a historical view of the process to begin with. He says, 'Over thousands of years, globalisation has contributed to the progress of the world through travel, trade, migration, spread of cultural influences, and dissemination of knowledge and understanding (including that of science and technology). These global interrelations have often been very productive in the advancement of different countries' (Sen, 2002). However, except may be in case of lunatic fringe, the contentions regarding globalisation have not been about its beneficial role and course over centuries, which any reasonable person would find acceptable. For that matter, in the modern world history, it is the working class movement that has been the foremost bearer of globalisation, forthrightly calling for the unity of the world proletariat irrespective of their national, ethnic and cultural boundaries. What needs to be addressed here are the contentions regarding the current phase of 'imperialist globalisation' (which extends from the colonial phase of globalisation). However, to Sen, imperialist nature is not the principal aspect of globalisation. He says, 'Of course, there are issues related to globalisation that do connect with imperialism (the history of conquests, colonialism, and alien rule remains relevant today in many ways), and a postcolonial understanding of the world has its merits. But it would be a great mistake to see globalisation primarily as a feature of imperialism. It is much bigger—much greater—than that' (Sen, 2002).

Once the primarily imperialist nature of present globalisation process is denied, then the need to oppose it on these grounds is also obviated and the adverse consequences of the process, howsoever daunting, are projected as mere distortions rather than as inevitable results thereof. In fact, Sen's assertion regarding the present phase of what we would categorically call as 'imperialist globalisation' goes much ahead, 'Indeed, we cannot reverse the economic predicament of the poor across the world by withholding from them the great advantages of contemporary technology, the well-established efficiency of international trade and exchange, and the social as well as economic merits of living in an open society. Rather, the main issue is how to make good use of the remarkable benefits of economic intercourse and technological progress in a way that pays adequate attention to the interests of the deprived and the underdog. That is, I would argue, the constructive question that emerges from the so-called anti-globalisation movements' (Sen, 2002).

Thus in one swathe he has resolved questions regarding control over contemporary technology, to whose advantage and at what cost to the environment and people (remember the widespread displacement of people brought about in putting to use this 'contemporary technology'): the imbalances, restrictive practices, ruining livelihoods of millions of families in the developing world and downright loot of the resources of the third world countries by the industrialised West through 'well-established efficiency of international trade and exchange' controlled by them. One has only to ask, and ask emphatically, how the 'underdogs' can make 'good use of the remarkable benefits of economic intercourse and technological progress' over which they do not have any control. Every effort is made to ensure that they cannot acquire such capability anytime in near future through effective enforcement of regimens like 'TRIPS', 'TRIMS' and if need be, the naked use of brute force. The understanding that in a world where relations between the nations continue to be defined by unabashed power play, and so long as pursuit of private profit continues to guide the use of 'economic intercourse and technological progress', and that the beneficial use of these processes for the betterment of humanity is impossible, is nowhere reflected in his views on globalisation. In a nutshell, it is the class dimension of the globalisation debate that is missing. Sen does criticise some of the globalisation measures as being obstructive for creation of a more just society, but having given away on the most fundamental contentions of 'imperialist globalisation' one can have little to complain on its natural outcomes.

Sen upholds the supremacy of markets. In his opinion, 'Even though the operation of a given market economy can be significantly defective, there is no way of dispensing with the institution of markets in general as a powerful engine of economic progress' (Sen, 2002). It may be true that market guided economy cannot be immediately dispensed with and indeed there might be a need for market-based exchange in some areas of trade between the nations for a long time to come. Is market the only forum for commodity exchange between and within the nations? Is there no feasibility of need-based exchange, at least in the most fundamental of the human wants? And if that indeed is the case, then one would expect a comment from the market worshippers on the socialist credo of, 'from each according to his ability, to each according to his need.'

Market-based exchange need not be the only way to satisfy human wants. As the productive capabilities at the disposal of man enable us to satisfy the needs of more and more people across the globe, every endeavour should be made to promote human need as the basis of exchange of commodities. This is all the more so when it concerns the most fundamental need like food for the hundreds of millions across the globe who are unable to constitute themselves effectively as part of markets, simply for the lack of purchasing power.

Sen however holds that defective market outcomes could be influenced by 'public policies in education, epidemiology, land reform, microcredit facilities, appropriate legal protections, et cetera, and in each of these fields, there is work to be done through public action that can radically alter the outcome of local and global economic relations.' A fuller exposition of this shared vision of 'public action' as a solution to the problems of market failure or development apathy, between Amartya Sen and Jean Drèze, is to be found in their book titled 'Hunger and Public Action' wherein they define public action as:

> not merely the activities of the state, but also social actions taken by members of the public—both 'collaborative' (through civic cooperation) and 'adversarial' (through social criticism and political opposition . . . But the reach of public action goes well beyond the doings of the state, and involves what is done by the public—not merely for the public. We also argue that the nature and effectiveness of the activities of the state can deteriorate very easily in the absence of public vigilance and activism (Sen and Drèze, 1989, Preface).

Such fine words, yet so simplistic in their assumptions. Public is thought of as though it is a homogenous mass of people, without divisions of class that make them take different views on public policies to suit their class interests or divisions of nationality, ethnicity, gender, race, region, religion and caste. These interests or divisions are so commonly used to keep the working masses divided so as to dissipate their class consciousness. The State is as though it is a neutral power rather than a coercive apparatus of class rule. In the world view of Sen and Drèze there seems to be infinite malleability of the State in adopting policies privileging the interests of the most marginalised, provided of course this homogenous public can be spurred into action to demand such policies.

All of this can be said only by way of inference, the distinguished duo can always dismiss the inference as imaginary. However, the entire debate on 'food security' in India that we have traced above does tend to prove our inferences to be right. At least the debate certainly does not acknowledge the fundamental conflict between the interests of India's ruling elite and those of India's poor and hungry.

It is not without reason that Sen's economic contribution is said to lie in enhancing the 'neoclassical notion of welfare by including rights and liberties, and more egalitarian notions of fairness' (Vakulabharanam and Motiram, 2000).

> While far from Marxist, his political leanings are definitely left of the mainstream economic tradition. Thus, though he has never explicitly rejected the capitalist mode of production, in many of his writings he mocks at a vulgar extension of market logic and egoistic behaviour into every aspect of human existence. In this manner of being an 'internal' critic of the mainstream tradition he has brought issues of starvation, famines, poverty and human development into the very heart of a remarkably callous economic tradition (Ibid).

However, it must be stated emphatically that in their theorisation both Sen and Drèze do not reject the basic premises of the present social, economic and political system. Hence, public action informed by such theory cannot but revolve within the structural limits imposed by the system.

Conservatism in theory cannot keep conservatism in policy far behind; its liberal form can at best be misleading. In the debate on poverty trends during the years of neoliberal economic reforms in India Angus Deaton, who has been a close associate of Drèze has sided with the claims of the ruling establishment that the reforms have led to decline in poverty levels in India (Deaton 2003a and 2003b). In what can be considered to be supportive of Angus Deaton's thesis on poverty reduction, we have already noted in Chapter 2 that as against the contention that the falling levels of per capita calorie consumption are a direct result of the rising poverty levels in the country, Deaton and Drèze have eminently argued that there is not enough evidence to support this hypothesis. Instead in the face of the evidence to the contrary, they go on to discuss various other factors being responsible for this decline (Deaton and Drèze 2009, 2010) in calorie consumption which have been shown by us not to withstand the test of available facts.

Likewise, talking of the moves for industrialisation of Bengal (read the Singur and the Nandigram anti-displacement movements) by the erstwhile CPM Government of West Bengal, Amartya Sen told the 'The Telegraph' in an interview, 'Ultimately, those who want to prevent industrialisation of Bengal do not look enough at the interest of the people of the state. They may intend well, but they are not serving the interest of Bengal's working class or peasantry. The prosperity of the peasantry in the world always depends on the number of peasants going down. That is the standard experience in the world' (*The Telegraph*, 2007). It is difficult to say if the then Prime Minister, Manmohan Singh took his cue from Sen in telling the journalists at his residence that:

> there is no such thing as a free lunch. India has no option but to industrialise . . . The only way we can raise our heads above poverty is for more people to be taken out of agriculture (Varadarajan, 2010).

Nonetheless, Sen's statement is remarkable in more ways than one; he simplistically paints people either as pro-industrialisation or anti-industrialisation. People's experience of how industrialisation has served them till now and their apprehensions regarding the loss of their livelihoods, especially given the fact of nearly jobless growth over the decades of neoliberalisation ought not to matter in their decision to support or oppose the industrialisation moves of the government. Coming as it does from a person of his stature, such a comment by Sen cannot be regarded as a casual comment and serves to dilute his contribution in expanding the 'neoclassical notion of welfare by including rights and liberties.'

Thus in the ultimate analysis the samaritans of the civil society and their ideologues exerting themselves to mitigate the pangs of hunger from India can at best be described in the words of Marx and Engels as 'bourgeois socialists.' They said in *The Communist Manifesto*:

> A part of the bourgeoisie is desirous of redressing social grievances in order to secure the continued existence of bourgeois society. To this section belong economists, philanthropists, humanitarians, improvers of the condition of the working class, organisers of charity . . . hole-and-corner reformers of every imaginable kind. This form of socialism has, moreover, been worked out into complete systems . . . The socialistic bourgeoisie want all the advantages of modern social conditions without the struggles and dangers necessarily resulting therefrom. They desire the existing state of society, minus its revolutionary and disintegrating elements (Marx and Engels, 1848).

The series of social sector programmes and schemes launched by the Government during the tenure of the UPA Government have been directed more at blunting the opposition to Government's policies rather than being reflective of a genuine desire on the part of the ruling elite to ameliorate the difficulties of the people. This is amply evident in the fact that, despite the evident adverse impact of the neoliberal policies, the government is going ahead with further intensifying their implementation and introducing newer policies, while at the same time the implementation of the social sector schemes leaves much to be desired.

The most likely reason behind the social sector initiatives seems to be that the rulers are aware that when the consequences of their policies become too disconcerting for the people to bear, the likelihood of their getting attracted towards more radical solutions also increases. The number of militant struggles against the 'economic policies' being encountered by the Governments at the Centre and in several states and the spectre of 'left wing insurgency' continuing to haunt the Governments bear testimony to this. However, the leopard cannot change its spots to become a sheep in order to deepen its loot of a country's resources in collaboration with their imperialist masters, the country's rulers cannot but intensify the implementation of neoliberal policies. Under the circumstances, the social sector reforms that promise the moon but deliver nothing more than crumbs to the oppressed, are perceived by the ruling elite as the best way out. Viewed this way, MNREGA does not just remain a poverty alleviation programme, but it serves the function of aborting land reforms from coming centre stage on the country's development agenda.

Under the circumstances, those indulging in the single minded pursuit of a 'welfare policy regimen' at the cost of a revolutionary transformation of the society, forget a very important lesson of history, that the western conceptualisation of a 'welfare state' also got centre staged when the oppressed masses first established a socialist state in the Soviet Union. The need to wean away their own workers from embarking on a more direct and resolute path became even stronger after World War II when more than a third of the globe turned red. The radical land reforms in Japan, South Korea and Taiwan after World War II, which laid the foundation for developing industrialised economies in these countries, were carried out under the tutelage of American agricultural economist Wolf Ladejinsky only when post-revolution China and North Korea had implemented thoroughgoing land reforms. Even that one prized attribute of developed bourgeois democracies 'universal suffrage' was made universal in many countries only when it was first granted as an inalienable right in the Soviet Union.

It is worth quoting the noted American sociologist Prof James Petras here:

> Immediately following the defeat of fascist-capitalist regimes with the defeat of Nazi Germany, the Soviet Union and its political allies in Eastern Europe embarked on a massive program of reconstruction, recovery, economic growth and the consolidation of power, based on far-reaching socio-economic welfare reforms. The great fear among Western capitalist regimes was that the working class in the West would 'follow' the Soviet example or, at a minimum, support parties and actions which would undermine capitalist recovery. Given the political discredit of many Western capitalists because of their collaboration with the Nazis or their belated, weak opposition to the fascist version of capitalism, they could not resort to the highly repressive methods of the past. Instead, the Western capitalist classes applied a two-fold strategy to counter the Soviet collectivist-welfare reforms: Selective repression of the domestic Communist and radical Left and welfare concessions to secure the loyalty of the Social and Christian Democratic trade unions and parties (Petras, 2012).

Today the most fundamental tenets of a 'welfare state' are crumbling in the West. In India 'welfare state' has never been anywhere comparable to that in the western bourgeois democracies, let alone the erstwhile socialist countries of Eastern Europe, Soviet Union or socialist countries of the Third World viz China, Cuba and Vietnam. Add to this the comprador character of the Indian bourgeoisie and the feudal class that is happy expediting the loot of the country's resources and its people in partnership with the imperialist bourgeoisie of the West.

That all sections of the ruling classes are broadly united on the questions of economic policies was once again evident in their response to the UPA Government's brazen policy initiatives to throw open multibrand retail to FDI, allow foreign investment in aviation and increase it further in the insurance sector and allow disinvestment in public sector undertakings. The various opposition parties, including the Parliamentary Left made much noise about this set of reforms, but backed off from bringing down the Government or coming out with a sustained plan for a determined agitation against such policies.

Under such circumstances what makes the civil society leaders believe that their appeals for compassion, concession and relief for the poor from the Government would succeed? One would hope for a situation where these partial demands are raised as part of an overarching struggle for societal change to confront the ruling classes and their State power by large scale mobilisation of the oppressed masses. It is only through such a political process that one can hope for conditions to obtain in the society where the poorest of the poor can realise their due. Public action has to be guided by 'revolutionary politics' rather than limit itself within the boundaries defined by the rulers.

There are examples from different parts of the world where such changes were attempted with varying levels of success. For reasons of the size of their populations and the enormity of the developmental challenges faced by both India and China in 1947 and 1949 respectively, it would be worth tracing their development histories with respect to satisfying the most basic human want—food.

This we shall do in Part II of the paper.

## References

Bandyopadhyay D, (2008): 'The relevance of land reform in post-liberalisation India', Infochange—News and analysis on social justice and development issues in India, April. Accessed on 15 March 2010 from http://infochangeindia.org/index2.php?option=com_content&do_pdf=1&id=7062.

Basu D. and Debarshi Das (2015): 'Austerity Triumphs Over Food Security: A Critique of Shanta Kumar Committee Report', Shanati.com, February 27. Available from http://sanhati.com/excerpted/12967/ on 14 September 2015.

Biswas N. (2006): 'On Funding and the NGO Sector', *Economic and Political Weekly,* 41(42): 4406-4408.

Deaton A. (2003a): 'Adjusted Indian Poverty Estimates for 1999-2000.' *Economic and Political Weekly,* Vol. 38 (4): 322-326.

Deaton A. (2003b): 'Prices and Poverty 1987-2000.' *Economic and Political Weekly,* Vol. 38 (4): 362-368.

Deaton A. and Drèze Jean (2010): 'Nutrition, Poverty and Calorie Fundamentalism: Response to Utsa Patnaik.' *Economic and Political Weekly,* Vol 45 (14): 78-80.

Deaton A. and Drèze Jean (2009): 'Nutrition in India: Facts and Interpretation', *Economic and Political Weekly,* Vol. 44 (7): 42-65.

Desrochers J. (2006): 'Social Movements Today: A Few Reflections from the Existing Literature.' *Integral Liberation* Vol. 10 (4): 244-252.

Dohrman and Jona Aravinda (2008): 'Special Economic Zones in India—An Introduction', *ASIEN* 106, S. 60-80.

Drèze J. (2010): 'Dissent note', *The Hindu,* 24 October.

*Economic and Political Weekly* (1996): 'Poverty Reduction by Manipulation', Vol. 31 (4).

FAO, 2008: 'What is Food Security? Food Security Concepts and Frameworks', EC-FAO Food Security Information for Action Program, p. 3.

Fernandes W. (1998): 'Land acquisition (amendment) bill, 1998: rights of project–affected people ignored', *Economic and Political Weekly,* Vol. 33 (42/43): pp. 2703-2706.

George Susan, 1984: 'Overcoming hunger—strengthen the weak, weaken the strong', in 'ill fares the land: essays on food, hunger, and power', institute for policy studies, Washington D.C., p. 1-15.

Government of India (2002): Ch. on, Agriculture, In the *Economic Survey 2001-02,* Ministry of Finance.

Government of India (2011): 'The National Food Security Bill, 2011, Draft', September. Available from http://www.prsindia.org/uploads/media/draft/Draft_National_Food_Security_Bill%202011.pdf on 14 September 2013.

Gupta S., 2010a: 'NAC meet tomorrow to discuss draft of food security bill', *The Hindu,* 29 August.

Gupta S., 2010b: 'NAC pares down its wish list on food security', *The Hindu* dated 31st August.

*Indian Express* (2008): 'We want capital, socialism not possible now: Basu', 5 January. Available from http://www.expressindia.com/story_print.php?storyId=258074, on 10 October, 2010.

*Indian Express*, 2010: 'NAC food security recommendation unfeasible: Panel', December 30. Available from: http://www.indianexpress.com/news/nac-food-security-recommendation-unfeasible/731026/ on 23 September 2011.

Jebaraj P. (2012a): 'Centre likely to sign deal with landless marchers on Jan Satyagraha at Agra', *The Hindu*, 10 October, 2012.

Jebaraj P. (2012b): 'Landless poor on long march to Delhi', *The Hindu*, 3 October.

Jebaraj P. (2012c): 'The Landless End March at Agra', *The Hindu*, 12 October.

Justice Wadhwa D.P. (2010): 'Justice Wadhwa Committee on the Public Distribution System: Report on the State of West Bengal', 29 November.

Karat B. (2011): 'Food Security Bill needs amendments', *The Hindu*, 22 July.

Kohli A. (2001): 'Introduction' In *The Success of India's Democracy*, Kohli A. (ed.), Cambridge University Press, Cambridge, 2001, p. 1.

Mander H. (2011): 'Ending Indifference: A Law to Exile Hunger?' *Economic and Political Weekly*, Vol. 46 (25): 45-50.

Marx K. and Engels F. (1848): Chapter 3, 'Socialist and Communist Literature' in *The Communist Manifesto*.

Mehdudia S. (2011): 'Take up export of food grains, recommends committee', *The Hindu*, 13 August.

Ministry of Rural Development (MRD) (Undated): 'Chapter IV. Committee on State Agrarian Relations and Unfinished Task of Land Reforms' Vol. I, Draft Report, Government of India, New Delhi.

Parsai G. (2011): 'Is ₹ 25 all that you need for a day?' *The Hindu*, 21 September.

Passell P. (1998): 'Economic Scene, The I.M.F. must go, critics say, but who will cope with crises?' *New York Times*, February 1998.

Patnaik U. (2007): 'Theorising food security and poverty in the era of economic reforms.' In *The Republic of Hunger and Other Essays*, Three Essays Collective, Gurgaon (Haryana), p. 188.

Petras J. (2012): 'The Western Welfare State: Its Rise and Demise and the Soviet Bloc.' Global Research, Centre for Research on Globalisation, 4 July. Available from: http://www.globalresearch.ca/the-western-welfare-state-its-rise-and-demise-and-the-soviet-bloc/, on 6th Oct. 2012.

Planning Commission (2012): 'Faster, Sustainable and More Inclusive Growth, An Approach to the Twelfth Five Year Plan (2012-17).'

Research Unit for Political Economy (2004): 'The Economics and Politics of the World Social Forum: Lessons for the Struggle against 'Globalisation'', Mumbai, September. Available from http://rupe-india.org/35/app1.html on 28 September 2011.

Right to Food Campaign, 2009: 'Right to Food: Essential Demands', 22 July. Available from http://www.righttofoodindia.org/data/rtf_act_essential_demands_of_the_rtf_campaign_220709.pdf on 12th Dec. 2010.

Right to Food Campaign website: 'Introduction to Right to Food Act,' Viewed on 5 September 2010 at http://www.righttofoodindia.org/right_to_food_act_intro.html.

Right to Food Campaign (2011a): 'Right to Food', *EPW*, Vol. 46 (33): 21-23.

Right to Food Campaign (2011b): 'Secretariat. Right to Food Campaign's Critique of the National Advisory Council's Note on the Draft National Food Security Bill', 7 March.

Sainath P. (2007): 'The Marie Antoinettes of Maharashtra', *The Hindu*, 15 September 2007.

Sainath P. (2009): 'The Age of the Everyday Billionaire', *Counterpunch*, 24 June. Available from http://www.counterpunch.org/2009/06/24/the-age-of-the-everyday-billionaire/ on 26 September 2011.

Sainath P. (2011a): 'Hard questions about soft questions', *The Hindu*, 21 February.

Sainath P. (2011b): 'The Union Cabinet gets healthier', *The Hindu*, 21 September.

Sainath P. (2012): 'To Fix BPL, Nix CPL', *The Hindu*, 26 March.

Sen A. (1998): 'Contextualising Welfare Economics', *Liberation*, Dec 1998.

Sen A. (2002): 'How to judge globalism: global links have spread knowledge and raised average living standards. But the present version of globalism needlessly harms the world's poorest.' *The American Prospect*, Jan 1, 2002 v13 i1 pA2(5). Available from http://www.sas.upenn.edu/~dludden/SenGlobalism.htm dated 28th Sept 2012.

Sen A. and Drèze J. (1989): Preface in '*Hunger and Public Action*', Oxford University Press.

*The Hindu* (2010a): 'NAC recommendations on Food Security Bill', 10 October.

*The Hindu* (2010b): 'Marxists not against market, FDI: Karat', 31 October. Available from http://www.thehindu.com/news/national/article859920.ece?css=print on 1 November, 2010.

*The Hindu* (2012): 'A different poverty trap', Editorial published on 22 March.

*The Telegraph* (2007): 'Prohibiting the use of agricultural land for industries is ultimately self-defeating', Monday, 23 July.

*The Telegraph* (2012): "Trickle down' will not work in tackling poverty: President Pranab Mukherjee", New Delhi, 25 July.

Tiwale S. (2010): 'Foodgrain vs Liquor: Maharashtra under Crisis', *Economic and Political Weekly*, Vol. 45 (22): 19-21.

Vakulabharanam V. and Sripad Motiram (2000): 'Progressive but Problematic: An Appreciation and Critique of Amartya Sen.' *Ghadar*, 4:1, 1 May.

Vanguard (1994): 'CPM's *Ganashakti*—Taking Refuge in Divya Shakti', April-June. Available from http://www.bannedthought.net/india/Vanguard/index.htm on 26 September 2011.

Varadarajan S (2010): 'Order on free grain to poor can't be executed: Manmohan Singh', *The Hindu*, New Delhi, 7 September.

# 8

# Hunger and Food Insecurity
## Structural Causes and their Remedies (Part II)

Chapter 7 traced the contours of the food security debate in the country and the political persuasions of its various proponents. It was also argued that the underlying politics of this debate is incapable of resolving the fundamental contradictions that beset the problem of food insecurity of the poor working masses of India. This obviously forces the question then—what is the way forward? This Chapter is all about that and we have used the comparative analysis of the trajectories taken by China and India since 1949 and 1947 respectively as the heuristic device to elucidate the possible alternatives. This is with the caveat that the authors are no apologists of the Dengite economic reforms post-1979.

## China and India: Similar Challenges but Diverse Ways

An argument in favour of comprehensive and equitable redistribution of societal resources, of which land reforms are an integral part, has been the running thread in this book. But at a time when fashionable preaching of reactionary economic and development policies, even by the Left section of the mainstream polity, has gained ascendency, it might be difficult for the readers to comprehend the real import of and the possibilities that our argument holds in store for the overall welfare of the people in India, especially insofar as securing their food security is concerned.

We present here some of the experiences of the People's Republic of China, where the kind of land reforms that we have argued for were carried out throughout China after the Revolution in 1949. A comparison is also presented between achievements of India and China in both food production and consumption, as also the overall welfare of the people.

The People's Republic of China was established in 1949 after the Communist Party of China under the leadership of Com Mao Zedong established a people's democracy in the country after defeating the comprador bourgeois represented by the Nationalist Party (the Kuomintang) that was led by the military dictator Gen Chiang Kai-Shek. As for the revolutionary classes in China, these comprised the peasantry, the working class and the nationalist bourgeois. However, the peasantry constituted the bulk of the revolutionary forces mobilised by the Chinese Communist Party and in this sense the Chinese Revolution was a 'New Democratic Revolution' where, unlike in the West, the task of vanquishing feudalism and establishing bourgeois democracy as a transitory phase towards establishing socialism was performed by the alliance of the peasantry and the working classes, led by the working class. The country-wide mobilisation of the oppressed working masses and their control over the State power through the Communist Party after the Revolution facilitated a radical and equitable distribution of the society's productive resources of which land reforms were primary. This removed gross disparities between social classes in the Chinese society and led to more equal opportunity for China's working masses for their social, economic and political development.

As opposed to this, the political process of transition of State power from the British colonialists to their Indian acolytes (who as we have already seen are now emboldened enough to openly praise the so-called beneficial effects of colonial rule) was anything but capture of the State power by the hundreds of millions of impoverished Indians or political forces representative of their class. India's Constituent Assembly was not a body elected through universal suffrage, much less, it was indirectly elected by the members of the provincial legislative assemblies, who in their turn were elected by an electorate that constituted only upper class Indians as per the 1909 'Indian Councils Act' of the British Parliament, also referred to as the 'Morley-Minto Reforms.' Just to give an idea how ridiculously unrepresentative the size of this electorate was, it needs to be noted that the total electorate in the 1934 General Elections held for the 'Central Legislative Assembly' in British India was a mere 1,415,892 (Hansard, 1942). More than a third of the Constituent Assembly members were nominated from the erstwhile princely states.

The Constitution that was drafted by the Constituent Assembly and took effect on the 26 January 1950, heavily borrowed its provisions from the 'Government of India Act, 1935.' Writing about the 'Constitution of India', Padma Bhushan awardee, Prof. M.V. Pylee says, 'The makers of the Indian Constitution drew . . . especially much from the British-made Government of India Act of 1935. Thus the Constitution of India is the result of considerable imitation and adaptation rather than of originality' (Pylee, 2003). He says further, 'The Constitution derives directly from the Government of India Act, 1935, many of its provisions almost verbatim' (Ibid: 5). It should be least surprising then that the current Prime Minister, Dr. Manmohan Singh finds reason in lavishing praise on lessons learnt from the British.

Unlike the Western bourgeois democracies the Parliament in India was not established as a result of the popular upsurge of the people against the erstwhile rulers. The fabled parliamentary democracy of India was established from above under British tutelage, through the acts of their Parliament—

the Indian Councils Act, 1909, the Government of India Act, 1919 and the Government of India Act, 1935. This gradual and controlled process of establishing the parliamentary form of government in India went hand in hand with co-opting the Indian elite in the evolving system of governance. Over the years, the naked power play backed by money and muscle power of the dominant classes, the representative parliamentary Democracy has become more and more non-representative of the aspirations of India's labouring masses.

Whatever else may be the import of these facts, it is clear that such a transition of State power was least amenable to equitable distribution of societal resources to leverage the interests of the overwhelming majority of impoverished Indians. The development strategy followed by India's ruling elite post-1947 has primarily enriched their interests. This of course left enough scope for pacifying the working masses by doling out some concessions, while at other times unleashing brutal repression on their political mobilisation and movements for seeking a more just society.

Thus while in China, the largely egalitarian social structure resulting from the policies adopted by the Revolutionary Government after 1949 laid down the basis for a more equitable distribution of the fruits of development, in India such egalitarianism was resorted to only in rhetoric and resisted in policy. The socio-economic disparities between different sections in the country have only increased so much so that even during the phase of 'Green Revolution' which is said to have made India self- sufficient in food, it is only the propertied sections among the peasantry that benefited, while the small peasants in the Green Revolution areas got further marginalised (Chowdhury, 1970, Jacoby, 1972).

The current phase of imperialist globalisation has only worsened the socio-economic inequities in India (Weiskopf, 2011).

## The Chinese Path

In 1949, China had 22% of the world population to feed with just about 5% of the earth's water resources and about 7% of its arable land (Zhang, 2011). While India had 14.2% of the world population in 1950 with second largest arable land mass after the US but only 4% of the world's renewable water resources (GOI, 2012). Table 8.1 gives the comparison between China and India as regards these parameters. These comparisons apart, both the countries faced immense problems of poverty, backward economies predominantly based on agriculture, lack of industrialisation and massive morbidity and mortality due to infectious diseases.

Famines, big and small were a common occurrence in China. In the following passage, Chen describes the scene that was not atypical of a Chinese village:

> . . . the annual spring famine, after the winter stores were eaten, merged into summer starvation that reduced animals and humans to walking skeletons of dried skin and bones. Without stamina to resist such hardships, the children and old folks died first and the able-bodied grew steadily weaker and more debilitated. Then, just as in times of flood, there were the same agonising questions or fateful decisions. Flee or stay? Sow a crop and chance that the rain would come in time and nourish it? Or chance it on the road, eating up your seed grain and then go begging? (Chen, 1973).

Lack of industrialisation and a predominantly agrarian economy meant that surplus to be ploughed into development of other sectors of the economy had to come from agriculture. This could only have put additional burden on land apart from feeding the hungry millions.

Soon after the Revolution the Communist Party of China (CPC) undertook extensive land reforms between late 1940s and 1952 which transformed China's land and income distribution system, thereby bringing forth the production

Table 8.1: Comparison of arable land and water resources of China and India.

| *Country* | *Arable land per capita (hectares per person)* | *TRWR (actual per capita ($m^3$/ year inhabitant)* | *Dependency ratio (%)* |
|---|---|---|---|
| China | 0.08 | 2258 | 0.6 |
| India | 0.13 | 1880 | 33.9 |

*Source:* Figures for arable land have been obtained from the World Bank data from the World Bank website. Figures for total renewable water resources (TRWR) and the dependency ratio of renewable water resources have been obtained from 'Review of world water resources by country, FAO, Rome, 2003.

*Note:* Arable land includes land defined by the FAO as land under temporary crops (double cropped areas are counted once), temporary meadows for sowing or for pasture, land under market or kitchen gardens, and land temporarily fallow. Land abandoned as a result of shifting cultivation is excluded.

*Dependency ratio:* That part of the total renewable water resources originating outside the country.

initiative of the Chinese peasantry. This was reflected in the rapid improvements in food production as also the dietary intakes of the Chinese (Wang et al., 1993). However, the average size of the landholding being too small meant that the produce from the land was not enough to mitigate the hunger of most of the peasant families let alone generate surplus for the country's industrial development.

Unlike the Indian rulers, who see the solution for the sickness in Indian agriculture to lie in taking more and more people out of land and promoting contract farming by big landlords or companies, the CPC had different plans for its agriculture. After land reforms, the CPC under Mao moved quickly on the collectivisation of agriculture. More than 100 million farm households joined collectives between 1954 and 1956. A further consolidation of collectivisation process was in the formation of 'rural people's communes' with the beginning of 1958 (Riskin, 1986).

Apart from inputting modern technology such as machinery and fertilisers, the Chinese Government sought to maximise the use of organic manure and concentrated on the organisation and maximum utilisation of human labour which was one resource that was available in plenty, in projects such as bringing newer lands under cultivation and on farm activities (Croll, 1983). Even at the cost of repetition we would like to emphasise the following information from a 1981 World Bank report, purely for the stark contrast in which it stands to the 'taking people out of agriculture' kind of approach of the Indian rulers and eminent economists. As is evident from Table 8.2, not only did China consistently add labour force to its agricultural sector at the rate of 2% per annum, but also it registered a handsome increase in net agricultural output and net output per worker (World Bank, 1981).

Table 8.2: Growth rates of net output, labour force and productivity in agriculture, 1953-79 (% p.a.).

| *Years* | *Net output* | *Labour force* | *Net output per worker* |
|---|---|---|---|
| 1952-57 | 4.9 | 2.2 | 2.6 |
| 1957-77 | 1.6 | 2.1 | –0.5 |
| 1977-79 | 9.4 | 1.0 | 8.3 |
| 1952-79 | 2.7 | 2.0 | 0.7 |

*Source:* World Bank (1981).

It needs mentioning here that in India and other developing countries that share similar social, economic or political structure, the limited extent to which land reforms have been implemented, were not accompanied by any substantive support through credit, marketing and other technical support to make the small and marginal farms viable. Resultantly, whatever land was distributed, much of it ended up being back with the landed gentry. Contrary to this, post-land reforms, in China the peasants were encouraged to pool in their resources and labour, thus the unit of production was sought to be moved from a household to a production team which was the lowest level of collectivisation unit. This in itself was a very laudable social goal. Collective production undermined the material basis of seeking individual rewards, meaning thereby that individual's well-being becomes integral to the collective well being of the people. This went hand in hand with means of collective consumption, for example, workers were encouraged to eat in large communal halls managed by the communes (Millman et al., 1990).

With collectivisation, the surplus labour was utilised in the construction of communal facilities in the communes. The peasant collectives supervised the allocation of different agricultural inputs, the credits as well as marketing. Unlike a market driven system where it is the purchasing power of the affluent sections that decides the nature of production, in socialist China 'certain staple foods were excluded from the market and distributed at least partly according to the need' (Croll, 1983: 5). As opposed to Sen's advocacy of market based exchange as being the most efficient means for increasing peoples' access to commodities, the socialist China did attempt to bring in the concept of need based exchange, free from vagaries of the market. The storage and redistribution of surplus foods were undertaken by either the commune or the State. Besides production and distribution of food, the Communes also played a pivotal role in the industrialisation of rural China with industries producing chemical fertilisers, agricultural machinery, cement etc being set up in communes. Thus the surplus agricultural labour was absorbed into these industries (Chen, 2009). This again stands out in sharp contrast to the prescriptions of our rulers to take people out of agriculture irrespective of whether alternative employment is generated for them or not.

Figure 8.1: The National Food System in China—1974

Levels of Food Production: Size

| *Level* | *Numbers in China* | *Production Brigade* | *Production team* | *House-holds* | *Persons* | *Hectares of lands* |
|---|---|---|---|---|---|---|
| Communes | 50,000 | 15 | 100 | 3,346 | 14,720 | 2033 |
| Production Brigade | 750,000 | – | 7 | 220 | 980 | 136 |
| Production Team | 5,000,000 | – | – | 33 | 145 | 20 |
| Household | 167,000,000 | | – | – | 4.4 | – |

Levels of Food Production: Functions

| | |
|---|---|
| Commune : | Management and organisation of production of grain staples.<br>Fulfilment of State grain procurement quotas, supervision of grain ratios.<br>Processing of grain (rice and flour mills)<br>Production of non-staples (fishing, animal husbandry, orchards, etc.) for sale and organisation of retail outlets.<br>Management and storage of reserves of staple foods.<br>Import of certain ingredients such as sugar, salt etc. for retail |
| Production : | Grain and edible oil processing, bean curd, noodles, food processing |
| Brigade : | Production of non staple foods—livestock, orchards, fish farms.<br>Management of supply and marketing co-operatives for non-staple foods. |

| | |
|---|---|
| Production Team | Production of grain staples, edible oil seeds, fruit, vegetables etc. for State and consumption of member households.<br>Raising livestock, fish and other foods for exchange.<br>Unit of accounting and distribution of staple foods and cash incomes*<br>Accumulation of reserves of staple foods<br>Production and distribution of non-staple foods (vegetables, fruit, meat, etc.) (Optional) |
| Household | Production of non-staple foods for consumption and exchange e.g. meat, fish, eggs, fruit, vegetables<br>Processing of food for consumption, preservation and cooking<br>Purchase of supplementary foods especially salt, sugar, etc.<br>Accumulation of reserves of staple grains. |

* In some areas the brigade may constitute the of unit of accounting.

*Source:* Figure 8.8 in 'The Porcelain Bowl: Food Consumption in Republican China' In *The Family Rice Bowl: Food and Domestic Economy in China,* UNRISD and Zed Press, London, 1983: p. 48.

The Figure 8.1 depicts different levels of food production in the National Food System of China and their respective functions. Once collectivisation of food production was realised, the production team was recognized as the basic accounting unit in which the distribution of income was done through a work point system. There were two kinds of work points—one that were given on the basis of the ability and the skill of the worker and were to be realised by the worker by putting in a day's work. Another kind of work point was given according to the nature of the task performed. A relative parity was maintained vis-à-vis the total work points earned by different households by giving different tasks to the different members of the family such that there was no gross disparity in the distribution of income. Privileging egalitarianism in income and distribution minimized the social friction that differential entitlements could have produced. In fact, the State put caps on personal income as a matter of policy.

At the harvest time the total income of the production team was calculated by deducting from the value of the total produce, the anticipated production cost, agricultural tax, contribution towards fund for purchase of capital inputs and that towards the welfare fund for indigent members in the production team households. Income thus derived was divided by the total work points earned by the team members to determine the cash value of each work point (Riskin, 1986).

Until collectivisation, the compulsion for survival itself constituted a potent incentive for production in private farming. However, the work point system under collectivised production obviated such incentives. At the same time the work point system did not entail any immediate individual payoff that would prove to be a bigger incentive compared to for example doing a task with highest work points. The ultimate reward under the work point system could come only through the 'values of cooperation and collective solidarity' in the process of production. Hence, the effectiveness of the work point system in a production team 'depended on the quality of team leadership and on the general social and political environment that shaped and limited team operations' (Ibid). In our opinion this implied that increasing production was more than a technological question. It required revolutionary politics to be kept in command, a need that was thoroughly repudiated by China's rulers after 1979, the time when communes were dissolved and family responsibility system was introduced instead.

Two methods of grain distribution were followed in the communes—one, known as the 'basic grain' in which grain was distributed for every individual member of the family based on the age and sex of the family members. Grain thus distributed was debited from the family's account with the collective. Basic grain had to be paid for at the time of post-harvest settling of family's account with the collective. The second component of the family grain was based on the total work points earned by the family and therefore depended on the earning power of the family in the production team. Different communes privileged one or the other method of grain distribution, thus communes emphasising the 'basic grain' method had a more equitable distribution of food among households (Ibid).

As girls were married out of the village, the elderly parents were taken care of by the sons. Households of elderly members not having sons, or a household having a higher dependency ratio were termed 'five guarantees' or 'hardship' households. The commune provided for such elderly people by guaranteeing their food, clothing, housing, medical care and burial expenses. In case of 'hardship' households a sideline employment and a plot of land as means of supplementary income were provided (Ibid).

The commune system also epitomised a model of democracy in the matters of most immediate concern to the people. For example, the production team leaders were not State bureaucrats or officials who exercised all control over the production teams and its decisions without being answerable to them. Riskin writes that the team leaders were 'paid out of team income like other commune cadres but more so, they owed their success not only to the ability to satisfy higher authorities, but also to their rapport with the villagers. The degree to which rural leaders exercised development initiative and also protected their constituents from the more arbitrary demands of the higher levels has probably been underestimated in recent indictments of the commune system' (Ibid).

One criticism that has been levelled against the commune is that it being the lowest level of State administration and at the same time a collective economic organisation, rendered a commune and thereby the peasants liable to dictates from the State (Ibid). However, one has to take a nuanced view of this criticism, for there has to be a mechanism for the State to get through its decisions in a planned economy down to the lowest level. Additionally, while the commune may be competent to take decisions regarding production commensurate with its economic and social interests, a commune may have inherent limitations in taking a view of the regional and national priorities that can best be adjudicated by regional and national level bodies of the State and the CPC. Almost every government in every country reserves unto itself administrative and economic mechanisms to get decisions implemented in accordance with its priorities. But this certainly does not happen in every country that the local communities get to elect their local administrators/bureaucracy and that such administrators exercise their power only so long as they enjoy the confidence of their constituency as seemed to be the case with communes in China.

## China and India: Comparative Achievements in Food Security

The commune system in China may appear ideal, but it would add up to little worth if it failed to create the material basis to provide for the people's needs. It will be our attempt in this section to compare the achievements of China and India in terms of food production and the consequent human well-being.

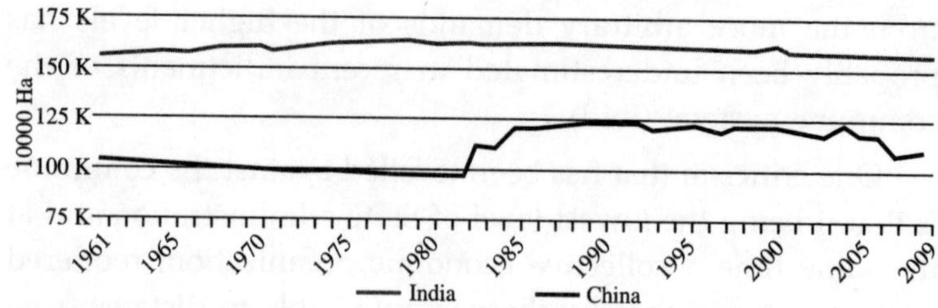


Figure 8.2: Comparison of total arable area between China and India since 1961.

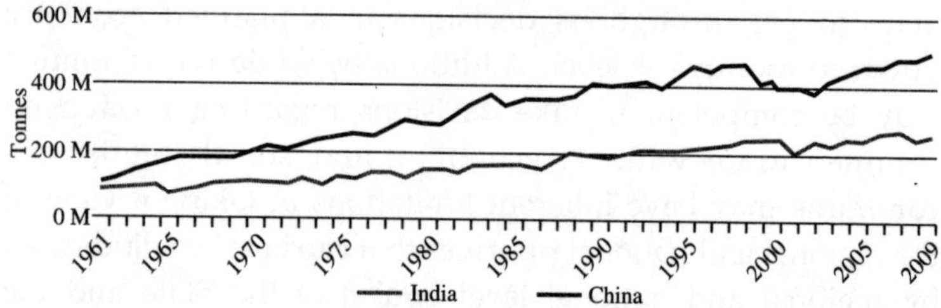


Figure 8.3a: Total cereals production in China and India since 1961.

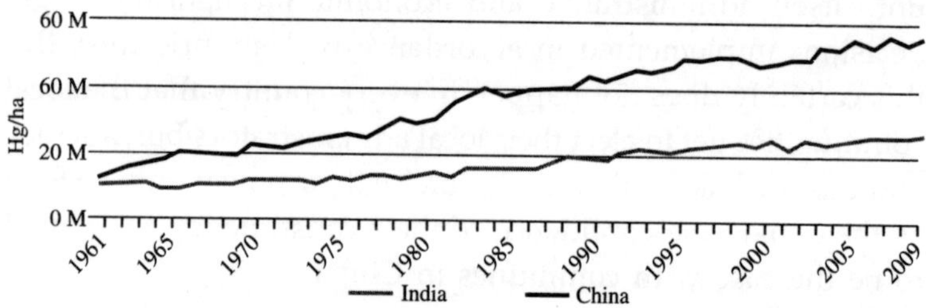


Figure 8.3b: Average yield for all cereals in China and India since 1961.

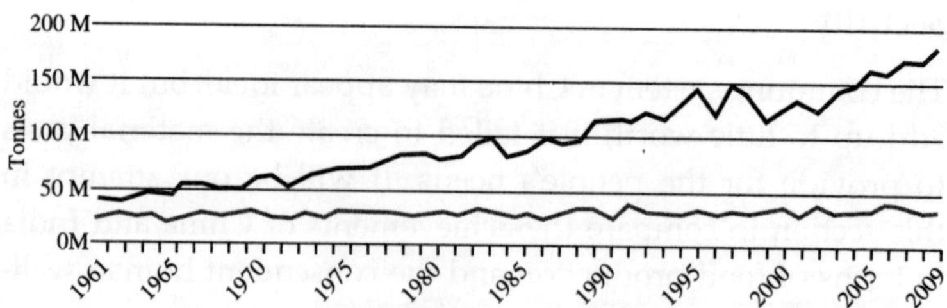


Figure 8.4a: Variation in total coarse grain production in China and India since 1961.

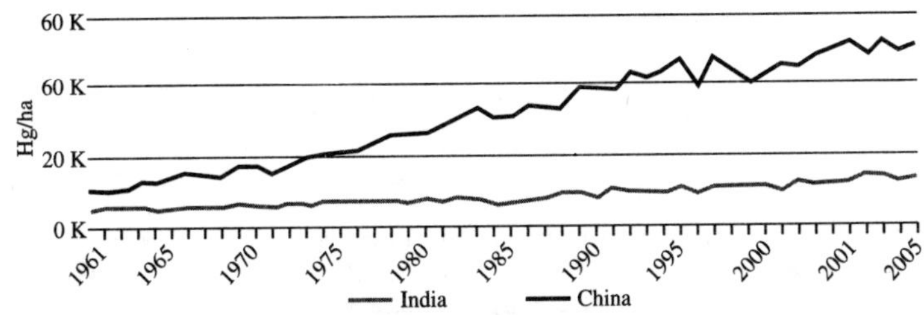


Figure 8.4b: Average yield for all coarse grains in China and India since 1961.

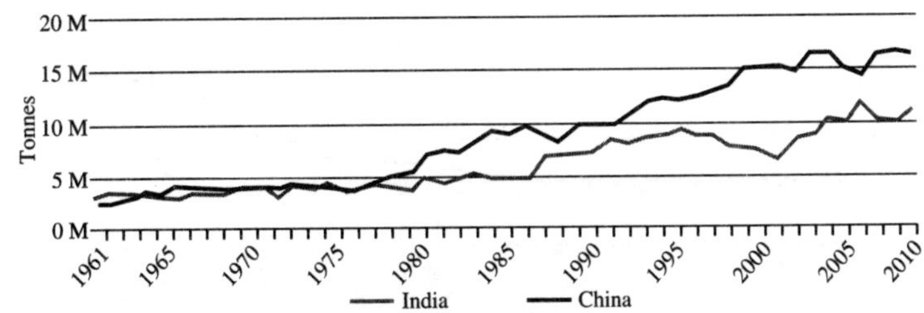


Figure 8.5a: Variation in total oil crops primary production in China and India since 1961.

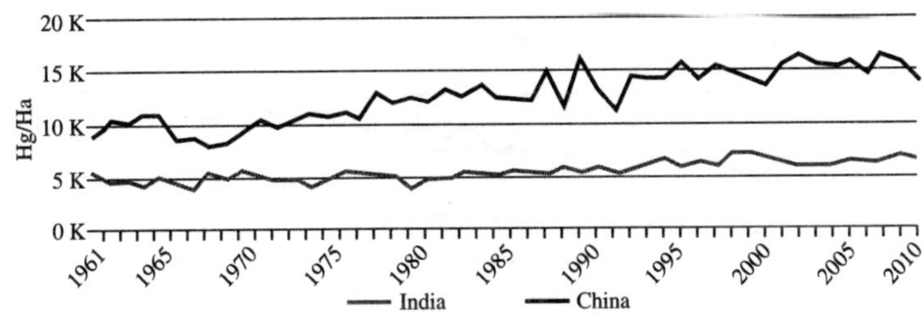


Figure 8.5b: Average yield of oil crops in China and India since 1961.

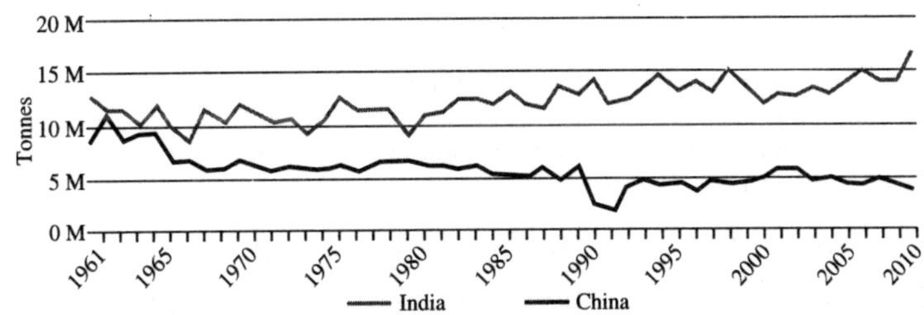


Figure 8.6a: Variation in total production of pulses in China and India since 1961.

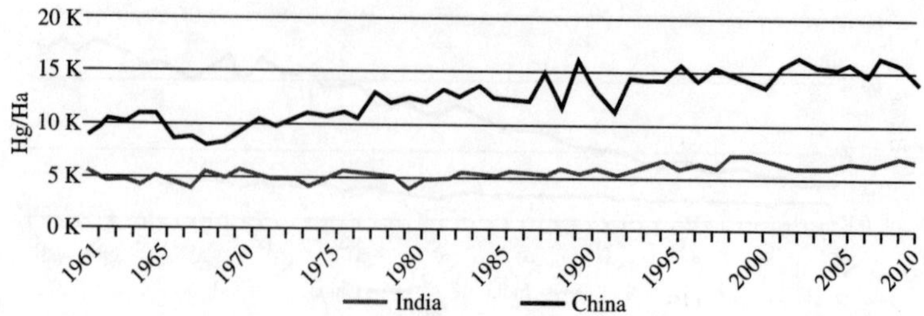


Figure 8.6b: Average yield of total pulses in China and India since 1961.

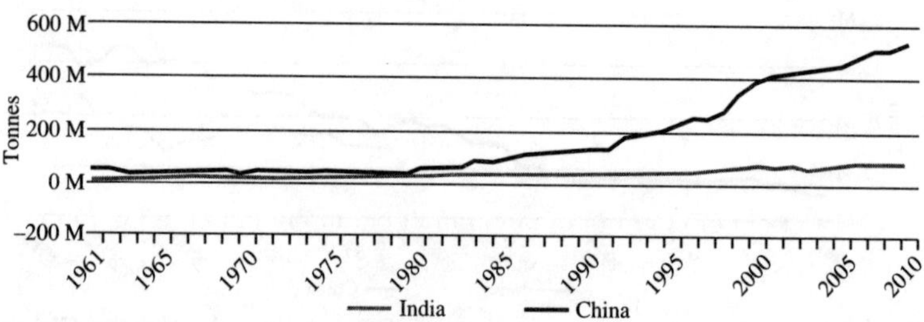


Figure 8.7a: Variation in total production of vegetables and melons in China and India since 1961.

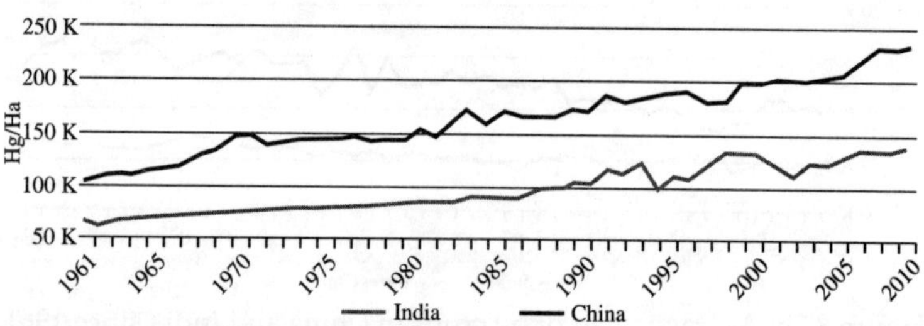


Figure 8.7b: Average yield of vegetables and melons in China and India since 1961.

*Source:* Figures 8.2 to 8.9b in this section are based on the FAO data for China and India. Since data prior to 1961 is not available with FAO, the data comparison is done beginning with the year 1961. Note: K = thousand, M = Million, Hg = Hectogram and Ha = Hectare.

Figures 8.3a to 8.7b very categorically tell the story of productivity of Chinese and Indian agriculture both in terms of total production and the yields. For most of the commodities, to begin with, China and India were very close in total production, with China having slightly higher levels of production except for oil crops and vegetables and melons. However, in subsequent years, the gap between China and India has progressively increased both in total production as well as yields. In fact, for coarse cereals, oil crops and pulses, the yields in India have remained almost stagnant. It is only in case of pulses that the total production in China has decreased progressively even though the yields have remained much higher than those in India. As we shall see shortly, the reason why production of pulses has decreased in China seems to be because of the fact that a large part of the dietary protein requirement of the Chinese has come to be met with by consumption of animal products. However, the yields of pulses in China have remained consistently higher than in India. It is worrisome that the overall production as also the yields of pulses has more or less remained stagnant in India, despite the fact that pulses are the most important source of dietary protein for a large number of Indians.

While China consistently increased the production as also the yields of coarse cereals as an important source of dietary energy, in India the graph for overall production as also the yields of coarse cereals has remained almost flat. This is so in spite of the fact that a large part of India's arable land mass is much more amenable to growing the hardy coarse cereals due to deficiency of water resources. One reason for this neglect of coarse cereals apart from the fact that the Government itself encouraged the shift to input intensive varieties of wheat and rice appears to be the gross disparity of purchasing power between the rich and the poor. Wheat and rice are the preferred cereals of the well-to-do sections and as they form the effective market for food grains, the production of food grains gets tilted towards these two crops. However, the fact that the Government has not privileged coarse cereals even for distribution through the public distribution network, has cost the country a viable mechanism for increasing the consumption and thereby the demand for coarse/nutri-cereals.

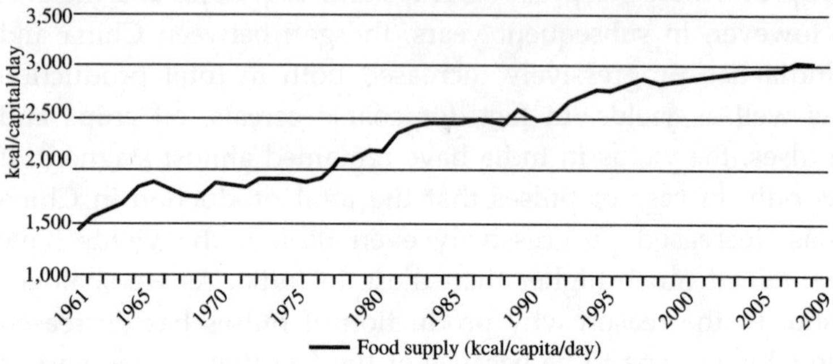


Figure 8.8a: Total per capita per day calories consumed in China since 1961.

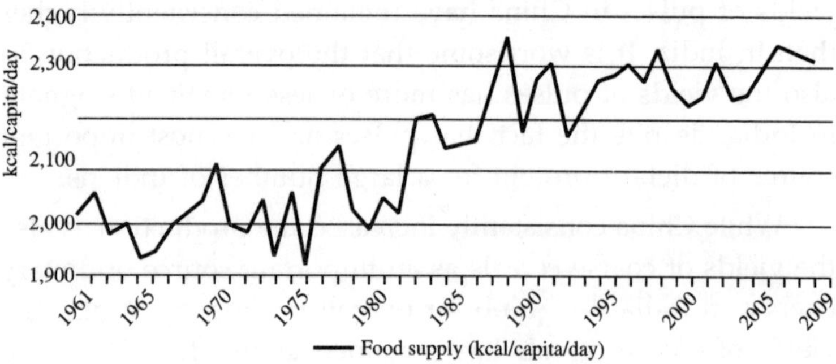


Figure 8.8b: Total per capita per day calories consumed in India since 1961.

The productivity of Chinese agriculture becomes all the more impressive compared to that of India because of the fact that China's arable land mass has consistently remained much lower to that of India as shown in Fig. 8.2. Even the fabled 'Green Revolution' does not seem to have helped much to increase the overall productivity of cereals in India.

Figures 8.8a and 8.8b show the trends in the total dietary energy consumption since 1961 in China and India. In 1961. the average total dietary energy consumption in China was far lower than in India due to the famine that lasted in China from 1959 to 1961. However, thereafter while we see a consistent and stable rise in total dietary energy consumption in China, in case of India, not only is the total dietary energy consumption a good 30% less than that of China in 2009, but the increase over the years has been very unstable, including during the years of 'Green Revolution' powered increase in production of wheat and rice.

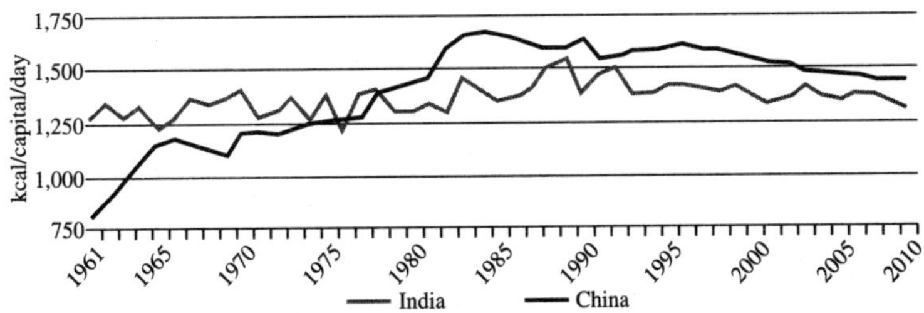


Figure 8.9a: Per capita per day dietary calories derived from cereals in China and India since 1961.

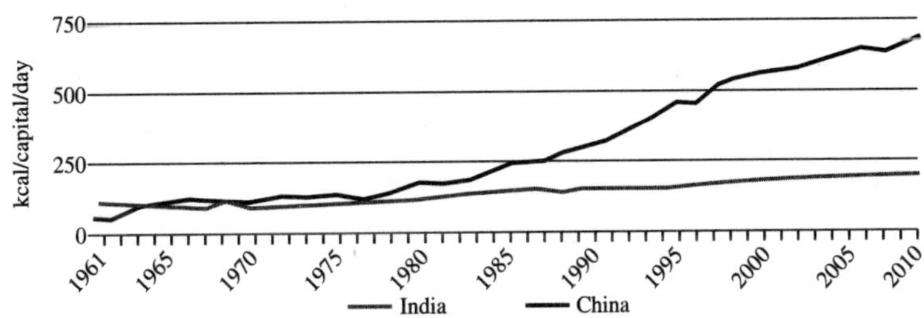


Figure 8.9b: Per capita per day dietary energy derived from animal products in China and India since 1961.

It is noteworthy that under the impact of the famine of 1959-61 China's per capita per day calorie consumption from both cereals and animal products in 1961 was less than that of India, with the former being as much as 66.7% less than that of India. In spite of the fact that the pre-famine dietary energy consumption levels could not be reached in China until the beginning of the seventies, the progress thereafter has been impressive, especially with regard to the consumption of calories from animal products.

Here there are lessons to be learnt by Indian policy wizards as regards the true meaning of 'diversification of diets.' We have dealt with the 'diversification of diets' controversy in the context of falling overall dietary energy consumption in

Table 8.3: Changes in Per Capita Per Day Dietary Energy Consumption from Different Sources of Dietary Energy Between 1961 and 2009

| *Dietary energy source* | *Country* | *1961* | *1971* | *1981* | *1991* | *2001* | *2009* |
|---|---|---|---|---|---|---|---|
| Animal products | India | 112 | 107 | 123 | 155 | 181 | 209 (86.6%) |
| | China | 56 | 125 | 177 | 329 | 565 | 694 (519.6%) |
| Fruits excluding wine | India | 30 | 31 | 31 | 34 | 45 | 63 (110%) |
| | China | 6 | 6 | 10 | 20 | 52 | 81 (170%) |
| Vegetables | India | 25 | 29 | 32 | 34 | 45 | 46 (84%) |
| | China | 60 | 36 | 42 | 70 | 158 | 205 (241.7%) |
| Cereals excluding beer | India | 1270 | 1278 | 1338 | 1468 | 1332 | 1318 (3.8%) |
| | China | 807 | 1209 | 1470 | 1546 | 1523 | 1447 (14%) |

*Source:* Compiled from data available at FAOSTAT Food Balance Sheets.

*Note:* The figures in parentheses are percentage rises in dietary energy from the given source as compared to the base year 1961. With the exception of vegetables where China's consumption was more than that of India in 1961, figures for India in 1961 have been taken as the base for China as well because due to the famine conditions in China in 1961, its own figures for the base year would be exceptionally low.

Chapter 2. The argument of some of the pro-establishment economists has been that the people in India have been opting for higher consumption of high value calories even at the cost of overall decline in the daily dietary energy consumption (as against the FAO Food Balance Sheets, the NSSO data shows that average per capita per day calorie consumption has been declining in India). Table 8.3 gives the changes in per capita per day dietary energy consumption from different sources of dietary energy between 1961 and 2009.

China's average per capita per day calorie consumption as of 2009 is still only 3,000 calories which is still much lower than 3,688 calories for US, its movement in the direction of diversification of diets has meant as huge an increase of 519.6% in calories from animal products, while those from fruits and vegetables have increased by 170 and 242% respectively. The increases from the same dietary sources in case of India are much too modest to sustain the claim of diversification of diets, especially as the number of people going hungry continues to be the highest in the world in absolute terms.

### *Impact on Human Welfare*

We could not get comparable data for both India and China for parameters like incidence and prevalence of infectious diseases, the infant mortality rates or levels of malnutrition etc to compare the impact of the level of food security in both the countries. However, Riskin (1986) describes the impact of food production and distribution in post-Revolution China in the following words:

> Rationing, an ethic of relative equality as well as frugality, and powerful state organisation have been credited with stretching meagre food supplies over China's enormous population so that the most extreme deprivation to be found in many other poor countries was on the whole avoided most of the time (the major exception, of course, being 1959-61).

Impressive statistics on life expectancy and infant mortality are consistent with this picture, and it is not contradicted by the observations of international observers.

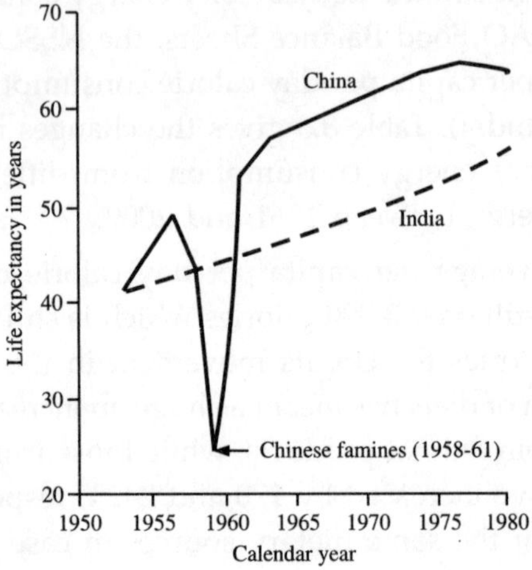


Figure 8.10: Variation in life expectancy in China and India between 1950 to 1980.

*Source:* Sen A (1987).

Life expectancy at birth can be a composite measure of people's welfare as it reflects improved nutrition, lesser morbidity and mortality as a result from improved healthcare and housing. Figure 8.10 shows the variation in life expectancy at birth for both China and India. Except for the dip in life expectancy from 1959 to 61, China's performance has by far exceeded that of India. The question here is how to account for the steep decline in life expectancy between the years 1959-61, especially as it is said to have led to excess mortality varying between 16.5 million to up to 30 million in China during the famine of 1959-61 (Banister, 1987, Coale, 1981, Ashton et al., 1984, Peng, 1987). Chang and Halliday in fact have gone miles ahead of others to claim in their book *Mao: the Unknown Story,* a total of 70 million deaths during the Mao's leadership of CPC, of which 38 million died in the famine of 1959 to 1961

(Chang and Halliday, 2005). For the purpose of our argument, we may also state that barring the estimates of Chang and Hallidy, Sen and Drèze agree with the estimates presented by Judith Banister and other American demographers referred to above (Sen and Drèze, 1989, 210).

Facts alone would not suffice to counter and defeat such malicious accusations against CPC and its tallest leader Com Mao Zedong, especially when the intent of those making such accusations, howsoever academically marshalled, is to target the politics and policies pursued by CPC for socialist development of China under the leadership of Com Mao. Under the weight of overwhelming evidence, many of these authors are obliged to accept the impressive achievements of China in its human development indicators. For example, Banister, the most prominent advocate of 'massive death toll' hypothesis of the Chinese Famine agrees that in 1973-75 the life expectancy in China was higher than that in many countries of Africa, Middle East, South Asia and South America. In a 1981 paper she along with Preston has described China as a super achiever in terms of increasing life expectancy of its people by an average of 1.5 years every year since the founding of the People's Republic of China in 1949 (Banister and Preston, 1981). Sen and Drèze acknowledge that 'as far as morbidity, mortality and longevity are concerned China has a large and decisive lead over India' (Sen and Drèze, 1989, 205).

As regards the achievements of the Chinese people under the leadership of Mao, the figures released by even his Chinese detractors, the Deng Xiaoping clique, only affirm to unprecedented growth of Chinese economy. Between 1952 to 1976 the Chinese industrial production increased on an average by 11.2% every year. In 1952 the industrial output made up barely 36% of the gross national output in China. However, in 1975 industry and agriculture contributed 72% and 28% respectively to the gross national output (Meissner, 1996). Table 8.4 below gives the achievements in agricultural production by China from 1961 till 1978 (the last year before CPC launched economic reforms and family responsibility system in agriculture under the leadership of Deng Xiaoping) along with comparison with US and India.

It can be seen from Table 8.4 that China's performance far outstrips that of India. Even during the famine year of 1961 the cereal crop yields in China were as much as 28% higher than those in India, while the total cereal production (absolute quantity) in China had almost reached the level equal to that of the US in spite of the fact the arable area of China which was 75% that of the US in 1961 got further reduced to only half the arable area of the US in 1978. This is in sharp contrast to India's arable area which was only 15% less than that of the US in 1978. While the scope for further increase in the yields and the total production of food grains may have been less in the US because of its already high levels of productivity, yet it is commendable that a poor resource strapped country like China at that time could almost equal its food grain production to that of the largest food grain producing country in the world.

It is worth giving a thought to whether such achievements are possible without active and conscious participation of the most ordinary people of the country, and whether the Government can elicit the cooperation and willing participation of the people by being insensitive to their misery, especially a misery that is said to have led to a loss of 30 million or more lives. The famine of 1959-61 in China is said to have had the maximum impact in the rural areas with little if any impact on the urban centres. It need be noted that in the 1950s China was still an agrarian economy and the prosperity of agriculture as a source of surplus was most important even for industrial development of the country. Hence, if one were to presume that the estimates of 'massive mortality' during the famine of 1959-61 were true then the industrial performance of China was managed despite the unprecedented tragedy

Table 8.4: Growth in Performance of Agricultural Sector and Food Supply—US, China, India.

| *Parameter* | *US* | | | *China* | | | *India* | | |
|---|---|---|---|---|---|---|---|---|---|
| | *1961* | *1978* | *% change* | *1961* | *1978* | *% change* | *1961* | *1978* | *% change* |
| Cereals total prod. (tonnes) | 163,619,996 | 276,603,574 | 69 | 109,659,981 | 273,038,121 | 149 | 87,376,500 | 142,964,700 | 63.6 |
| Cereals total yield (Hg/Ha) | 25,222.93 | 41,097.84 | 62.9 | 12,110.05 | 28,019.53 | 131.4 | 9,472.84 | 13,701.81 | 44.6 |
| Cereals-Excluding Beer-Food supply (kcal/capita/yr) | 627 | 616 | –1.8 | 807 | 1387 | 71.9 | 1270 | 1480 | 16.5 |
| Animal prod.-Food supply (kcal/capita/yr) | 1,010 | 948 | –6.1 | 56 | 139 | 148 | 112 | 112 | 0 |
| Arable land* | 180,630 | 188,755 | 4.5 | 103,397 | 97,221 | –6 | 155,806 | 163,635 | 5.02 |

*Source:* Compiled from FAOSTAT data. Note: *Land in thousand hectares. The figures are given from 1961 onwards only because FAOSTAT does not have figures for earlier years.

that was unfolding in rural China. This is something that defies rational thinking.

Sen and Drèze state, 'The remarkable aspect of the famine is its continuation over a number of years without an adequate recognition of the nature of the crisis (and without leading to the necessary changes in public policy)' (Sen and Drèze, 1989, 211). World War II caused as many as 65 to 75 million deaths over five years and we all know the kind of disruption it caused across the globe. Here we have around 30 million excess deaths taking place in a single country over a period of three years and yet it passes off 'without an adequate recognition of the nature of the crisis.' One is likely to say that World War II was a war, while what happened in China was a peace time tragedy. But what is not intelligible is that how come people simply chose to die silently, in the numbers that is claimed, in the villages without making attempts to escape to the cities and urban areas. In fact, Chang and Hallidy claim that—'The traditional possibility of escaping a famine by fleeing to a place where there was food was now blocked off' by Mao (Chang and Halliday, 2005). If this indeed were true and if the government had tried to prevent the migration of people to cities per force, then given the size of the population of China such coercion could only have led to an explosive situation hard to ignore.

Based on his own study Prof Han Dongping of the Department of History and Political Science, Warren Wilson College, US puts a poser:

> The Great Leap Forward ended up in a unprecedented grain shortage under the Communist rule in China. But it was not the only thing that was unprecedented. There were no grain riots, no peasant rebellion, no grain hoarding for profits, no selling of children and wives, which would have been normal occurrence with a famine like that in Jimo and in China in general. It was so unlike China that even today many younger people still asked their parents

> why they did not storm the government granaries which were not even guarded by any military forces. Is not this something worth studying too? Mao did not talk about ending tuanjie (security and order) at the time, as the current Chinese leaders do today, but his government was able to maintain order and security in the face of such unprecedented national disaster. Why? (Dongping, 2003).

In his interviews with peasants in the provinces of Shandong and Henan they said:

> Without the organized relief efforts of the Maoist state, the impact of the natural disasters of 1959, 1960 and 1961 would have been much greater in Jimo for all we know. That was why many farmers say, 'Without the Government's relief efforts, more people would have died' (Ibid).

Dongping further says:

> Mao's mistakes and Mao's merits were paradoxically entwined to such an extent that any effort to separate the two would be simply impossible. For that reason, few Chinese workers and farmers ever blamed Mao for what happened during the Great Leap Forward. It is not that Chinese farmers and workers are too dumb to know any better, as many Chinese elites suggest. It is their wisdom to see both Mao's mistakes and his merits at the same time (Ibid).

Lest we presume Dongping to be a blind Mao sympathiser, it needs to be stated here that two of his grandparents perished during the 'The Great Leap Forward' famine, and indeed at times he sounds more critical of Mao than the peasants he interviewed for his study.

That there was excess mortality during the years of 'Great Leap Forward' seems to be true though the jury is still out on the number of people who perished. Everyone seems to be picking a figure as per one's own persuasion. The Government during Mao's regime accepted that 30% of the economic problems were caused due to human error, while 70% was caused by the natural disasters; under Deng this was made just the other way round i.e. 70% due to human error and 30% due to natural disasters. The western scholars make the natural disasters seem inconsequential and put the entire blame on human error due to policies implemented under 'Great Leap Forward' (Ibid).

The 'massive death toll' thesis of the Chinese famine of 1959-61 came to be taken more seriously after the Deng Xiaoping regime released the death rates in China for the decades of 1950s and the 1960s (Banister, 1987). As per these death rates, the excess mortality in China between 1959 and 1961 was as much as 16.5 million. Later these 'official' Chinese figures were picked up by American demographers Ansley Coale, John Aird and Judith Banister who processed them further to come out with an estimate of 30 million deaths during the famine (Ball, 2006). As regards the official Chinese data, no information was available as to the methodology involved in their collection more than twc decades after the famine occurred or the authenticity of these figures in general. As to the further spin given to these figures by the American demographers, many agencies like the CIA, the private American Foundations like the Rockefeller, academic institutions propagating neo-liberalism and the established academic journals played their due role in the process.

Anyone interested in a more balanced handling of the issue and an academic critique of the 'massive death toll' thesis can read the 2006 article by Joseph Ball that was published in the *Monthly Review* (Available from: http://monthlyreview.org/commentary/did-mao-really-kill-millions-in-the-great-leap-forward). Another source for a more matter of fact and academic assessment of Mao's China can be had from Gregor B. and Chun L., eds. (2009): *Was Mao Really a Monster? The academic response to Chang and Halliday's Mao: The Unknown Story*, Routledge, London, UK.

Those insisting on denigrating the attempts made by Chinese people to develop socialism in their country under the leadership of Mao may well discover yet more sophisticated ways of estimating the death toll during the 'Great Leap Forward.' However, the significance of the policies adopted as part of the 'Great Leap' cannot be judged by the number of dead in the famine or the various omissions and commissions of policy alone. To make a judgement on the 'Great Leap Forward' we need to keep politics in command. The revolutionary politics of the 'Great Leap Forward' needs to grasped for more than historical and academic reasons. All those genuinely interested in carrying forward the struggle for emancipation of working masses beyond the limits that are sought to be imposed by 'bourgeois socialists' need to understand the politics of the social and economic change that was attempted as part of the 'Great Leap Forward' in China under the leadership of Com Mao, as also the politics of the 'bourgeois socialists.'

## Two-Line Struggle in China and the Circumstances Leading to the 'Great Leap Forward'

With the success of the Chinese Revolution under the leadership of Mao in 1949 the task of the 'New Democratic Revolution' in China was accomplished.[i] Therefrom what direction should the Chinese revolution have taken has been a hotly contested ideological, philosophical and public policy issue (CPC, 1973, Hsueh-ping, 1969). One section of the Party led by Mao was in favour of carrying forward the 'New Democratic Revolution' to merge into a 'Socialist Revolution' in order to develop China into a modern socialist state through rapid modernisation of its agriculture and building the country's industrial base with social ownership of the means of production (Hsueh-ping, 1969). As part of this strategy after implementation of land reforms, Mao led China in the collectivisation of agriculture that went up to the process of organisation of communes in the rural areas. Alongside development and modernisation of agriculture, socialist construction of industry was also undertaken on a large scale both in the urban areas as also the rural communes.

As opposed to Mao's line of 'Socialist Construction' Liu Shao-chi and his acolyte Deng Xioping forwarded the 'Theory of Productive Forces' their contention being that building socialism in a backward country like China cannot be possible unless forces of production are fully developed under capitalism. On socialist development of agriculture Liu Shao-chi held, 'that steps should be taken gradually to shake the foundations of private ownership, weaken it until it is nullified and raise the mutual aid organisations for agricultural production to the level of agricultural producers' cooperatives as a new factor for 'overcoming the peasants' spontaneous tendency.' This is an erroneous, dangerous and utopian conception of agricultural socialism (Renmin Ribao, Hongqui and Jiefangjun Bao editorial departments, 1968, 1969).[ii]

Shao-chi propagated—'Question of Socialism is a matter of future. It is too early to raise it now . . . Capitalism in China today is still in its youth and it is high time to give full play to its historical and positive role and let it make its contribution' and that 'the capitalists should exist and develop for decades' without restriction (Hsueh-ping, 1969). Its ideological trappings apart, such a line only implied that having captured the political power, the workers and the peasantry in China should hand over this power to the capitalists. After all Mao termed Liu Shao-chi and Deng Xiaoping as capitalist roaders for no mean reason.

These were not just theoretical differences of opinion, but posed problems at every stage of implementation of policies for 'Socialist Construction.' For example in 1955 even as the movement for forming agricultural cooperatives was gaining strength in China, in the month of May, Liu Shao-chi along with Deng Xiaoping bared their hostility to the 'agricultural cooperation movement by formulating the retrogressive policy of 'holding up', 'contraction' and 'checking up', as a part of which a plan for reducing the number of cooperatives was formulated and in a little over two months, 200,000 cooperatives were dissolved in the country (Renmin Ribao, Hongqui and Jiefangjun Bao editorial departments, 1968). Even as the 'Great Leap Forward' was launched in 1958 for establishing of the rural communes and boosting up both agricultural and industrial production in rural China, these capitalist roaders tried every measure in the book to defeat the laudable objectives of the 'Great Leap.' They propagated and tried to implement the system of 'individual household responsibility' in agricultural production (Ibid: 14-18). It is during this phase that Deng Xiaoping made his famous comment, 'So long as it raises output 'going it alone' is permissible. Whether the cats are white or black, so long as they can catch mice, they are good cats' (Ibid: 16).

Such circumstances could not have but complicated further the situation created by the natural disasters that occurred during the period of the 'Great Leap Forward.' It would seem prudent to conclude that a large part of the human error of the 'Great Famine' of China was in fact made up of the disruption caused by the capitalist roaders rather than the policies of 'socialist development' of the 'Great Leap.'

Apart from the opposition within, the ideological split with the Soviet Union was eminently clear by 1957, after Khrushchev signalled capitalist restoration in Soviet Union during the 20th Congress of the Communist Party of the Soviet Union (CPSU). Mao held on to the 'Revolutionary Spirit' of Marxism-Leninism against the line adopted by the CPSU. In response the Soviets withdrew all technical assistance from the ongoing industrial projects in 1960, including even the blueprints of the plants. China was denied the much needed spare parts for many industries. The question that faced CPC and the Chinese people was whether to give in to such blackmail or to push ahead with an independent path of building Socialist China by relying on the twin resources China had in abundance—'its human resources and its enthusiasm.'

## The Paradox of Socialising Consumption

In what appears to be the most laudable and yet, paradoxically the most controversial policy initiative taken during the 'Great Leap Forward' is that of establishing 'Community Dining Rooms.' This was the first such initiative by the State at 'socialising consumption' on the communes by transforming the old way of 'individual living' into a new way of communal dining. Yet it is paradoxical that such a laudable initiative has been blamed by various authors as being one of the important causes of food scarcity. Again, as in case of numbers of deaths during the famine, it is difficult to separate grain from the chaff to know the extent to which 'communal dining' led to grain shortages? However, there are enough reasons to see the establishment of 'communal dining halls' as signs of remarkable success of the Government's policies to hasten the 'Socialist Construction' of China.

The need for establishing 'communal dining halls' was borne out of the objective conditions resulting from the success of the policies of socialist construction followed up to the time of 'Great Leap Forward.' It is said:

> The appearance of mess halls is not a chance phenomenon, but is dictated by objective conditions. Since last winter, an unprecedented and all-round great leap forward has been achieved in agricultural production. The enlargement of the scale of production, the increase in undertakings and the need for more intensive farming make the shortage of labour power keenly felt. In order to resolve this contradiction, it is essential, in addition to large-scale improvement in farm

> tools, to tap the great labour resource provided by women (Beijing Ribao, 22 July 1958).

Further:

> In the wake of expanding socialist enterprise the necessity of lightening the household burdens of women as much as possible has come to the fore of public attention (Renmin Ribao, 2 June, 1958).

In the words of Elizabeth Croll, the official publications of the Communist Party like Renmin Ribao, 25 and 29 October 1958, Hebei Ribao dated 7 September, 1958 explained the rationale of the 'communal dining halls' thus:

> The hitherto individual and dispersed peasant way of life, with its concomitant small-producer, narrow and parochial interest in food supplies was to be replaced by community co-operation and a mutual responsibility for each other's sustenance and welfare. Party members and cadres were therefore exhorted to participate in the mess halls and assume responsibility for establishing and infrastructure that would allow for some democratic management of the mess halls (Croll, 1983).

The community dining halls played a great role in securing the food security and nutrition of the rural households, especially the ones that were grain-deficient due to lesser number of working hands, or larger number of dependents or old people in the family. They are said to have led to savings in food, fuel and labour and 'equalisation of consumption.' However, the role played by dining halls in the emancipation of women was exceptional. While paid labour increased their financial independence and social status, at the same time it relieved the demands of petty domestic chores placed on women and created scope for leisure (Ibid). Highlighting this role of the 'community dining halls' the leadership of the 'National Women's Organisation' opined that the dining halls had been instrumental in resolving the contradiction between the participation of women in social production and their role in servicing the needs of individual households. A statement of the Chairwoman of the National Women's organisation published in *Peking Review* stated:

> We are setting up community dining rooms, nurseries, kindergartens and so on not to negate the significance of household work, but to change household work originally carried out on an individual scattered basis into collective social work both in form and essence (*Peking Review*, 9 December 1958).

It is regrettable that this novel experiment in the socialisation of consumption did not last for long. The reasons are stated to be many. It is said that overconsumption by peasants and workers during the initial period led to scarcity later on, moreover workers are said to have become casual towards agricultural production for making this food available for such socialised consumption. The dining halls put additional burden on the meagre resources of the production teams as the expenditure that was earlier incurred by the households was now to be borne by the production teams and the earlier unpaid domestic labour of women was now socially paid work. Indeed the reasons were many, but the point here is—does such an endeavour become worthless only because difficulties were encountered during its implementation? Or should we insist on such laudable social projects being implemented only on the fulfilment of as impossible a condition as that there shall be no mistake, no setback in their implementation? The authors certainly do not think so.

Whatever may be the dilemmas in this regard, at least the peasants in China do not seem to think so. This is what the peasants in two of the worst affected provinces—Shandong and Henan had to tell Prof Dongping regarding their experience of the communes:

> There was no evidence to suggest that the public dining halls actually caused the famine by itself, or that the public dining halls were unpopular among farmers. In fact, many farmers recalled the beginning of public dining halls with fond memories. Some farmers said that they never had eaten so well in their life, and never before could they eat as much as they wanted. The food was much better than at home, with meat and tofu dishes and fried cakes (Dongping, 2003).

Whatever else may be the disagreements with the policies pursued during the 'Great Leap Forward', the foregoing description should enable us to see through the designs of authors like Jun Chang and Jon Halliday and who they speak for while writing in their book *Mao: the Untold Story* (2005) on the deaths that occurred during the Chinese famine. Whatever else may be the conclusions we can now say with assurance that the deaths were not part of a deliberate plan. Yet this book calls Mao a 'liar, ignoramus, fool, philistine, vandal, lecher, glutton, hedonist, drug-peddler, ghoul, bully, thug, coward, posturer, manipulator, psychopath, sadist, torturer, despot, megalomaniac and the greatest mass murderer of the twentieth century.'

Attempts such as these to malign the historically unprecedented achievements of the Chinese working masses under the leadership of Mao, or for that matter any revolutionary upheaval of the oppressed people on the globe and their leadership that are perceived as the most stoic threat by the oppressors, can only expect to be maligned in the most malignant of the terms. For us in India, who have among us the largest number of hungry people in the world, it is worth wondering as to when we will be able to create conditions for realising socialised production and socialised consumption in our own villages and towns such that the interests of the most marginalised among the marginalised are taken care of. We also need to ponder over as to when we can overcome the boundaries that are sought to be imposed on the way we think of the security of our bread and butter.

As to the lessons of the 'Great Leap Forward', someone has talked of French Revolution to the effect that, 'we might only be beginning to learn its lessons now.' While the 'Great Leap' may have fumbled on some of its objectives in the immediate sense, it afforded a precious opportunity to the working masses around the world to learn from the experience gained during the implementation of the 'Great Leap Forward' policies. As Dongping says:

> The critics of the collective farming system in China often use the tragic failure of the Great Leap Forward to condemn the idea of collective farming in China. They did not pay attention to the fact that the Great Leap Forward only represents a short learning curve of the collective farming years, and many of the experiments that failed during the Great Leap Forward flourished during the Cultural Revolution years' (Dongping, 2003).

## The Politics of our 'Bourgeois Socialists'

We have dealt in detail above the development trajectory of China in order to draw appropriate lessons for India. One aspect that emerges very clearly from the experience of China is that its working masses have been the motive force behind its impressive achievements in the social sectors like health, education, livelihood development and food security etc. No doubt the leadership was provided by the CPC and its tallest leader Mao, but they tapped the enthusiasm and capabilities of the Chinese people to enable these achievements.

A critical appraisal of China's achievements in human development would require an understanding of the politics, the processes and the factors that facilitated galvanising people to shape their own destiny, rather than just an appreciation for the end result of their efforts. Indeed if the end results are desirable, then the politics, the processes and the factors that led to these results should at least be worth studying. The attitude that people take towards this politics and processes would in a way be indicative of the extent to which they are committed to any meaningful change in our own society.

Alternatively, if we have a better alternative or difference of opinion, it should be clearly articulated. In this section, drawing from the experiences of China, we try to focus attention on the kind of politics and economic thinking that have informed the various welfare measures that have been initiated by the Central Government over the last ten years or so. We have focussed our arguments largely around the views expressed by Amartya Sen and Jean Drèze over the period as they have been the foremost development economists who have exercised a great deal of influence in shaping development policies in the country apart from the pro-government economists of the neoliberal persuasion.

Talking of the processes that led to social change in China, the following observations should appear agreeable in the light of the foregoing:

- The success of the Revolution in 1949 led to a massive campaign for an equitable distribution of means of production in the society, of which the land reforms programme was the most important given the fact that China was overwhelmingly an agrarian economy with an overwhelming number of its people residing in villages.
- Equitable distribution of productive resources was fundamental to creating an egalitarian society in which all the members not only enjoyed equality before law, but also equality of opportunities to develop their capabilities. Such a situation undermined the possibility of exploitative relations of production in the society.
- Unlike subsidy driven charity, much of the resources required for the implementation of the social welfare

measures were generated by the benefactor communities themselves by socialising production and appropriation of surplus and socialised consumption. This arrangement was more in line with the principle of 'enabling people to take care of themselves' as against 'we taking care of the people.'

- Newer forms of organising production and consumption like production teams, production brigades, the communes and 'communal dining' etc. that were formed, despite their possible shortcomings ushered in much greater participation of the people in regulating matters of their daily life. Far greater practical measures seemed to have been taken towards emancipation of women, for developing rural industry to absorb surplus labour from agriculture and provide employment to all.

It would be reasonable to presume that these constituted steps towards ushering in real time functioning democracy in the lives of the majority of people in China and certainly went far beyond conceptualisation of democracy as one man one vote a vote that is manipulated in every possible manner through use of money, muscle and societal fault lines of caste, class, region, religion and ethnicity. Simultaneously, the relationships of dependence, subjugation and exploitation continue to be strengthened by systemically and systematically maintaining high levels of poverty, illiteracy and ill health.

In their comparison between China and India, Sen and Drèze do recognise the vast lead that China has over India in terms of controlling morbidity and mortality and vastly increasing the life expectancy of average Chinese with the support of much enhanced nutrition (Sen and Drèze, 1989). They have examined two possible reasons for China's success in enhancing the well-being of its citizens—one, economic growth led social security and secondly support-led security. Their verdict is clearly in favour of support-led security. They say:

> The network of health services introduced in post-revolutionary China in a radical departure from the past—involving cooperative medical systems, commune clinics, barefoot doctors, and widespread public health measures—has been remarkably extensive . . . these and other medical resources are distributed more evenly across the country (even between urban and rural areas), with greater popular access to them than India has been able to organize . . . Food distribution is, in fact, a part of a far-reaching programme of social security that distinguishes China from India . . . and it is plausible to see China's success story as one of support-led security (Sen and Drèze, 1989).

But there are problems with this verdict. It is much too succinct. While it takes note of the huge infrastructure of social support built by China to develop its human resources, it totally eclipses the politics and the profound social changes that were brought in the wake of success of Chinese Revolution in 1949. More importantly, ensuring 'support-led security' entailed massive political mobilisation of the working masses of China both in the villages and the cities. In the absence of highlighting these developments, it would seem that 'support-led security' is something that can be ordered top down and people cannot but be passive recipients of State's largesse.

This certainly is not true that persons of Sen and Drèze's erudition are ignorant of the underlying process behind China's achievements. In his 1982 article—'How India is doing', not only does Sen acknowledge that in India the power actually rests in the hands of the elite, which while being a minority are still numerous. He writes:

> In so far as elitism is seen as one of the main problems with India, a comparison with China is obviously relevant. With the establishment of Communist China, anti-elitism immediately became one of the major emphases of its official policy, and during the Cultural Revolution this aspect of Chinese policy became particularly prominent. Certainly

> anti-elitist achievements of China are very substantial. The traditional rural power structure was smashed effectively, the hold of the urban elite quite transformed. Schooling and medical services have expanded rapidly and are much more widely spread than in India. The general level of nutrition has vastly improved. Life expectancy—between sixty-four and sixty-nine years according to various recent estimates—is much higher than India's miserable fifty-two years' (Sen, 1982).

He then goes on to pose the question:

> But in view of the price that India has to pay for its political system, it could be asked: are these liberties (emphasis ours) worth it? Would not better feeding, clothing and health for the Indian population compensate for the loss of liberty (emphasis ours) which after all effectively concerns only a minority? (Ibid).

Sen gives two reasons in answer to this question:

> First, there is little evidence that matters of liberty do not concern most of the people even in the poor countries. Indeed, the response of Indian voters to Mrs Gandhi's 'emergency' rule demonstrated the wider concerns of one of the poorest electorates in the world . . .
>
> Second, the choice posed is unreal. A regime in which basic liberties (emphasis ours) are severely suppressed and in which the Government cannot be voted out of office no matter what it does, is deeply unpredictable, and there is no guarantee that even large-scale starvation and famines would not occur under such a regime. Indeed, there is clear evidence now that in China during the three years from 1959 to 1961 a great many people died from lack of food (Ibid).

We would agree with Sen that 'matters of liberty' not only concern most of the people, but they concern the poor the most, for these liberties play a crucial role in enabling the poor to safeguard their lives and livelihoods. However, both in his question and the second part of its answer, Sen seems to be distinguishing his 'basic liberties' from rights like feeding, clothing and health. Apparently, what he means by 'basic liberties' are—the right to vote (to be able to vote a government out of office) and the right to free expression (to criticise a government's policies without fear). From the tenor of his submissions it is obvious that people in China lacked these 'basic liberties.'

In 1989 Sen and Drèze reaffirmed their faith in parliamentary democracy characterised by political opposition and adversarial journalism as a potent weapon against hunger and famine. They postulate:

> A political 'triggering mechanism' which brings the protection system into play and indeed which keeps the public support system in a state of preparedness . . . Given the political system of post-independence India, it is extremely hard for any government in office—whether at the state level or at the centre—to get away with neglecting prompt and extensive anti-famine measures at the first signs of a famine. And these signs are themselves more easily transmitted given India's relatively free media and newspapers, and the active and investigative role that journalists as well as opposition politicians can and do play in the field (Sen and Drèze, 1989).

Assessing the aforementioned submissions of Sen and Drèze is important to know the directions they provide for 'Public Action.' The thrust of the argument forwarded by both seems to be that whatever be the liberating impact of achievements of the Chinese people in the fields of healthcare, education, nutrition, tackling unemployment, emancipation of women and the rapid economic advances under Communist rule (at least till the end of Mao's period), these still do not add up to be recognized as equivalent to or facilitating the 'basic liberties' which people in democracies like India can freely enjoy. The 'basic liberties' (right to vote and the freedom of expression) in India can meaningfully and effectively operate even as people are illiterate, unemployed, hungry and crippled with disease, even as oppression based on economic status, caste, gender and religion continues to have a free run. The proof is provided in the form of Indira Gandhi being voted out of power in 1977 for the excesses committed during 'Emergency.' It is another matter that those who were voted in were not any revolutionaries who threatened the monopoly of the elite on political power and the productive resources, they were just another section from within the ruling classes, several of them being erstwhile Congress leaders not until far back in time.

It is acknowledged that the nature of Indian society and polity is basically elitist and that the elite have a vice-like grip on power. They have used this power to further their social and economic interests even as they have devised mechanisms in the form of 'affirmative actions' to co-opt the foremost minds from among the traditionally oppressed sections in the ruling set-up controlled by them. While the elite have been responsive enough to avoid any precipitate situation like famines, yet they have effectively blocked the avenues for the socio-economic emancipation of the oppressed working masses to ensure their interests (Sen, 1982).

In spite of so much being ascribed to Indian elite, yet under similar circumstances the Communists in China, under the leadership of Mao smashed the power structure of the elite of China to implement land reforms. They did it to sweep aside a 'millennia of social tradition' with the birth of the commune (Hesketh and Zhu, 1997): to emancipate Chinese women from centuries of slavery to domestic labour and make them equal participants in the building of a new society; to develop Chinese industry and agriculture for the prosperity of the commonest Chinese rather than serve the profit motive of the elite to make the city-based intellectuals who despised the Chinese peasant, go to the villages and use their knowledge for the uplift of the poorest of the poor Chinese and being responsive to their needs (Hesketh and Zhu, 1997). All of these actions do not seem to usher in the quality and level of democracy that exist in India. Communists made all Chinese, irrespective of their social status, eat together, even as we may still only be able to find an occasional village in which a Brahmin or a Rajput or any upper caste person would be willing to have meal together with a dalit publically without fear of retribution from his/her own community. When Mao saw that the Communist Party leadership itself had become an obstacle in the realisation of the development of the Chinese masses and their liberties, he gave the slogan—'Bombard the Headquarters' (Headquarters of the Communist Party) while launching the 'Cultural Revolution.' The most ordinary peasants and workers stood up to the authority of the government officials, village heads, production team leaders and Commune leaders and made them accountable for their mistakes. The officials were supposed to labour with the peasants and workers to understand their problems rather than just order them around. Cultural Revolution brought in a new wave of democratisation in the Chinese society (Dongping, 2003). These facts need only be contrasted with the image of a Dalit landless labourer, a small or marginal peasant begging for help with folded hands before petty officials in the collectorate or block headquarters in a district in India.

Yet all of this still does not add up to the worth of the 'basic liberties' enjoyed by the working masses of India, their poverty, illiteracy, hunger and squalor and centuries old exploitation notwithstanding. These developments in Chinese society are yet not worthy of being acknowledged as any process of democratisation of the Chinese society. No doubt that during this march of hundreds of millions of ordinary

Chinese working masses to build a new society there were many mistakes, even encesses which we now condemn can with the benefit of hind right; but then as Mao said:

> A revolution is not a dinner party, or writing an essay, or painting a picture, or doing embroidery, it cannot be so refined, so leisurely and gentle, so temperate, kind, courteous, restrained and magnanimous. A revolution is an insurrection, an act of violence by which one class overthrows another.

But our bourgeois socialists would have nothing of this. In their conceptualisation of 'democracy', rather than smash the power base of the elite, which they themselves acknowledge as being responsible for the miserable condition of the working masses of India, they would rather have poor masses of India use their 'basic liberties' to keep changing the governments through vote, even if this has increasingly come to mean that Indians have only the right to choose their favourite millionaire with the prospects of any real alternative being thrown up being next to none. The unity of all the ruling class political parties on the implementation of the neoliberal economic policies is just a case in point.

Given the conditions as they obtain in the present time, the reliance placed by Sen and Drèze on the 'political 'triggering mechanism' of political opposition and adversarial press in preventing famines or situations akin to them looks increasingly simplistic. As regards the political parties in the electrol arena, the more numerous they are, the more the same they look. Even on issues like corruption which at one time ]did result in the overthrow of governments, there hardly appears any difference between ruling parties or alliances and those in the opposition in present time. We have allegations of corruption being thrown around against leaders of all the major political parties. The role of the 'free press' in taking up the real issues of the people—those of poverty, unemployment, hunger and health, agrarian crisis etc. is stark only by its absence. Over the years, especially during the years of neoliberalism, common interests have come to span across business, politics and the media with the role of money in the conduct of politics and media acquiring gigantic proportions. In this scheme of things the poor have been reduced to a state of being helpless onlookers, except in those situations/areas where they are politically organised under the leadership of revolutionary forces or their independent organisations and are waging resolute struggles against predatory policies of the ruling elite and challenging the power base of the elite.

It could be added here that with the kind of resources and the logistical capacity available with large modern states like India and China, occurrence of famines may well have become a relatively distant possibility. There are a large number of other factors/problems to which the much valued 'political trigger mechanism' ought to be sensitive to and effective in preventing. This trigger mechanism has just not failed in tackling the issues of mass hunger, malnutrition, frequent disease epidemics, political corruption, loss of lives and livelihoods on a large scale through the kind of development paradigms being pursued in the country but what is shocking is there is an increasing brazenness among the elite on all these issues. Even in cities like Delhi, vector borne disease epidemics occur every year with their associated casualties, yet the failure has been total in preventing these in the national capital let alone in preventing yearly epidemics like that of Japanese Encephalitis occurring in large parts of eastern UP that have been killing and maiming people for years. Allegations of corruption against sections of elite in power are countered not by the assurance of investigating these and taking appropriate action, but by assertions that the Government also has evidence of corruption against those making allegations. The General Secretary of Congress, the principal party of the earstwhile ruling coalition at the Centre, Mr Digvijay Singh said in a television talk show:

> There were lot of things, which came out during the NDA regime (the first NDA government under the leadership of Sh Atal Bihari Bajpai. But did Congress party ever use that. We will never use this...If I say, I do not have it (evidence against kin of Advani and Vajpayee), then it is not correct (*Outlook,* 2012).

For two mega scams unearthed during the region of earsthwhile UPA government, (2G Spectrum and the 'Coalgate's scam totalling 3.62 lakh crore (2G scam ₹ 1.76 lakh crore, Coalgate ₹ 1.86 lakh crore) the Government had the temerity to field senior ministers in its defence who claimed that there had been no loss at all in spite of the Government Auditor giving official reports to the contrary. The then ruling coalition managed to take the sting out of allegations of corruption against the companies of the son-in-law of the first ruling family by exposing scams committed by the companies owned by the President of the principal opposition party. The story of scams has become a veritable race of riding a tiger, where the accused can hope to survive only by exposing bigger scams of his/her adversaries even as they keep running faster and faster outdoing each other in perpetrating more scams.

As regards the elitist character of media, the less said the better. There has been a lock, stock and barrel dumbing down of the media where the issues of the working masses are the least priority or are invariably construed in a manner to present the concerns of the elite as for example on the issues of strikes and agitations by the workers and peasants. The Neera Radia tapes in the case of the 2G Spectrum scam only present a glimpse of the way the nexus between big business, the fourth estate and the ruling polity operates to rob the country and its people of its precious resources. Innovations like paid news have seriously undermined the credibility of the Indian news media. The worst is that in spite of all these exposures, there appears to be little effort on the part of the powers that be to remedy the situation. The import is that one simply has to live with it. The political trigger mechanism of Sen and Drèze is irreparably short-circuited. No doubt, both the authors have criticised the components of this trigger mechanism from time to time, and yet they provide credibility to them by being associated with the charmed inner circles.

Under the circumstances how long can we abhor the path seeking to smash the power base of the Indian elite to facilitate the redemption of India's working masses? Devoid of any vision to usher in a larger societal change, merely exhorting people to fight for enactment of newer laws in the quest for 'support-led social security'—when the ruling elite have had little intention to implement security that the existing laws provide—amounts to serious mischief. The mischief lies in disarming the working masses ideologically by weaning them away from a revolutionary change on the one hand and weaving illusions of a 'caring elite' on the other.

It is in this context that the far greater democratic changes that came about in the lives of the ordinary Chinese in the wake of the success of the Chinese Revolution of 1949 are sought to be portrayed as less than democratic, while the so-called democracy in India is made to appear still desirable in spite of all its shortcomings. Moreover, there is an implicit understanding that these shortcomings can be overcome by enacting entitlements assuring various social securities—health, employment, food etc. Not only that the practical experience of the people belies such hopes, but also it is remarkable that in spite of alluding to the elitist nature of the Indian State, Sen and Drèze still have high hopes from this elite to implement comprehensive social security schemes. Under the circumstances, if one indeed believes (which Sen and Drèze do) that smashing the power base of the elite in China after the success of the 1949 Revolution led to 'substantial' social sector achievements for the Chinese people and that the elitist character of the State and polity in India have been the biggest impediments in alleviating the condition of the masses, then the natural result of such an understanding would be that one should emphasise on taking practical measures towards linking the struggles for partial demands with the struggles seeking broader societal change, of which there are many in our country. However, such an effort on the part of the movements like the 'Right to Food', with which Drèze has been openly associated, is not evident in any recognisable manner. The desperate attempt rather seems to be that—'Please enact entitlements lest those fighting for changing the system take us too close to the precipice.'

We cannot really make sense of the fact that in spite of clearly recognising that the problem lies with the present system, Sen and Drèze still attempt to salvage it by asserting that the present social, economic and political order in the country is yet the better choice, even if a devil's choice, rather than going the way China did after 1949. To our understanding, the attempt clearly is to dissuade people from taking to the revolutionary path.

Sen and Drèze seem to unquestioningly accept the 'massive death toll' thesis of the Chinese famine of 1959-61. In 1982 Sen wrote:

> Indeed, there is clear evidence now that in China during the three years from 1959 to 1961 a great many people died from lack of food. The exact size of the extra mortality caused by the food problem remains controversial . . . recently available Chinese data, suggests that 'the net loss in 1960-61 would have to be no less than 23 million' though other evidence suggests that 'the losses during the crisis may not have been as acute' (Sen, 1982).

These claims are reiterated in 1989 in the book *Hunger and Public Action* co-authored by Sen and Drèze. As already mentioned earlier, the Chinese data that Sen and Drèze refer to is the data that was released by the Deng Xiaoping regime in the 1980s, more than 20 years after the famine. The fact is that Deng along with Liu Shao-chi had consistently opposed Mao's policies of building socialism in China arguing for capitalist development of China in the name of developing productive forces. That this data could have been fabricated and could have been a deliberate overestimation of the actual mortality especially as the methodology of collection of the data is not known, are factors that do not seem to have crossed Sen and Drèze's minds.

This is only further helped by the fact that both the authors hardly discuss the politics behind the developments in China. Such a discussion could have at least obliged them to discuss the motivations behind the policies like the 'Great Leap Forward' and the 'Great Proletarian Cultural Revolution' rather than simply condemn them on the basis of selective discussion on some adverse consequences. A closer political scrutiny would have also made them realise that there was a genuine possibility of the most well intentioned policies also facing serious problems, especially when those were being attempted with little experience in the process of building a socialist society in a backward agrarian country that had just emerged from a semi-feudal and semi-colonial society.

The other route that these authors could have adopted was to accept their bias against the development trajectory adopted by revolutionary China and defend their bias more robustly. However, given the way things have been dealt with by them, they have even attempted a misleading presentation of Mao's words to strengthen their argument. In their chapter comparing China and India in the book 'Hunger and Public Action' Sen and Drèze write:

> The misinformation also contributed to the non-revision of production and distribution policies and to the absence of any emergency entitlement protection programme[35] (Sen and Drèze, 1989).

The footnote number 35 mentioned here is as follows:

> In 1962, shortly after the famine, when the recent experiences were being reviewed, Mao Zedong noted the problem of informational failure for planning in the absence of local democracy (emphasis ours): "If there is no democracy and ideas are not coming from the masses, it is impossible to establish a good line, good general and specific policies and methods . . . without democracy you have no understanding of what is happening down below. The situation will be unclear and you will be unable to collect sufficient opinions from all sides. There can be no communication between top and bottom and the top-level organs of leadership will depend on one-sided and incorrect material to decide issues. Thus you will find it difficult to avoid being subjectivist and it will be impossible to achieve unity of understanding and unity of action, and impossible to achieve true centralism' (Mao Zedong, 1974).

In the above sequence 'misinformation' leading to 'non-revision of production and distribution policies' is automatically linked to what is made out to be a confession of sorts by Mao regarding the absence of 'local democracy' in the Chinese society. Whereas the fact in Mao's own words is as follows, 'The central point that I have spoken about is the question of how to realise 'democratic centralism' and how to promote democracy within and without the Party (Mao, 1962)[iii].

'Democratic Centralism' is the key organisational principle of a communist party that can be and needs to be emphasised time and again among the party members to improve upon the functioning of the Party. In his speech he even stressed the need for this emphasis on explaining 'Democratic Centralism' in view of the fact that 80% of the party membership had joined the Party after the Revolution. The emphasis on 'Democratic Centralism' by Mao can in no way be construed to be an admission of lack of democracy either in the Party or in the Chinese society. Needless to say, one can always stress the need for greater democracy either inside the Party or in Party's relationship with the society. In fact in the same speech Mao says:

> Generally speaking our Party is very good. Our Party is mainly composed of workers and poor peasants. The great majority of our cadres are good, they all work industriously, but we must also see that in our Party there still exist some problems, we mustn't imagine that everything is good with the state of our Party (Mao Tse-tung, 1962).

Mao does make a mention of the experience during the great Leap Forward:

> Comrade Liu Shao-chi said in his report that in the past four years our line was correct. and that our achievements were the main feature, we made some mistakes in our practical work and suffered some hardships, but we gained experience, therefore we are stronger than before, not weaker (Mao Zedong, 1962).

Explaining the dialectical understanding of the process of 'socialist construction' attempted during the 'Great Leap Forward', Mao says:

> . . . understanding the laws of socialist construction must pass through a process. It must take practice as its starting point, passing from having no experience to having some experience, from having little experience to having more experience, from the construction of socialism, which is in the realm of necessity as yet not understood, to the gradual overcoming of our blindness and the understanding of objective laws, thereby attaining freedom, achieving a

> flying leap in our knowledge and reaching the realm of freedom (Ibid).

Explaining the laws of socialist construction further, Mao says:

> Our understanding of the objective world must pass through a process. First of all we do not understand, or do not completely understand it, but after repeated practice and after we have obtained results through practice, when we have won victories and also had tumbles and setbacks, we are able to compare our victories and defeats. Only then is there a possibility of developing to the point of achieving complete understanding or relatively complete understanding. By that time we shall be exercising more initiative, we shall be freer and we shall become more intelligent. Freedom means the recognition of necessity and it means transforming the objective world. Only on the basis of recognising necessity can man enjoy freedom of activity, this is the dialectical law of freedom and necessity. What we call necessity is an objectively existing law. Before we recognize it our behaviour cannot be conscious, it has elements of blindness. At this time we are stupid, during the last few years haven't we made many stupid blunders? (Ibid).

As a great teacher, Mao leaves his mark in so lucidly explaining the dialectical nature of the process of development and the need for the party members to grasp this process. Even as he acknowledges the 'blunders' that were committed during 'socialist construction' attempted during the 'Great Leap Forward' he asserts that such mistakes are inevitable and indeed it is only though such a process of achievements and failures, victories and setbacks, that we can grasp the objective reality of the laws of development.

Even as he acknowledges the mistakes, there is no reason to believe that Mao accepted lack of democracy in China, let alone the banal allegation that tens of millions perished during the 'Great Leap Forward.' In fact, there are lessons to be learnt for us here in India from what Mao had to say regarding the experiences gained through the development path adopted in China. Redemption of the working masses of India is much more complicated than a struggle for enactment of a few laws guaranteeing some entitlements for the poor. The emancipation of the working masses of India cannot but be guided by the objective realities of class contradictions in the Indian society. Rather than grappling with these questions and organising the struggles of the workers and the peasantry even on their partial demands as an integral part of the larger struggle for societal change, the attempts of the civil society are to pre-empt the struggles for larger societal change, especially any revolutionary upheaval. Even as the Government is withdrawing from committing itself to fulfil the meagre entitlements provided for in the recent social sector legislations, civil society mavericks are busy rallying the people to make ever more fervent demands for relief from the Government but without breaking the safe limits for this struggle set by the system. Such tactics can only lead to defeatism among the people.

## How has China Done Under the Reforms?

After Mao's death, the capitalist roaders were quick to gain power in the Party as well as the Government. In agriculture, the collective organisations were dissolved and individual household responsibility system introduced under the new dictum propagated by Deng's regime, 'letting some get rich first.' The result was that the households with superior skills, more labour power and political access forged ahead, whereas those less endowed in such attributes were left behind. The inequities have increased in China and with the dissolution of the communes the elaborate system of social security has all but disappeared (Riskin, 1987). Passion for economic liberalism has weakened the resolve to provide public support measures for the population. Riskin (1988) notes that, 'The style is a hybrid one involving a strange mixture of residual socialist rhetoric and Chicago School Values.' But the socialist rhetoric has been distinctly in retreat in recent years.

We shall present the impact of market reforms with the help of just two examples—changes in the per capita grain production and the crude death rates in China before and after the reforms that were launched in 1978.

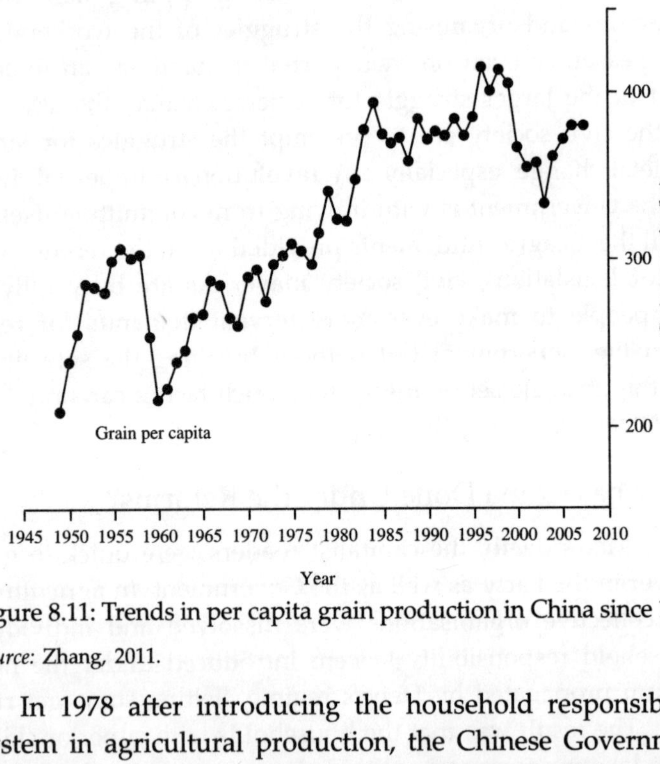


Figure 8.11: Trends in per capita grain production in China since 1950.

*Source:* Zhang, 2011.

In 1978 after introducing the household responsibility system in agricultural production, the Chinese Government doubled the procurement prices for food grains which resulted in a steep rise in production of food grains until 1985. But thereafter the per capita food grain production has stagnated due to non-remunerative prices and rising costs of inputs (Dongping, 2003).

In terms of human welfare we can see from figure 8.12 that the crude death rate was the lowest in China in 1977-78, and thereafter the crude death rate rose marginally and remained more or less stagnant until 2004, when it rose further. The difference between the CDRs of China and India is worth noticing for the period up till the beginning of the 21st century. This difference would imply an excess mortality in India over all these years that is many times larger than the claimed 'massive death toll' during the Chinese famine of 1959-61.

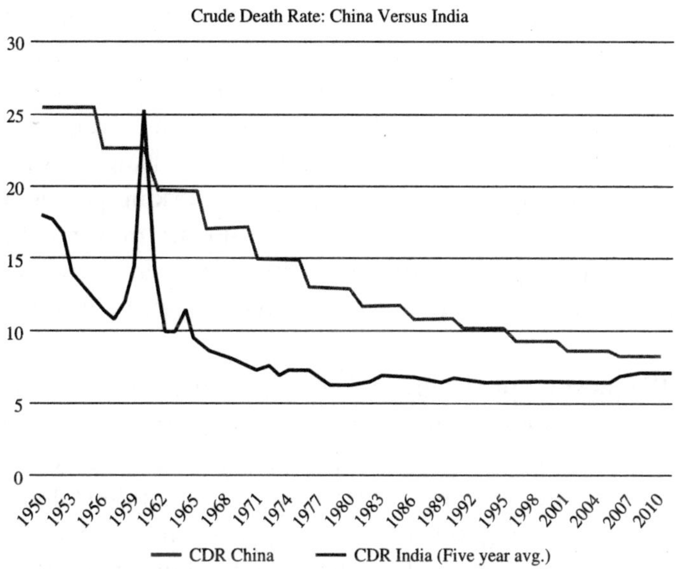


Figure 8.12: Comparison of trends in crude death rates between China and India.

Figure 8.12 is based on statistics available from National Bureau of Statistics of China: *China Statistical Yearbook 2011*, Chapter 3: Population, Available from: http://www.stats.gov.cn/tjsj/ndsj/2011/indexeh.htm, For India five year average crude death rate available from United Nations (2011): 'World Population Prospects, the 2010 Revision', Population Division, Population Estimates and Projections Section.

## Conclusion

Given the thrust of the argument presented in this paper, some might remark rather derisively, 'Oh! So you mean everything should wait until revolution takes place, for the measures you suggest may not be possible under the present dispensation.' Nothing could be farther from the truth and a bigger travesty of the struggle for food security than this.

Principally, what needs to be understood is that there is a need to bridge the distance between 'aaj ki ladai' (fight for the pressing immediate issues) and 'raaj ki ladai' (fight for the rule of the working class), without being derisive towards the undeniable need for a revolutionary change of the highly unjust social, political and economic order of the day. Let this be clear that without a resolute struggle for the immediate needs/partial demands of the working people, we cannot hope to build a powerful revolutionary movement for establishing their class rule. Likewise, a-one sided emphasis on partial demands amounts to setting the people in pursuit of a chimera.

We most emphatically affirm to the crucial importance of strong redistributive policies in tackling the immediate crisis along with addressing the 'real structural roots', however to go silent about the latter, or turn them into an understatement while emphasising the former is to disarm the people in their fight for a just and honourable solution to their food insecurity and it is in this sense that it amounts to supplanting a 'revisionist agenda' in place of a 'revolutionary agenda' in the sphere of food security. The struggle for the partial demands ought to be conducted in a manner as to expose the limits of the present system and not to set limits to the struggle itself.

To translate this into practice means to understand that today there is a broad unity among the different parties of the ruling classes from the extreme Right to the Left, within the parliament over the anti-people economic policies.

The struggle against these policies has moved outside the realm of Parliamentary politics as reflected by the different struggles mentioned above, none of which is led in the main or exclusively by any party represented in the Parliament. Hence, to build a fighting alliance one has to look towards forces outside of the Parliament. There is a need to build a 'New Democracy' in the country in place of the one we have at present.

There might still be some who may scoff at us saying, 'The government is not willing to increase the entitlement from 25 kg to 35 kg and you talk of redistributing land.' To this we would like to conclude by recounting another story: that of a lion cub who was abducted by jackals and was subsequently rescued by other lions. Unable to hunt as he was, the other lions exhorted, 'you may not be able to hunt, but you are a lion cub, you can at least roar.' Our exhortation is that we all must roar and roar in defence of the people's rights.

## Endnotes

i. 'Old China was a semi-colonial and semi-feudal country in which the productive forces were at a very low level and had long stagnated. This resulted mainly from cruel oppression and exploitation by imperialism, feudalism and bureaucrat-capitalism. When we have political power we have everything. The decadent and backward relations of production could be fundamentally changed and the productive forces greatly developed only when the masses were armed with Mao Tse-tung Thought and when the proletariat (through the Communist Party) led the masses (mainly the peasant masses) in carrying out the revolution, i.e., the new-democratic revolution, against the three main enemies—imperialism, feudalism and bureaucrat-capitalism—to seize political power throughout the country' (Hsueh-ping, 1969). In classical European history the task of demolishing feudal mode of production was performed by the bourgeoisie, leading to the establishment of bourgeois democracies. However, with the coming into being of imperialism in the colonial countries the imperialists used the alliance of local comprador bourgeoisie (bourgeois) and the local feudal classes to rule these countries. Hence, the local bourgeoisie was incapable of overthrowing either the colonial rule or the local feudal classes with whom it shared power after the erstwhile colonies turned into semi-colonies due to the erstwhile colonial powers resorting to indirect ways to exploit the newly independent third world countries. Simultaneously, feudal relations of production also evolved into semi-feudal relations. As the bourgeoisie in these countries is incapable of overthrowing the feudal classes, the task of completing the bourgeois democratic revolution also has to be performed by the working class in alliance with the peasantry which forms the overwhelming mass of the exploited people in these countries. Completion of bourgeois democratic revolution under the leadership of the working class is called a new type of democratic revolution and hence—'New Democratic Revolution.'

ii. Comment on the report submitted by Shansi Provincial Party Committee: 'Raise the Mutual—Aid Organisations in the Old Liberated Areas to a Higher Level', 3 July, 1951.

iii. This reference is to the same speech of Mao as is cited (Mao Tse-tung, 1974: 164).

## References

Ashton B., Hill K., Piazza A. et. al. (1984): 'Famine in China 1958-61', *Population and Development Review*, 10, 613-645.

Banister J. (1987): *China's Changing Population*, Stanford University Press.

Banister J. and S. Preston (1981): 'Mortality in China' in *Population and Development Review*, Vol. 7 (1): 98-110.

Ball J. (2006): 'Did Mao Really Kill Millions in the Great Leap Forward?', *Monthly Review*, September 21. Available from: http://monthlyreview.org/commentary/did-mao-really-kill-millions-in-the-great-leap-forward on 18 October, 2012.

Beijing Ribao 22 July (1958): quoted in Croll E (1983): Appendix 1—'A Rural Experiment in Socialising Consumption: The Community Dining Room' In *The Family Rice Bowl: Food and Domestic Economy in China*, UNRISD and Zed Press, London, 1983, p. 343.

Chang J. and J. Halliday (2005): *Mao: The Unknown Story*, Johnathan Cape.

Chen J. (1973): *A Year in Upper Felicity*, Macmillan, p. 90.

Chen Y. (2009): *Transition and Development in China: Towards Shared Growth*, Ashgate Publishing Ltd., p. 38.

Chowdhury B.K. (1970): 'Disparity in Income in Context of HYV.' *Economic and Political Weekly*, Vol. 5 (39): pp. A90-A91+A93+A95-A96.

Coale A. (1981): 'Populataion Trends, Population Policy and Population Studies in China', *Population and Development Review*, Vol. 7. (1): 85-97.

Communist Party of China (CPC) (1973): *Three Major Struggles on China's Philosophical Front (1949-64)*, Foreign Languages Press, Peking.

Croll E. (1983): The Procelian Bowl: Food Consumption in Republican China. In *The Family Rice Bowl, Food and Domestic Economy in China*, UNRISD and Zed Press, London, 1983: p 45.

Ibid, p. 5.

Government of India (2012): 'Draft National Water Policy (2012) as Recommended by National Water Board in its 14 Meeting Held on 7 June, Ministry of Water Resources.

Gregor B. and Chun L., eds. (2009): *Was Mao Really a Monster: The Academic Response to Chang and Halliday's Mao: The Unknown Story*, Routledge, London, UK.

Hansard (1942): 'Central Legislative Assembly (Electorate)', 10th Nov. Available from: http://hansard.millbanksystems.com/written_answers/1942/nov/10/central-legislative-assembly-eeectorate on 7 November 2012.

Han Dongping (2003): *The Great Leap Famine, the Cultural Revolution and Post- Mao Rural Reform: the Lessons of Rural Development in Contemporary China*. Available from http://chinastudygroup.net/2003/04/the-great-leap-famine-the-cultural-revolution-and-post-mao-rural-reform-the-lessons-of-rural-development-in-contemporary-china on 31 May, 2012.

Hsueh-ping H. (1969): 'Revolutionary Mass Criticism: The Essence of "Theory of Productive Forces" Is to Oppose Proletarian Revolution', *Beijing Review*, Vol. 12 (38): pp. 5-8, September 19.

Hesketh T. and Zhu W.X. (1997): 'Health in China: from Mao to Market Reform', *BMJ*, 314:1543.

Jacoby E.H. (1972): 'Effects of the 'Green Revolution in South and South-East Asia.' *Modern Asian Studies*, Vol. 6 (1): pp. 63-69.

Marx K. and Engels F. (1848): Chapter 3—'Socialist and Communist Literature' in *The Communist Manifesto*.

Millman S., Aronson S.M., Fruzzetti L.M. et. al. (1990): 'Organisation, Information and Entitlement in the Emerging Global Food System' In *Hunger in History, Food Shortage, Poverty and Deprivation*, Newman L.F. (ed.), Blackwell Publishers, Cambridge, USA, p. 320.

Meissner M (1996): *The Deng Xiaoping Era. An Enquiry into the Fate of Chinese Socialism, 1978-1994*, Hill and Wray, New York. 1996.

Mao Tse-tung, (1962): 'Talk At An Enlarged Working Conference Convened By The Central Committee of The Communist Party of China', Jan 30. Extracted from *Peking Review*, No. 27, July 7, 1978.

Mao Zedong (Tse-tung) (1974): *Mao Tse-tung Unrehearsed, Talks and Letters: 1956-71*, Penguin Books, London.

*Outlook* (2012): 'Won't Use Evidence against Kin of Vajpayee, Advani: Digvijay', October 21st. Available from: http://news.outlookindia.com/items.aspx?artid=778723 on 24 Oct 2012.

Pylee M.V. (2003): *Constitutional Government in India*, S. Chand & Company, Delhi, p. 3.

Ibid, p. 5.

Peng X. (1987): 'Demographic Consequences of Great Leap Forward in China's Provinces.' *Population and Development Review*, Vol. 13 (4): 639-670.

Riskin C. (1986): 'Feeding China: The Experience since 1949', Revised version of paper prepared for UNU/WIDER conference on Hunger and Poverty—The Poorest Billion, Project on Food Strategies, Helsinki, 21-25 July 1986.

Riskin C. (1987): *China's Political Economy: the Quest for Development Since 1949*, Oxford University Press, Oxford.

Riskin C. (1988): *Reform: Where is China Going?* mimeo, Columbia University.

Renmin Ribao, Hongqui & Jiefangjun Bao editorial departments (1968): *The Struggle between the Two Roads in China's Countryside*, Foreign Languages Press, 23 November, p. 9.

Ibid., p. 11.

Ibid., pp. 14-18.

Ibid., p. 16.

Renmin Ribao, 2 June (1958): Appendix 1—'A Rural Experiment in Socialising Consumption: The Community Dining Room' In *The Family Rice Bowl: Food and Domestic Economy in China*, UNRISD and Zed Press, London, 1983, p. 343.

Sen A. (1987): 'Food and Freedom', Sir John Crawford Memorial lecture, Washington D.C., October 29.

Sen A. and Drèze J (1989): Preface in *Hunger and Public Action*, Oxford University Press, Delhi.

Sen A. and Drèze J. (1989): *Hunger and Public Action*, Oxford University Press, Delhi, pp. 210-212.

Ibid., p. 205.

Ibid., p. 211.

Ibid., pp. 204-225.

Ibid., p. 209.

Ibid., p. 213.

Sen A. (1982): How is India Doing? *The New York Review of Books*, 21 (Christmas Number).

Weiskopf T.E. (2011): 'Why worry about the inequality in the booming Indian economy.' *Economic and Political Weekly*, Vol. 46 (47): pp. 41-51.

Wang Q., Jensen H.H., Johnson S.R. (1993): 'China's Nutrient Availability and Sources, 1950-91, Working Paper 93-WP 113, Sept 1993, Centre for Agricultural and Rural Development, Iowa State University.

World Bank (1981): 'China: Socialist Economic Development', Report No. 3391-CHA, Annex C: Agricultural Development, June, pp. 72-73.

Zhang J. (2011): 'China's success in increasing per capita food production.' *Journal of Experimental Botany*, Vol. 62(11): 3707-11.

# Index